# Victoria's Wars

# Victoria's Wars

## The Rise of Empire

SAUL DAVID

*To Colin,*
*with best wishes*

*[signature]*

VIKING
*an imprint of*
PENGUIN BOOKS

VIKING

Published by the Penguin Group
Penguin Books Ltd, 80 Strand, London WC2R 0RL, England
Penguin Group (USA) Inc., 375 Hudson Street, New York, New York 10014, USA
Penguin Group (Canada), 90 Eglinton Avenue East, Suite 700, Toronto, Ontario, Canada M4P 2Y3
(a division of Pearson Penguin Canada Inc.)
Penguin Ireland, 25 St Stephen's Green, Dublin 2, Ireland (a division of Penguin Books Ltd)
Penguin Group (Australia), 250 Camberwell Road,
Camberwell, Victoria 3124, Australia (a division of Pearson Australia Group Pty Ltd)
Penguin Books India Pvt Ltd, 11 Community Centre,
Panchsheel Park, New Delhi – 110 017, India
Penguin Group (NZ), cnr Airborne and Rosedale Roads, Albany,
Auckland 1310, New Zealand (a division of Pearson New Zealand Ltd)
Penguin Books (South Africa) (Pty) Ltd, 24 Sturdee Avenue,
Rosebank, Johannesburg 2196, South Africa

Penguin Books Ltd, Registered Offices: 80 Strand, London WC2R 0RL, England

www.penguin.com

First published 2006
1

The acknowledgements on pp. ix–xii constitute an extension of this copyright page
Endpapers: *Sebastopol from the Extreme Right of the Trench Attack* by William Simpson.
Private collection/The Stapleton Collection/Bridgeman Art Library

Set in 12/14.75pt Monotype Bembo
Typeset by Rowland Phototypesetting Ltd, Bury St Edmunds, Suffolk
Printed in Great Britain by Clays Ltd, St Ives plc

A CIP catalogue record for this book is available from the British Library

ISBN-13: 978-0-670-91138-7
ISBN-10: 0-670-91138-0

*For Benedict and Tess*

# Contents

# List of Illustrations

## Section One

## Section Two

## Section Three

# Maps

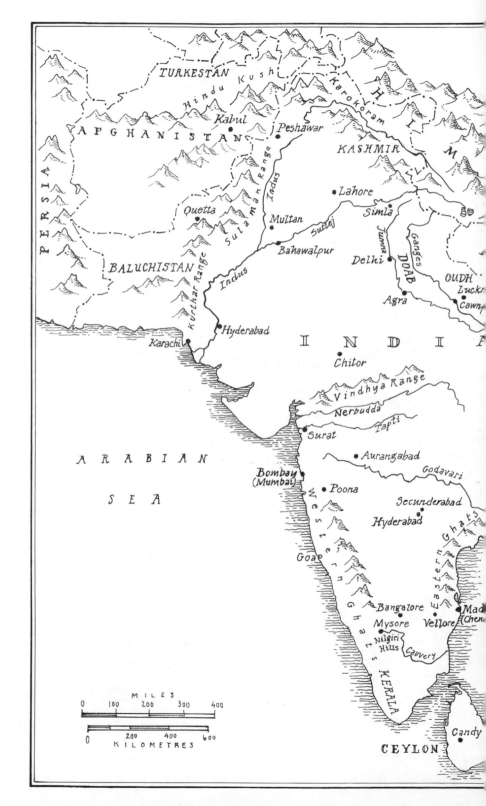

# THE INDIAN SUBCONTINENT

TIBET

HIMALAYAS

CHINA

NEPAL

Brahmaputra

Ganges

AR

ASSAM

MANIPUR

BENGAL

Chittagong

BURMA

Calcutta

Irrawaddy

Ava

RISSA

Mouths of the Ganges

Pagan

madi

ARAKAN

Prome

Donabyu

Pegu

Bassein

Rangoon

SIAM

BAY OF

BENGAL

INDIAN      OCEAN

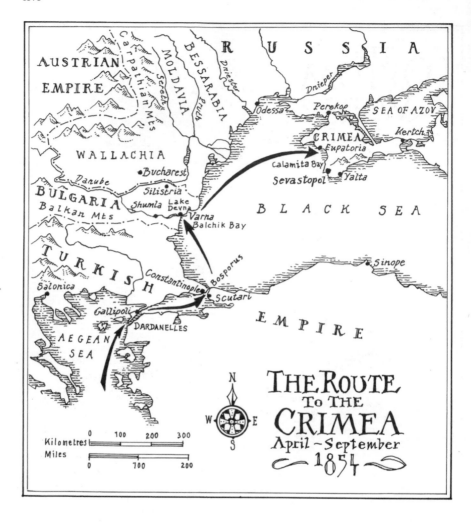

THE ROUTE TO THE CRIMEA

April – September 1854

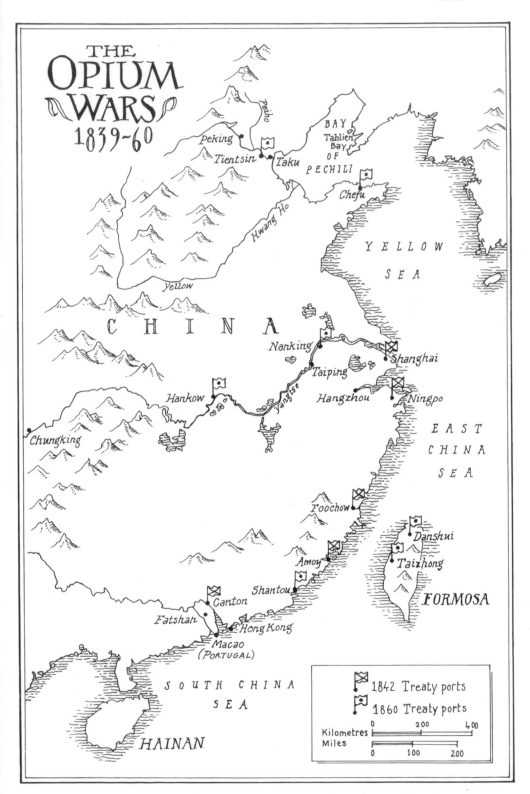

# Prologue

Shortly before six in the morning on 20 June 1837, a carriage drew up in front of Kensington Palace in central London. It had come from Windsor Castle and contained two men: Lord Conyngham, the portly lord chamberlain, and Dr William Howley, the septuagenarian archbishop of Canterbury. Let in by liveried servants, the pair asked to speak to the duchess of Kent, a German-born princess who in 1818 had taken as her second husband a younger son of the 'mad' King George III. The duchess appeared and, after a brief conversation, returned to the bedroom she still shared with her eighteen-year-old daughter, Princess Victoria. The princess was woken – with a kiss, according to her mother – and told that two men were there to see her. She rose quickly, threw a dressing-gown over her nightdress and, with her fair hair still loose about her shoulders, received the two visitors in her sitting-room. She was, as she recorded pointedly in her journal, '*alone*'. She added: 'Lord Conyngham (the Lord Chamberlain) then acquainted me that my poor Uncle, the King, was no more, and had expired at 12 minutes past 2 this morning, and consequently that I am *Queen*.'

There were no tears. They had flowed the night before when Prince Ernest of Hohenlohe-Langenburg, her half-sister's husband, had informed her that William IV, the popular but ineffectual 'Sailor King', had only a few hours to live. Instead the young queen felt mostly relief: that her kindly uncle had been relieved of his suffering; and that she, at last, was her own mistress. Constrained, hitherto, by the strict system imposed upon her by her widowed mother and her mother's scheming private secretary (and some say lover), Sir John Conroy, she was now free to make her own decisions. Her first had been to speak to the two envoys without her mother being present; the trick was repeated at nine, after breakfast, when she received Lord Melbourne, the handsome 58-year-old Whig prime minister, '*quite alone*, as I shall *always* do all my Ministers'. As Melbourne kissed her hand, she told him it had long been her intention to retain both him and his government, and that 'it could not be in better hands than his.' He stooped to kiss her hand a second time in gratitude.

Melbourne then read the young queen the draft of her declaration to the Privy Council.* He had composed it himself and she thought it 'very fine'. Indeed her overall impression of Melbourne could not have been more favourable. 'I like him very much', she recorded, 'and feel confidence in him. He is a very straightforward, honest, clever and good man.'

The Privy Council met in the palace's Red Saloon at 11.30 a.m. Attending were two of Victoria's three surviving uncles – the dukes of Cumberland and Sussex – and most of the senior political, military, legal and ecclesiastical officers of the realm. It was hard for them not to be impressed by the self-assured and dignified manner with which this slight young girl, clad in black, assumed the responsibilities of state. 'Everyone appeared touched with her manner,' noted one cabinet minister, 'particularly the Duke of Wellington and Lord Melbourne. I saw some tears in the eyes of the latter.' Victoria recorded that she was 'not at all nervous' as she read out the declaration and swore in the members of the council. That night, after a quiet supper and another 'very important' conversation with Melbourne, she slept alone for the first time in her life. The Victorian Age had dawned.

When the young, politically naive but fiercely dutiful Queen Victoria ascended the throne in 1837, Britain was the world's leading industrial power, with apparently limitless supplies of coal and iron, and a virtual monopoly on steam power. London was not only the largest city in the world but also its principal financial exchange. Victoria's navy was recognized as the ultimate arbiter of

---

* A (largely honorary) body of advisers appointed by the monarch. Most members had held, or still held, high political, legal or ecclesiastical office.

world affairs, while her army basked in the reputation it had won at Waterloo.

Yet Britain's empire was, if anything, in decline. The American Revolution had helped to sour the notion of empire, and powerful commercial interests were arguing for free trade and against the protectionism of the eighteenth-century imperial system. In 1837 the empire consisted of a jumbled collection of territories acquired in bits and pieces over the generations, administered partly by government and partly by chartered companies. 'It was', wrote James Morris, 'an unsystematic affair, an empire in abeyance, possessing no unity of purpose or sense of whole.' It nevertheless covered some two million square miles and possessed a population in excess of a hundred million.

The greatest imperial presence was in India, where, by a process of conquest and treaty, the Honourable East India Company (HEIC) had completed its transformation from trading company to sovereign power and was directly ruling more than half of the subcontinent as the agent of the British government. Less buoyant were Britain's West Indian possessions, including the sugar islands; these had underpinned domestic prosperity in the eighteenth century but were now, following the abolition of slavery in 1834, in rapid decline. There were the 'white' colonies in Canada and Australia – all of which would soon demand a measure of self-rule – and there was Ireland, nearer to home and ruled by the English since the twelfth century.

Cape Colony in southern Africa had been British since 1806, and a Cape Town trading company had recently founded Port Natal (later Durban) in south-east Africa. Other new acquisitions included Ceylon (part of the peace settlement in 1815) and Singapore (founded by Sir Thomas Stamford Raffles in 1819). In Europe the Union Jack fluttered over a string of key naval bases: Heligoland, Gibraltar, Malta and the Ionion Islands. Elsewhere British possessions were confined to a hotchpotch of islands, trading stations and strategic strongpoints, amongst them Penang, Arakan, the Falklands, the Seychelles, Mauritius, Gambia, the trading forts of the Gold Coast, St Helena, Norfolk Island and Bermuda. An estimated 1.2 million Britons were living abroad, including 56,000 soldiers in imperial garrisons (a large proportion of them in India).

During the period known as the 'Dual Monarchy' – from Victoria's accession in 1837 to the death of her husband Albert in 1861 – the empire almost quintupled* in size thanks to territorial acquisitions in Asia, Africa, the South Sea and the Far East. Its cities, canals, railways and telegraphs were changing the face of continents. It was well on the way to becoming the greatest empire the world had ever seen.

This is the story of that extraordinary quarter century of imperial conquest and the people who made it happen: the politicians, colonial administrators, businessmen, generals and ordinary soldiers. It is, in particular, the story of the two major and nine medium-sized wars† that were fought in the name of trade, civilization and the balance of power. Of those many conflicts, only the Crimean War of 1854–6 was not strictly an imperial war, though it was fought with the security of empire in mind. (Of course the gap between the perception and the reality of a genuine threat to 'imperial' interests was no less yawning in 1838, when the British launched an unprovoked war in Afghanistan, than it was in 2003, when the British and Americans did the same in Iraq.)

When Victoria became queen, the British Army was fighting battles in a manner its seventeenth-century forebears would have recognized. But her reign was to coincide with some of the greatest technological advances of any period of history. By 1861 the advent of steamships, telegraphic communications, rifles and breech-loading cannon had revolutionized the business of war. Tactics and uniforms had to evolve to keep pace. But the conservative nature of the British Army meant that it rarely learnt from its previous campaigns; it preferred to adapt on the job. All of Victoria's early wars were successful but often only after initial setbacks. Incredibly, the greatest industrial nation in the world

---

* From two to nine and a half million square miles.
† The British fought thirty campaigns during this period. But most of them were little more than border skirmishes or punitive expeditions.

did not always enjoy either a tactical or a technical superiority over its foes.

The one constant in this period of unprecedented change, always at the centre of the ever-expanding imperial web, was the formidable figure of Queen Victoria herself: shaping, supporting and sometimes condemning her government's foreign policy – but never ignoring it. And through all this she was helped and guided by her talented and hugely underrated husband, Prince Albert.

# 1. The Young Queen

The unlikely chain of events that brought the daughter of George III's fourth son to the British throne was set in motion on 6 November 1817, when Princess Charlotte, twenty-one, the only child of the prince regent (later George IV), died shortly after giving birth to a stillborn son. This double tragedy not only deprived the country of two heirs apparent but left the incapacitated King George III,* the father of fifteen children, without a legitimate grandchild. Only two of the regent's six surviving brothers were legally married – the dukes of York and Cumberland – and neither had fathered a child. The so-called 'Race for the Throne' was on.

It was won by fifty-year-old Edward, duke of Kent. A tall, stout, attractive man with a bald head and a fringe of hair he was wont to dye black, he had made his career in the army, where he became notorious as a martinet. It all came to an abrupt end in 1803, when his harsh regime at Gibraltar resulted in the death of a sergeant from flogging. The duke was quietly removed from the active list. Yet he had earlier served with distinction in the French West Indies (for which he was mentioned in dispatches) and eventually retired a field marshal.

His private persona could not have been more of a contrast. He was generally regarded as a warm, humane man whose 'liberal' views were at odds with those of his Tory brothers. The duke of Wellington, while disagreeing with his politics, considered him one of the most eloquent conversationalists he knew. Edward

---

* He had suffered for most of his adult life from a mysterious illness that modern doctors have diagnosed as the metabolic disorder known as porphyria (whose symptoms include severe stomach pain, fever, racing pulse and delirium). A particularly severe attack in 1810 resulted in the regency of his eldest son, George, prince of Wales, which lasted until George III's death in 1820.

excelled at after-dinner speeches and indulged his interfering nature (and kept his three private secretaries busy) with a constant stream of complaints and suggestions to government departments. His domestic arrangements were similarly unorthodox. For the previous twenty-seven years he had lived a quiet and unobtrusive life with his French mistress, Thérèse-Bernadine Montgenêt, better known as Madame de Saint-Laurent, who was seven years his senior. But, like his brothers, he was a spendthrift and constantly in debt. Convinced that parliament would increase his already generous annual income of £27,000* if he married, he had been on the lookout for a wife since 1815. His preferred choice was Princess Charlotte's sister-in-law,† the Dowager Princess Victoire of Leiningen (née Saxe-Coburg-Saalfeld), a thirty-year-old widow with two children. He proposed on their first meeting but was rejected. Charlotte's death caused him to press his suit with renewed vigour.

This time Princess Victoire accepted – partly swayed by inaccurate rumours that the prince regent had given his blessing – and the couple were married in Coburg on 29 May 1818. The duke had been hoping for an increase to his allowance of £25,000 a year, and a £12,000 grant to pay for his 'outfit' and marriage expenses. Instead the House of Commons voted him an extra £6,000 and nothing for his 'outfit'. The duke of Wellington was not surprised, describing the royal dukes as the 'damnedest millstone about the necks of any government that can be imagined'. He added: 'They have insulted – *personally* insulted – two thirds of the gentlemen of England, and how can it be wondered at that they take their revenge upon them when they get them in the House of Commons.'

Two other royal dukes were married by the summer of 1818: the duke of Clarence, George III's third son (and the future King William IV), and the duke of Cambridge, his youngest surviving

---

* Roughly equivalent to £1m today.
† In 1816 Charlotte had married Victoire's brother Prince Leopold, the third son of the duke of Saxe-Coburg-Saalfeld, a minor German principality.

son. Cambridge's union was the first to produce a healthy child – christened George – on 26 March 1819. But Prince George would inherit the throne only if neither of his father's newly married elder brothers had children. In the event, the duke of Clarence produced two daughters, but both died in infancy. The duke of Kent had better fortune. On 24 May 1819, after a straightforward six-hour labour, his wife gave birth to 'a pretty little Princess, as plump as a partridge'. At the insistence of the prince regent she was christened Alexandrina Victoria: the first name in honour of the Russian Tsar Alexander, the second a sop to her mother. Known as 'Drina' in her infant years, the family eventually plumped for Victoria, or 'Vickelchen', as her German mother called her.

Victoria never knew her father. He died of pneumonia when she was just seven months old,★ leaving his widow the onerous task of raising a future queen. The duchess was assisted by the handsome and insinuating Captain (later Sir) John Conroy, the duke's former equerry, who became her private secretary and, some say, her lover. It was Conroy who convinced the duchess that her daughter needed to be isolated from other members of the royal family: partly to protect her from their low moral stan-dards and partly because, he said, Victoria's life was in danger from some of her designing uncles, particularly the quarrelsome duke of Cumberland, who would become king if she died first. Conroy's long-term plan, however, was to retain such an exclusive hold over the young princess that when she became queen he and the duchess would rule by proxy. Thus was instituted the so-called 'Kensington system' – named after the palace in which she lived – whereby the young princess was kept apart from other children, rarely left alone and never allowed to see any visitor without a third person present. And yet, despite this lonely upbringing in a state of virtual house arrest, Victoria developed into an affectionate, self-possessed and dutiful young woman. Nothing better illustrates

★ The duke of Kent died on 23 January 1820, six days before his father, George III.

her extraordinary mixture of humility and responsibility than the journal entry she made on her eighteenth birthday, just a month before becoming queen. 'How old!' she wrote, 'and yet how far am I from being what I should be. I shall from this day take the *firm* resolution to study with renewed assiduity, to keep my attention always well fixed on whatever I am about, and to strive to become every day less trifling and more fit for what, if Heaven wills it, I'm some day to be!'

That the duchess of Kent and Sir John Conroy had miscalculated the effect their 'system' would have on Victoria is clear from the speed with which the young queen asserted her independence. Her mother was banished to a distant bedroom, while the hated Conroy was denied an official position and eventually induced to 'retire' from the duchess's household by the promise of an Irish peerage.* The man who instead became the queen's mentor and chief adviser was William Lamb, the second Viscount Melbourne. A handsome, urbane and cultured man, Melbourne had experienced more than his share of private misfortune. He had married, against his family's wishes, the beautiful, eccentric and headstrong Lady Caroline Ponsonby, daughter of the earl of Bessborough. Her affair with, and unrequited love for, the poet Lord Byron had scandalized society and embarrassed her husband; yet he had forgiven her and only her descent into insanity had caused their separation. She died in 1828 and was followed to the grave a year later by her sickly and feeble-minded son, Augustus, Melbourne's only child. Melbourne sought solace in his career as a leading Whig politician and in 1835 became prime minister for the second time in two years. He would remain in office until 1841, and was therefore on hand to guide Victoria through the crucial early years of her reign.

Some observers feared that Melbourne would abuse his position to make himself, in effect, king. But they misread his essen-

---

* Conroy left the duchess's service in 1839 but, thanks to the queen's veto, never received his Irish peerage. He died in 1854.

tially honourable and patriotic nature. Charles Greville, the celebrated diarist and clerk to the Privy Council, best summed up Melbourne's feeling towards the queen when he wrote:

I have no doubt he is passionately fond of her as he might be of his daughter if he had one, and the more because he is a man with a capacity for loving without having anything in the world to love. It is become his province to educate, instruct, and form the most interesting mind and character in the world.

Melbourne threw himself into the task with singular enthusiasm, spending as much time enthralling the young queen with his endless fund of amusing stories and love of literature as he did tutoring her in the art of politics and her role as a constitutional monarch. For no longer could a monarch make or break governments, as George III had done. The steady erosion of royal patronage and the changes brought about by the great parliamentary Reform Act of 1832 (particularly the expansion of the electorate to one in seven males and the abolition of 'rotten' boroughs*) had increased the House of Commons' influence over the government and weakened that of the monarch. But the traditional social elites – the aristocracy and greater gentry – still dominated both houses, and, for them, the period between the Reform Acts of 1832 and 1867 was a political golden age. The worst of the 'rotten' boroughs had been disenfranchised, but influence and money still talked at election time, ensuring either uncontested seats or ballots in which the most 'generous' candidate prevailed. Centrally organized political parties were beginning to emerge to take account of the expanded electorate, but it was only after the passing of the 1867 Act (which gave one in three men the vote) that they were able to exert discipline over their members. All this left Victoria in a curious constitutional position: nominally powerful but in

---

* A 'rotten' or 'pocket' borough was one in which the electorate was so small that it could be dominated by a single landlord who, in effect, had the MP in his pocket.

reality the weak partner in the precarious balancing act between monarch, government and parliament. Yet monarchs still had – in the words of Walter Bagehot, the great constitutional historian – 'three great rights': to be consulted, to encourage and to warn. As her reign progressed, Victoria would make full use of these rights to influence government policy.

In 1837, however, Victoria still had much to learn. When told that the 1838 parliament would open on 9 January, she declared her intention not to attend. 'Oh, you must,' implored Melbourne. 'That would never do.' Reluctantly – but sensibly – she acquiesced. The key to influencing Victoria was to gain her trust. This Melbourne achieved from the very beginning. 'Talked with him about many important things,' she noted on 2 July 1837. 'He is indeed a most truly honest, straightforward and noble-minded man and I esteem myself *most* fortunate to have such a man at the head of the Government; a man in whom I can safely place confidence. There are not *many* like him in this world of deceit!' Many contemporaries suspected Victoria of falling in love with her charismatic prime minister. Her feelings, wrote Greville, 'are *sexual* though She does not know it'. Possibly. She had lost her father at an early age and was clearly susceptible to a father figure. But if she did feel for Melbourne anything beyond 'daughterly' love, it was clearly of the schoolgirl-crush variety.

A month after her accession, Victoria moved from Kensington Palace to Buckingham Palace, a large mansion at the top of St James's Park that had been bought by her grandfather, George III, and enlarged by his son George IV. Though the refurbishment of this large and draughty house, begun by William IV, was not yet complete, Victoria insisted on moving in July because her old house was not grand enough for a ruling monarch. She was 'much pleased' with her 'high, pleasant and cheerful' new apartments.* But she did not leave the place of her birth – where she had enjoyed 'pleasant balls and *delicious* concerts' – without

---

* They consisted of her bedroom, her private sitting room and an audience room. The duchess of Kent had separate apartments.

regrets. 'I have gone through painful and disagreeable scenes here, 'tis true,' she wrote, 'but still I am fond of the poor old Palace.'

The high point of Victoria's first year as queen was her coronation at Westminster Abbey on 28 June 1838, for which parliament provided the handsome sum of £200,000 (four times the amount given to her predecessor). London, with its population of one and a half million swelled by 400,000 visitors, was bursting at the seams. Greville wrote on 27 June:

There was never anything seen like the state of this town; it is as if the population had been on a sudden quintupled; the uproar, the confusion, the crowd, the noise, are indescribable. Horsemen, footmen, carriages squeezed, jammed, intermingled, the pavement blocked up with timbers, hammering and knocking, and falling fragments stunning the ears and threatening the head; not a mob here and there, but the town all mob, thronging, bustling, gaping, and gazing at everything, at anything, or at nothing; the park one vast encampment, with banners floating on the tops of the tents, and still the roads are covered, the railroads loaded with arriving multitudes.

On the day itself the queen was woken at four by cannons firing the royal salute and was unable to get back to sleep because of the noise from countless bands and the growing crowds. She finally rose at seven and, after a light breakfast, dressed in her coronation robes of white satin and red velvet, and placed a circlet of diamonds in her hair. At ten she climbed into the gold State Coach with two attendants and began the slow procession, via Constitution Hill, Piccadilly and Whitehall, to Westminster Abbey. The crowds exceeded anything she had 'ever seen'. Their 'good humour and excessive loyalty' made her proud to be queen of '*such* a Nation', and her only worry was that some might be injured in the crush.

Amidst 'deafening cheers' she reached the west door of the abbey at 11.30 and went straight to the robing room, where she put on a long red mantle lined with ermine. Followed by her eight young train-bearers and Lord Conyngham, and preceded by Lord Melbourne carrying the Sword of State, she walked slowly towards the altar. The scene was magnificent: the abbey decorated with crimson and gold tapestries; the rows of peeresses 'quite beautiful in all their robes, and the peers on the other side'; the altar covered with gold plate. Victoria was received by the archbishop of Canterbury, who proclaimed her 'the undoubted Queen of this realm'. This drew the universal response: 'God Save Queen Victoria.' Having taken the oath to maintain the Protestant religion, the queen withdrew to the nearby St Edward's Chapel, where she replaced her robes and diamond circlet with a linen shift and a supertunica of cloth of gold. Returning bareheaded to the altar, she sat in St Edward's Chair as four knights of the Garter held a gold canopy over her head and the archbishop performed the Ceremony of the Anointing. Then the dalmatic golden robe lined with ermine was clasped around her, and she was handed the orb, sceptre and ruby ring. Unfortunately the ring was too small for her fourth finger, having been measured for the fifth, and had to be screwed on by the flustered archbishop as she winced in pain. Finally the archbishop placed the crown of state on her head. As he did so, the peers and peeresses donned their coronets, causing shafts of light from the candles to criss-cross in the gloom. Trumpets and drums sounded, and outside cannon fired as the crowds roared, 'God Save the Queen.'

# 2. Afghanistan

Nine months earlier, as the young queen was still settling into her new London residence, a lone British horseman neared the Afghan capital of Kabul, thousands of miles away in central Asia. As he approached, a large noisy retinue emerged from the city gates to welcome him. At its head, seated atop a splendid elephant, was Akbar Khan, son of the amir, who greeted the rider with 'great pomp and splendour'. Together, mounted on separate elephants, the pair entered the city as large crowds strained for a sight of the mysterious foreigner. His name, it emerged, was Captain Alexander Burnes.

Born in Montrose in 1805, the son of the provost,★ Burnes had served in India since the age of sixteen. Though slight of frame and undistinguished looking, he had caught the eye of the Indian authorities and was eventually transferred from his Bombay regiment to the elite Political Department. Intelligent, resourceful, robust and daring, he was also a natural linguist and fluent in Persian, Arabic and Hindustani. He had made his name in 1832 by carrying out a daring intelligence-gathering mission through Afghanistan and into the fabled central Asian khanate of Bokhara, travelling on across the Turcoman Desert to the shores of the Caspian Sea, from where he returned to India, via Persia. So important was the information he gleaned that he was sent back to London to report in person. There he was dubbed 'Bokhara Burnes' by the press, lionized by society and granted audiences with both the prime minister and the king. He was even introduced to the then fourteen-year-old Princess Victoria, who thought his tales 'very interesting'.

In 1835, having published *Travels into Bokhara* to great acclaim

★ Mayor.

a year earlier, Burnes returned to India and his old job as assistant to the resident at Cutch. But in late 1836 he received orders from the new governor-general, Lord Auckland – a man he had met on his recent trip to Britain – to undertake a mission to Kabul. 'I came', he wrote after his arrival, 'to look after commerce, to superintend surveys and examine passes of mountains, and likewise *to see into affairs and judge what was to be done hereafter.*' He was sent, in other words, under the cover of a commercial mission. But his real reason for going was political: to see which way the land lay at the amir's court.

George Eden, second Baron Auckland, was a 51-year-old bachelor when he arrived in India in March 1836. The son of a distinguished politician who had held cabinet rank under various prime ministers – including Pitt, Addington and Grenville – Auckland never quite achieved the same prominence, though he had been a member of Lord Grey's and Lord Melbourne's governments. He was, in the opinion of a contemporary, 'quiet and unobtrusive in his manners, of a somewhat cold and impassive temperament, and altogether of a reserved and retiring nature'. Another described him as a hard-working, well-intentioned man but one of limited judgement. He was certainly sincere when he announced at his leaving dinner his intention of 'extending the blessings of good government and happiness' to India's millions.

Although an appointee of the British government, Auckland was technically an employee of the Honourable East India Company, the former trading house that had, by a process of treaty and conquest, come to dominate the subcontinent.* Its three presidencies – Bengal, Bombay and Madras – now covered more than half of India. Of the remaining Indian princely states, only the Sikh kingdom of the Punjab posed a serious challenge to British hegemony. But it was the external threat to British India,

---

* Since the India Act of 1784, the executive control of Indian affairs had passed from the HEIC's Court of Directors to a Board of Control in London. Its president was a cabinet minister and therefore answerable to parliament. But the Court of Directors retained its monopoly of patronage, and officials in India still enjoyed considerable freedom of action.

particularly from Russia, that came to dominate Auckland's thinking during his early months in charge. For much of the previous century tsarist Russia had been expanding its eastern empire at Persia's expense, notably by acquiring Georgia in 1800 and territory in the Caucasus thirteen years later. Persia's attempt to reverse the trend in 1826 had ended in another humiliating defeat. Worse was to follow in 1836, when the new shah of Persia was encouraged by the Russians to seek compensation for his losses by conquering the Afghan province of Herat, commonly known as the 'Gate of India'. An ultimatum was duly sent to the ruler of Herat, Shah Kamran, who summarily rejected it. War was inevitable.

Lord Palmerston, the British foreign secretary, was well aware that Russia was using Persia as its stalking horse, testing Britain's resolve to maintain Afghanistan's territorial integrity. The best way to foil Russian designs, he decided, was to counter a pro-Russian ruler in Persia with a pro-British ruler in Afghanistan. This was the gist of the briefing he gave to Lord Auckland before the latter's departure for India in early 1836. More explicit instructions were sent to him by the secret committee of the HEIC's Court of Directors: he was to 'judge as to what steps it may be proper and desirable for you to take to . . . counteract the progress of Russian influence in a quarter which, from its proximity to our Indian possessions, could not fail, if it were once established, to act injuriously on the system of our Indian alliances, and possibly even to interfere with the tranquillity of our own territory'. He could accomplish this task, he was told, by sending a confidential agent to Dost Mohamed, the amir of Kabul, 'merely to watch the progress of events, or to enter into relations with this chief, either of a political or merely, in the first instance, of a commercial character'.* Alexander Burnes was the obvious choice as agent: he had travelled extensively in Afghanistan, knew the language and had

---

* In the late 1830s, when early steamships and the express route across the Suez Isthmus were used, it took up to three months for instructions from London to reach Calcutta. This time delay gave the local authorities a great deal of latitude when it came to implementing policy.

met Dost during his previous visit to Kabul. His mission was one
of the first acts in what came to be known as the 'Great Game',
the often secret struggle between Britain and Russia for control of
the central Asian gateways into India.

The enthusiastic greeting given to Burnes on his arrival at Kabul
in September 1837 was a sign that the amir needed friends. Not
only was Persia advancing on Herat with Russian support, but
Dost's brother had recently lost the fertile province of Peshawar,
at the head of the Khyber Pass, to the formidable Sikh ruler Ranjit
Singh, the 'Lion of the Punjab'. If the British could help him
regain Peshawar, Dost told Burnes, he would willingly assist their
commercial and political aims. But Burnes knew that the Indian
government would never jettison its strong alliance with Ranjit in
return for Dost's friendship, and was therefore unable to offer more
than vague assurances.

In the midst of these delicate negotiations appeared Captain Yan
Vitkevich, a Lithuanian-born officer in the Imperial Russian Army,
who had travelled from Orenburg in the Urals with a letter for
Dost from Tsar Nicholas I himself. On hearing of his approach,
Dost had asked Burnes whether he wanted the Russian arrested or
expelled. Burnes said neither. Instead he wanted Dost to listen to
what the Russian had to say and then report back. Dost agreed,
but the news, when it came, was not what Burnes wanted to hear.
'We are in a mess here,' he confided to a friend. 'The Emperor of
Russia has sent an envoy to Caubul to offer Dost Mahomed Khan
money to fight Runjeet Sing!!! . . . I sent an express at once to my
Lord A., telling him that after this I knew not what might happen,
and it was now a neck-and-neck race between Russia and us.'

Auckland's unhelpful response was to rule out the possibility of
forcing Ranjit to hand back Peshawar. At the same time Burnes
was instructed to warn Dost that were he to enter into an alliance
with the Russians, or any other power, that might be considered
detrimental to British interests, then he would be forcibly removed
from his throne. An outraged Dost refused to bow to Auckland's
demand that Vitkevich be expelled, not least because the governor-
general had offered nothing tangible in return. Instead, on 21 April

1838, he received the Russian envoy with every mark of respect at his Bala Hissar palace. Six days later, conceding defeat to his rival, Burnes left Kabul to report to his superiors.

By now the Persian siege of Herat was in its seventh month and the city's fall was daily expected. Writing in May 1838, Auckland felt he had three options: he could leave Afghanistan to its fate, though that would simply invite 'Russian and Persian intrigue upon our frontiers'; he could save Afghanistan by supporting the existing chiefs of Kabul and Kandahar, though that would 'give power to those who felt greater animosity against the Sikhs than they did against the Persians'; or he could allow Ranjit's Sikh armies to advance on Kabul with the intention of restoring the former ruler, Shah Shuja,★ who was then in exile in the British frontier town of Ludhiana. Incredibly – and despite the opposition of experienced politicals like Claude Wade, the British agent on the North-West Frontier, who preferred to support Dost – Auckland chose the last option.

The governor-general had been heavily influenced in his thinking by Sir William Macnaghten, secretary to the Secret and Political Department in Calcutta (and therefore Burnes's boss), a man described by Auckland's sister Emily as '*our* Lord Palmerston'. The son of an Indian Supreme Court judge, Macnaghten had joined the HEIC's army as a sixteen-year-old cadet and later transferred to the political branch, where his industry and linguistic ability secured him rapid promotion. Now forty-five, with spectacles, a heavy moustache and a sharp nose, he was ambitious enough to promote a risky policy that, if it turned out well, would bring him fame and further honours. Macnaghten conducted negotiations with Ranjit and Shuja in person, signing treaties with them for a joint march on Kabul in June and July respectively.

★ Shuja ul-Mulk, a Saduzai, ruled Kabul from 1803 to 1812, when he was overthrown by his elder brother Mahmoud. Mahmoud was toppled, in turn, by Dost Mohamed of the rival Barukzai clan, though he maintained a foothold of power in Herat, where his son Kamran still held sway. The exiled Shuja had made a number of attempts to recapture his throne, most recently in 1833, when his troops were defeated outside Kandahar by Dost Mohamed.

Burnes had made his own feelings clear in a letter to Macnaghten in early June, pointing out that the situation in Kabul could not remain as it was, and that nothing but 'decided remonstrance' would deter Russian encroachment. As for Shuja, the British government had only to send him to Peshawar with an agent, two of its own regiments as an escort and 'an avowal to the Afghans that we have taken up his cause, to ensure his being fixed for ever upon his throne'. But, he added, 'we must be *directly* concerned.' In other words, British troops should be part of the invasion force. And yet his favoured course of action would have been to support Dost. 'He is a man of undoubted ability', wrote Burnes, 'and has at heart a high opinion of the British nation, and if half you must do for others were done for him . . . he would abandon Russia and Persia to-morrow.'

Burnes, however, was overruled by Macnaghten, his assistant Henry Torrens and John Colvin, Auckland's private secretary, who was destined to play a leading if inglorious role in the great sepoy★ rebellion of 1857. The only one of Burnes's suggestions that Macnaghten and his cohorts did agree with was that British troops should also take part. Auckland duly consulted his commander-in-chief, General Sir Henry Fane, who, according to his ADC,† warned against such a 'wild and unmeasured expedition'. Even if an initial invasion was successful, argued Fane, it would be 'next to impossible' to 'maintain large bodies of troops in countries so distant, and which hardly produce sufficient food for a very scanty population'. When Fane realized that Auckland was determined to proceed regardless, he insisted on assembling as large a British force as possible. In the event the so-called 'Army of the Indus' was drawn from both the Bombay and Bengal presidencies and was originally comprised of six regiments of cavalry, eighteen of infantry, two brigades of artillery and supporting units.

★ An Indian infantry soldier in the employ of the HEIC; from the Persian *sipahi*, or soldier.
† Aide-de-camp or personal staff officer.

The opening moves in the conflict were precipitated by Auckland and his closest advisers in the face of much local opposition. They had come to the extraordinary conclusion that the best way to carry out London's instructions – namely to prevent Russia from gaining a foothold in Afghanistan, and thereby threatening the security of British India – was the substitution of Shuja for Dost. An additional benefit was the forging of new trade links with Afghanistan. But these commercial interests could have been achieved by negotiation with Dost. The chief aim of the war was regime change: the replacement of an (allegedly) anti-British amir with a pro-British one. Two key questions, however, had not received a satisfactory answer: how would the fiercely independent Afghan tribes react to the imposition by British bayonets of a former ruler of doubtful popularity? And how would the British, even if they succeeded in conquering Afghanistan, be able to hold on to it? Such doubts were clearly in the mind of Mountstuart Elphinstone, the enlightened former governor of Bombay who had turned down the vacant governor-generalship in 1835, when he wrote to a friend:

I used to dispute with you against having an agent in Caubul, and now we have assumed the protection of the state as much as if it were one of the subsidiary allies in India. If you send 27,000 men up the Bolan Pass to Candahar (as we hear is intended), and can feed them, I have no doubt you will take Candahar and Caubul and set up Soojah; but for maintaining him in a poor, cold, strong and remote country, among a turbulent people like the Afghans, I own it seems to me to be hopeless.

Auckland's perspective was more short term. On 1 October, with the Bengal portion of the Army of the Indus gathered at Ferozepur, he set out the reasons for invasion in his Simla⋆ Manifesto: to overthrow Dost Mohamed, who had formed schemes

---

⋆ Simla was a hill station in the foothills of the Himalayas, where the governor-general spent much of the hot season between June and October.

of 'aggrandizement and ambition injurious to the security and peace of the frontiers of India', and who had given his 'undisguised support to the Persian designs in Afghanistan'; and to replace him with Shah Shuja, whose popularity in his own country had been proved, and whose power would now be supported 'against foreign interference and factious opposition by a British army'. Only once Shuja had been 'secured in power, and the independence and integrity of Afghanistan established' would British troops be withdrawn.

The news, in mid October, that the Persians had raised their siege of Herat made little difference to Auckland's plans beyond reducing the size of the invasion force. But it was the last straw for Sir Henry Fane, the commander-in-chief, who did not support the policy of armed intervention but who thought that, if it did take place, it should be done properly. The official reason for his replacement as commander of the Army of the Indus by Lieutenant-General Sir John Keane, head of the Bombay Army, was ill-health. But Fane was dissatisfied, telling Auckland that such a small army did not require his services, and complaining that Macnaghten, who was to accompany the expedition as political chief, had usurped his authority. The 'principal and real reason' that Fane relinquished the command, wrote his ADC, 'was disgust at the extraordinary power, both civil and military, delegated to Mr McNaghten – such power as would have rendered the commander-in-chief of all the armies in India a mere cipher or tool in the hands of a civil secretary to Government'.

The army that General Keane would take with him into Afghanistan was a heterogeneous mix of Queen's troops, Britons and Indians in the employ of the HEIC, and Shah Shuja's local levies. But, like all commanders in India, Keane would rely most on his regiments of British infantry: the 2nd (Queen's), 3rd (Buffs) and 17th (Leicestershire) Foot, and 13th (Somersetshire) Light Infantry. Red-coated infantrymen had been the backbone of the British Army for the previous century and a half, during which time their appearance, equipment and tactics had changed very little. They still wore tight red coatees,★ buff leather cross-belts and close-fitting grey trousers; constricting their necks were black leather stocks and atop their heads sat tall shako dress caps that – with their brass rim, scales and badge – weighed up to three pounds and resembled inverted coal scuttles. Their remaining equipment – musket, ammunition pouches, water bottle, bayonet and haversack – brought the total burden for a fully laden soldier to a back-breaking seventy pounds.

The infantryman's musket was essentially of the same Brown Bess design that had been in service since the 1730s.† A muzzle-loading, smooth-bore flintlock, it was short of range (effective to only 200 yards), slow to use (two to three shots per minute) and wildly inaccurate (though effective enough in a European conflict against compact bodies of troops). It was also heavy (twelve pounds) and, with a barrel of thirty-nine inches, extremely long and unwieldy. But its large bore – .753 calibre, the biggest in Europe – packed a considerable punch, and the duke of Wellington, for one, was an ardent admirer. He described it as the 'most efficient' musket yet produced, adding: 'The fire from it [is] . . . the most destructive known. It is durable, it bears all sorts of Ill-Usage; is easily repaired, and kept in Repair and Serviceable; and besides its Power as a Missile, its length is an advantage in the use of the Bayonet.' But even the bayonet was a weapon of questionable reliability: sixteen inches long, triangular in shape and iron in construction, it was heavy and had a tendency to bend and work itself loose in combat.

Officers wore similar uniforms to those of their men – though more elaborate and without cross-belts – and were armed with swords and pistols. The latter were single-shot, inaccurate and unreliable. So ineffective were they, in fact, that the 1833 cavalry

---

★ Swallow-tailed coats with buttons and facings specific to a particular regiment. In the case of the 2nd (Queen's Royal) Regiment of Foot, the buttons were stamped with a crown and the number '2', and the facings were blue.

† The British Army was in the process of converting its muskets from the flintlock to the percussion ignition system, which would improve range and reliability. But the new muskets would not reach regiments serving in India for a number of years.

regulations defined the pistol as 'merely a useful standby at close-quarters if the sword or sword-arm were disabled'.

The social origins of officers in the British Army could not have contrasted more with those of their men. Officers came, on the whole, from the traditional ruling castes: the aristocracy, landed gentry and rich middle classes. This was the direct result of the purchase system, whereby commissions had to be bought for a certain fixed amount (though an unofficial surcharge was often paid, particularly in the more fashionable guards and cavalry regiments). In theory an officer could purchase the next rank only when he had become the senior of the rank below. But rich and unscrupulous officers could get round this by bribing their senior but less affluent colleagues to waive their right to purchase. The fabulously rich seventh earl of Cardigan – of 'Light Brigade' fame – was one of the chief exponents of this financial chicanery, rising from cornet to lieutenant-colonel in just six and a half years (it usually took about twenty). Citing Cardigan and others as examples of how the purchase system favoured wealth over merit, Radical members of the post-reform parliament of the 1830s made a number of attempts to abolish it. But they all failed thanks, in no small part, to the opposition of the conservative duke of Wellington, who insisted that the purchase system was the surest way to protect the social and political status quo. 'It is the promotion by purchase', he told a House of Commons committee in 1833, 'which brings into the service men of fortune and education, men who have some connection with the interests and fortune of the country . . . It is this circumstance which exempts the British Army from the character of being a "mercenary army".'

Not every promotion was paid for: commissions were purchased only up to the rank of lieutenant-colonel, and brevet (or non-substantive) rank could be awarded for meritorious service at home or in the field. But the vast majority of officers paid for their initial commissions, which, in 1837, cost a minimum of £450 (or roughly £20,000 today). Because of this, and because they were expected to supplement their modest pay with a private income, most officers were from wealthy backgrounds.

Non-officers, or other ranks, came from the opposite end of the social spectrum. Poor pay, harsh discipline and long service abroad ensured that only those on the very lowest rung of society were tempted to enlist. Most were former agricultural labourers, with unemployed artisans, servants, miners, 'thoughtless youths, petty delinquents' and 'men of indolent habits' making up the balance. For the penniless, a strong incentive to join up was the remittance of all debts under £30 and the payment of bounty money. Not all recruits were desperate: a few wanted to see the world, serve their country and better themselves by promotion. But such ambitious and adventurous types were always in a minority. Wellington's infamous description of his soldiers in 1813 as 'the scum of the earth' referred as much to their lowly social origins as it did to their indiscipline after the Battle of Vitoria in the Second Peninsular War.

To keep such unpromising material in order, he and other senior officers insisted upon a draconian system of punishments. The cornerstone of the system, and the ultimate sanction, was the lash. Radical MPs made a number of attempts to abolish flogging in the 1820s and 1830s. All were defeated, but the popular clamour did result in the setting up of a Royal Commission in 1836 that limited the number of lashes a general court martial could award to 200* (prior to 1829 it had been 1,000). In the native armies of the HEIC, by contrast, flogging was abolished altogether in 1835 by Lord William Bentinck on the grounds that it deterred 'young men of respectable connections' from joining up. The social standing of the average Indian recruit was, to be fair, much higher than that of his British counterpart: the vast majority of Bengal soldiers, for example, were high-caste Hindus. But Wellington's fears were realized when the discipline of the Indian Army deteriorated, and Lord Hardinge, then governor-general, felt he had no option but to reintroduce flogging on a limited scale in 1845.

Infantry tactics had changed little since Waterloo and were specifically adapted to European war and the perceived inadequacies

* The limit for district and regimental court martials was 150 and 100 respectively.

of British weapons and troops. They relied upon close-order formations of the line for firing and charging, columns for manoeuvre
and the square as a defence against cavalry. What tactical innovation
there had been during the Napoleonic Wars – notably the use of
riflemen and light infantrymen to screen regular infantry – was the
preserve of a small number of units. And yet a war against Afghan
tribesmen could not have been more unsuitable for close-order
fighting. Hardy hillmen, familiar with arms from boyhood, the
Afghans were natural fighters who knew instinctively how to make
the best use of cover, and who could move from rock to rock with
the nimbleness of a mountain goat. Though their long-barrelled
matchlock muskets – known as *jezails* – were of ancient design
and had a tendency to burst, they had the crucial advantage of
being able to shoot further than British muskets. And they were
better shots, one English officer describing them as 'perhaps the
best marksmen in the world'. They were also skilled horsemen,
something of a necessity in a country that had no navigable rivers
and was too rugged for wheeled traffic. All in all they presented a
formidable foe with their mobility, fieldcraft and marksmanship.
They were, in effect, mounted infantrymen par excellence and
presented the British Army with the same sort of challenge at the
beginning of Victoria's reign as the Boers would at its end. Siege
operations might not be such a problem, but to combat them in
the field the British would need more than their traditional virtues
of discipline, courage and massed firepower. They would require,
in particular, the skills learnt by their riflemen and light infantry in
the two Peninsular Wars of 1808–14, when each company* knew
how to skirmish and to act independently.

The invasion of Afghanistan began on 10 March 1839, when the
Bengal Contingent of the Army of the Indus – 10,000 strong
– entered the formidable Bolan Pass, the gateway to southern
Afghanistan, 'a huge chasm, running between precipitous rocks to

* A British infantry regiment was divided into eight companies, A to H, of
roughly a hundred men each.

the length of seventy miles, and rising in that distance to the height of 5,637 feet above the plains below'. The plan was for Sir Willoughby Cotton to make the initial incursion; Keane, with the Bombay troops and Shuja's Contingent, would follow in his wake. It had been intended that Sikh troops would make a simultaneous advance up the Khyber Pass, but the ailing Ranjit Singh changed his mind, and this would not now take place. The British were on their own.

Once under way, the invasion force stretched for miles, a vast unwieldy column of soldiers, beasts, wagons and camp followers, the last outnumbering the fighting troops by three to one (as was usual in the subcontinent). Swelling the baggage to an alarming extent was the personal gear of the British officers, most of whom ignored Fane's suggestion to travel light. Even the junior officers were followed by as many as forty servants – cooks, bearers, dhobis and water-carriers – and camels laden with luggage. Among their 'necessities' were cigars, jams, pickles, potted fish, tinned meats, plate, glass, crockery, candles, table linen, books, dressing-cases, cologne and Windsor soap. Senior officers were just as culpable, with one brigadier-general requiring no fewer than sixty camels to transport his belongings.

Accompanying Cotton as political adviser was the recently knighted Sir Alexander Burnes. He had planned ahead by buying the cooperation of the local chieftain, the khan of Khelat, whose usual style was to plunder passing travellers. But, even without armed opposition, the slow pace of the column, the harshness of the rocky terrain and the absence of water and forage meant the march towards Kandahar quickly descended into chaos. It was, in the understated words of one officer, 'attended by great trouble, many privations and heavy loss in camels, hundreds and hundreds having died, consequently Govt. and many officers suffered very severely by the loss of tents and baggage'. Their subordinates were hit where it hurt most: in the stomach. British soldiers had their bread ration reduced, sepoys were put on half-rations and camp followers even less. The column was saved from starvation by Burnes's purchase of 10,000 sheep from a reluctant khan and

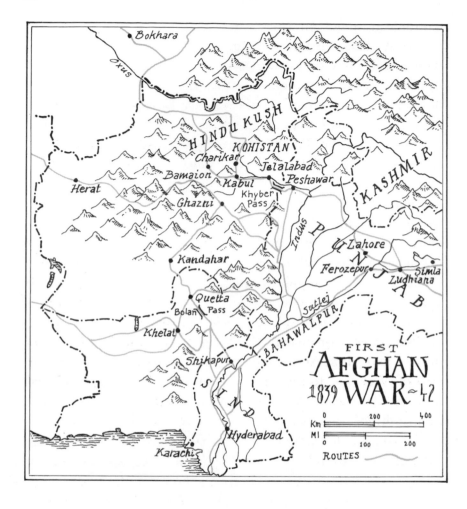

Cotton's insistence on a series of forced marches. On 24 March the Bengal troops reached Quetta, 'a most miserable mud town, with a small castle on a mound'. They were joined in early April by Keane and the Bombay Contingent, who had suffered serious supply problems of their own. The solution suggested by the ruthless Shuja was to reap the unharvested crops, leaving the inhabitants to starve. This was vetoed by Macnaghten, who, wisely, chose not to alienate the locals. But Shuja's contemptuous attitude towards ordinary Afghans – describing them as 'a pack of dogs, one and all' – did not bode well for the future. 'We must try', wrote Macnaghten, 'and bring him gradually round to entertain a more favourable view of his subjects.'

On 9 April the combined Army of the Indus moved on towards Kandahar with its supplies as meagre as ever: just fifteen days' rations for a march of fifteen days. Any delay in the capture of Kandahar would, according to one officer, have caused the army to disintegrate. Fortunately Dost's brothers chose not to defend the city, and, on 25 April, Shuja entered in apparent triumph to the cries of 'Welcome to the son of Timur Shah! Kandahar is rescued from the Barukzyes!' Much of this enthusiasm had been paid for by British gold, and a truer indication of local feeling was given on 8 May, when a grand review of troops on the plain outside Kandahar was attended by fewer than 500 Afghans. Even more worrying, noted a British colonel, was the fact that 'none of the Sirdars or men of rank have yet come in to tender their allegiance, all having fled with their followers.' Shuja's authority, as a result, did not 'extend beyond the gates of Candahar, and would be weak enough there were it not for the British camp outside'.

For two months the army languished at Kandahar, waiting for the harvest to ripen and replenish its supplies. The British troops, in particular, found the city and its inhabitants risible and charmless. 'Candahar is a square', wrote one staff officer, 'with four broad streets meeting in the centre with bastions and walls of mud, a lower wall and a contemptible ditch. We could have demolished the wall in no time. The city is beastly dirty, so are the people. They are cunning, avaricious, proud and filthy, notwithstanding all the romantic descriptions of Burnes, Connolly★ [*sic*] & Co.'

It was with a feeling of relief, therefore, that the army resumed its advance on 29 June. But Afghan opposition was beginning to stiffen, and the next British objective would prove a much tougher nut to crack than Kandahar. Two hundred and thirty miles distant, astride the road to Kabul, lay the formidable fortress town of Ghazni. During the British delay at Kandahar its defences had been strengthened, its garrison increased to 3,000 men under Dost's son Hyder Khan and provisions laid in for six months. Dost assumed the British would cover Ghazni with a small force and continue their advance. But Keane had been assured that the city was weakly held, and he was determined to capture it. To assist a direct assault he had begun the invasion with some heavy 24-pounder siege guns. Macnaghten, however, had persuaded him to leave them behind at Kandahar on the strength of reports from spies – 'some no doubt from and instructed by the Enemy' – that Ghazni had been 'abandoned' and 'no resistance' would be offered. It was a mistake, as Keane himself acknowledged in a letter to Sir Jasper Nicolls, Fane's successor as commander-in-chief of India:

On the morning of the 21st July the Army in three columns moved close to the outworks of the place, and instead of finding it, as the accounts had stated, very weak and incapable of resistance, a second Gibraltar appeared before us. A high rampart in good repair built on a scarped mound about 35 feet high, flanked by numerous towers, and surrounded by a well constructed [escalade] and a wide wet ditch. In short we were astounded, but there we were.

Keane ordered the twenty-two cannon he did have with him – a variety of 6- and 9-pounders – to open up on the fort, but they had little effect on its thick walls and were soon outgunned by a heavy counter-fire. Keane was in a fix. He could not leave such a

---

★ Captain Arthur Conolly, another intrepid 'political', who had written about his adventures in the region, including a visit to Kandahar in 1830. It was Conolly who first used the phrase the 'Great Game' in a letter to a friend.

strong position astride his line of communication, and yet did not have the guns to mount a direct assault. While he mulled over the problem, he put his troops under cover in nearby villages and gardens, and instructed his chief engineer to look for chinks in the fort's armour. One was found: the Kabul Gate on the north side of the town, which, though protected by a barricade, was 'assailable' and had the additional advantage of high ground screening its approach.

Keane resolved to attack, and, having received their instructions, the troops began to move into position at midnight on the 22nd. By 3 a.m. all was ready. Three engineer officers and a party of Indian sappers approached the Kabul Gate unseen and stacked up 300 pounds of gunpowder. With Keane's light artillery and a decoy force to the south creating a diversion, one of the officers lit the powder train. Captain James Douglas, a staff officer with the reserve column, recorded:

The scene at this moment was magnificent. The fire was unremitting on both sides. It was not yet daylight, and the indistinctness of objects, the rude walls, and queer figures formed a picture more beautiful, more grand, than anything I have ever imagined. Suddenly an explosion, louder than thunder, broke through the road of artillery; then a pause; then a cheer; the unmistakable English cheer, rent the air; then the old walls and battlements illuminated with the flash of arms, and then the busy musketry went chattering through the streets.

No sooner had the Kabul Gate exploded in a cloud of smoke, broken masonry and shattered timber than a bugle sounded 'Charge!' and the storming party – light companies from three British and one Bengal European regiment – were haring towards the breach. There they encountered stiff resistance from a dense body of sword-wielding Ghazis★ who left one section of thirty-two

★ Religious fanatics who fought under the green banner of Islam and who believed that death in battle with the infidel would guarantee them a place in Paradise. Not unlike the extreme Muslim terrorists of today.

British troops with only a single man unwounded. But ultimately the Ghazi scimitars were no match for British volley fire
and bayonets, and the breach was cleared. It took some time for
the main British column to enter the city, 'the gateway being
blocked up with rubbish and dead bodies, mostly Afghans', and
more time still for the remaining pockets of resistance to be
crushed. But by sunup the citadel was in British hands. Keane
reported:

The Afghans are desperate behind walls and were severely punished. We
buried 600 within the walls and the loss outside in the outworks and cut
by the cavalry trying to escape was 400 more. Our loss is about 200
including officers. So what was said to be secure for a year against any
power, was ours in two hours. And what I could hardly believe, but is
God's truth, not a woman was violated. Young Hyder was found con-
cealed, when order was restored, in one of the towers, and brought
prisoner to my tent. The poor youth was dreadfully low . . . I told him
by way of a little comfort that he was a brave soldier and had made a
gallant defence . . . He said he could bear his capture and that of his
fortress with resignation, but being obliged to appear before Shah Soojah
. . . was a death blow to him.

Hyder was 'shaking like a leaf' as Keane led him into Shuja's
presence. He need not have worried. Having listened to Keane's
advocacy, Shuja announced that the son of his mortal enemy
would be 'well treated'. Handed over to Burnes for safekeeping,
the young Afghan prince was so relieved by the 'kind treatment
he had met with' that he at once wrote to tell his father.

    Hyder was not the only Afghan treated well. No fewer than
1,500 defenders were taken prisoner, and, as Keane thought worthy
of mention, not a single Afghan woman was raped. Even for British
soldiers this was unusually restrained, particularly in the heat of a
battle with Asiatics. Major Henry Havelock, the teetotal Christian
soldier who would be immortalized for his exploits during the
Indian Mutiny, put it down to enforced temperance. 'The character of the scene in the fortress and citadel would have been very

different,' he wrote, 'if individual soldiers had entered the town primed with arrack, or if spirituous liquors had been discovered in the Afghan depots.' It helped too that the soldiers' daily rum ration had run out two weeks earlier. The only sour note was the wholesale pillage of Ghazni by Keane's camp followers, who 'managed to scale the walls before the firing had well ceased and plundered the place of every description of property'.

The sudden loss of the seemingly impregnable Ghazni was, however, a mortal blow for Dost's regime. 'Our success', wrote Captain Douglas, 'has electrified the people of the country who expected, at least, a siege of some months. They say we must have gained the place by magic or treachery . . . The news reached Cabool within 24 hours and this day Jabbur Khan, the brother of Dost Mahomed Khan of Cabool, came to our camp to treat for terms.' Jabbur demanded for Dost the hereditary title of vizier – or chief minister – long held by the Barukzai clan, in return for his abdication. Shuja refused and offered instead an 'honourable asylum' in British India. This was rejected by an indignant Jabbur, who declared his intention, and that of his brother, to fight to the death. Unfortunately for Dost, his troops did not see it that way, and as the British approached Kabul they began to melt away. Further resistance was hopeless, so, with a small band of followers, he abandoned Kabul and rode north towards the Hindu Kush.

Having detached a small force to garrison Ghazni, Keane's army arrived before the walls of Kabul on 6 August. A day later Shuja entered the city on a magnificent white charger, his gold robes glinting with precious stones. He was flanked by Macnaghten and Burnes – who would henceforth serve as British envoy and resident respectively – both in full diplomatic fig, 'a cocked hat fringed with ostrich feathers, a blue frock coat with raised buttons, richly embroidered on the collar and cuffs, epaulettes not yielding in splendour to those of a field marshal, and trowsers edged with very broad gold lace'. Such finery failed to impress the citizens, who gave the returning shah an ominously lukewarm reception. 'It was more like a funeral procession', wrote a contemporary, 'than the entry of a King into the capital of his restored dominions.' But

Captain Douglas★ was not particularly worried. 'Shah Shuja has not from the first met with that degree of personal attachment and active support which our Government anticipated,' he admitted to his father.

But . . . now that the King is seated on his throne and all the rebel chiefs expelled, it is evident that all the peaceable and industrious classes of the people are highly satisfied with the change . . . Many say, 'Who is Shah Shuja that we should love him. He is an Afghan and, for all we know, may become as great a tyrant as those he has displaced. But give us justice, security of property and moderate Government and we will be thankful and contented.' I have asked hundreds of respectable men if they were pleased with the Shah's return. The invariable answer has been: 'You are the people we look to. You are just, liberal and wise. We are weary of oppression and misrule. Give us protection and we ask not who is King.'

Dost, however, was still at large. Until he had been captured, and the country properly pacified, there was little chance that Auckland would have his wish – expressed in a memo of 20 August – of withdrawing all British troops back across the Indus. In the end it was decided to leave the whole Bengal Contingent to prop up the Shuja regime. But this did not take the gloss off what, on the surface, appeared to have been a brilliantly conceived and executed military campaign that had attained all the political objectives it had been set. Russia and Persia were no longer in any doubt that Afghanistan was, and would remain, a British sphere of influence. The official rewards for such an achievement were suitably lavish: Auckland was made an earl, Keane a baron and Macnaghten a baronet; Cotton was advanced in the Order of the Bath from KCB to GCB, three brigadier-generals were knighted (KCB) and a further fourteen senior officers were made CB. But the newly ennobled Baron Keane of Ghazni was not taken in by the façade

---

★ Douglas was killed during an expedition to subdue an Afghan tribe known as the Surga Khail in early 1841.

of tranquillity. As he prepared to hand over command to Cotton and return to Bombay, he remarked to a young subaltern: 'I cannot but congratulate you for quitting the country; for, mark my words, it will not be long before there is here some signal catastrophe!'

Queen Victoria's knowledge of the unfolding events in Afghanistan was limited to the occasional snippet from Lord Melbourne. On 7 October 1838, for example, he told her that the cabinet had agreed that Sir John Hobhouse, the president of the Board of Control,★ would write to Auckland to the effect that '*no* expedition should be sent into Persia, but to strengthen and protect our Indian Possession on the side of Afghanistan and Cabul.' In other words the government was fully supportive of the Afghan incursion but did not want it to go any further. Three weeks later the prime minister referred again to the Afghan crisis by asking the queen if she was 'uneasy' at the movement of 'these two great armies'. It was undoubtedly 'very serious', she replied, and was not he worried? He said no but admitted it was a 'great crisis' and a 'stroke for the Mastery of Central Asia'. Auckland, he added, had surely done the 'right thing' by mobilizing his troops.

Victoria did not refer to the subject again in her journal until 7 April 1839, by which time the invasion of southern Afghanistan had begun, though the news would take two months to reach Britain. As before, the conversation was led by Melbourne. 'You should see the Indian papers, to see what Auckland's about,' he advised the queen. There was going to be a 'great war', he added, the outcome of which would determine who, of Britain and Russia, was to have 'possession in the East'. At this stage, clearly, the British government was firmly behind Auckland's policy of armed intervention. The queen, on the other hand, was still too young and inexperienced to take an active role in British diplomacy, and was content to follow the advice of her prime minister. It was an agreeable situation for the government but one that would not last.

★ In effect, the secretary of state for India.

Victoria was, in any case, much preoccupied by the fallout of what came to be known as the Hastings Affair. The person in question, Lady Flora Hastings, the clever and attractive elder daughter of the marquess of Hastings, had been the duchess of Kent's lady-in-waiting since 1835. Regarding her as little more than a spy, Victoria had never warmed to her, and when, in February 1839, she noticed that Lady Flora's stomach was swollen she leapt to the unmerited conclusion that the unmarried 29-year-old was 'with child'. The queen blamed the hated Sir John Conroy, who had recently travelled overnight in a post-chaise with Lady Flora, and eventually insisted on an examination by two doctors. They cleared the unfortunate lady-in-waiting of any impropriety, but could not explain the swollen stomach. When the story leaked out, Victoria was vilified in the press as the vindictive persecutor of an innocent woman. The opprobrium only increased when it was discovered that the true cause of Lady Flora's indisposition was liver cancer. But by then the queen had a more appalling prospect in view: the loss of her mentor, Lord Melbourne.

On 7 May, having the previous day won a motion to suspend the unruly legislature of Jamaica by just five votes, Melbourne resigned. The queen pleaded with him to reconsider, but his mind was made up. His Whig ministry had been under pressure in parliament for some while, and its defeat, he believed, was simply a matter of time; better to go now, at a moment of his choosing, than to endure a lingering death. He left the distraught queen with one piece of advice: to insist that none of her household, except those engaged in politics, be removed by the incoming Tory government. If acted upon, and it was, this suggestion was bound to cause trouble. The ladies of the queen's household were all wives of prominent Whigs. It was only natural that Sir Robert Peel, the new prime minister, would want to replace at least some of them with Tories. But Victoria refused to budge. Did she mean to keep *all* her ladies? asked an incredulous Peel. '*All,*' she replied. Even the duke of Wellington, the grandest of Tory grandees, was unable to change her mind. But he and Peel made it clear that, if she would not give in, she would have to look elsewhere for her ministers. She was delighted, and at once invited Melbourne to remain in office. Incredibly he agreed. 'It is', wrote Greville, 'a high trial of our institutions when the caprice of a girl can overturn a great ministerial combination.'

Coming so soon after the Hastings Affair, the so-called 'Bed-chamber Crisis' reduced still further the queen's popularity. It received another blow in early July, when, shortly after Lady Flora's death on the 5th, the queen was insensitive enough to attend the Ascot races. Two women made their displeasure known by hissing at the queen and calling her 'Mrs Melbourne'. A furious Victoria told the prime minister that she would gladly have seen them flogged. She had, after all, 'done nothing' to kill Lady Flora. She felt the need to make reparation, none the less, and sent representatives to the funeral and £50 to Lady Flora's maid. The money was returned by the Hastings family.

Events in the latter part of the year, however, were more to Victoria's liking. First came the news from Afghanistan, enthusi-astically received by the British public, that Keane had captured Ghazni and entered Kabul unopposed; then the visit of her first cousins Princes Ernest and Albert of Saxe-Coburg-Gotha in October. Her favourite uncle, Leopold, the widower of Princess Charlotte, who had since become king of the Belgians, had made no secret of his wish that she should marry his nephew Albert, the younger of the two brothers. But Albert, several months her junior, had made little impression on Victoria during his previous visit to Britain in 1836, beyond falling asleep during supper and retiring early from a ball. On learning of her cousins' visit, Victoria spelt out the various obstacles to a match in a letter to her uncle of 15 July. She was, she wrote, in no hurry to marry, nor was the country anxious 'for such an event'. Two or three years hence would be early enough. There was also the question of Albert's suitability as a husband. 'I may not', she warned, 'have the feeling for him which is requisite to ensure happiness. I *may* like him as a friend, and as a *cousin*, and as a *brother*, but not *more*.'

Her fears were groundless, though the visit did not begin well. On 10 October, after a particularly rough Channel crossing, the brothers reached Windsor Castle without their luggage. It had somehow gone astray, and without suitable clothes they were unable to appear at dinner. Victoria was unconcerned. Having met the pair at the top of the stairs, she was amazed by how much they had 'grown and changed', particularly Albert, whose strikingly handsome looks she regarded as *'beautiful'*. The brothers were presented after dinner and again the queen marvelled at how 'handsome and pleasing' Albert was. Was it true, she asked Melbourne, that Albert was like her in appearance? 'Oh! yes he is,' replied the prime minister; 'it struck me at once.'

The queen was smitten, and the following day, after the brothers had visited her in her sitting room, she was in raptures over Albert's 'beautiful blue eyes', 'exquisite nose', 'pretty mouth' and 'beautiful figure, broad in the shoulders, and a fine waist'. That evening, after dinner, he impressed the queen with his elegant dancing. The more time the queen spent with Albert, the more about him she liked: his intelligence, charm, love of music and staunch (though not intolerant) Protestantism. After just three days she was forced to confess to Melbourne that her opinion on marriage had changed and that she would make her decision 'soon'. He suggested she should leave it a week, and she agreed. But a day later she told him she was determined to marry Albert. 'I think it is a very good thing,' replied Melbourne with tears in his eyes, 'for a woman cannot stand alone for long, in whatever situation she is.'

Albert did not learn of his fate for a further twenty-four hours. He had just come in from hunting when the queen sent for him. She recorded:

He came to the closet where I was alone, and after a few minutes I said to him, that I thought he must be aware *why* I wished them to come here, and that it would make me *too happy* if he would consent to what I wished (to marry me). We embraced each other over and over again, and he was *so* kind, *so affectionate*. Oh! To *feel* I was, and am, loved by such an *Angel* as Albert was *too great a delight to describe!* I told him I was quite unworthy of him and kissed his dear hand. He said he would be very happy *'das Leben mit dir zu zubringen'* and was so kind and seemed so happy, that I really felt it was the happiest brightest moment of my life, which made up for all I had suffered and endured . . . I told him it was a great sacrifice, – which he wouldn't allow.

Nor was it a sacrifice. As the younger son of an insignificant German princeling – Coburg had fewer than 300,000 inhabitants – Albert's marriage prospects were hardly bright. With no realm or fortune, he had only his youth, looks and charm to recommend him. Victoria, on the other hand, was queen of the world's most powerful nation and could not have been more of a catch. She was bright, young and far from unattractive (if you liked your women plump and homely, more milkmaid than courtesan). Even her short stature – a little over five feet – was not incompatible with Albert's modest 5' 7". And as Victoria's husband he would want for neither prestige nor comfort. Influence was another matter. The consort of a constitutional monarch could expect to have little or no say in the affairs of state, and finding a worthwhile occupation would not be easy. Fortunately Albert had few illusions. 'My future lot is high and brilliant,' he wrote to a friend, 'but also plentifully strewn with thorns.'

How thorny he would soon find out. First his proposed annuity of £50,000 was defeated in the House of Commons and reduced to £30,000 (little more than half that given to his uncle Leopold at the time of his marriage to Princess Charlotte). Then he was denied a suitable title. The queen wanted him to be made king consort; Melbourne would not hear of it. 'For if once you get the English people in the way of making kings,' he explained, 'you will get them in the way of unmaking them.' The cabinet, aware that parliament was determined to deny Albert a political role, would not even recommend him for an English peerage. Victoria blamed the 'abominable infamous Tories'.

The marriage went ahead as planned. Albert, having settled his affairs in Coburg, returned to London on 8 February 1840, to the queen's obvious delight. She embraced him at the door of Buckingham Palace, took him by the hand and led him up to her sitting room. Two days later they were married in the Chapel

Royal at St James's Palace: Victoria wore a white satin gown, diamond necklace and earrings, and orange flowers in her hair; Albert the gorgeous red and gold uniform of a British field marshal, the honorary rank to which the queen had appointed him. Greville estimated that only five of the 300 guests were Tories. That number included the duke of Wellington, who had been added to the list only after special pleading by Melbourne. Any further the queen would not go. 'It is MY marriage,' she is said to have told the prime minister, 'and I will have only those who sympathize with me.'

The day went well, despite early-morning showers, with large crowds cheering the royal couple as they returned to Buckingham Palace for the wedding breakfast. 'Nothing could have gone off better,' Melbourne told the queen. Finally, at 4 p.m., the newly-weds set off for their four-day honeymoon at Windsor Castle. At last the queen had Albert to herself, and he would not disappoint. 'I do not think it is *possible* for any one in the world to be *happier*, or AS happy as I am,' she wrote to her uncle Leopold the following day. 'He is an Angel, and his kindness and affection for me is really touching.' The wedding night was obviously a success, because six weeks later the queen discovered she was pregnant, an 'unhappy condition' she would experience eight more times and never enjoy. On 21 November 1840, after a twelve-hour labour, she gave birth to a daughter: Princess Victoria. 'Never mind,' said the queen on learning the sex, 'the next will be a Prince.' It was: Prince Albert ('Bertie') Edward, prince of Wales, was born less than a year later on 9 November 1841.

# 3. The Retreat from Kabul

The British garrison at Kabul, meanwhile, had settled down to the life of a typical Indian hill station, with concerts, horse races, wrestling and cricket matches. They even felt confident enough to send for their wives and families, with Lady Macnaghten and Lady Sale, the wife of Brigadier-General Robert Sale, two of the first to arrive. Shuja followed suit by bringing his harem from India. To house them he persuaded the overconfident Macnaghten to vacate the fortress of Bala Hissar, which had been occupied by British troops since the autumn of 1839. It was the first, and perhaps the most serious, in a catalogue of British blunders.

The troops were moved from the Bala Hissar to a new cantonment about a mile to the north-east of the city. It could not have been a worse location. The ground selected was low and swampy, commanded on every side by hills and forts; between it and the city was a patchwork of orchards and gardens, criss-crossed with irrigation ditches and particularly unsuited to the rapid movement of men and guns. Nor was the design of the cantonment by Lady Sale's son-in-law, Lieutenant John Sturt of the Bengal Engineers, much of an improvement. The main position was a rectangle 600 by 1,000 yards, surrounded by a low rampart and narrow ditch, and with a defensive perimeter of almost two miles. This was far too large to be manned effectively by the garrison available, and the problem was compounded by a second enclosure, half as big again, that jutted out from the northern rampart and contained the bungalows of Macnaghten and his staff. It was poorly defended and put at risk the northern face of the main compound. And, if that was not bad enough, the commissariat stores were placed in a separate fort 300 yards away.

Not everyone accepted the new arrangement with equanimity. Brigadier-General Abraham Roberts, commanding Shuja's levies,

was shocked by the indefensibility of the new site when he returned from leave in India. Not one to hide his feelings – he
had been particularly critical of the decision to dissipate British
forces in numerous isolated garrisons – he was eventually recalled
at Macnaghten's insistence and replaced by the more compliant
Brigadier-General Thomas Anquetil.

For a time Roberts's fears seemed groundless. In December 1840,
soon after defeating a British force in Kohistan, Dost Mohamed
surrendered to Macnaghten in person and was exiled to Ludhiana,
where, in a neat irony, he was housed in the same quarters that
Shuja had occupied. Dost urged his sons to follow his example,
and only Akbar Khan, the eldest, refused to come in. He remained
an outlaw beyond the Hindu Kush, biding his time until events
were more conducive to winning back his father's throne.

But the warning signs were there for the British. As early as
May 1840, reports were coming in of local chiefs plundering 'all
travellers and caravans' on the road between Kandahar and Ghazni.
Then, in January 1841, an uprising by the Durani clan was nipped
in the bud thanks to the swift reaction of Major-General William
Nott, a tough, no-nonsense officer in command in Kandahar.
Nott was the obvious choice to replace General Cotton in overall
command when the latter retired from the service in the spring of
1841. But he was overlooked because of his abrasive nature and
lack of respect for Shah Shuja, whom he once described in a letter
to his daughters as 'most certainly as great a scoundrel as ever
lived!' It did not help Nott's cause that he was an 'Indian', rather
than a Queen's, officer, commissioned into the army of the HEIC.

The officer chosen to succeed Cotton, Major-General William
Elphinstone, had obvious advantages over Nott. A grandson of the
tenth Baron Elphinstone and cousin of Mountstuart Elphinstone,
the former governor of Bombay, he had commanded the 33rd
Foot with distinction at the Battle of Waterloo. Yet he had been
on half-pay for most of the intervening period, returning to the
active list only on his promotion to major-general in 1837. Posted
to India two years later, he was commanding at Meerut, the most
northerly division of the Bengal Army, when he was informed of

his new appointment. His reaction was less than enthusiastic. 'The climate there is good,' he told his brother, 'and there is some additional pay but in the present state of things I think I should have preferred staying here. But we must go when ordered.'

With Afghanistan apparently pacified, Elphinstone saw little opportunity for military glory. He was, in any case, nearly sixty and far from well. Lord Auckland's sister Emily, who saw him shortly before his departure for Kabul, noted he was 'in a shocking state of gout, poor man' with 'one arm in a sling and very lame'. Any reservations that Auckland might have felt about Elphinstone's health were outweighed by the general's amiable disposition and the likelihood that he would get on with Macnaghten and Shuja.

Elphinstone's earliest impressions of both, and of his mission in general, were formed at Jelalabad in early April 1841. They were not particularly favourable:

My command I do not think enviable. It is one of extreme responsibility and anxiety . . . The Political Agents (generally young officers) are frequently proposing schemes for the execution of which they are not responsible . . . I saw [Macnaghten] today and he still thinks, if I recommend it, an advance will be made [to Herat], but I do not. He is a cold and reserved man, but well spoken of by those who know him, and I believe very clever . . . Shah Soojah I saw two days ago. A stout, careworn looking man. He received me in a wretched garden. His house appeared bad and uncomfortable, as indeed are the most here. No one except Sir Wm. Macnaghten possesses more than a mud hut.

The general's spirits were further depressed when his arrival in Kabul, on 30 April, coincided with a particularly severe attack of rheumatic gout, which left him bedridden for much of May. On his feet by the 19th, he was shocked by the weak military position that Cotton had left:

The City is extensive, very dirty & crowded & a great deal of business apparently going on in the Bazar. It is situated in a hollow, surrounded by high mountains . . . The cantonment is . . . not very defensible without a number of men, as people can come in from without at many points. This, in the event of troops being required elsewhere, would be very inconvenient, & I am a good deal puzzled what is now the best thing to be done. ·

Elphinstone has generally been dismissed by historians as an incompetent and weak-willed commander. He signally failed, they say, to prepare adequately for the coming storm. But many of the mistakes – such as the siting of the cantonment – had been made before his arrival, and there is evidence that he made some effort to repair the damage. He wrote later: 'At different periods during this time I wrote to Lord Auckland, pointing out the deficiencies in cantonments, and making various suggestions viz., the necessity of having a citadel to overawe the city, sufficient ground to be purchased around the magazine fort to form a glacis giving the command of both roads, and a sufficient space round the fort. These were objected to on the score of expense.' Elphinstone's request for a second brigade to be stationed at Kabul was also ignored.

And, if bureaucratic niggardliness were not enough, Elphinstone had also to contend with his failing health. A second attack of rheumatic gout on 6 June, this time accompanied by a 'violent fever', would confine him to bed for much of the summer. On 26 July he wrote to his kinsman Lord Elphinstone: 'My medical attendants tell me that I cannot recover in this country, and that I ought to leave it . . . If this opinion is borne out by the Medical Committee which assembles next month, I shall deeply feel obliged to give up a command I should have liked had I been possessed of health to perform its duties. It is one of interest & excitement, requiring great activity, mental and bodily; but my stay would be useless to the public service & distressing to myself.' The medical committee duly met on 6 August and confirmed that the general was unfit for service. But in the time it took for Auckland to authorize Elphinstone's return to India, events had moved on.

Back in Britain, Melbourne's tottering Whig administration

finally fell in August 1841 after a general election had returned a Tory majority of seventy-six. Sir Robert Peel was prime minister at last, much to the queen's obvious discomfort. But the switch had been inevitable for so long that Victoria was grimly resigned when it came. 'I am quiet and prepared,' she wrote to her uncle Leopold, 'but still I feel very *sad*, and God knows! very wretched at times, for myself and my country, that *such* a change must take place.'

Fearing that the Afghan adventure would ruin the heavily indebted HEIC, which was footing the bill, Peel demanded economies. Macnaghten responded in September by halving the £8,000 annual subsidy paid to the eastern Ghilzais, the tribesmen who controlled the most direct route to India through the Khyber Pass. Their predictable response was to plunder the next caravan from India. But Macnaghten, anxious not to delay taking up his new post as governor of Bombay, played down the threat. The Ghilzais, he wrote to Auckland, were simply 'kicking up a row about some deductions which have been made from their pay' and would be 'well trounced for their pains'.

The opportunity came in early October, when, to save a few more pennies, Macnaghten weakened the British presence in Kabul by ordering Sir Robert Sale's brigade, at the end of its tour of duty in Afghanistan, to march through the territory of the troublesome Ghilzais to meet its relief in Peshawar, rather than the other way round. It was confidently assumed that 'Fighting Bob' Sale would sweep aside the Ghilzais, enabling Macnaghten and Elphinstone to return to India in his wake. In the event, Sale's brigade came off worst and took refuge in the village of Gandamak, en route to Jelalabad and the Khyber Pass. Elphinstone later claimed to have had 'frequent conversations' during this period with both Macnaghten and Burnes 'regarding the extent to which this disaffection might have spread', and in particular about the 'state of feeling in the city'. He was assured by both, but especially by Burnes, that the 'disaffection was not widely disseminated and did not extend to Cabool'. They had been misinformed.

★

At dawn on 2 November, the day before Macnaghten and Elphinstone were due to depart for India, the insurrection exploded in Kabul with an attack on the British Residency, a large courtyarded mansion in the heart of the city. Burnes had been warned by his Hindu secretary the night before that his life was in danger and that he should move into the cantonment. He had refused, saying he had done the Afghans no injury; why, then, should they harm him? It did not occur to him that many Afghans held him personally responsible for bringing British bayonets to Afghanistan; nor was he aware that one of the leading conspirators was Abdulla Khan, a local chief whom he had recently insulted. At first the angry crowd that surrounded the residency hurled nothing more lethal than insults and brickbats. Convinced he could talk himself out of trouble, Burnes ordered his sepoy guard not to shoot. As a precaution, however, he sent a message to the cantonment that he was under siege and needed assistance.

When word of the rising reached the cantonment, Macnaghten discussed with Elphinstone how best to react. Macnaghten's secretary, Captain George St Patrick Lawrence, was all for sending a regiment of troops into the city to rescue Burnes, disperse the mob and seize the ringleaders. The suggestion was dismissed by Elphinstone and his staff as 'pure insanity', though they did agree to his next proposal: to send a force under Brigadier-General John Shelton, Elphinstone's deputy, to occupy the Bala Hissar, 'from whence it would be in a position to act as circumstances required, and as might be directed by the King and the General'. The move would take place, however, only once Shah Shuja had given his permission. Lawrence was sent to obtain it. But when he reached the Bala Hissar, having been shot at on the way, Shuja explained that a force had already been sent into the city, under his son and prime minister, which would surely 'suppress the tumult'. It did not, though it made good early progress, and was eventually recalled by Shuja. Only then did Lawrence ride to Shelton with instructions to march on the Bala Hissar. The latter did so – with a mixed force of cavalry, infantry and guns – but would go no further. He seemed paralysed by the situation and unsure what to do. When

Lawrence urged him to enter the city 'at once', he refused. 'My force is inadequate,' he replied, 'and you don't appear to know what street fighting is.' It was, in any case, far too late to save Burnes.

Soon after sending the message, Burnes had gone out on to his balcony to advise the mob to disperse. Flanked by his younger brother Charles, an Indian Army subaltern on a visit to Kabul, and Major William Broadfoot, his political assistant, he appealed in vain. Some of the bolder spirits had already scaled the compound walls and were in the process of setting fire to the stables. Suddenly a shot rang out and Broadfoot collapsed, clutching his chest. Burnes and his brother dragged him inside, but he was already dead. Only at this point did Burnes give his sepoy guard permission to open fire. Their bullets had little effect. With the house ablaze and the mob tearing across the courtyard, Charles Burnes tried to fight his way out. He got as far as the garden, killing six assailants in the process, before he was 'cut to pieces'. His elder brother is said to have donned native dress in an attempt to escape. But he was quickly recognized and hacked to death, as were the remaining members of his guard. The mob then turned its attention to the building next door, which housed Shuja's treasury. Once they had overwhelmed the guard, the insurgents helped themselves to £17,000 of government money, many returning home laden with plunder. Now was the opportunity to restore order; it was never taken, and George Lawrence blamed the military:

How easily we could have quelled the insurrection had we only firmly and instantaneously used the powerful force at our disposal! But alas! vacillation and incapacity ruled in our military councils, and paralysed the hearts of those who should have acted with energy and decision. By their deplorable pusillanimity an accidental émeute [riot], which could have been quelled on the moment by the prompt employment of a small force, became a formidable insurrection.

In fact it was Macnaghten, Lawrence's senior, who was largely responsible for downplaying the seriousness of the outbreak on 2 November, telling Elphinstone at their early-morning meeting

that he 'did not think much' of the city insurrection and that it
would 'shortly subside'. It was also Macnaghten, mindful of the
political implications, who insisted that Shuja be consulted before
troops were sent into the city to quell what was, at that stage, a
civil disorder. And it was Shuja himself who lost his nerve when
his own force was making good headway against the insurgents. If
any senior officer deserves censure for indecision that day, it is
surely Shelton and not Elphinstone.

The following day an attempt was made to open up communications with the Bala Hissar. It met heavy opposition and was
ultimately forced to retrace its steps, because, according to Lawrence, Shelton disobeyed instructions to meet it halfway. The siege
of the cantonment now began, with more than 4,500 British and
Indian troops, not to mention 12,000 camp followers, cooped up
in a wholly inadequate defensive position. Their predicament was
made infinitely worse on 6 November, when the nearby commissariat fort fell to the rebels. Henceforth the troops were put on
half-rations.

Elphinstone, it is true, did not display the type of energetic
and decisive generalship that might have rescued the situation.
He should, at the very least, have ensured that the commissariat
supplies were brought into the relative safety of the cantonment.
But by then he was a sick man and 'unable to get about without
difficulty except on horseback & then not easily'. A heavy fall
from his horse, while inspecting the guards during the evening of
the 2nd, had only made matters worse. And so, feeling himself
'not equal' to the performance of his duties, he agreed to Macnaghten's suggestion that Brigadier-General Shelton should be
recalled from the Bala Hissar to shoulder some of the burden. The
brigadier duly arrived on 9 November with two guns and a regiment of Shuja's infantry. But, from the outset, Elphinstone did not
receive from Shelton 'the cordial cooperation & advice' that he
had a right to expect. 'On the contrary,' wrote Elphinstone, 'his
manner was most contumacious from the day of his arrival. He never
gave me information or advice, but invariably canvassed & found
fault with all that was done, condemning all orders before officers,

frequently preventing and delaying carrying them into effect.'

Despite a couple of successful skirmishes against the insurgents, including a tardy but ultimately successful action by Shelton to clear the Behmaru Hills of Ghilzais on 13 November, Elphinstone regarded the situation as hopeless and had for some time been urging Macnaghten to treat with the rebels. This plea was given added urgency when two wounded officers – Major Eldred Pottinger, the political agent in Kohistan, and the adjutant of a Gurkha regiment – stumbled into the cantonment during the morning of 15 November. They and a lone sepoy were the sole survivors of a 600-strong British force. Word soon arrived of a second disaster: the 150-man garrison at Shekabad, just thirty miles from Ghazni, had been slaughtered to a man. Macnaghten's response was to try to split the rebel camp by offering gold to one of its more powerful tribes, the Kuzzilbashes, through the medium of Mohun Lal, the late resident's Indian secretary. The attempt came to nothing.

On 19 November, by which time it was clear that neither Sale nor Nott was in a position to march to the Kabul garrison's assistance, Macnaghten urged Elphinstone to reject any idea of retreat. Such a course of action would be, he said, 'not only disastrous but dishonourable', as it would necessitate abandoning vast amounts of government property as well as Shah Shuja, 'to support whom was the main object of our original entrance into Afghanistan'.

He pointed out [wrote Lawrence] that even if we could make good our retreat, we could carry with us no shelter for the troops, who would in consequence, at this inclement season, suffer immensely, while our camp followers, amounting to many thousands, must inevitably be utterly destroyed. As to any hope of successful negotiations, it appeared to him in vain, so long as there was no party among the insurgents of sufficient strength and influence to insure the fulfillment of any treaty we might enter into.

Macnaghten thought the 'wisest course' would be to throw themselves into the Bala Hissar. But he was prepared to wait another

eight or ten days before making a decision, presumably to give his
scheme to divide the rebels time to mature. Inertia, however, was
soon no longer an option. On 22 November the enemy appeared
in front of the village of Behmaru, to the east of the cantonment,
whence the British were obtaining most of their supplies. To
prevent the rebels from capturing Behmaru and completing the
cantonment's encirclement, a force was sent to occupy the village.
But the attack was not pressed home with any vigour, and, after
some inconclusive skirmishing, it returned to the cantonment.

That night there was more bad news: Akbar Khan, Dost's eldest
son, had arrived in Kabul to assume the leadership of the insurrection. Events had reached a critical juncture. At a hurriedly
convened council of war, Macnaghten argued forcefully for the
immediate occupation of Behmaru. Shelton opposed the manoeuvre, pointing out that the troops were exhausted and the inevitable casualties could not be justified. But Elphinstone backed
Macnaghten, and, at dawn the following day, Shelton marched
out of the cantonment with a mixed force of around 1,100 men
and a single horse artillery gun. His initial objective was the high
ground above Behmaru, from where he could shell the rebel
position. This part of the operation was a success, forcing many
of the rebels to withdraw through the village. But when urged
to order an assault on the village itself, thereby flushing out the
remaining rebels, Shelton hesitated. By the time he gave the order,
the rebels had returned in force, and the attack was a failure.

It was now light, and the rebels, emboldened by the feebleness
of the British attack, occupied a neighbouring hill and opened fire
with their long-range jezails. Shelton's extraordinary response was
to form his infantry into two squares, one behind the other, with
the cavalry to the rear. As one British officer commented, the
square was designed to repel cavalry, and yet it was used at Behmaru
'to resist the *distant fire of infantry*, thus presenting a solid mass
against the aim of perhaps the best marksmen in the world, the
said squares being securely perched on the summit of a steep and
narrow ridge, up which no cavalry *could* charge with effect'. With
their muskets hopelessly out-ranged, the British squares soon began

to sustain heavy casualties. For a time the lone British artillery gun kept the enemy at bay. But it eventually overheated and fell silent, allowing the Afghans to close to within a few yards. A sudden rush and it was taken, only to be retrieved by a costly counter-attack. All the while Shelton was being urged by his officers to order a bayonet charge. He would not. When the Afghans charged instead, the demoralized British troops cracked. 'Our squares broke,' wrote Lawrence; 'all order was at an end, and infantry and cavalry fled down the hill together.' Many were cut down by the pursuing Afghans, and few would have survived had the rebel cavalry commander Osman Khan, 'one of the chiefs then in communication' with Macnaghten, not called off the attack.

The operation had been a disaster, with more than 300 of Shelton's men killed. Amongst the dead was Lieutenant-Colonel Thomas Oliver of the 5th Native Infantry, a mixed-race officer whose estranged Eurasian wife, Frances, had had six children by a brother officer.* Oliver had been one of the garrison's leading 'croakers', or doom merchants, and seems to have had something of a death wish. 'For when our men were ordered to lie down on the hill to shelter them from the enemy's fire,' wrote Lawrence, 'Oliver could not be persuaded to screen himself, but stood erect until shot down.' Grossly overweight, he presented an easy target.

The following day, buoyed by their success, the rebel chiefs sent two emissaries to discuss terms. Elphinstone urged negotiation, telling Macnaghten that he considered it 'impracticable' to defend the cantonment without reinforcements, and that their best hope was to seek terms with the outwardly friendly Osman Khan. Macnaghten, however, could not bring himself to accept the humiliating terms on offer – 'requiring us to abandon Shah Soojah, lay down our arms, and surrender unconditionally, our lives only being spared' – and the talks were broken off on 27 November, with the envoy declaring: 'I prefer death to dishonour.'

---

* Lieutenant-Colonel (later Major-General Sir) Hugh Wheeler. Oliver's death enabled his wife to marry Wheeler. Both were killed during the Cawnpore massacres of 1857.

It was now that Macnaghten suggested a withdrawal into the more secure Bala Hissar. But Elphinstone was against the move – on account of 'a want of carriage' to transport the 650 sick and wounded, 'the strength and vigilance of the enemy' and doubts as to whether the Bala Hissar 'would yield provisions and fuel sufficient for the increase of numbers' – and it never took place. Instead, on 8 December, having surrendered yet more ground to the enemy, Elphinstone told Macnaghten that 'no more military operations could be undertaken' and that 'no time should be lost in negotiating a safe retreat to Hindostan.' The envoy did not want to abandon Shuja but agreed to reopen negotiations on hearing that a relief force from Kandahar had been forced back by bad weather.

On 11 December, at a spot 200 yards from the cantonment, Macnaghten met with Akbar Khan and the other leading rebels. The envoy's terms were as follows: all British garrisons would withdraw from Afghanistan and Dost Mohamed would be allowed to return from exile; in return the Afghans would guarantee the British safe passage, undertake not to ally with any foreign power without the consent of the British and give Shah Shuja the option of remaining in Afghanistan on a pension or returning to India with the British. As long as suitable supplies were furnished, added Macnaghten, they would 'evacuate the cantonment within three days'. The rebels agreed in principle, and the meeting broke up.

But little or no supplies were brought in, and the chiefs began to increase their demands, requiring the British to surrender their guns and ammunition, and to leave behind all married officers and their families as hostages. These delays prompted Macnaghten to revive his plan to split the rebel chiefs by renegotiating a separate deal with Akbar Khan. The initial approach, in the form of a letter signed by Akbar, was made during the evening of 22 December. Akbar's offer was: Shah Shuja to remain as king, with Akbar as his chief minister; the British troops to be allowed to delay their departure until the spring; and Aminulla Khan, the chief ringleader, to be handed over to the British. Given the weakness of the British position, these terms were ludicrously generous. But Macnaghten failed to smell a rat, and by giving his assent he sealed his fate. For Akbar had deliberately offered up Aminulla Khan to test Macnaghten's faith.

The following morning Macnaghten told Elphinstone of his plan. Were the other rebel chiefs aware of the deal? asked the general. No, said Macnaghten, they were not in on the 'plot'. Elphinstone was alarmed by the use of the word 'plot' and begged to know if there was any danger of 'treachery'. 'None whatever,' replied Macnaghten. 'Leave it all to me. I understand these things better than you do.' He added that he was about to meet Akbar Khan to conclude the deal, and that he would appreciate it if the general had two regiments and two guns ready to move at a moment's notice.

At noon Macnaghten left the cantonment with three political officers – Captains George Lawrence, Robert Trevor and Colin Mackenzie – and a tiny escort of ten Indian cavalrymen. They met Akbar Khan at a spot about 300 yards from the cantonment, close to the Kabul River. After exchanging the usual pleasantries, the Britons were invited to recline on some horse blankets that had been spread on the ground. They did so. But, on noticing that there were an 'unusually large number of armed Affghans' in the vicinity, Lawrence asked if they might not be removed. 'Oh, we are all in the same boat,' said Akbar, 'and Lawrence Sahib need not be the least alarmed.' No sooner had he spoken than Lawrence was pinioned from behind and disarmed. 'If you value your life,' said his assailant, 'come along with me.' Lawrence recalled:

I turned round and saw the Envoy . . . struggling to rise, and his wrists locked in the grasp of Mahomed Akbar, horror and consternation being apparent in his face. Trevor and Mackenzie I noticed also in the same predicament as myself. Comprehending at a glance that resistance was useless, I said 'Lead on; I will follow you.' At the same moment, swarms of Affghans, armed to the teeth, sprang up all around, yelling, and demanding that I should be given up as a 'koorban' – a sacrifice to their vengeance. They were with the utmost difficulty kept off.

Mounted behind a Ghilzai chief, Lawrence reached the relative safety of a nearby rebel fort, where he was later joined, in a cell, by a bruised Mackenzie. Macnaghten and Trevor were not so fortunate. Determined not to be taken, the envoy had struggled free of Akbar's grip, pushing the Afghan chief in the process. Akbar's response was to draw a double-barrelled pistol – one of a pair, formerly owned by Lawrence, that Macnaghten had given him as a gift – and shoot the envoy twice in the chest. Other Afghans closed in with knives to finish the job. Trevor, meanwhile, had been dragged off a horse and butchered in the snow. Later that day a mob appeared outside Lawrence and Mackenzie's cell, brandishing a severed European hand and shrieking, 'Your own will soon be in a similar plight.' It was Macnaghten's. His head and limbs were being paraded in triumph through the streets of Kabul, while his trunk was hanging, alongside Trevor's corpse, from a meat-hook in the bazaar.

Macnaghten had only himself to blame. By agreeing to Akbar's offer, and going back on his earlier agreement, he had shown he could not be trusted. Yet Akbar had not intended to murder Macnaghten and did so only when the latter refused to go quietly.

When Elphinstone learnt that Macnaghten had been seized and taken into the city, he assumed he had gone there 'for the purpose of negotiating'. He therefore did nothing beyond ordering the troops to remain under arms and the cantonment to be cleared of all Afghans, thereby releasing a number of prisoners. Only when a letter arrived from Lawrence the following day did he learn the truth. But even then he took no punitive action, preferring to swallow Akbar's assertion that the uncontrollable Ghazis were responsible for the envoy's death. Instead he resumed negotiations with Akbar on the grounds that the troops were so 'weakened, harassed and depressed' they could offer no effective resistance.

Only Major Pottinger, the senior surviving political, and a few of the junior officers were bent on revenge. Pottinger urged an immediate assault on Kabul, which the troops, incensed by the murders, 'would no doubt have stormed and carried'. Akbar was not to be trusted, he said, and the only way to save both their honour and their lives was either by marching to the Bala Hissar and holding out until the spring, or by forcing their way through to Jelalabad. Elphinstone did not agree and was backed by a council of senior officers, who condemned Pottinger's suggestions as 'impracticable'. The negotiations continued.

On New Year's Day 1842, as heavy snow fell, an agreement was reached with Akbar and the leading Afghan chiefs. In return for 14½ lakhs* of rupees the British would be given safe passage to Peshawar. Apart from their personal weapons, they could take with them only six artillery pieces and three mule-borne mountain guns; the rest, along with the surplus muskets and ordnance stores, would be left. Six officers would also remain behind as surety for Dost Mohamed's return to Afghan soil.

Shah Shuja tried to persuade Elphinstone to hold his ground, warning him that the chiefs were not to be trusted. But the general's mind was made up, and, at 9 a.m. on 6 January 1842, the 'troops moved off, a crouching, drooping, dispirited army, so different from the smart, light-hearted body of men they appeared some time ago'. Of the 4,500 British troops, only 700 were Europeans, mostly members of the 44th (East Essex) Foot and the Royal Horse Artillery. The rest were sepoys of the HEIC and members of Shuja's own infantry and cavalry. They were accompanied by thirty or so European women and children – travelling with the advance guard – and more than 12,000 camp followers. To reach their immediate destination – the garrison at Jelalabad – they would have to march more than eighty miles through snow-covered passes held by potentially hostile tribesmen.

Despite the promise of protection, the Afghan escort failed to turn up, and the unwieldy column was hounded from the start. The rearguard was fired on as it left the cantonment, and the rest of the column was attacked throughout the day by Afghan

---

* A lakh was 100,000 rupees, or £10,000, making a grand total of 1.45m rupees, or £145,000. The money was paid in government bills that could be redeemed only on the safe arrival of the troops in Peshawar.

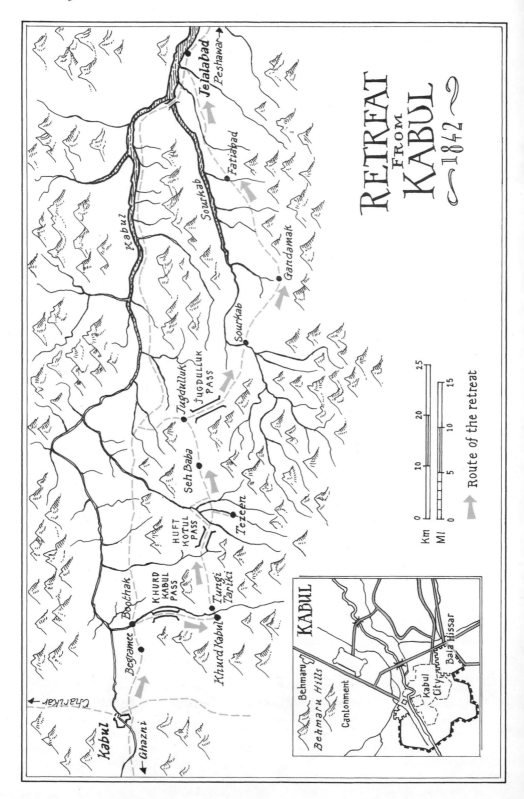

RETREAT FROM KABUL ~1842~

Route of the retreat

Jelalabad
Peshawar
Fatiabad
Gandamak
Sourkab
Sourkab
Kabul
Jugdulluk
JUGDULLUK PASS
Seh Baba
Tezeen
HUFT KOTUL PASS
KHURD KABUL PASS
Boothak
Tungi Tariki
Khurd Kabul
Begramee
Charikar
Kabul
Ghazni

Km
MI

KABUL
Behmaru Hills
Behmaru
Cantonment
Kabul City
Bala Hissar

horsemen who, darting in like wolves, drove off baggage animals and slaughtered stragglers. Soon the snow was marked by a trail of bloody corpses and scattered belongings. By nightfall the march had covered just six miles. 'There were', recalled Lady Sale, 'no tents, save two or three small palls that arrived. All scraped away the snow as best they could, to make a place to lie down on. The evening and night were intensely cold: no food for man or beast procurable, except a few handfuls of bhoosa,* for which we paid five to ten rupees.'

By dawn, scores had died of exposure, and many more were frostbitten. The Indian soldiers, in particular, were suffering, because Elphinstone had ignored Pottinger's suggestion that horse blankets should be cut up and used as puttees.† Long before the advance guard moved off without orders at 7.30 a.m., hundreds of sepoys and camp followers had already left, and most of Shuja's troops had deserted. 'Already all discipline and order had ceased,' wrote George Lawrence, who was in charge of the European civilians, 'and soldiers, camp followers, and baggage were all mingled together. More than half of the sepoys were, from cold and hunger, unable to handle their muskets, and throwing them away, mixed themselves up with the mass of non-combatants.'

Shortly after departing the camping ground, the rearguard was attacked and the three mountain guns were shamefully abandoned, a detachment of the 44th 'not firing a shot to defend them'. It had been Elphinstone's intention to push on that day through the dreaded Khurd Kabul Pass, five miles long and hemmed in by steep cliffs. But the attack on the rearguard had cost valuable time, and he decided to stop after just five miles. As night was closing in, Akbar Khan and 600 horsemen appeared, claiming to be the promised escort and blaming the column's misfortune on its premature start. Provisions would be sent, said Akbar, if Elphinstone

* Chopped straw, or chaff.
† A long strip of cloth worn spirally round the leg from the ankle to the knee, used for protection and to provide warmth.

agreed to halt until news had arrived of Jelalabad's evacuation. (Akbar had earlier induced Elphinstone and Pottinger to write to Brigadier-General Sale and request the withdrawal of the Jelalabad garrison.) Elphinstone refused, owing to the 'extreme inclemency of the Season'. With the temperature falling to ten below zero, the night was the worst yet, with most of the officers and all the men 'forced to lie down upon the snow, without food or fuel'. Some sepoys burnt their equipment and even their clothes in a desperate attempt to keep warm.

The following morning, as the advance guard was about to move off, Afghan tribesmen opened fire from the flank but were driven off by the 44th and a gallant cavalry charge led by George Lawrence. It was his last significant contribution, because, shortly after, he received word from General Elphinstone that he was wanted by Akbar Khan as a hostage, together with Brigadier Shelton and six others. This was to ensure that the column would not march beyond Tezeen, the other side of the Khurd Kabul and Huft Kotul Passes, where 'supplies of every kind' would be provided. At first Lawrence refused to go, 'saying that I would much prefer remaining with the force', and Major Pottinger went in his stead. But Akbar was determined to have Lawrence and the other senior political, Colin Mackenzie, and they were ordered to comply. Elphinstone 'said he was sorry to lose me,' remembered Lawrence, 'but go I must'. On their arrival at Akbar's camp, messengers were at once dispatched with orders for the firing to cease. The respite, however, was temporary.

As the column – with its effective fighting strength now down to 2,000 men – entered the Khurd Kabul Pass, Ghilzai tribesmen opened fire from the heights. Some of the Afghan chiefs, accompanying the advance guard, shouted at the Ghilzais to stop shooting. But they were ignored, and all order disappeared as the column surged forward in blind panic. Lady Sale and her twenty-year-old daughter, Alexandrina, were riding in the vanguard with the irregular cavalry, and had donned poshteens* and turbans, like the

★ Sheepskin jackets.

Indian troopers, to avoid drawing attention to themselves. Both made it through the pass, though Lady Sale was shot in the wrist, and Mrs Sturt's pony wounded in the ear and neck. Thousands of others were not so lucky, including a number of European women and children who were separated from their camels and captured by the Afghans. Elphinstone wrote later:

The pressure of non-combatants and cattle rendered vain all attempts to restore order. The horse artillery had unfortunately got some spirits and many of them dashing with their swords at all who opposed progress. Towards the end of the pass the firing increased and the line of march presented the appearance of a rout. The rear guard, H.M. 44th and 54th N.I., suffered very severely, and were at length obliged to find their way up to the main body as best they could. They were aided in so doing by a gun which was turned with good effect near the outlet ... As we reached the bivouac, snow fell and continued during the night. Nothing could be done for the wounded, and we had to pass another night on the snow, without tents, food or firewood.

More than 500 soldiers and 2,500 camp followers were killed in the pass. The dead included Lieutenant Sturt, Lady Sale's son-in-law, and Major John Paton, a senior member of Elphinstone's staff. Akbar insisted that he had tried to stop the slaughter, but Pottinger was not fooled by the charade. He heard Akbar shouting 'Slay them!' in Pushtu while at the same time ordering the tribesmen to stop firing in Persian, 'imagining that we should understand the last, and not the first'. The scene in the pass, as the hostages rode through it later that day, was one of unimaginable horror. 'Sepoys and camp followers were being stripped and plundered on all sides,' wrote Lawrence, 'and such as refused to give up their money and valuables were instantly stabbed or cut down by the ruthless enemy with their long knives. On seeing us the poor creatures cried out to me by name. But what could we do? We ourselves were quite helpless.'

Dawn on the 9th revealed a scene of appalling suffering. 'The flesh from the men's feet and hands was peeling off in flakes,' recorded a British officer. 'Scores had been frozen to death in the night and many who were frost bitten threw away their arms and accoutrements and mingled with the camp followers.' This unruly crowd set off for Tezeen without orders, only to be recalled by Elphinstone, who, out of desperation, had bowed to Akbar's request to halt until an escort and supplies could be provided. Later that morning Akbar further 'proposed that the ladies and their husbands, the children, and the wounded officers should be made over to him, and he would protect them, and afterwards forward them under escort to Jellalabad'. Elphinstone agreed at once, 'being desirous to remove the ladies and children, after the horrors they had already witnessed, from the farther dangers of our camp'. Many thought him a fool to trust Akbar. But he saw in him the best hope of preserving the non-combatants' lives, and events would prove him right. The promise of food and fuel, however, was not fulfilled, and the column 'passed another night on the bare snow without food, covering or fire'.

When the march resumed at 7 a.m. on 10 January, the fighting force was down to about a thousand men. The survivors of the 44th led the way, but no sooner had they passed the village of Tungi Tariki than the main body was attacked and all but annihilated. 'Little or no resistance was made by the sepoys,' wrote Elphinstone, 'most of whom had lost their fingers or toes, their muskets covered with frozen snow would have been of little use could the men have handled them. The slaughter was frightful and when we reached Kubber Jubber, fighting men were with difficulty distinguishable from camp followers. Most had thrown away their arms and accoutrements.' At Kubber Jubber, Elphinstone sent one of his officers, Captain James Skinner, to remonstrate with Akbar for allowing the attacks to continue. Akbar's response, wrote the general, was that he greatly 'regretted his utter inability to control the Ghilzees, but as the force was now composed of few but Europeans he would guarantee their safety to Jellalabad if I would send them to him without arms'. Unwilling to abandon the remaining sepoys and camp followers, Elphinstone refused, and the chaotic march continued.

At Tezeen, Elphinstone tried once more to negotiate a truce. But when Akbar tried to exclude the Indian troops, the general decided to press on through the night, leaving behind the remaining field gun and a 'great number' of the camp followers, who 'would not, or many could not, move further'. Taken by surprise, the Afghan tribesmen provided little opposition until 3 p.m. on the 11th, by which time the column had almost reached the village of Jugdulluk. A running fight continued into the village itself, where the remnants of Elphinstone's command took refuge in a handful of ruined buildings. At 5 p.m., with the battle still in progress, Captain Skinner arrived with a message from Akbar, inviting Elphinstone, Brigadier-General Shelton and Captain Johnson to a face-to-face meeting. Non-attendance would, warned Akbar, almost certainly lead to the destruction of the remaining men. Elphinstone later claimed that his initial reaction was 'strongly adverse'; those senior officers he did consult, however, 'gave it as their decided opinion that no effort of ours could release the small remnant of the army from its perilous predicament, and urged me in the most pressing manner to waive my personal objections'. Skinner further assured Elphinstone that there would be 'no objection or obstacle' to his immediate return to camp, should his interview not produce the desired result. He therefore agreed and, having made over the temporary command of the troops to Brigadier-General Anquetil, set off for Akbar's camp with Shelton and Johnson in tow. History has condemned Elphinstone for abandoning his men in this way. But, in truth, he had little option. The fighting force now numbered fewer than 300 men,* most of them members of the 44th Foot; of the few sepoys that remained, not one had a rifle, while the Europeans had 'only a few rounds in pouch and no spare ammunition'. Their destruction was certain unless the general could broker a deal.

At Akbar's camp, Elphinstone was 'courteously received' by the

---

* Elphinstone gave their numbers as '160 to 180' of the 44th Foot, '50 or 60' of 5th Light Cavalry and '30 or so' horse artillery (first Elphinstone memorandum, no date, OIOC, MSS Eur/F89/54).

Afghan prince, who promised to send supplies to the troops and to obtain a safe conduct from the Ghilzais. But no supplies were forthcoming; nor was the general allowed to return to his camp. Instead he was summoned, the following morning, to a conference with the Ghilzai chiefs, who were loud in their 'vociferations of enmity, declaring that they wanted our blood'. Eventually, re-called Elphinstone, after much angry discussion, Akbar 'apparently' forced from the Ghilzais 'an unwilling consent to a cessation of hostilities, and for our safe conduct to Neemlah, on my promising to write and endeavour to procure the evacuation of Jellalabad and paying two lakhs of rupees for distribution among the Ghilzees'. But the meeting was adjourned 'before anything final had been settled', because Elphinstone needed time to consult Skinner, who, unbeknownst to the general, had been murdered by Ghilzais on his way back to the British position at Jugdulluk. Soon after the meeting reconvened, in the afternoon, the sound of heavy firing could be heard from the British camp, and messengers brought word that the remaining British troops, 'impatient' at the general's 'unexpected detention', had pushed on towards Gandamak.

Dr William Brydon, the thirty-year-old assistant surgeon of a regiment of native infantry, was with the bedraggled group that left Jugdulluk under the cover of darkness. He was under the impression that Brigadier Anquetil had given the order to march after receiving from Elphinstone a note 'telling us to push on at all hazards, as treachery was suspected'. No such note was ever sent, though it is possible that Anquetil got wind of Skinner's murder. At the top of the Jugdulluk Pass the Ghilzais had constructed a thornbrush barricade that, not expecting a night march, they had left undefended. But the alarm was raised as the soldiers struggled to break through it, and a furious attack was made on the British rear. Brydon recalled:

We had not gone far in the dark before I found myself surrounded, and at this moment my Khidmutgar [butler] rushed up to me, saying he was wounded, had lost his pony, and begged me to take him up. I had not time to do so before I was pulled off my horse and knocked down by a blow on the head from an Afghan knife, which must have killed me had I not a portion of Blackwood's Magazine in my forage cap. As it was a piece of bone about the size of a wafer was cut from my skull, and I was nearly stunned, but managed to rise upon my knees, and seeing that a second blow was coming I met it with the edge of my sword, and I suppose cut off some of the assailant's fingers, as the knife fell to the ground. He bolted one way, and I the other, minus my horse, cap, and one of my shoes. The Khidmutgar was dead; those who had been with me I never saw again. I rejoined our troops, scrambled over a barricade of trees made across the Pass, where the confusion was awful, and I got a severe blow on the shoulder from a fellow who rushed down the hill and across the road, and here I picked up a 44th cap.

The badly injured Brydon was saved by clinging on to the stirrup of a fellow officer's horse, which dragged him clear of the mêlée. He then came across a sowar★ who told him he was 'wounded and dying', and begged him to take his pony 'or somebody else would'. As Brydon tried to 'encourage' him, he toppled to the ground dead, taking with him one of the stirrups. So Brydon mounted and, a little further ahead, met Brigadier-General Anquetil, who asked him 'how they were getting on in the rear'. Brydon's blunt response caused Anquetil to ride back to see what he could do. He was never seen again.

Only about a hundred soldiers and twice that number of camp followers made it through the pass. The thirty or so mounted men, Brydon amongst them, pushed on ahead under the command of Captain Henry Bellew, the last remaining staff officer. At daybreak the riders reached Gandamak, where a dispute arose as to which direction to take. Brydon knew the area well and recommended the road over the hills to Jelalabad; but a clerk in one of the public offices disagreed, saying the road through the Neemlah Valley was the 'safest'. Unable to decide, the party split into two almost equal halves, with Bellew, Brydon and fourteen men taking the hill road and the clerk leading the rest into the valley. This latter party was

★ Indian cavalry man.

attacked en route and all but the clerk killed. He was later taken to Jelalabad by friendly Afghans but died of fever.

Those on foot did not reach Gandamak until mid morning. They were met by a fusillade of shots that forced the small party of soldiers – about twenty officers, fifty men of the 44th Foot, a handful of horse artillerymen and five or six sepoys – to take up a position on high ground to the left of the road. Amongst them was Lieutenant Thomas Souter, who had wrapped one of the 44th's Colours* around his midriff in an attempt to save it. He recalled:

Some Affghan horsemen appeared, to whom we made a sign to come to us, which they did. Firing ceased, Major Griffiths and a Mr. Blewitt accompanied the party to negotiate with a neighbouring chief for a certain sum of money to let us proceed to Jellalabad. A great number of Affghans came up the hill, and appeared friendly with our people until they commenced snatching swords and pistols from the officers; this we could not stand, but drove them from the hill, and the fight commenced again. After two hours, during which we drove the Affghans several times down the hill, our little band (with the exception of about twenty men and a few officers of different regiments) being either killed or wounded, the enemy suddenly rushed upon us with their knives and an awful scene took place, and ended in the massacre of all except myself, Serjeant Fair (our Mess Serjt.) and seven men, that the more than usual humanity displayed by Affghans were induced to spare.

Souter put his deliverance down to the fact that his poshteen flew open during the hand-to-hand fighting, exposing the gorgeous Queen's Colour beneath. 'Thinking I was some great man from looking so flash,' he wrote, 'I was seized by two fellows (after my

* Each British infantry regiment had two gold-fringed silk standards, 6' 6" long by 6' deep, that it carried into battle: the Queen's Colour, which consisted of a large Union flag with a royal cipher in its centre; and the Regimental Colour, which was the same shade as the regiment's facings, and was decorated with the Union flag in its upper canton and a badge in its centre.

sword dropped from my hand by a severe cut on the shoulder, and my pistol missing fire), who hurried me from this spot to a distance, took my clothes off me, except my trousers and cap, and led me away to a village.'*

Dr Brydon's party, meanwhile, had made it over the hills and into the lush valley beyond without incident. On approaching the village of Fatiabad, just fifteen miles from their destination, Bellew said he would ride ahead to 'inquire into the state of the country'. He returned with good news: the villagers were friendly and had promised to bring bread. But it was a ruse to delay the riders while armed reinforcements were sent for, and by the time Bellew realized his mistake it was too late. Seeing Afghan horsemen converging from all sides, he urged the group to stick together before riding back towards the village, where he was promptly killed. Only Brydon and four others managed to cut their way clear. But the group soon split, with the three best mounted – led by Captain Frederick Collyer – leaving Brydon and Lieutenant William Steer behind, saying they would 'send us help'. Before long, however, Steer announced that he could go no further, as he and his mount were 'done'. He would, he said, hide in a cave. Brydon tried to dissuade him, but to no avail, and he was forced to continue alone. A little further along the road he was blocked by a group of twenty Afghans. Fortunately they were armed with nothing more than knives and stones, and Brydon was able to gallop through them. Yet his ordeal was far from over. He recorded:

A little further on I was met by another similar party who I tried to pass as I did the former, but was obliged to prick the poor pony with the point of my sword before I could get him into a gallop. Of this party, one man on a mound over the road had a gun, which he fired close down upon me, and broke my sword, leaving about six inches on the

* One of the men who spared Souter later returned the Colour, 'though divested of the tassels and most of its tinsel'. A month after the massacre Souter and the handful of survivors were handed over to Akbar Khan and reunited with Elphinstone and the other hostages (Souter to his wife [n.d.], NAM, 6912-6).

handle. But I got clear of them, and then found that the shot had hit the poor pony, wounding him in the loins, and he could hardly carry me, but I moved on very slowly and saw some fine horsemen, dressed in red. Supposing they were some of our Irregular Cavalry I made towards them, but found they were Affghans, and that they were leading off Captain Collyer's horse.

Brydon tried in vain to escape, but his pony would 'hardly move'. Fortunately only one Afghan gave pursuit, quickly overhauling the doctor and slashing at him with his sword. In parrying the cut, Brydon lost the remainder of his broken blade and was reduced to throwing the hilt as the tribesman made a second pass. It was enough to disturb the Afghan's aim, his sword missing Brydon's body but cutting into his left − or bridle − hand. 'Feeling it disabled,' wrote Brydon,

I stretched down the right to pick up the bridle. I suppose my foe thought it was for a pistol, for he turned at once and made off as quick as he could. I then felt for the pistol I had put in my pocket, but it was gone, and I was unarmed, and on a poor animal I feared could not carry me to Jellalabad. Suddenly all energy seemed to forsake me, I became nervous and frightened at shadows, and I really think would have fallen from my saddle but for the peak of it and some of our people from the fort coming to my assistance.

He had been spotted from the rooftop of the highest house in Jelalabad Fort by an eagle-eyed staff officer. 'As he got nearer,' wrote Major Henry Havelock,

it was distinctly seen that he wore European clothes and was mounted on a travel-hacked yaboo, which he was urging on with all the speed of which it yet remained master. A signal was made to him by someone on the walls, which he answered by waving a private soldier's forage cap over his head. The Caubul gate was then thrown open and several officers, rushing out, received and recognised in the traveller the first, and it is to be feared the last, fugitive of the ill-fated force at Caubul in Dr. Brydon.

Havelock's fears, in one sense, were realized. Of the 16,000 or so men, women and children who set out from Kabul, only a handful reached the safety of Jelalabad; Brydon was the sole European who lived to tell the tale.

The doctor's first thought, on reaching safety, was for his fellow fugitives. Hearing how things stood, Brigadier-General Sale immediately dispatched a party to 'scour the plains'. But it could do no more than recover the bodies of Collyer and his two companions; of Steer there was no sign. Brydon, meanwhile, had had his wounds dressed and been given his first square meal in days. As he ate, he told Sale and his staff the appalling details of the retreat. 'This day', recorded one officer, 'my ears were saluted with perhaps the most awful account known or heard in the annals of our Indian warfare. The whole Cabul force has been destroyed!'*

On 8 January 1842, as General Elphinstone's army was fighting for its life in the Khurd Kabul Pass, Queen Victoria received the first official news of the Afghan rebellion in the form of a letter from Lord Fitzgerald, the president of the Board of Control. 'Many valuable officers have fallen the victims of a widespread conspiracy,' lamented his lordship, 'which seems to have embraced within its confederation the most warlike tribes of the Afghan nation.' The full scale of the disaster did not become clear until early March, when Fitzgerald confirmed the death of Sir William Macnaghten, the evacuation of Kabul and the loss, almost to a man, of Elphinstone's command.

The queen was horrified. But of greater concern to her now was the fate of the hostages, particularly the women and children. A similar thought had for weeks been occupying the mind of Lord Auckland, who, some say, never recovered from the news of the disastrous retreat. With just a few weeks of his governor-generalship left to complete – Lord Ellenborough, the new Tory

---

* Brydon recovered from his wounds to take part in the reconquest of Afghanistan. His gallant pony did not: no sooner was it stabled than it 'lay down and never rose again' (Brydon Diary, 13 Jan. 1842, NAM, 8301–60).

appointee, was already en route to Calcutta – both his Afghan policy and his reputation were in tatters. How 4,000 British troops could be overwhelmed by 'only twice or thrice as many ill-armed Afghans' he was at a loss, he wrote, to understand. A reconquest of Afghanistan, however, was out of the question. Auckland had already committed troops, including three of his British regiments, to fight in China,★ and the potential cost of a second Afghan War – both in terms of men and money – was too great to contemplate. Instead his chief priorities were to extricate the remaining British garrisons – at Kandahar, Ghazni and Jelalabad – and to negotiate, if possible, the release of the hostages.

The man given the task of achieving these limited aims was Major-General George Pollock, an experienced Company officer who arrived in Peshawar to take command of British reinforcements in late January. But of the two brigades available to him, one had recently failed in its attempt to reach Jelalabad, and it took time to restore its morale and wait for the winter snows to melt. It was not until early April, therefore, that Pollock at last entered the Khyber Pass. There he demonstrated his mastery of irregular warfare by using flanking parties to scale the heights and get round the back of every Afghan force that offered resistance. Jelalabad was finally 'relieved' on 16 April, as Pollock's troops marched in to the ironic strains of the old Jacobite tune 'Oh, but ye've been lang o'coming'. For in truth the garrison had saved itself by trouncing Akbar's besieging army on 8 April. Inevitably the plaudits went to 'Fighting Bob' Sale. The real hero of the defence, however, was the senior political, Captain George Broadfoot, whose brother had died with Burnes. It was Broadfoot – a heavily built, red-haired and bespectacled Scotsman from Orkney – who alone had prevented a negotiated withdrawal in February, and who, along with Havelock, had persuaded a reluctant Sale to attack Akbar on the 8th.

Of the remaining two British garrisons, only Kandahar, under

---

★ In a conflict that was sparked by the imperial Chinese government's attempt to suppress the lucrative British-dominated opium trade. It became known as the First Opium War.

the pugnacious General Nott, was still holding out. The Ghazni troops had capitulated in March, upon the receipt of a letter from Elphinstone requesting them to do so, and were promptly butchered by their treacherous foes. Just ten officers survived the massacre, including a young ensign destined for great things by the name of John Nicholson. The hostages, meanwhile, had been moved from Budiabad, where they had been held for six weeks, to a fort in Tezeen. There, on 23 April, a broken General Elphinstone breathed his last. 'He was wounded at Jugdulluk on the 11th or 12th of last January,' wrote Major Pottinger to one of the general's brothers,

and being invited to a conference with the Affghan leader he was made prisoner and taken to [Budiabad] where he was laid up with a severe fit of the gout (rheumatic) brought on by the hardships he had been exposed to. This together with the sufferings from his wound which was irritated to the highest degree by having to ride 70 miles without getting it dressed, reduced him to such a degree of weakness that he was unable to bear the fatigue consequent on him accompanying the Affghan Army on its retreat from Jellalabad & sunk under an attack of diarrhea which came on him about the 19th.

The general had impressed all, said Pottinger, by the 'noble fortitude with which he bore the great reverse of fortune & excessive bodily pain' and 'the constant self denial he showed during his prolonged illness in regard to the wants & cares of others'.

Enclosed in Pottinger's letter was a copy of a memorandum that Elphinstone had written before his death. An attempt to explain the disaster that had befallen his command, it listed a number of factors: his physical incapacity, not helped by a 'severe fall' from his horse on the day the rebellion began; the 'indefensible' nature of the cantonment; the lack of artillery officers; the lack of support provided by Brigadier-General Shelton; and, a veiled criticism of Macnaghten, the fact that he was 'wholly dependent on the Envoy & others for information'. Referring to the memorandum, Pottinger said that its 'opinions' coincided with those 'held by the unprejudiced in the Army'. This admission is important, because Pottinger is often cited by historians as the general's severest critic.

The debate over Elphinstone's personal responsibility for the disaster will continue to rage. Captain Lawrence blamed the 'military leaders' as a whole, citing their 'incompetency, feebleness, and want of skill'. But then Lawrence's loyalty was always to the memory of his murdered chief, Macnaghten. Pottinger, on the other hand, had no axe to grind, and his tacit acquittal of Elphinstone should carry greater weight. It was an opinion concurred with by Henry Loch, a director of the HEIC, after reading the more detailed of the two Elphinstone memorandums. 'It is extremely interesting', he informed the dead general's brother, 'and places many circumstances in a new light and favourable to your brother's judgement and conduct.'

But if Elphinstone was not chiefly to blame for the disaster, who was? The prime candidates are surely Lord Auckland, for unnecessarily invading Afghanistan in the first place; the new Tory administration, for demanding the retrenchments that reduced the number of troops and provoked the rebellion; General Cotton, Elphinstone's predecessor, for allowing the cantonment to be sited in such an untenable position; Brigadier-General Shelton, for his insubordination and indecisive leadership; and, last but not least, Sir William Macnaghten, for playing down the threat of a rebellion and, when it came, attempting to play one rebel chief off against another.

That Britain was able to withdraw from Afghanistan with even a modicum of honour intact was down to her two generals in the field, Nott and Pollock. Lord Ellenborough, the new governor-general, had started by making all the right noises, declaring on 15 March, three days after Auckland's departure, his determination to inflict upon the Afghans 'some signal and decisive blow'. But, on hearing of the fall of Ghazni and the repulse of a small force en route from Quetta to Kandahar, he changed his mind and instructed both generals to withdraw from Afghanistan 'at the earliest practicable moment', leaving the hostages to their fate.

Fortunately both commanders delayed long enough for Ellen-borough to give them, in early June, the option of withdrawing via Kabul. The responsibility for such a risky venture, however, would be theirs alone. Ignoring this ignoble sleight of political hand, the generals converged on Kabul from different directions.

Pollock arrived first, on 15 September, having defeated Afghan armies at the Jugdulluk Pass and Tezeen; Nott marched in two days later. In both of Pollock's battles his troops had ignored the inferior range of their muskets by swarming up the heights and closing with the bayonet, displaying the type of steely determin-ation that a thirst for revenge often produces. For all along the road from Fatiabad lay the remains of the Kabul garrison, the corpses 'in heaps of fifties and hundreds, our gun-wheels passing over and crushing the skulls and other bones of our late comrades at almost every yard'. Pollock's men responded with an orgy of pillage and murder, burning rebel villages and executing all male occupants over the age of fourteen.

It only remained to secure the release of the remaining 105 hostages at Bamaion, a hundred miles west of Kabul, and this was achieved on 17 September by a detachment of Pollock's cavalry. Two days later Lady Sale enjoyed an emotional reunion with her husband. 'To my daughter and myself', she wrote, 'happiness so long delayed as to be almost unexpected was actually painful, and accompanied by a choking sensation, which could not obtain the relief of tears.' On their return to Britain in 1844, the Sales were accorded a hero's welcome with civic receptions in Londonderry, Liverpool and Southampton, and a private audience with the queen.

Before departing Kabul in mid October, Pollock blew up the magnificent Great Bazaar, where Macnaghten's dismembered body had been displayed a year earlier. Thus did he comply with Ellenborough's instructions to leave 'some lasting mark of the just retribution of an outraged nation'. Yet Pollock and Nott's withdrawal to Peshawar was far from a procession, as the implacable Ghilzais harried them all the way. One of the last officers to die, in an attack on the British rearguard in the Khyber Pass, was Ensign

Alexander Nicholson of the 30th Native Infantry. The following
day John Nicholson, recently released from Afghan custody, had
the misfortune to discover his brother's mutilated corpse with its
severed genitalia protruding from its mouth in accordance with
local custom.

In late December 1842 Pollock's force, the so-called 'Army of
Retribution', finally reached the Indian border town of Ferozepur,
where Lord Ellenborough was waiting to congratulate it. But most
of the governor-general's praise was reserved for Sale and his
'Illustrious Garrison', much to Pollock and Nott's irritation. As for
future policy, Ellenborough had already announced in October
that British troops would 'be withdrawn to the Sutlej' and the
Afghans left to themselves 'to create a government amidst the
anarchy which is the consequence of their crimes'. He added,
without a trace of irony: 'To force a sovereign upon a reluctant
people would be as inconsistent with the policy as it is with the
principles of the British Government.' Dost Mohamed was duly
released from British custody and reinstalled as amir. His usurper,
Shah Shuja, had been murdered in Kabul in April 1842. Apart
from one brief wobble during the Second Sikh War, Dost remained
a friend to the British, and hostile to the Russians, until his death
in 1863. His son Akbar predeceased him by sixteen years.

Yet the Afghan fiasco had seriously damaged Britain's prestige
in the East. 'There is', wrote the duke of Wellington, 'not a
Moslem heart from Peking to Constantinople which will not
vibrate when reflecting on the fact that the European ladies and
other females attached to the troops at Kabul were made over to
the tender mercies of the Moslem Chief who had with his own
hand murdered Sir William Macnaghten . . . It is impossible that
that fact should not produce a moral effect injurious to British
influence and Power throughout the whole extent of Asia.' Just
how 'injurious' would soon be apparent.

The summer of 1842 was an anxious one for Queen Victoria as she
awaited news of the hostages in Afghanistan. But the ever-present
danger to her own person, and to that of her husband, Albert, was

brought home to her on 30 May when a deranged cabinet-maker by the name of John Francis shot at and missed the royal couple as they drove in an open carriage up Constitution Hill.* Despite a warning that a potential assassin – Francis as it turned out – had been spotted aiming a pistol at her carriage two days earlier, the queen had gamely decided not to change her schedule, though plain clothes policemen were 'distributed in and about the parks, and the two Equerries riding so close on each side that they must have been hit, if anybody had'. The queen attributed her deliverance – the second time in four years she had survived an assassination attempt† – to divine intervention. 'God is merciful,' she remarked; 'that indeed we must feel daily more!'

A week later came mixed news from India, with Sale's 'signal victory' outside Jelalabad and Pollock's successful forcing of the Khyber Pass counterbalanced by the fall of Ghazni and the repulse of the Kandahar relief column. The outlook was a little brighter in early July – the day after yet another (though less serious) attempt had been made on the queen's life by a deformed youth named Bean – when Lord Fitzgerald reported that Brigadier-General Richard England's column had succeeded in reaching Kandahar at the second attempt. Not until late November, however, was the queen told of Pollock and Nott's 'brilliant exploits', including the recapture of Ghazni and Kabul, and the rescue of '*all*' the British hostages. The news coincided with equally welcome intelligence from the Far East, where British victories on sea and land had forced the Chinese government to cede Hong Kong and open up five further ports to foreign trade. Such 'brilliant successes' deserved recognition, the queen told Sir Robert Peel, and she was only too happy to approve his recommendations, including knighthoods

---

* Francis was apprehended at the scene, tried and convicted of treason. His death sentence was later commuted to life imprisonment.
† The previous occasion was on 11 June 1840, when, in an uncanny parallel of the later incident, the royal couple were shot at from close range as they drove up Constitution Hill. Both bullets missed, and the would-be assassin, a young waiter called Edward Oxford, was seized by onlookers. Found guilty but insane, he was sentenced to life in prison.

for Nott and Pollock, a pension for Sale and a baronetcy for Major-General Sir Hugh Gough, the commander of the China expedition. She also gave permission for her own troops to wear the Afghanistan campaign medals that Lord Ellenborough had had struck for the Indian Army. Active service medals were, at the time, extremely rare. A Waterloo Medal had been struck in 1816 and a Peninsular Medal would be, retrospectively, in 1846. Thanks to the example set by the HEIC in 1842, campaign medals with battle bars would become the norm. Yet the queen could not help feeling, or so she told Peel, that it would have been more appropriate if the Afghan Medal had come from herself and not from the governor-general of India.

# 4. Sindis and Sikhs

In June 1843, having recently given birth to Princess Alice, her third child in four years, Queen Victoria was cheered by yet more glad tidings from India: Major-General Sir Charles Napier, she was told, had 'completely routed' the rulers of Sind.

Sind was a large independent state to the north-west of British India; it straddled the Lower Indus River, which Calcutta had long considered ripe for commercial exploitation. A former province of the Mughal Empire, its million or so inhabitants were mostly Muslim and ruled by two amirs from the Baluchi Tulpur clan. This pair had allowed British troops to use Sind as a base of operations for the original invasion of Afghanistan in 1839. But British encroachment had steadily increased with the seizure of Karachi and the establishment of a chain of garrison towns along the route from Sukkir to Quetta. With rumours of an impending Sindian backlash, many of them hearsay, Ellenborough sent General Napier to the territory in the autumn of 1842 to secure an agreement that would, if granted, have reduced the amirs to little more than British clients. The hawkish Ellenborough was determined to secure this vital frontier zone: either by subjugating the amirs or, if they resisted, by conquering them and annexing Sind.

Sir Charles Napier, the man sent to do Ellenborough's bidding, was a highly unorthodox soldier. A former Radical MP and cousin of the famous Whig politician Charles James Fox, Napier had once described the HEIC's administrators as leeches sucking India's lifeblood. He had even less time for the amirs of Sind, whom he regarded as brutal, untrustworthy and corrupt. A Bible-thumping Christian, he saw himself as an instrument of God and felt he had a divine mission to rid Sind of its wicked rulers. His appearance was no less eccentric than his views. One soldier described him wearing a helmet 'the shape of a jockey's cap with a white quilted cover', a 'blue frock coat' covered in gold braid, and a pair of thigh-length brown leather boots. Of his face, only the nose and eyes were visible, the rest 'being covered' with a moustache, whiskers and beard, the last reaching down to his waist. Napier likened himself to Oliver Cromwell, another Soldier of the Lord, and their ascetic lifestyles were not dissimilar. Unlike most officers of the period, Napier campaigned with the bare necessities. A subordinate wrote: 'His tent is but a small single poled one, same as a staff-sergeant's. The furniture consists of a cotton floor-cloth; small Bengal hearth-rug; a cot about 2 feet high, worth a rupee, with a very scanty share of bedding; an old champagne case forms his only table & an empty brandy case his seat.' Such frugality endeared him to his men, as did his impressive record of service in the Peninsular Wars and the American War of 1812.

Napier, however, was no diplomat, and he soon clashed with the senior political officer in Sind, Major James Outram, who contested his claim that the amirs were secretly plotting war. They were being driven to resist, said Outram, because of the soldier-envoy's heavy-handedness. For Napier was not only demanding the cession of various towns, including Karachi and Sukkir; he also wanted the abolition of duties on Indus traffic and an acknowledgement that only the HEIC could settle disputes between the amirs. As if that was not enough, one of the amirs was also expected to hand over the large chunk of territory that the British had promised to the ruler of Bahawalpur in return for help during the recent Afghan War. Incredibly the amirs signed the one-sided treaty on 12 February 1843. But still Napier was not satisfied. The concentration of armed Baluchis near the southern stronghold of Hyderabad was, he felt, a sufficient provocation for him to invade Sind with a modest force of 3,000 men. The ensuing clash took place at Miani, seventeen miles south of Hyderabad, on 17 February.

Small-arms technology had undergone something of a minor revolution in recent years, with the British Army's switch, in 1839, from the flintlock to the percussion ignition system. The flintlock had a slow discharge, often hanging fire for a few seconds, because of the delay between the flash of the priming powder in the pan★ and the explosion of the main charge in the barrel. Its flash also tended to obscure the firer's view, as well as warn the intended target, and in rain the weapon was almost useless because the priming powder got wet and refused to ignite. The percussion ignition system – first developed by the Reverend Alexander Forsyth at the turn of the century and later refined by George Lovell, inspector of small arms – solved all these problems by using a sealed copper cap as its primer. The cap was ignited when struck by a hammer, which replaced the flintlock's cock. In regimental trials the converted muskets – still of the same muzzle-loading Brown Bess design but with percussion cap locks – were not only far less prone to misfiring and hanging fire, they were also more accurate, with an effective range of up to 300 yards. But so low had the British Army's store of weapons become, in the wake of post-war retrenchment, that it took many years to re-equip all the British (and HEIC) units serving abroad. Most of the regiments that fought in the Sind War, for example, were still armed with the old flintlock muskets.

Miani, therefore, was won by the traditional British tactic of closing with the enemy so that cold steel and volley fire could do their work. Outnumbered by more than three to one, Napier opened the battle with an artillery barrage that softened the Baluchi flank and enabled his infantry to advance on the main position. There the bayonets of the single British infantry regiment, the 22nd (Cheshire) Foot, proved decisive, though supporting units from the Bombay Army wavered for a time. Eventually the Baluchi matchlockmen were driven into a river bed, where they were shot down in their hundreds. With the battle won, Napier marched on to Hyderabad; there, on 20 February, he announced the summary deposition of the two amirs and the annexation of their lands. They kept up a limited resistance but were finally defeated in a

★ Hence the expression 'flash in the pan' when the initial explosion did not result in a full discharge.

one-sided battle near Hyderabad on 24 March. The famous brief punning dispatch – '*Peccavi*' ('I have sinned') – that Napier is said to have sent to the governor-general after the Battle of Miani was in fact the invention of a seventeen-year-old schoolgirl, Miss Catherine Winkworth.

Lord Ellenborough was delighted with the acquisition. Not so Peel's government, which had forbidden the annexation of more Indian territory, or the directors of the HEIC, Ellenborough's nominal bosses, who were horrified by the cost of garrisoning the unruly new province. In February 1844, backed by Outram's claim that Napier had deliberately engineered an unnecessary war, the veteran campaigner Lord Ashley introduced a motion of censure into the House of Commons, describing the conflict as a 'foul stain' on Britain's honour. Though the motion was defeated by 134 votes – with Benjamin Disraeli and his 'Young England' colleagues voting against the government – Ellenborough's fate was sealed. He was recalled in April, with the HEIC directors criticizing his overbearing manner, warmongering and theatrical love of display. They were particularly alarmed by his ill-concealed desire to take advantage of the political chaos in the Punjab by launching another war of conquest.

The queen was strongly opposed to the sacking, telling Sir Robert Peel that she thought it '*very* unwise at this critical moment, and a very ungrateful return for the eminent services Lord Ellenborough has rendered to the Company in India'. But the directors would not back down, and the returning governor-general had to be content with a GCB and an earldom.

Ellenborough was replaced by his former brother-in-law, Lieutenant-General Sir Henry Hardinge. An experienced soldier, the 59-year-old Hardinge had served with distinction as a staff officer in the Peninsular Wars and had, as British commissioner to the Prussian Army, lost a hand at Ligny during the Waterloo campaign. Since becoming an MP in 1820, however, his energies had been largely devoted to politics, including two stints in government as secretary-at-war. He was still in the latter post, and loath to leave it, when Peel offered him the governor-generalship. Personal

1. Khurd Kabul Pass, five miles long and hemmed in by steep cliffs. More than 500 British and Indian soldiers and a further 2,500 camp followers perished in the pass during the disastrous retreat from Kabul in January 1842.

2. The Advance on Kabul.

3. Nathaniel Bancroft in the splendid, if impractical, uniform of the Bengal Horse Artillery. He enlisted as a boy soldier in 1833, saw action in all the major battles of the First Sikh War and retired as a staff sergeant in 1858.

4. Sergeant John Pearman fought with the 3rd Light Dragoons ('the Mudki-Wallahs') in both Sikh Wars. He later joined the police and rose to the rank of chief constable.

5. Lieutenant-General Sir Hugh (later Viscount) Gough, the brave but tactically naive British commander during both Sikh Wars. He appears here in the famous white 'fighting coat' that he always wore in battle so that his men could recognize him.

6. Dewan Mulraj, the semi-independent ruler of Multan, whose abdication sparked the Second Sikh War. This is a calotype (an early form of photography) by Jethro McCosh, an army surgeon, of 1849.

7. Sketch by Captain Walter Unett, 3rd Light Dragoons, of the mêlée in which he was badly wounded during the Battle of Chilianwalla, 13 January 1849.

8. Ensign Alick Pennycuick, 24th Foot, standing over the corpse of his father, Brigadier-General John Pennycuick, on the battlefield of Chilianwalla. Moments later Pennycuick junior was shot in the back and killed. Their bodies were found side by side.

9. 'Funeral of the duke of Wellington. The Funeral Car Passing the Archway of Apsley House, 18 November 1852', colour lithograph by T. Picken after Louis Haghe, 1853.

10. 'The Principal Approach to the Great Dragon Pagoda at Rangoon', engraving by T. Fielding after Joseph Moore, 1825.

11. The allied commanders, Lord Raglan (*with white hat*) and General Pélissier (*with cocked hat*), on the steps of the British Headquarters, a modest farmhouse on the Chersonese Plateau, summer 1855. Photograph by Roger Fenton.

12. A private of the 28th Foot in full marching order, by Roger Fenton. He carries waterbottle, ammunition pouch, knapsack, rolled blanket, haversack and Minié rifle.

13. Balaklava Harbour with the huts of the Guards' camp in the foreground.
Photograph by James Robertson.

14. The Charge of the Heavy Brigade at the Battle of Balaklava, 25 October 1854.
Oil on canvas by Godfrey Douglas Giles, 1897.

15. Soldiers of the 47th Foot in winter dress, by Roger Fenton.

16. The Malakhov Tower, one of the keys of the Russian defensive system at Sevastopol, by James Robertson. It was finally taken by the French on 8 September 1855, forcing the Russians to evacuate the southern half of their great naval base.

17. The interior of the Grand Redan after the British failed to capture it on 8 September 1855, by James Robertson. It was abandoned the same day by the Russians when the neighbouring Malakhov Tower fell to the French.

18. Queen Victoria presenting Lieutenant-Colonel Sir Thomas Troubridge, 7th Fusiliers, with his Crimea Medal on Horse Guards Parade, 18 May 1855. Troubridge lost both feet at the Battle of Inkerman.

reasons were behind his unwillingness to go, notably his advanced age – he would become the oldest governor-general – and devotion to family and home. But three factors changed his mind: the prestige of the most powerful job in the British Empire, a far larger salary and his personal loyalty to Peel. Hardinge was not the first soldier–politician to become governor-general of India: recent predecessors included the marquess of Hastings and Lord William Bentinck. But he was the first not to hold the dual appointment of commander-in-chief. This, as we shall see, would put the actual commander-in-chief, General Sir Hugh Gough, in an invidious position in time of war: senior in military rank but under Hardinge's political authority.

A paternalist Tory, Hardinge arrived in India in September 1844 full of good intentions. His achievements, during his four-year term of office, were many: advances in education, with more schools and universities, and promises of government employment for college-educated Indians; a massive public works programme, with construction begun on the Ganges Canal and a national railway network; and the extension of social reforms to the princely states, such as the discouragement of suttee,★ infanticide and human sacrifice. Yet it is for the first hard-fought war against the redoubtable Sikh nation of the Punjab that Hardinge's governor-generalship is chiefly remembered.

The Punjab – or 'Land of the Five Rivers' – was a largely flat territory, triangular in shape, which extended from its north-east base in the foothills of the Himalayas to near the confluence of the Indus and Sutlej Rivers in the south-west. The land in between was intersected by the remaining four great rivers that fed the Indus (from south to north): the Beas, Ravi, Chenab and Jhelum. The ethnic make-up of the territory was a mixture of Pathans, Punjabi Muslims, Hindus and the dominant minority group, Sikhs, who made up about a sixth of the population. The Sikhs (or 'Disciples') had been formed as a peaceful religious sect amongst

---

★ The self-immolation of Hindu widows on their husbands' funeral pyres. Suttee had been outlawed in British India in 1829.

the Hindu Jat★ community of the Punjab by the first guru Nanak
in the late fifteenth century. Nanak rejected the rigid caste system
and polytheism of Hinduism, preferring to worship the one in-
visible God and to uphold the principle of universal toleration
and social equality. By the late seventeenth century, however, the
threat of Muslim persecution had forced Govind Singh, the tenth
and last guru, to transform the Sikhs into a military order known
as the Khalsa (or 'Army of the Free'). His intention was to create
a loosely democratic organization in which all men were equal. Its
rules were known as the 'five Ks', after the initial letter of the
Punjabi words denoting them: no man was to cut his hair or beard;
shorts and a steel bangle (on the right wrist) were to be worn; and
a comb and sword (or short dagger) always carried. All members,
in addition, were to adopt the last name of 'singh' (lion).

The beginning of the Sikh rise to prominence was the Khalsa's
defeat of its Afghan overlords in 1763, giving the Sikhs control of
the territory between the Sutlej and Jumna Rivers (later known as
the Cis-Sutlej States). More victories over the Afghans left the
Sikhs, by 1793, undisputed masters of the whole of the Punjab
proper. But it was under the leadership of Ranjit Singh, the son
of a minor chieftain who had made his name fighting the Afghans,
that the Sikhs reached the zenith of their power. An unimpressive-
looking man, blind in one eye and illiterate, Ranjit was nevertheless
a fine horseman and a charismatic leader. He was also a notorious
drinker, drug-taker and womanizer, excesses guaranteed to endear
him to his macho male subjects. In 1801 Ranjit took the first step
towards creating a unified Sikh state when he declared himself
maharaja of Lahore. His second was the creation of a large standing
army on the European model, which he achieved by hiring military
advisers from across Europe and the United States, but particularly
Frenchmen and Italians who had served under Napoleon. By the
late 1830s these men had built up a modern, well-trained regular

---

★ Tall, well built and famed for their military prowess, the Jats are a race
of farmers and nomadic herdsmen who live primarily in north-west India.
Predominantly Hindu, they are said to be the predecessors of European Gypsies.

army of 70,000 men, comprised of tactically flexible all–arms brigades. Though Sikhs were in a majority, the army also contained Hindu, Muslim and even Gurkha units. Half of all the artillerymen, for example, were Muslim. In time of war the regulars could be joined by up to 16,000 irregular cavalrymen, or *goracharras*, bringing the grand total to nearer 85,000 men.

Even as Ranjit was plotting the extension of his military and political influence, he was wily enough to come to terms with the British as the dominant power in the region. In 1809, for example, he signed a treaty confirming a British protectorate over the Sikh states of Malwa, to the south of the Punjab, enabling the British to establish garrisons at Ferozepur, Ludhiana and Ambala. This left him free to expand his domain north of the Sutlej with a series of campaigns that won him the valuable provinces of Kashmir, Multan and Peshawar, and the sobriquet 'Lion of the Punjab'. At its height the Sikh state covered more than 8,000 square miles, with a population of five million and an annual revenue of between £2m and £3m.

Yet Ranjit's death in 1839 – from a stroke brought on by excessive drinking – left the ship of state rudderless. None of his many reputed sons had the strength of character and prestige required to hold the country together. So began a vicious power struggle, with Ranjit's successors succumbing, one by one, to assassination and suspicious death. Into this power vacuum stepped the Khalsa. The in–fighting at court had left the country's finances in chaos, and the army was owed several months of back-pay. The ordinary soldiers responded by electing five-man committees – or *panches*★ – to uphold their interests, which were, in effect, substantial and regular pay. The panches, in turn, sent representatives to an army council, which replaced the generals as the effective head of the Khalsa. The army council soon became the dominant force in Punjabi politics and, in December 1844, supported the regency

---

★ From the traditional *Panchayat*, or court of five, usually a jury or village council. The panches were similar to the elected representatives of the New Model Army in 1647 and the soviets of the Russian Army in 1917.

of Maharani (or Rani★) Jindan, the mother of six-year-old Dalip Singh, the fourth and last of Ranjit's acknowledged sons. The daughter of a kennel-keeper, Jindan had come to Ranjit's notice as a dancing girl. The maharaja maintained scores of dancing girls, many of them Kashmiri, whom he organized, along with his favourite catamites, into a faux royal bodyguard complete with tinsel armour and toy bows. Jindan was his favourite and just twenty-one when Dalip was born in September 1838. Yet she was notoriously licentious – described by Hardinge as 'a handsome debauched woman of 33,† very indiscriminate in her affections, an eater of opium' – and there is no guarantee that Ranjit was Dalip's real father. The maharaja believed himself to be so, however, and that was all that mattered. At Ranjit's funeral, Jindan wisely chose not to join the four wives and five dancing girls who, in accordance with the rites of suttee, which would not be outlawed in the Punjab until 1847, threw themselves on to the pyre. She had the dynastic claims of her ten-month-old son to consider.

During the early part of 1845, with the Khalsa's backing, Jindan ruled supreme in Lahore. But the state treasury was empty – thanks, in no small part, to official corruption and recent hikes in army pay – and there was a growing conviction within the Khalsa that a war with the British might offer a solution. Many Sikhs regarded such a war, in the light of recent British disasters in Afghanistan and the annexation of neighbouring Sind, as not only inevitable but winnable. First, however, the backbone of the Lahore government needed to be stiffened. The weakest link was considered to be Jawahir Singh, Jindan's brother, who had been appointed vizier. Jawahir was a vicious, corrupt individual who was every bit as debauched as his sister; he was wont to dress as a dancing girl and was implicated in a number of courtly assassinations. The reckoning came on 21 September 1845, when the army council summoned Jindan, her son and Jawahir to a meeting at the Mian Mir Parade Ground on the outskirts of Lahore. Flanked by 400 horsemen,

---

★ The wife or widow of a maharaja, equivalent to queen.
† She was in fact twenty-eight.

Jindan and her brother arrived on separate elephants, the latter holding Dalip Singh in his arms. They found regiment after regiment of the Khalsa drawn up in immaculate order. On the council's instructions, troops advanced to remove the royal escort and surround the two elephants. Jindan was then instructed to get down from her howdah.* What happened next was related by Alexander Gardner, an American-born adventurer who had joined Ranjit's army as an artillery adviser in 1832. Now sixty, the son of a Scottish surgeon who had fought against the British during the American War of Independence, Gardner (or 'Gurdana Khan', as the Sikhs called him) was an eccentric figure who often wore a suit and turban made from the tartan of the 79th Highlanders. He recorded:

The Rani was dragged away, shrieking to the army to spare her brother. Jawahir Singh was next ordered to descend from his elephant. A tall Sikh slapped his face and took the boy from his arms, asking how he dared to disobey the Khalsa. Duleep Singh was placed in his mother's arms, and she, hiding herself behind the walls of her tent, held the child up above them in view of the army, crying for mercy for her brother in the name of her son. She flung the child away in an agony of grief and rage . . . he was caught by a soldier. A soldier had gone up the ladder placed by Jawahir Singh's elephant, stabbed him with his bayonet, and flung him upon the ground, where he was despatched in a moment with fifty more.

Jawahir's brutal assassination was the beginning of the end for the Khalsa. Thereafter, fearful of its power, the Lahore durbar† made little effort to curb the dogs of war. Far from it: there is strong evidence to suggest that the new vizier, Lal Singh, who also happened to be Jindan's lover, and Tej Singh, a leading sirdar‡ who had gained the confidence of the Khalsa, deliberately encouraged the army to fight a pre-emptive war in the expectation that

* A seat, usually covered, for two or more on the back of an elephant.
† The court or inner government of an Indian ruler; a hall or place of audience.
‡ Political or military chief.

it would be defeated. By contributing to that defeat, by means of treasonable communications with the British, they would not only remove the Khalsa from Punjabi politics but would also ensure their prominence in any post-war Lahore government. If, on the other hand, the Khalsa was victorious, then they and the rani would at least have the consolation of ruling, however tenuously, over a much more powerful Sikh state. That, at least, was the plan.

Sir Henry Hardinge had known for several months, from reports sent by his agents in Lahore, that trouble was brewing. Yet he had made strenuous efforts not to provoke the volatile Khalsa. He knew that the HEIC directors were anxious to avoid another costly war (as was Peel's government), and that the morale and discipline of the Indian Army had not fully recovered from the disasters in Afghanistan.★ If the Sikhs launched an unprovoked attack, however, he needed to be ready. As early as March 1845 he had 'silently collected' a force of 30,000 troops on the frontier 'for *defensive* operations'. He had also, in his opinion, saved young Maharaja Dalip Singh's life by his threat 'not to recognize a successor if he be removed by violence'.

In September, with the situation worsening, Hardinge left Calcutta for the frontier. En route he overruled his commander-in-chief, Sir Hugh Gough, who, in response to reports of a build-up of Sikh forces across the Sutlej, had ordered part of the Meerut garrison to march north. Hardinge also ignored requests for re-inforcements from the general commanding the frontier garrison at Ferozepur, telling the HEIC's secret committee on 4 December that he did not expect any Sikh aggression. But four days later, by which time he had reached the frontier town of Ludhiana, he changed his mind and ordered the 80th (South Staffordshire) Foot to move north from Ambala. It had hardly begun its march when Hardinge learnt that the Sikhs had crossed the Sutlej in force on

★ The recent disaffection among Bengal regiments ordered to Sind over the issue of *batta* (or field allowances) − resulting in the disbandment of one and disciplinary proceedings in several others − was evidence of this.

12 December. A day later, citing a breach in the 1809 Anglo-Punjabi Treaty, Hardinge declared war.

The British, thanks to Hardinge's wariness, were now in a ticklish position. About 50,000 Sikhs had crossed the Sutlej and were concentrated near the village of Ferozeshah, ten miles west of the main British frontier garrison at Ferozepur, under Major-General Sir John Littler. The British forces, by contrast, were split between a number of locations at varying distances from the river and each other: closest to the Sutlej were the garrisons of Ferozepur and Ludhiana, 7,000 and 5,000 strong respectively but divided by a distance of eighty miles; a further eighty miles separated Ludhiana from the main British striking force at Ambala, 10,000 men under the personal command of Sir Hugh Gough. The last remaining reserve of 9,000 troops was at Meerut, 130 miles east of Ambala. The British were not only heavily outnumbered but also danger-ously divided. Hardinge and Gough knew that unless they were given enough time to concentrate their army, the Sikhs would surely destroy them in penny-packets (or 'in detail', as military theorists have it).

Fortunately for the British, the Sikhs chose not to make an immediate attack on Ferozepur. Lal Singh hinted at the reason when he sent a message to Captain John Nicholson, serving as one of Gough's commissariat officers, describing his intentions and expressing the hope that they would remain friends. Many his-torians have taken this as proof of treachery on the part of the two Sikh commanders, both of whom were high-caste Hindus. Yet Lal, in typical Eastern fashion, may simply have been taking out an insurance policy in case of defeat. The commanders were not, in any case, completely inactive: having crossed the Sutlej, they split their forces, Tej taking the smaller portion to mask Ferozepur while Lal awaited the main British force in a strong defensive position at Ferozeshah. Given the marked superiority of Sikh artillery, in both number of pieces and calibre, it made good sense to fight a defensive battle.

By 17 December the main British Army, with both the com-mander-in-chief and governor-general in attendance, had reached

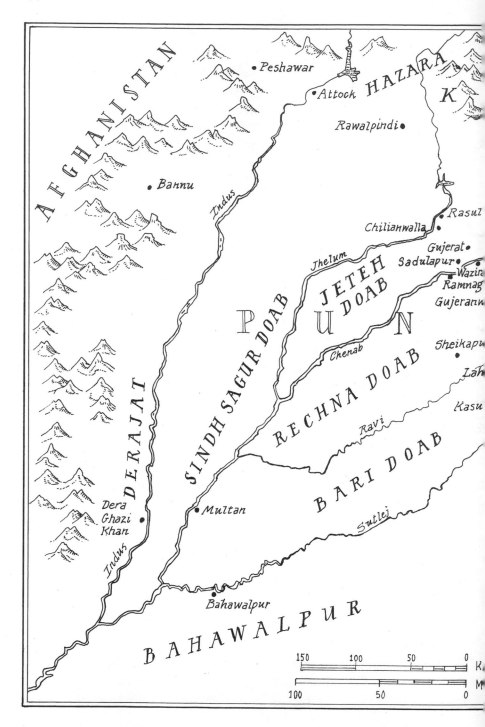

KASHMIR

Srinigar

Chenab

Jammu

PUNJAB

Indus

Ganges

INDIA

ARABIAN SEA

BAY OF BENGAL

Ravi

A

B

Kangra

Amritsar

Beas

Jullundur

JULLUNDUR DOAB

Sutlej

braon

Ferozepur

Aliwal

Simla

Ferozeshah

Ludhiana

Mudki

Kasauli

Sirhind

MALWA

Patiala

Ambala

Dehra Dun

Jumna

Ganges

THE
SIKH WARS
1845-9
THE PUNJAB
& surrounding districts

Meerut

Delhi

N

W    E

S

Badhni, fifty miles south-east of Ferozepur. Despite being re-inforced by troops from Ludhiana, it numbered only forty-two guns and 12,000 men, less than a third of whom were British. Most of the force had covered the hundred or so miles from Ambala in just four days, an incredible feat given the poor state of the roads (many of which were little more than sandy tracks), the inadequate water supplies and the wildly fluctuating temperatures.* One sol-dier of the 31st (Huntingdonshire) Foot was so tormented by the ordeal that he took off his leather stock without permission and, when ordered to replace it, chose to shoot himself instead. Above all, the march was a triumph of logistics. An army of 12,000 men were accompanied by at least three times as many camp followers, 'besides numerous elephants, camels, bullocks, horses, ponies etc.'. The amount of food needed to sustain this number of humans and beasts was scarcely credible. A typical regiment of British cavalry, 800 horses strong, required 8,000 pounds of corn a day. And all of it had to be transported in carts and wagons that themselves required extra livestock to pull. And so on.

The uneasy command structure was also a potential problem, for never before had the commander-in-chief of India been accom-panied on campaign by a governor-general who also happened to be an experienced, if slightly junior, soldier. In theory Sir Hugh Gough was in charge of all military operations; yet he must have feared that his political superior would intervene at the critical moment (and his fears proved correct). It helped, however, that Gough was one of the doughtiest and most experienced fighting soldiers in the British Army. Of Irish gentry stock, and still pos-sessed of a slight brogue, he had received his first commission at the age of fourteen and his first adjutancy a year later. He had fought in numerous theatres, including South Africa, the West Indies, the Peninsula, China and, most recently, in India during the Gwalior War of 1843, when he had twice beaten the once-mighty Maratha armies at the Battles of Maharajpur and Panniar.

---

* Even in the cold season, which runs from October to March, midday tempera-tures in northern India can be extremely hot.

It was in the Peninsula, however, that he first rose to prominence, commanding the 87th (Royal Irish) Fusiliers at the victories of Barossa, where he captured a French Eagle, and Vitoria, where he went one better and captured the baton of Marshal Jourdan, the French commander. Seriously wounded at Nivelle in 1814, he was compensated with a knighthood and a pension.

But, for all his service under that great exponent of war, the duke of Wellington, Gough was a soldier of little subtlety. He preferred brute force to clever tactics in the sure knowledge that British courage and discipline would eventually win the day. He was, as one historian has put it, a disciple of the 'Ritchie-Hook'★ school of warfare, which held that victory came after constantly 'biffing' the enemy. In Gough's eyes this meant rapidly closing with the enemy whenever, and wherever, he could be found. Such basic tactics were all well and good against an enemy possessing inferior equipment and training; but the Sikhs were not like any other Asian foe that Gough had encountered.

Gough was, however, extremely popular with his men. They were convinced he had their welfare at heart and that he would always share their discomfort and danger. He repaid that faith by wearing a long white 'fighting coat' in battle so they would know he was amongst them. A jovial man, with his white whiskers and easy manner, the men had nicknamed him 'Tipperary Joe'. They would follow him anywhere, and, in a close fight, such blind devotion was often the difference between victory and defeat.

On 18 December, after a long 21-mile march, Gough and his men were approaching the village of Mudki when cavalry scouts reported it occupied by the enemy. At first Gough ordered his exhausted troops to form up for battle. But the order was rescinded when word arrived that the enemy troops were only cavalry, and that they were withdrawing. Aware that a larger Sikh force must be near, he gave fresh orders for patrols to be sent out and the column to camp on the outskirts of the village. The ground chosen

---

★ The reference is to the fictional character Brigadier Ritchie-Hook. See Evelyn Waugh's *Men at Arms* (1952).

was mostly flat and open, with a mile or so of undulating ploughed fields between it and a broad belt of dense jungle.

Arriving in camp at this nervous time was a 35-year-old Bengal sapper called Captain Robert Napier, yet another soldier destined for great things, who had just completed the 120-mile journey from Ambala in three days. He recorded:

Arrived at Moodkee at about 3½ p.m. Apparently an inextricable confusion of troops, elephants, camels, and baggage. The Governor-General and staff, and Major [George] Broadfoot [the senior political officer], assembled under a tree. The latter said, to one of the former, that his latest intelligence of the enemy informed him that they were aware that the discipline of the feringhees★ was too powerful for them in open field, but that, man to man, they were as brave and skilful as ourselves, and that they intended a night attack. Met Colonel Haughton who kindly invited me to General Gilbert's quarters . . . I had scarcely taken the bridle from my horse when Major Codrington [one of Gilbert's staff officers] said that the Seikh army were advancing to the attack; a cloud of dust announced their approach, boldly adopted at the moment when our troops were harassed from the extraordinary length of their march, and in apparent confusion.

The rapidly approaching Sikh force was made up of around 10,000 men – mainly cavalry – and twenty-two guns. Its task was to delay the British and give Lal Singh more time to prepare his defences at Ferozeshah. Though outnumbered, the Sikhs were partially screened by a belt of jungle and had the advantage of surprise. Gough responded by pushing forward his horse artillery and cavalry towards the edge of the jungle, while his infantry, some of which had not even arrived, was formed into line.

There were no units of Royal Artillery in India at that time, and among the Bengal Horse artillerymen who galloped forward that day was a tall, black-haired gunner called Nathaniel Bancroft. Born in India in 1823, the son of a soldier, Bancroft had followed

---

★ *Feringhis*: literally 'Franks' or 'foreigners', a derogatory term for a European.

in his father's footsteps by becoming a recruit at the age of nine. For nine years he served with various units of field artillery, but his ambition was always to join the horse artillery, the *corps d'élite*, and on 7 December 1841 he got his wish. That day, he wrote,

when leather breeches and long boots, brass helmets with red horse-hair manes, and jackets with ninety buttons . . . were the favourite dress of the Bengal horse artillery, who vaunted themselves, and with justice and reverence be it spoken, the finest specimens of that arm in the world; when shaven chins and upper lips, and mutton-chop whiskers (according to regulation) were the order of the day – the reader's very humble servant attained the mature age of 18 years, and his service began to count towards a pension.

Horse artillery had been created by Frederick the Great in the eighteenth century as a mobile reserve that could be rushed to any part of the battlefield more quickly than field artillery; its chief role, however, was to support cavalry. The first British units of horse artillery (RHA) were formed in 1793. Seven years later the Bengal Army followed suit, and by the outbreak of the First Sikh War there were thirteen troops of Bengal Horse Artillery: nine European and four Indian. Each troop was armed with six muzzle-loading, smooth-bore guns: five 6-pounders, firing roundshot and canister, and one 12-pounder howitzer that lobbed exploding shells. (The heavier batteries of field artillery, by contrast, had five 9-pounder guns and one 24-pounder howitzer.) The guns were attached to limbers* and drawn by teams of six horses, most of which were mounted by members of the gun team. Only the gun commander – usually a sergeant – rode a separate horse. In action the guns would be galloped to within 400 yards of the enemy and then unlimbered, with the horse team stationed just behind the gun in case it needed to be moved.

The action of firing the gun was a highly skilled – not to say

---

* The detachable forepart of a gun carriage, consisting of two wheels and an axle, a pole for the horses and a frame for the ammunition.

hazardous – procedure. First the commander (or No. 1) would lay, or aim, the gun over open sights by moving the trail laterally and adjusting the elevating screw. The loader (No. 3) would then place the charge and projectile into the muzzle for the spongeman (No. 2) to ram home. Next it was the turn of the ventsman (No. 4) to pierce the charge through the vent hole with a small spike known as a 'pricker'; that done, he would insert an explosive tube into the vent. Last, having received the order from the commander, the firer (No. 5) would light the tube with his slow-burning portfire.★ No sooner had the gun settled from its recoil than its bore was sponged with water to extinguish any burning fragments of gunpowder. If any of these tasks was poorly performed or badly coordinated, the gun team risked maiming or death.

At Mudki no fewer than five troops of horse artillery and two batteries of field artillery, forty-two guns in all, were pushed forward to engage the Sikhs. 'We sustained many casualties in this purely artillery duel,' recalled Bancroft, 'and there were many narrow escapes.' Few narrower than his own, when a musket ball passed through the ear of the horse he was riding and killed the mounted gunner behind. But none of the gruesome sights that assailed young Bancroft during his first battle was grimmer than that of a ventsman 'running about disembowelled', a shell fragment having ignited the powder bag that he wore at his waist. The most notable gunner casualty was Lieutenant Robert Pollock, son of the hero of Kabul, who refused to have his shattered leg amputated and died the following day.

With his artillery gradually gaining the upper hand, Gough ordered a general attack, a move for which he was sharply criticized after the battle by one of his divisional commanders, Sir Harry Smith. If he had remained on the defensive, argued Smith, he would have forced the advancing Sikhs into the open. With only

---

★ A cylindrical holder containing a slow-burning incendiary composition. When the troop received the order 'prepare for action', an even slower burning match – held on a staff called a 'linstock' that could be stuck in the ground – was ignited. The firers ignited their portfires from the linstocks.

two hours of daylight left, there was, in any case, hardly time to win a decisive victory. Yet Gough's instinct was to take the initiative, and he knew, in addition, that the superior range of his percussion muskets was negated by the more powerful Sikh artillery pieces. So he attacked, with the cavalry on both flanks leading the way.

Not content with breaking through a far superior body of Sikh horse on the right, the 3rd Light Dragoons wheeled left and charged across the Sikh rear, overrunning some guns and capturing a Sikh standard in the process. (It was this charge that earned the 3rd their nickname 'Mudki-wallahs'.) Close behind the 3rd was a squadron of the Governor-General's Body Guard, whose adjutant, 23-year-old Reynell Taylor, recalled:

Conceive a brigade or column of troops galloping through a thick thorn jungle enveloped in clouds of dust so dense that the standard of my squadron was the only landmark I could recognize, approaching nearer and nearer to the thundering batteries of the enemy and the yelling crowd protecting them . . . Loud shouts of friend and foe arose on our right as our gallant dragoons dashed in, clearing all before them, and in another second we were in a mass of bloody-minded Sikh horse and foot, chiefly the former . . . I believe the men we were opposed to were, or thought themselves to be, cut off from escape by the dragoons, and they fought most furiously. I was personally engaged with five men at different times, and after a tussle of some seven or eight minutes in which our adversaries were all cut down, shot, or driven off, I found myself wounded in three different places, my reins cut and my horse 'Pickle' severely wounded by a sabre.

Meanwhile the infantry had passed through the line of British guns, with the right division, Sir Harry Smith's, the furthest forward. His men inevitably suffered the severest casualties, particularly the 50th (Queen's Own) Foot on the extreme right, which, at one point, formed square when threatened by Sikh cavalry. But the 50th continued to advance, as did the 31st Foot of its sister brigade, both units firing a final volley before charging the Sikh guns. The sepoy regiments in support did not perform so well, many hanging back and causing British casualties with their wild fire. A measure of their lacklustre showing is the fact that the 47th Bengal Native Infantry, brigaded with the 31st Foot, had fewer than 10 per cent of the British unit's casualties.

As dusk was falling, the Sikhs withdrew, leaving the British in possession of the field and seventeen enemy guns. But victory had its price: 872 casualties, 506 of whom were British, with the 3rd Light Dragoons losing almost a quarter of their total. Many of those wounded and unhorsed in the epic charge had been killed out of hand by the Sikhs, prompting a similar ruthlessness, and the cry 'Remember Mudki', when the 3rd next took the field.

Among the senior British fatalities were a divisional commander, Sir John McCaskill, two brigadier-generals and the quartermaster-general, Sir Robert 'Fighting Bob' Sale, the 'hero' of Jelalabad, who had returned to India with his wife and daughter in 1844. Though a senior staff officer with no business in the thick of the action, Sale had 'attached himself' to Smith's division and paid the ultimate price when a grapeshot shattered his thigh. 'Most deeply do we lament the death of Sir Robert Sale,' wrote the queen on hearing the news, 'and most deeply do we sympathise with that high-minded woman, Lady Sale, who has had the misfortune to lose her husband less than three years after she was released from captivity and restored to him.' The queen granted Lady Sale, who had published her Afghan journals to great acclaim in 1843, a special pension of £500 a year. She died on a visit to Cape Town in 1853, the inscription on her tombstone reading: 'Underneath this stone reposes all that could die of Lady Sale.'

Those casualties who survived the Battle of Mudki were not well cared for. The army had advanced without field hospitals, and the regimental surgeons had to make do with the limited resources in Mudki Fort. 'There were NO arrangements made for the wounded previous to this march of our Troops from cantonments,' wrote one officer. 'The suffering of the wounded from the want of attendance [was] dreadful and in many cases fatal.' Hardinge would later criticize Gough's staff for its inadequate preparation, noting that 'no supplies had been laid in on the route to Feroz-poor.' That was partly deliberate, so as not to alarm the Sikhs, but there was no excuse for the failure to bury all the Mudki dead, a number of whom were still lying where they had fallen a full month after the battle.

Like Smith, Hardinge now had serious misgivings about Gough's generalship. They were heightened the morning after the battle, when a dust cloud seemed to herald a fresh Sikh attack. Typically Gough ordered the troops out; he was just as quickly overruled by Hardinge. It was a scene that Captain Napier hoped 'never again to witness'. He wrote: 'Orders were given by the C. in C.; counter orders by the Governor-General. Troops were told to go to their lines to cook, then to stand fast, then to cook, until the Sipahis [sepoys] wearied, said they preferred to remain where they were.' It eventually proved to be a false alarm, but the men did not return to camp until 3 p.m.

A day later Hardinge was heartened by the arrival in camp of a British officer recently released by the Sikhs. He was Captain George Biddulph of the 3rd Bengal Irregular Cavalry, and his tale was scarcely credible. He had been captured and beaten by enemy horsemen during the morning of the 18th and taken to the huge Sikh camp at Ferozeshah. There he was paraded before the ill-tempered multitude, who abused and struck him anew. He was convinced that he would have been killed, there and then, had his escort not defended him. Eventually he was taken to the tent of the Sikh commander Lal Singh, whom he recognized from his 'splendid dress'. But when he spoke to Lal he received 'no answer'. Instead Lal ordered him to be placed in chains and handed over to General Bekani Ali Khan, the Muslim commander of artillery. That evening, chained to a gun, Biddulph listened nervously to the distant roar of the Mudki battle. As the artillerymen stood to their guns with lighted matches, he expected every moment to be his last. 'I expected my head to be rolling on the ground,' he wrote, '& in breathless anxiety, hoped to hear the Hurrah of our Dragoons & the clangour of their charge into the Sikh camp. The

3rd Dragoons did actually charge not very far from me, but darkness came on, & the guns ceased roaring.'

The following day, when it became clear that the Sikhs had lost the battle, Biddulph experienced less abuse and was even offered 'employment in their army'. To keep him warm through the chill nights the artillerymen built a fire and gave him tobacco to smoke. Finally, on 20 December, General Khan announced his imminent release. As word spread, a crowd gathered and threatened to kill him. Fortunately the gunners stood firm and said they would fight anyone who attempted to harm him. Eventually a horse was brought and, escorted by the general's brother, Biddulph rode out of the camp and over to the British, where he received a joyous reception he would 'never forget'.

At dawn on 21 December – after three days' rest at Mudki, burning captured gun carriages and storing cannon in the fort – the British resumed their march towards Ferozepur. Gough and Hardinge's plan – for the latter was inevitably consulted – was to link up with the Ferozepur garrison, under Major-General Sir John Littler, and then attack one or other of the two Sikh armies. There was always the danger, of course, that Littler's force would be destroyed before it could join hands with Gough's; or that the Sikhs would concentrate first. Either way the Sikh commanders would need to take the initiative; yet, in their constant secret messages to the British camp, they seemed only too eager to remain on the defensive. But could these treasonable communications be trusted?

Gough's force came within sight of the main Sikh position at Ferozeshah, a powerful horseshoe entrenchment, at around 10.30 a.m. on the 21st. There was no sign of Littler, who, thanks to a mix-up, had only left Ferozepur at 8 a.m. and still had some distance to cover. Gough was unconcerned and, after a brief reconnaissance of the Sikh defences, ordered an immediate attack. Fortunately for his troops, and possibly the fate of British India, Hardinge again intervened. No attack could take place, the governor-general insisted, until Littler had arrived. Gough was furious, not to say humiliated, but he bowed to his political superior. It was a wise move. Without Littler, the British had 13,000 men and forty-four guns; the Sikhs had the same number of troops but many more guns and the advantage of the defence. Even with the extra troops the battle could go either way.

The junction was made with Littler's division – 5,500 men and twenty-one guns – a couple of miles south-east of Ferozeshah, at 1.30 p.m. The army was then deployed for battle: Major-General Sir Walter Gilbert's division on the right, Brigadier-General Newton Wallace's in the middle, Littler's on the left and Smith's in reserve; the cavalry were placed on each wing. But the broken terrain made movement difficult, and it was not until 4 p.m. that the tired and thirsty British troops began their attack. As at Mudki, the battle opened with an artillery duel,★ and, once again, the Sikhs got the better of it. Gunner Bancroft recalled:

It being found that our light six-pounder guns produced but slight effect on the enemy's heavier metal . . . our major, evidently with the object of ascertaining how close it would be necessary for him to advance, laid one of the guns himself, ordering it to be fired; he stepped aside to note the result, which must have disappointed him, as he was observed to stamp his food impatiently. He turned round in search of his horse, and not seeing it, he said, 'Bancroft, where is my horse?' Pointing to the direction in which the animal was standing, the writer answered: 'There he is, Sir!' The words were scarcely uttered, when he saw the gallant major lying at a little distance from his horse – headless! . . . At the same moment the writer felt a dreadful shock on his right side, and his right arm involuntarily whirled round his head.

Bancroft had been hit by the same roundshot that decapitated his major. Fortunately for him, it passed between his body and right arm, 'carrying away his pouch and belt on one side, and the soft

★ Because most independent states in India possessed powerful artillery, and none more so than the Sikhs, it was standard procedure for Indian artillery, when attacking, to engage the enemy's guns so as to remove the threat of anti-personnel fire. British artillery, by contrast, still clung to the traditional tactic of engaging the enemy's infantry.

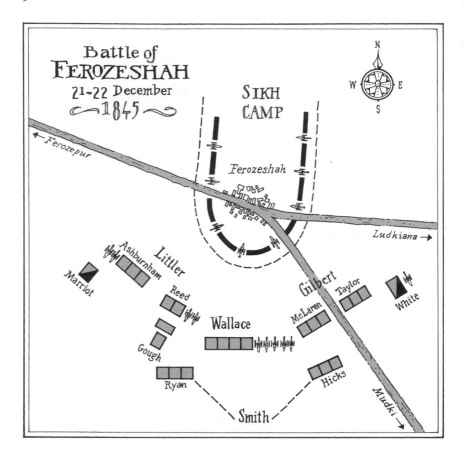

parts of the arm itself on the other'. He watched the rest of the battle from the hazardous vantage of a limber-box.

The confusion caused by the heavy Sikh bombardment may explain why one of Littler's brigades attacked prematurely, with disastrous results. With scant support from its two sepoy battalions, the 62nd (Wiltshire) Foot advanced virtually alone into a storm of grape and musket balls, losing sixteen officers and 283 men in a matter of minutes. Exposed in the open, their left flank threatened by Sikh cavalry, the survivors were ordered to withdraw. Littler's other brigade was made up entirely of Indian soldiers, and only one battalion, the 33rd Native Infantry, advanced with any vigour. But it too was repulsed, and the whole division moved to the rear and took no further part in the battle. The only exception was a group of about fifty men of the 33rd, who joined a regiment in the neighbouring division.

At this point, with his left flank disintegrating and disaster looming, a less steadfast general might have cut his losses and ordered a retreat. But Gough knew only one battlefield manoeuvre – attack – and so ordered his remaining divisions to advance, with Smith's replacing Littler's on the left. Rising up from the ground, where they had been lying to avoid the heavy Sikh bombardment, the men of Gilbert's and Wallace's divisions raced forward, with Hardinge and Gough, unmistakable in his white 'fighting coat', leading them on. Once again the infantry advanced in echelon from the right, eighty yards between battalions, with the 29th (Worcestershire) Foot in the van. Advancing steadily and firing by files, the men of the 29th passed through the remnants of the horse artillery and paused only when they came to the hundred yards of open ground that lay between the edge of the jungle scrub and the Sikh entrenchment. This gave the neighbouring 80th Foot time to catch up, and, ignoring a hail of bullets, the two regiments charged together across the open ground, fired a last close-range volley, then broke through the wooden barricade, crossed the shallow ditch and rushed the Sikh gun platforms. The Sikh gunners fought desperately, but their swords were no match for the British bayonets, and they were soon overcome. Beyond the gun line the

British were opposed by massed ranks of Sikh infantry, their first rank kneeling to fire a volley. So determined was the British charge, however, that the Sikh formation was quickly broken, and hundreds fled to the rear.

By now the neighbouring British brigade, led by the recently joined 1st Bengal Europeans, had also entered the Sikh camp. They were ably supported by the sepoys of the 16th Grenadiers, but the remaining regiment of Native Infantry, the 45th, held back during the advance and inflicted a number of 'friendly fire' casualties with its wild volleys. Major David Birrell, commanding the 1st Europeans, recorded:

On passing our Artillery, the gunners gave us a cheer, and when some distance past them, I prepared to charge, giving the word 'Charge' when about 200 paces from the enemy's Batteries. At 80 paces or so all our front rank gave a volley from the hip almost as we received a volley of grape shot which caused many casualties in our ranks. We then rushed on capturing the guns in gallant style, the Siek gunners who had stood to the last being bayonetted and shot by our men who had reserved their fire.

Mounted on his horse, Birrell was one of the first over the trench and almost paid with his life. Attacked by two sword-wielding Sikhs in succession, he was saved by the intervention of his men, who bayoneted one and shot the other. He also narrowly avoided being blown to pieces by an exploding Sikh magazine, which killed a number of his soldiers as they advanced towards the village of Ferozeshah. An important factor in the successful advance of Gilbert's division was the cover given to its right flank by the men of the 3rd Light Dragoons, who won fresh laurels by charging a battery of guns that could have been used to enfilade the British infantry. But, having sabred the gunners, the dragoons careered on through the supporting infantry, and many were shot down.

Units of the other two divisions also penetrated the Sikh camp, though Wallace's men, particularly the 9th (East Norfolk) Foot, were badly cut up as they advanced over the same ground that had defeated the 62nd Foot. Again the performance of the sepoy battalions in the brigade was patchy. The 26th Native Infantry did well but not the vaunted 2nd Grenadiers. Among the latter's officers was Ensign William Hodson, a 24-year-old Cambridge graduate, only recently arrived in India, who wrote home in disgust: 'In the most dense dust and smoke, and under an unprecedented fire of grape, our Sepoys again gave way and broke . . . The Colonel, the greater part of my brother officers, and myself were left with the colours and about thirty men immediately in front of the batteries.' It was, he added, a 'fearful crisis', and only the 'bravery of the English regiments saved us'. So mistrustful of Indian troops did this experience leave Hodson that, after the war, he insisted on transferring to the 1st Europeans.

Lieutenant E. A. Noel of the 31st Foot, part of Smith's division, described the battle as 'murderous, but glorious, the excitement of charging right into the mouth of the guns you cannot conceive'. But he, like Hodson, had only contempt for his Indian comrades. 'The Sepoys are fit for nothing,' he wrote; 'most of them bolted and their officers joined us. The papers of course will praise them, but this is only policy.'

The breaching of the Sikh defences, however, was far from the battle's final act. British regiments became mixed up in the dust and smoke, and the Sikhs launched a number of counter-attacks. One was mistaken for friendly fire, and, in consequence, the 29th Foot was ordered not to shoot back. The mistake was compounded – according to Captain Robert Napier, acting chief engineer, who had entered the entrenchment with Gough and his staff – when Hardinge and his chief political officer, Major George Broadfoot, the hero of Jelalabad, 'rode forward, as they supposed, to stop the fire of *our regiment* in front, as if they would have fired outward or to the rear, had they been our own'. Broadfoot was shot and killed; Hardinge narrowly escaped. Only now did the 29th advance and drive back the Sikhs.

With darkness falling, his units scattered and the Sikh camp a dangerous place to linger with its exploding magazines, Gough ordered his troops to withdraw 300 yards and bivouac in the open.

They were, as a result, forced to abandon the guns they had captured at such great cost, many of which were turned on them by returning Sikh gunners. There was little order and no attempt to take up a defensive position. 'Had the enemy known the condition of our troops and attacked them,' wrote Napier, 'they would have been slaughtered like sheep.' One particular gun was causing havoc in Gilbert's division. Eventually, on Hardinge's orders, it was captured and spiked by the 80th Foot with the 1st Europeans in support. 'After this,' noted Major Birrell, 'the force near [Hardinge and Gough] rested free from much annoyance from midnight to daybreak – but the troops with Sir H. Smith were exposed to a heavy fire nearly all night.'

The crisis for the British was far from over. Gough's army had suffered heavy casualties,★ and many of its units were disorganized and out of touch. At any moment Tej Singh's army might arrive to tilt the balance decisively in favour of the Sikhs. Little wonder that Hardinge later described that night as one in which 'the fate of India trembled in the balance.' So unsure was he of ultimate British success that he dispatched to the rear a reluctant Prince Waldemar of Prussia, who had been serving on his staff as an observer. He also sent back Napoleon's sword, a present from the duke of Wellington, and ordered all state papers at Mudki to be burnt.

At dawn on the 22nd, word went round the British camp that Gough was about to withdraw to Ferozepur. Napier was horrified. 'I consulted several of the staff,' he recalled, 'and then went to [Gough] and submitted my opinion, that if we moved we lost the fruits of our victory; that we could hold our present position, and find food in the enemy's camp, prepare and make use of his artillery, and that our communication was open with our rear at Moodkee, and as good with Ferozepoor as if we were actually there.' Gough voiced his agreement, and said he would do 'all in

---

★ The British suffered 2,415 casualties (694 killed) during the two-day Ferozeshah battle. Only a third were Indian troops, though they made up three fifths of the army's total. The Sikhs lost around 3,000 men.

his power to remain', but 'political considerations' would have to come first. In fact it was the governor-general who was pressing a hesitant Gough to remain; not vice versa. 'The C.C. came to me,' recalled Hardinge, '& told me he felt the perilous & critical state in which we were – triumphant on the ground we had so severely contested but apparently surrounded by thousands of Sikhs.' But, as Hardinge was determined to 'fight it out', orders were given to re-enter the Sikh camp. There was little opposition, and the guns, many of which had not been spiked, were soon retaken. With the camp in British possession, Gough and Hardinge were cheered to the echo as they rode along the line.

But, just when it seemed that the battle was won, scouts reported the approach of Tej Singh's huge army from the west: he had appeared at last. Gough was now in a desperate position. His ranks were depleted, his remaining men tired and thirsty, and his ammunition almost exhausted. The Sikhs, on the other hand, were fresh and apparently eager for battle. To combat the mass of cavalry on each Sikh flank, Gough ordered his infantry to form squares in front of the entrenchment. Tej responded with long-range artillery fire, killing a brigadier-general, amongst others. The British troops lay down as their artillery was brought forward. But the guns were low on ammunition and out-ranged. 'Seeing that we were losing men and horses every minute,' wrote Captain G. H. Swinley of the BHA, 'we retired under cover of the village and the entrenched camp.'

Gough made a desperate attempt to draw the fire from his infantry by riding out to a flank in his conspicuous white fighting coat. The bold gesture had little effect, beyond endangering his life. A number of camp followers began to vote with their feet, and they were followed by not a few sepoys and a whole regiment of Indian cavalry, which rode to the rear. To reduce casualties, Gough withdrew his infantry to the line of the entrenchments (where they probably should have begun the fight). Then, when it seemed that the situation could hardly get worse, most of the British guns and cavalry on the left of the line began to move off in the direction of Ferozepur. A junior staff officer, some say

affected by sunstroke, had reissued Gough's original orders without
authority, and, incredibly, they were obeyed. 'Can you imagine
such a thing', wrote Swinley to his sister, 'as the whole of the
artillery and very nearly all the cavalry of an army leaving the field
of battle with the C–in–C and all the infantry still engaged?'

At this critical moment, the 3rd Light Dragoons came to the
rescue once again by charging a much larger body of Sikh horse
on the right flank. The Sikh riders fled, and before long the whole
Sikh Army was in retreat. Tej later claimed to have issued the
order because he did not think his troops were capable of driving
the British from their defensive position. But he would never get
a better opportunity to defeat Gough, and many historians suspect
him of duplicity. The 'verdict' must be, wrote one, 'that the Sikhs
were deprived of the victory that their valour had richly deserved
by the treachery of their leaders'. Tej followed Lal Singh back
across the Sutlej, leaving the relieved, not to say astonished, British
in possession of the field. Captain Swinley summed up the thoughts
of many when he wrote: 'It is a perfect riddle how a disciplined
army like ours could have become so completely disorganized
and not annihilated and still more wonderful is it that a battle
was won.'

Gunner Bancroft was among the hundreds of British casualties
taken by bullock cart and elephant to hospital tents in Ferozepur
Fort. 'The sights', he wrote later, 'were most harrowing. Most of
[my] comrades of the horse artillery who were taken out of the
carts had died on the field from loss of blood and scarcity of water,
and some of them were at the door of death, gasping their last.
They were all placed side by side on the ground; several of them
had their limbs shattered with round shot and grape; and after the
moribund had breathed their last, they were again put into carts
and taken outside the fort to be buried in a pit dug for the purpose.'

With more reinforcements on the way from Meerut, Gough
was in no hurry to re-engage the Sikhs, and on 27 December his
army halted five miles from the Sikh bridgehead over the River
Sutlej at Sobraon. Though Hardinge liked Gough as a person and
admired his bravery, he did not think he was the right man to win

the war. 'We have been in the greatest peril,' he informed Sir Robert Peel in a confidential letter of 30 December, '& are likely hereafter to be in great peril, if these very extensive operations are to be conducted by the com.-in-chief.' His recommendation was for Gough to be replaced by Sir Charles Napier, who, at the time, was governor and military chief of Sind. The cabinet disagreed, preferring Hardinge to assume dual political and military control. But by the time its decision reached India the war was over.

Gough was reinforced by 10,000 men from Meerut on 6 January 1846. Thus strengthened, he moved closer to the Sikh bridgehead at Sobraon, which itself had been massively reinforced. He was keen to attack before the Sikhs could complete a bridge across the river. But the ferocity of the Sikh response to his initial bombardment on 14 January caused him to postpone the assault until his heavy guns had arrived. Instead he dispatched a column under Sir Harry Smith to counter various Sikh forays over the Sutlej to the east. While Smith was thus engaged, Gough received word of a much larger Sikh incursion in the vicinity of Ludhiana. Anxious to safeguard his slow-moving siege train, he at once ordered Smith to block the threat. But en route to Ludhiana, Smith blundered into the Sikh invasion force and, realizing he was hopelessly outnumbered, did his best to avoid battle. He could not, however, prevent Sikh irregulars from attacking his baggage train and causing about 200 casualties. On 28 January, with his column swelled by reinforcements to 10,000 men and forty guns, Smith met and decisively defeated the Sikh army of 13,000 men near the village of Aliwal, fifteen miles west of Ludhiana.* This time the sepoys fought well, and the 500 British casualties were shared equally between Smith's Indian and European troops. The Sikhs again lost 3,000 men and almost seventy guns.

---

* Smith was rewarded with a baronetcy and, after the war, was appointed governor and commander-in-chief of the Cape Colony. The Natal town of Ladysmith, famous for its epic siege during the Anglo-Boer War of 1899–1902, was named after his remarkable Spanish wife, Juana, who was just fourteen when they met during the Peninsular Wars, and who accompanied him on all his subsequent campaigns.

Gough was now free to turn his attention to the Sikh bridgehead south of Sobraon. The Sikhs had not been idle, and the position now consisted of three lines of semicircular entrenchments, their flanks resting on the Sutlej. The 3,000-yard front line was the strongest: a ditch protected by a high earth bank that had been revetted (or strengthened) by wood. In most places the bank rose to an imposing ten feet; but on the right, where the soil was sandiest, it reached only six feet. Given that this was the position's weak spot, it is odd that Tej Singh chose to protect it with his irregular infantry, who were less reliable; the regulars were massed in the centre and on the left, with the majority of the artillery also in the centre. To protect the flanks, and to cover the fords, the Sikhs had placed their cavalry and the rest of the artillery, under Lal Singh, on the far side of the river. Both banks were linked by a recently constructed bridge-of-boats.*

Hardinge preferred to outflank the position by crossing the Sutlej near Ferozepur. Keen to avoid the inevitable casualties of a frontal attack, he may also have been influenced by recent communications with Gulab Singh of Jammu, the new vizier at Lahore, who was keen to negotiate a peace. But Gough was having none of it: a flanking manoeuvre would leave both his lines of communication and various British garrisons vulnerable to attack; far better to destroy the bulk of the Sikh Army while he could. By 10 February he was ready to attack. His siege train of nineteen heavy guns had arrived on the 7th, and Smith rejoined with his victorious troops a day later. Gough now had 15,000 men and about eighty guns. The total Sikh force on both banks was, according to Hardinge, 'at least' 35,000 men and up to a hundred guns. Yet Gough was unperturbed, and his plan of attack was, for him at least, a model of subtlety: to concentrate his main effort on the weak Sikh right, while simultaneous diversionary attacks were made on the centre and the left.

The British bombardment began as the morning mist lifted at

---

* A temporary river crossing comprised of boats moored abreast and covered with a wooden road.

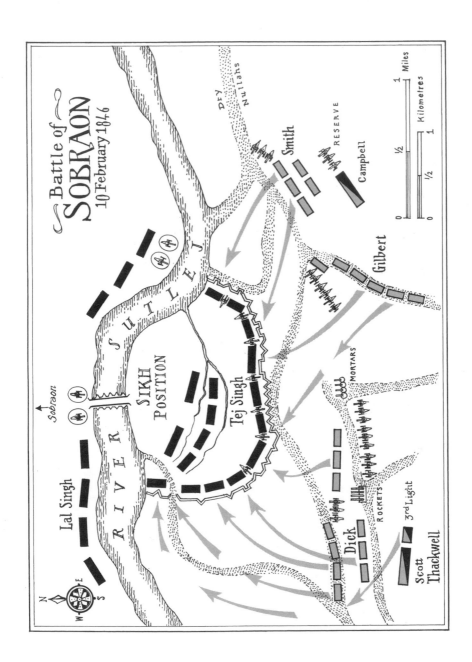

Battle of SOBRAON
10 February 1846

Sobraon

SIKH POSITION

SUTLEJ RIVER

DRY Nullahs

Lal Singh

Tej Singh

Smith

RESERVE

Campbell

Gilbert

MORTARS

ROCKETS

3rd Light

Dick

Scott
Thackwell

Miles
Kilometres
0 ½ 1
0 ½ 1

8.30 a.m. But inadequate ammunition supplies caused the barrage to be cut short and, with the fire slackening at 10.30, Major-General Sir Robert Dick was ordered to begin the main attack on the Sikh right. 'Thank God,' Gough is said to have remarked on being told of the ammunition shortage, 'then we'll be at them with the bayonet.' The troops in Dick's leading brigade might not have agreed. The initial advance went well, as men of both the 53rd (Shropshire) and the 10th (Northern Lincolnshire) Foot broke through the first line of the Sikh defence. But they were soon halted by enfilade fire from the far bank and from within the entrenchments. Then Dick himself was killed, urging his troops on, and a determined Sikh counter-attack forced the British to concede some ground. In desperation, Gough ordered the diversionary attacks on the Sikh centre and left to be made in earnest. They too were beaten back. Attacking in the centre, as part of Gilbert's division, was Major Birrell of the 1st Europeans, who recalled: 'Their guns opened upon us, but did little or no injury the shot going over us, but on getting about 60 or 70 yards from their entrenchment, the Infantry poured so destructive a volley of musketry upon us that it actually staggered the Regt. and in less than three or four minutes, 11 officers and 200 men of my Corps were killed and wounded, being half of the numbers engaged. This heavy loss compelled us to fall back a little and reform.'

But eventually the pressure on the centre and left told, as the Sikhs rushed troops across from their right, which in turn enabled Dick's division to retake the ground it had lost. Prominent in the fight, as ever, was the 3rd Light Dragoons, which used a ramp to cross into the entrenchments before charging the enemy in concert with two units of Bengal light cavalry. Trooper John Pearman, a 26-year-old former railway guard who had just joined the 3rd with a draft from Britain, recorded:

On we went by the dead and dying, and partly over the poor fellows, and up the parapet our horses scrambled. One of the Sikh artillery men struck at me with his sponge staff but missed me, hitting my horse on the hindquarters, which made the horse bend down. I cut a round cut at him and felt my sword strike him but could not say where, there was such a smoke on. I went with the rest through the camp at their battalions which we broke up.

With Gilbert's and Smith's divisions also making headway, the Sikhs were being squeezed back into an ever-smaller area. Some fought on, but most followed Tej Singh's lead by fleeing towards the bridge. It was quickly choked and began to break up, forcing whole regiments to swim for their lives. 'We drove the enemy into the river,' recalled an officer of the 63rd Native Infantry (part of Dick's division), 'where thousands of them were killed by our file-firing and by the grape and canister of 4 troops of Horse Artillery; and a great number must have been drowned.' Gunner Bancroft, recovered from his wound at Ferozeshah, described the water as a 'bloody foam, amid which heads and uplifted hands were seen to vanish by hundreds'. No quarter was given, and Sikh losses were put as high as 10,000 men and all sixty-seven guns. British casualties were similar to those at Ferozeshah: 2,383 (but with just 320 killed).

The power of the Khalsa had been broken, and the road to Lahore was open. It was only left for Hardinge to decide on the severity of his terms for peace. He had no intention, he told his stepson two days after the battle, of annexing the whole of the Punjab. Such a move was contrary to government and HEIC policy and would, in any case, have required the presence of British bayonets at Lahore to enforce British rule, a state of affairs repugnant to Hardinge. Instead he proposed to 'clip the state which has shown itself too strong, punish & disband the army, & give the Hindoos another chance'. The exact terms were thrashed out at a meeting between Hardinge and Gulab Singh at Kasur, on the road to Lahore, on 16 February. They included: the annexation of the Jullundur Doab, between the Sutlej and Beas Rivers; the restriction of the Sikh Army to twenty-five battalions, 12,000 horse and twenty-five guns; the imposition of a war indemnity of £1.5m; the stationing of a British garrison in Lahore until the end of 1846 (to guarantee the payment of the indemnity); and an undertaking by the Lahore government not to make war or peace without British permission. Gulab Singh – described by Hardinge as 'the ablest scoundrel in all Asia' – agreed to these harsh terms in return for the title of maharaja of Jammu. Uppermost in Hardinge's calculations, of course, was the security of British India, and, to him at least, the emasculation of Sikh power and the establishment of a resident in Lahore seemed the best ways to achieve it.

As a sign of submission, Gulab had brought with him to Kasur the young maharaja of Lahore, Dalip Singh. 'Conceive a beautiful little boy of 8 years old', wrote Hardinge, 'brought into the midst of cannon & feringees, amongst strangers represented as monsters who eat cows & destroy Sikhs by thousands. The brave little fellow showed no fear; I coaxed him & made him laugh, a great Eastern indecorum, gave him a musical box with a bird & trays of presents, which he looked at with curiosity. The talk was diplomatic, of old Runjeet his father (who was not his father), & after an hour the boy retired with a salute of 21 guns.' With Dalip in tow, Hardinge and Gough entered Lahore and took possession of its magnificent red fort – built by the Mughal Emperor Akbar in the sixteenth century – on 20 February. The city was less impressive, with one officer describing it as the 'dirtiest place I ever saw'. He added: 'The streets are so narrow that two elephants could not pass each other, and in the centre there is a little drain full of stagnant water from which the smell is very offensive.'

The formal signing of the Lahore Treaty took place in a large marquee outside the city on 9 March. The British guard of honour was provided, fittingly enough, by the 3rd Light Dragoons, resplendent in their dark blue double-breasted coatees with scarlet facings, dark blue overalls and black beaver shakos.★ 'In the tent', recorded Trooper Pearman, 'were Sir Henry Hardinge, Sir Hugh Gough and the staff officers, and about two hundred of us with drawn swords. The Sikh chiefs also had their guard of honour.

---

★ Tall, cylindrical peaked caps with chain chinstraps and a regimental crest in the form of a Maltese cross. On campaign they were worn with a white quilted cover.

It was a grand sight. The ceremony took two and a half hours, and then Sir Henry Hardinge ordered the durbar to be broken up.' Henceforth the government of the reduced Punjab would be conducted in Dalip's name by a regency council. The newly promoted Colonel Henry Lawrence, Broadfoot's successor and the eldest of the famous Lawrence brothers, was the British resident appointed to keep it in line.

## 5. 'I know it to be just, politic, and necessary'

Victoria and Albert were at Osborne House, their recently built private residence on the Isle of Wight, when the first reports of the hard-fought victories at Mudki and Ferozeshah reached Britain in early March 1846. The queen pointedly made no mention of Gough in her letter of congratulation to Hardinge, confining her remarks to an 'admiration' of the governor-general and his troops, and sorrow at the loss of so many distinguished officers. She looked forward to the 'next news', she wrote, with 'great anxiety'.

It would not last long. On April Fool's Day, the relieved queen gave permission for the guns in Hyde Park to be fired in celebration of the crushing victory at Sobraon. To Hardinge she expressed 'her extreme satisfaction at the brilliant and happy termination of our severe contest with the Sikhs', adding, 'The Queen . . . knows how much she owes to Sir Henry Hardinge's exertions.' Again no mention of Gough, though governor-general and commander-in-chief would each be rewarded with a peerage: Hardinge a viscountcy and Gough a barony.

A crisis in domestic politics, however, soon drove all thought of colonial wars to the back of the queen's mind. Sir Robert Peel, whom she had come to admire and trust, had recently introduced a bill for the repeal of the protectionist Corn Laws over a period of three years. First brought in on a sliding scale in 1828, the Corn Laws ensured that the duty on imported grain rose as the domestic price fell. In 1842 Peel had reduced the duty at the lower end of the scale, and within four years was completely won over to the argument that free trade would benefit all classes in Britain. But the majority of his party was fiercely opposed to the bill, regarding it as a betrayal of landed interests, and these protectionists were led in the Commons by an obscure MP called Benjamin Disraeli.

Born in December 1804, the son of prosperous and literary

Sephardic Jews (hence his father's surname, D'Israeli), Disraeli had converted to Christianity at the age of twelve, thereby removing the bar to political office.* After three failed attempts, he finally entered parliament as the MP for Maidstone in 1837, but Peel had consistently denied him office, and he was better known for his campaigning novels and foppish dress than he was for his political career. Now all that would change. On 22 January 1846, the day the bill was announced, Disraeli gave a masterful speech in which he portrayed Peel, in Robert Blake's words, as a 'slightly pompous, priggish mediocrity who was betraying the party by which he had risen'. He sat down to Tory cheers that lasted three minutes. Battle had been joined, and Disraeli, hitherto anonymous, had launched himself on the path to greatness.

Victoria and Albert were strongly supportive of Peel's measure, chiefly as a means of alleviating the Irish Famine. The queen had already donated £2,000 of her own money to a Famine relief fund; Albert topped this by providing moral support at one of the earliest Corn Law debates from the gallery of the House of Commons. The gesture was unmistakable, causing one Tory to complain from the floor that the prince's presence gave 'the semblance of a personal sanction of her Majesty to a measure which, be it for good or for evil, a great majority, at least of the landed aristocracy of England, of Scotland, and of Ireland, imagine fraught with deep injury, if not ruin, to them'. The prince had overstepped the constitutional mark by betraying his, not to mention the queen's, political bias. He would not make the same mistake again.

Royal support might have helped the measure pass through parliament; but it could save neither Peel's government nor his party. On 25 June, the day the Corn Importation Bill became law – Whig, Irish and Radical support having helped it pass its third reading in the House of Commons a month earlier by ninety-eight votes – the Tory rebels took their revenge by combining with the

---

* Until Catholic Emancipation in 1829, only Protestants were admitted to public office and military service. Jews had to wait another twenty-nine years for their emancipation.

opposition to defeat a government initiative to restore law and order in Ireland. Peel was forced to resign, and the queen, much against her will, asked Lord John Russell to form an alternative administration. He managed this by forging an alliance between his own Whig Party and the Radicals. But an attempt to broaden further the base of the new government by offering cabinet posts to prominent free-trade Tories like Lord Aberdeen and Sir James Graham, both ministers under Peel, did not succeed. Not that it mattered. Peel's repeal of the Corn Laws had split the old Tory Party into two opposing factions: the protectionists, led by Disraeli and Lord George Bentinck in the Commons and Lord Stanley in the Lords; and the free-trade Peelites. The Conservatives – as the protectionist rump became known – would not enjoy another majority government until 1874.

The queen was distraught. 'I had to part with Sir R. Peel and Lord Aberdeen,' she informed her uncle Leopold, 'who are irreparable losses to us and the Country . . . We felt so safe with them. Never, during the five years that they were with me, did they *ever* recommend a *person* or a thing which was not for my or the Country's best, and never for the Party's advantage only; and the contrast *now* is very striking; there is much less respect and much less high and pure feeling.' She was referring in particular to Lord Palmerston, the new foreign minister, whom she and Albert regarded as anti-French, arrogant and self-serving, though her opinion of the government as a whole was not high. It was 'weak', she told Leopold, and Russell did 'not possess the talent of keeping his people together'. Yet she had managed to extract one concession: that the newly ennobled Viscount Hardinge of Lahore would be allowed to continue as governor-general of India. Apprising him of this, she lamented: 'One of the most brilliant Governments this Country ever had has fallen at the moment of victory!'

Back in Lahore, meanwhile, Henry Lawrence was finding the job of resident much more difficult than he had expected. His attempt to reform the civil administration of the Punjab, particularly the legal code and the system of revenue collection, was being frustrated by the 'venal and selfish' regency council at every turn. Dominated by the queen mother, Rani Jindan, and her lover Lal Singh, the vizier, the council was a hotbed of corruption and intrigue. One British political officer wrote of Lal:

I have seldom seen a better looking man . . . He is, I should say, about thirty years of age, strongly built, tall, and very soldier-like, though as cunning as a fox; talks in a bland, kind tone, which could not hurt a fly, though he would just as soon cut a man's windpipe as look at him. Every one of the sirdars [chiefs] hate him, and make no secret of their dislike, but say with the greatest coolness that Lal Sing's life is not worth two hours' purchase after the withdrawal of the British troops from Lahore.

Misgovernment by Lal and the rani, together with the cost of the recent conflict, had placed the treasury in a parlous state and in no position to pay the huge war indemnity in the time allotted. The council's solution was to offer instead the former Afghan province of Kashmir, conquered by Ranjit Singh in 1819 and left in the hands of a Muslim governor. But the Indian government had neither the men nor the money to secure such a rugged outpost, a sort of mini-Afghanistan, and so Lawrence suggested giving it to Maharaja Gulab Singh,★ the ruler of neighbouring Jammu, in return for half of the Sikh war indemnity. Hardinge and Gulab both agreed, and so it was that a Muslim-dominated province was sold to a Hindu ruler, thereby sowing the seeds of the factional strife that still persists in Kashmir to this day.

No sooner had Gulab arrived at his new capital of Srinagar with a British escort in July 1846 than it became obvious that the Muslim majority did not want him. 'We had not been many days in the city', recalled his escort commander John Nicholson, 'before we

★ A Dogra Hindu from the hills between the Punjab and Kashmir, Gulab joined the Sikh Army as a trooper and rose to the rank of general. In 1820, as a reward for his service, he was put in charge of the recently conquered hill state of Jammu by Ranjit Singh.

learnt that the governor had made up his mind to drive Gulab Singh's small force out of the valley and seize us. We had great difficulty in effecting our escape, which we did just in time to avoid capture.' In truth the hasty withdrawal of Gulab's Dogra troops over the mountains to Jammu was more a rout than a retreat. Hardinge now had little option but to enforce the deal he had made with Gulab by sending a much larger force of 10,000 men to quell the rebellious province. Led by Henry Lawrence and a handful of young political officers – with Patrick Vans Agnew, Harry Lumsden, William Hodson and Nicholson amongst them – the force included a large proportion of former members of the Sikh Army whose loyalties were far from certain. Lawrence summed up the hazards of the mission as follows: 'Half a dozen foreigners taking up a largely subdued mutinous army through as difficult a country as there is in the world to put the chief, formerly their commander, now in their minds a rebel, in possession of the brightest jewel in their land.' As it happened, the Sikh troops behaved beautifully and the Muslim governor surrendered without a fight, leaving the unscrupulous Gulab in charge of Kashmir.

It was then discovered that Lal Singh and Rani Jindan had encouraged the governor's opposition to Gulab's rule. Tried by a British court martial, Lal was found guilty of duplicity and exiled in January 1847. The rani had already been stripped of most of her powers by a new settlement, the Treaty of Bhairowal, that Lawrence concluded with Tej Singh and the leading sirdars on Boxing Day 1846: in return for giving them unconditional owner-ship of their vast estates – they had formerly held them as fiefs in return for money and services – they would pay for the British garrison to remain in Lahore until 1854, the period of the young maharaja's minority, and would also hand over control of the civil and military administration to Lawrence, who became, in effect, the ruler of the Punjab. The rani opposed the new treaty in vain and was eventually exiled to Sheikapur on a pension of 48,000 rupees a year.

Over the coming year, in the name of good government, Law-rence reduced the authority of the young maharaja and his council still further, until they were little more than ciphers. He also, in October 1847, placed Rani Jindan under house arrest on suspicion of fomenting opposition to British rule. She was not alone in suspecting him of annexation by the back door. 'Why do you take possession of the kingdom by underhand means?' she asked him in a letter. 'Why do you not do it openly? On the one hand you make a show of friendship and on the other you have put us in prison?' Lawrence and Hardinge, however, would not remain in India to reap what they had sown.

They returned to Britain on the same ship in January 1848: Lawrence on sick leave and Hardinge for good. Their respective replacements were Sir Frederick Currie and Lord Dalhousie, the latter arriving in India in February. Lawrence had left his capable brother John as acting resident and head of the regency council; but the decision was overruled by the incoming governor-general, who appointed Currie, a high-ranking civil servant with little diplomatic experience, instead.

James Andrew Broun Ramsay, the tenth earl of Dalhousie, was just thirty-five years old when he arrived in India. A Lowland Scot, the son of a former commander-in-chief of India and governor-general of Canada, he had been a rising star of the Tory Party until the upheavals of 1846. He supported the repeal of the Corn Laws, having just entered Peel's cabinet as president of the Board of Trade, and became, almost by default, a Peelite. He was one of the former ministers that Russell tried, without success, to tempt back into government. But he was prepared to accept the onerous post of governor-general of India, believing he was young enough, talented enough and energetic enough to make a difference. An additional factor was Russell's promise to leave him 'entirely free in respect of political opinions'. Like one of his recent predecessors, Lord William Bentinck, he was a strong advocate of the political philosophy of Utilitarianism: a belief that human legislators were required to 'assist men to avoid harmful acts by artificially weighing such acts with the pain of punishment'. This Utilitarian passion for 'uniformity of management and unity of authority' would cause Dalhousie to introduce during the six years of his governor-generalship a number of administrative and political reforms that were highly unpopular among ordinary Indians. But all that was in the future.

A more immediate problem was the growing antagonism towards British 'rule' in the Punjab, particularly from those unemployed former soldiers and disgruntled sirdars who feared a steady erosion of their economic and political power. Foremost among the latter was Dewan Mulraj, the semi-independent ruler of the southern province of Multan, who had done a deal with Lawrence to pay the government a smaller succession fee – twenty lakhs of rupees instead of thirty – in return for a third of his territory and a higher revenue assessment. As if these terms were not harsh enough, Lawrence then abolished Mulraj's right to levy transit dues and hear appeals against his legal decisions.

In December 1847, partly as a ruse to avoid paying revenue arrears, Mulraj announced his intention to abdicate in favour of his son. But he was persuaded to delay his decision until Sir Frederick Currie, the new resident, had reached Lahore. Currie duly arrived in March 1848, but made no attempt to get to the bottom of Mulraj's machinations. Instead he simply announced that Mulraj had been replaced by a Sikh governor, Sirdar Khan Singh, and his local levies with regular troops from Lahore. Two HEIC officers, Lieutenants Patrick Vans Agnew and William Anderson, would accompany Singh to Multan as his political and military advisers. Trouble was inevitable.

Vans Agnew and Anderson reached Multan on 18 April and were received by Mulraj with every sign of friendship. But a day later, as they were being given a tour of Multan Fort, the two British officers were attacked and badly injured by mutinous Multani irregulars. Saved from certain death by Sirdar Khan Singh and his mounted escort, they were taken to a nearby mosque, from where they sent urgent requests for help. But that night their Gurkha guard melted away, leaving them at the mercy of Mulraj's mutinous troops. Vans Agnew was sitting beside Anderson's bed, holding his hand, when the mob broke in and hacked them to death with swords. Though probably not part of the original conspiracy, Mulraj quickly took control of the revolt, presenting Sirdar Khan Singh with a sack containing Vans Agnew's severed head, and telling him to return to Lahore with 'the head of the youth he had brought down to govern at Mooltan'.

Herbert Edwardes, the political officer closest to hand, advised Currie to send a British force to crush the rebellion. Currie's reply, quoting Lord Gough at Simla, was that no force could march until the end of the hot and rainy seasons, a delay of at least six months. 'Postpone a rebellion!' exploded Edwardes. 'Was ever such a thing heard in any government? Postpone avenging the blood of two British officers! *Should* such a thing be ever heard in British Asia?' But heard it was, and it is hard not to conclude that Dalhousie wanted the rebellion to spread so he could have an excuse for annexing the whole of the Punjab.

Left to his own devices, Edwardes raised a large force of Muslim irregulars and used them to defeat Mulraj's undisciplined troops not once but twice, driving the survivors back into Multan. The Lahore durbar, meanwhile, had sent a large force under Raja Sher Singh, a leading Sikh sirdar, to support Edwardes; but it was known to be unreliable and kept well to the rear. Not until 12 August did the lead elements of a British column, under Major-General William Whish, finally arrive at Multan, and a further seven weeks would elapse before a half-hearted attempt was made to storm the city. It failed, though part of the suburbs was captured. As Whish pondered his next move, Sher Singh defected to the rebels, causing the British commander to raise the siege and withdraw to the south.

By now the flames of insurrection had spread north to the Sikh garrisons in Peshawar, Bannu and Hazara, the last commanded by Sher Singh's father, Chattar Singh, who had been thwarted by Currie in his intention to marry his daughter to the young Maharaja Dalip Singh. In early October, Sher marched north to join his father, taking most of the Sikh and Hindu troops in Multan with him. But a body of Pathan Horse, under Captain John Nicholson, had managed to secure the fort at Attock Ferry, and for a time prevented Chattar from crossing the Indus and heading south. So Sher

Singh made for Gujeranwala, about thirty-five miles north of Lahore, to await reinforcements from the north. They would eventually include 5,000 Afghan horsemen, dispatched by Dost Mohamed, who hoped to recover his lost province of Peshawar.

Only now, with the situation desperate, did the Indian government begin to concentrate its troops. In early October, shortly before leaving Calcutta for the Punjab, Lord Dalhousie had told a public banquet: 'Unwarned by precedents, uninfluenced by example, the Sikh Nation have called for War and on my word, sirs, they will have it with a vengeance.' In a private letter, however, he voiced his concern about Gough's generalship:

*Because* my predecessor represented the unfitness of the C.-in-C., and the Government proposed to discontinue him, he must be continued now though they still believe him unfit, and though we are on the brink of events which may sorely test his fitness. This seems to me neither logical nor just: nor yet either handsome or fair towards an officer on whom they cast enormous responsibility, and with it force on him instruments by which he is to act, who are in their own estimation wholly unfit for the task before them. The C.-in-C. has been all I could wish hitherto. What he may be when he gets into the field remains to be seen.

He would not have to wait long to find out. Gough crossed the Sutlej River on 9 November and reached Lahore on the 13th. Three days later he marched north with his Army of the Punjab: twenty-one regiments of infantry, twelve of cavalry and eleven batteries of artillery. He now knew that the government policy was annexation, though a proclamation to the people of the Punjab had referred rather vaguely to the British intention of 'restoring order'.

Still too weak to face the main British Army, Sher had withdrawn further north to the small village of Ramnagar, where there were fords over the River Chenab. There he was joined by the Bannu troops, bringing his total force to 6,000 men and thirty guns: amongst them mutinous regulars, disbanded former members of the Khalsa and disaffected sirdars with their retainers. As Gough approached, Sher began to move the bulk of his army across the river. But the deployment was still taking place when the British vanguard, under Brigadier-General Charles Cureton, made contact with Sikh outposts south of the river on 22 November.

Cureton had had an extraordinary career. Embroiled in a debt scandal while a young Militia officer, he had resigned his commission, faked his suicide and enlisted as a trooper in the 14th Light Dragoons under an assumed name. By the time his true identity became known, he had been wounded three times in the Peninsular Wars and promoted to sergeant. He was offered a commission in the infantry, but later transferred to the 16th Lancers and rose to command a cavalry brigade in the Gwalior and First Sikh Wars. He was said to be the best cavalry leader in India, but his actions on 22 November 1848 make such a claim hard to sustain.

It was the cold season, and the River Chenab was little more than a narrow channel in a wide sandy bed, flanked by high banks and deep nullahs.* To cover his withdrawal over the ford, Sher had posted artillery on the north bank, and infantry on an island halfway across the river and in the broken ground to the south. But, ignoring both the difficulty of the terrain and Gough's order not to attack until the main force had come up, Cureton sent his cavalry and horse artillery forward to investigate. Seeing a body of Sikhs near the river bank, a squadron of the 3rd Light Dragoons charged and sent them scuttling back across the ford. Heavy fire from the far bank, however, soon forced the squadron to withdraw. The recently promoted Corporal Pearman recalled:

A party of the enemy horse with lances came in our rear. One was behind me. My horse was nearly beat, but I formed a right rear guard with my sword to parry off his lance should he point, as he was only about six feet from me. We kept like that some distance. My horse at this time could only go about six miles an hour, but the lancer did not close up with me. Private William Hacken was behind him and he put his sword through him, putting a stop to his gallop.

* Deep ditches or dry river beds.

Meanwhile some irregular Sikh horse had crossed a ford to the British right, and the 14th Light Dragoons and 5th Bengal Light Cavalry were sent to disperse them. In this they were successful, but the commander of the 14th, Colonel William Havelock, brother of Henry, then exceeded his orders by charging into a deep nullah occupied by Sikh infantrymen. Brigadier Cureton saw the danger and tried to stop him. But he was killed by a musket ball as he rode forward, and the charge continued. It succeeded in over-running the Sikh position but quickly got bogged down in the soft sand beyond, and a number of dragoons were killed, including Havelock. Gough, who had ridden forward to observe the battle, claimed 'astonishment' at Havelock's action. But it later emerged that Gough himself had said to Havelock: 'If you see a favourable opportunity of charging, charge.'

With Cureton dead, the divisional command devolved on Brigadier-General Colin Campbell, one of the most experienced warriors in the British Army. Born in Glasgow in 1792, the illegitimate son of a well-born Scottish lady and a carpenter named Macilver, he had mistakenly been given the name of his uncle, Colonel John Campbell, at the time of his first commission. He had since seen action in numerous campaigns, including the ill-fated Walcheren expedition, the Peninsular Wars, the American War of 1812 and the First Opium War of 1839–42. But, lacking money and social standing, it had taken him thirty years to rise from captain to colonel. Now an acting divisional commander, he was anxious to join the fray. Gough could see that the light was failing, however, and ordered the action to be broken off.

A stand-off developed as Gough brought forward the rest of his troops, and Sher Singh dug in on the far bank. Instead of launching his customary frontal assault, Gough attempted to outflank the Sher's position by detaching a column, under Major-General Sir Joseph Thackwell, and ordering it to cross the river further upstream. Thackwell managed this at Wazirabad, on 2 December, but without his heavy guns. He was at a marked disadvantage, therefore, when Sikh guns engaged him en route to the Sher's position on 3 December. Fortunately these batteries

were covering the withdrawal of Sher's army and did not remain
in action for long. By nightfall Sher had taken up a new position
on the Jhelum River. Thackwell followed as far as Heylah, ten
miles to the south, but Gough kept his main force south of the
Chenab to await reinforcements and supplies.

While Gough was reasonably happy with the progress he had
made, his political master felt differently. 'The C.-in-C.'s movement was excellent,' wrote Dalhousie, 'his success important, but
it was not a victory, and I cannot call it so, however vexed he
may be.' He was also concerned that Gough had marched from
Ferozepur to the Chenab before his 'commissariat and other
department arrangements were complete, and in spite of remon-
strances of heads of departments'. The expected supplies had
'totally failed him', and on 24 November even Gough had admitted that his army was in a 'most critical position'. Dalhousie,
moreover, had been left with only two British regiments to cover
the 1,100 miles that separated Ambala from Calcutta. To provide
Gough with a reserve of six regiments he had had to transfer three
from the Madras Presidency and to move a Bengal unit from the
coast of Arracan. Such was the state of Gough's supplies and
supports.

On 18 December, having at last overcome his logistical difficulties, Gough moved his main force up to Heylah to join
Thackwell. With Dalhousie urging caution, he decided not to risk a
battle until he had been reinforced. All eyes were turned, therefore,
towards Multan. The arrival of a column of Bombay troops –
bringing the total British force to almost 16,000 men – enabled
the new commander, Brigadier-General the Honourable Henry
Dundas, to reopen the siege of the city on 27 December. After a
number of breaches were made in the city walls, a general assault
was launched during the afternoon of 2 January 1849. Despite
the confusion of night fighting, heavy casualties and a lacklustre
performance by some of the Bengal troops, it eventually succeeded
in driving the defenders back to the sanctuary of the fort. But the
brutal treatment of innocent citizens did the assaulting troops little
credit. A corporal of the 32nd (Cornwall) Foot wrote:

Every one was plundered whom our men could lay their hands upon, regardless of their pitiful cry, and in some instances were women and children shot down amongst the men . . . One of my fellow-corporals, who never was worthy of the jacket he wore, was guilty of cold-blooded murder. He shot a poor, grey-headed old man, while he was begging that he would spare, and not hurt, his wife and daughters; nor take away the little property they possessed, consisting of a few paltry rings, upon their fingers and in their ears. The fellow pulled the rings off in the most brutal manner.

The same corporal knew of at least one case of rape by an Irish private of his regiment, who 'went into a room, and took a young girl from her mother's side, and perpetrated the offence, for which he has to answer before the God who heard that poor girl's cries and petitions'. If the corporal had been present, he would have 'shot him dead'.

With the city in British hands, a fresh siege began, with heavy batteries and mortars constantly battering the fort's defences. On 22 January, with its walls in ruins and Dundas's men poised to attack, the fort at last surrendered. Mulraj was imprisoned, pending an inquiry; all those suspected of involvement in the attack on Vans Agnew and Anderson were hanged. The rest of the garrison was disbanded.

Dundas's success was down in no small part to the quality of his Bombay troops. Even Bengal officers compared them favourably with their own sepoys, noting their superior discipline and their willingness to put duty before caste by working in the trenches. The Bombay gunners also had the advantage of using a revolutionary new propellant called guncotton. For years scientists had been experimenting with ways to make gunpowder – a mixture of sulphur, charcoal and purified saltpetre – more powerful. They knew that saltpetre provided the oxygen necessary for combustion; the trick was to find a replacement for saltpetre that would make the mixture burn more rapidly. In 1845 a celebrated German chemist called Christian Schönbein thought he had found the solution when he treated cellulose with nitric acid to produce a substance known as guncotton (or nitrocellulose). As well as being practically smokeless, it significantly increased muzzle velocity. So impressed was the Board of Ordnance, during a demonstration by Schönbein at Woolwich in 1846, that it authorized the construction of a guncotton factory at Faversham in Kent. Some of the finished product had already made its way out to the Bombay Presidency by the time a disastrous explosion wrecked the Faversham works in 1847. Though used with some success during the siege of Multan,★ guncotton in its original form was no longer considered a safe and reliable replacement for gunpowder. For that, European armies would have to wait for the introduction of the smokeless propellant known as cordite in the late 1880s.

The fall of Multan was a welcome boost for the British, but a far more important battle had already been fought on the Jhelum. Gough's original intention had been to wait for reinforcements from Multan before launching his attack. Three factors forced him to change his mind: news that Attock Ferry had fallen to the Sikhs, opening the way for Chattar Singh's troops and the Afghan cavalry to link up with Sher Singh; pressure from Dalhousie, who was concerned that Indian public opinion was turning against the war; and reports that Sikh agents were attempting to undermine the loyalty of his Bengal sepoys. During the morning of 13 January, therefore, he marched his army of sixty-six guns and 12,000 men towards the Sikhs' entrenched position on the south bank of the Jhelum. Unbeknownst to him, the whole Sikh Army, sixty-two guns and 30,000 men, had advanced from their trenches to a well-screened position on the back fringe of a belt of jungle. Sher's numerical superiority, however, was partially offset by the fact that at least half of his troops were newly raised and not to be compared with the magnificently trained and disciplined Khalsa of 1845.

★ One private of the 32nd Foot wrote: 'As soon as it was dark the effect produced by the new explosive material was very remarkable; a broad flash intimated the discharge of the gun, and this was followed by the bright track of the fuse, which, on reaching its destination, was succeeded by a vivid flash, showing that the missile was doing its work of destruction' (Swinson (ed.), *The Memoirs of Private Waterfield*, 78).

Advancing through jungle, the British took more than four hours to cover the eight miles that separated their bivouac from the village of Chilianwalla, opposite the Sikh centre. It was well after midday when Gough made his preliminary reconnaissance by ascending a small mound to the front of the village. From there he could see that the Sikhs had come out of their trenches and were, in Dalhousie's words, 'formed in an extended line in and on the edge of a jungle'. Dalhousie added: 'The enemy's left was rested on a low range of hills full of ravines, his right (distant six or seven miles from his left) rested on very thick jungle; he was in great force.' As it was getting late, Gough decided to postpone his attack until the following day, when he would have more information about the Sikh position. Orders were given to halt and make camp.

As [Gough] was making his arrangements [wrote Dalhousie], the enemy pushed some of his batteries forward and opened a fire. The heavy guns were ordered to the front, their practice was beautiful, they were making great execution, and rapidly silencing the enemy, when the C.-in-C. stopped them, and ordered *an advance in line of his whole force* with only two regiments Native Indians in reserve. In vain he was reminded of the time of the day; in vain he was shown the enemy were ready enough to fight; in vain he was reminded of his own plan which he was abandoning; in vain the efficacy of the fire of the heavy guns was pointed out, and he was implored to confine himself to them till the next day. His answer to my agent [Major Mackeson] was, 'I am C.-in-C. of this army and I desire you to be silent.' Although he had been told over and over again that fighting in jungle was the sorest trial to sepoys, 'Advance.' So they advanced, a line of 3 miles against a line of nearly 7! in thick jungle, in and behind which the enemy were posted with all their guns, and with their intrenched position to retire upon.

It was Mudki all over again, with an exhausted British Army caught on the hop and its commander determined to attack a Sikh force of unknown size and location. Poor reconnaissance was chiefly to blame, for which Gough must take responsibility. Better observation of the Sikh position would have told Gough that its weak

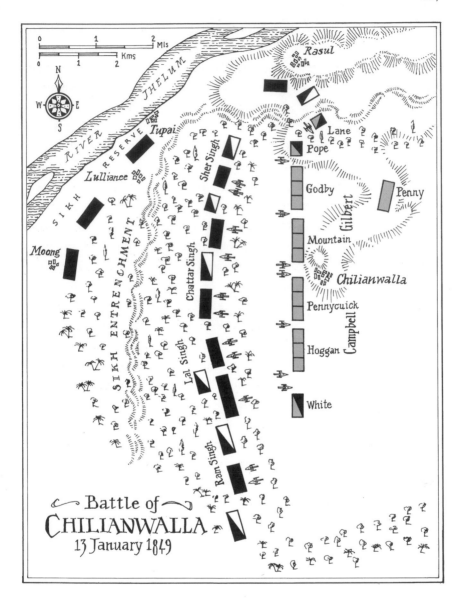

Battle of
CHILIANWALLA
13 January 1849

point was its open right flank, held by Ram Singh's Bannu troops. Unaware of this, and heavily outnumbered, he decided to attack the centre of the line in the hope of splitting the Sikh Army into two and driving it back towards the river. He formed up his own modest force of two infantry divisions – Campbell's on the left and Sir Walter Gilbert's on the right – and placed a cavalry brigade on each flank. Brigadier-General Nicholas Penny's infantry brigade was in reserve. Gough's plan was to soften the enemy defences with artillery fire before ordering a frontal attack. But, during the preliminary bombardment, an unidentified staff officer moved a battery of field artillery from the centre of Campbell's position to the left flank in support of some hard-pressed horse artillery. This had the desired effect of subduing a Sikh battery to its front, but it also left Campbell's infantry without sufficient artillery support. The only other notable action on the left flank at this time was a gallant charge by a squadron of the 3rd Light Dragoons against a much larger body of irregular Sikh cavalry. Corporal Pearman recalled: 'Well away we went. Captain [Walter] Unett shouted, "Come on, boys! Now for it!" But he was soon cut down, and so was Lieutenant Sisted, and young Gough was also on the ground, the first and second badly wounded. The enemy formed a complete wedge, and we had to cut our way through them for quite a hundred yards before there was any clear ground.' Once through, the remnants of the squadron turned and charged back the way they had come. Pearman added:

I had a bayonet wound in the right arm as we cut our way back to the regiment – a slight flesh wound near the elbow . . . The fellow would have shot me as my horse was plunging and my sword was in the fellow's shoulder, but Sergeant Wild, coming up, cut off the back of his head, and down he went. Wild said to me, 'Come on Jack,' and away we went, about seven of us, and got safe to the regiment, where I got a bandage put round my arm. What men got back, got back by three or five or six or seven at a time, some one way and some came another. I can never forget this charge. Such a mass to get through. How any of us did get back was a wonder.

Of the 106 men who charged that day against an enemy force at least seven times their number, only forty-eight were still in their saddles at the end of the action.★

At about 3 p.m., with the artillery duel an hour old, Gough ordered his infantry divisions to advance. Campbell chose to accompany his left brigade, under Brigadier-General Hoggan, partly because he thought the scrubby terrain would make divisional control impossible, and partly because Hoggan was shortsighted. It was a mistake, because it left his right brigade, under Brigadier-General John Pennycuick, to its own devices. And, to make matters worse, Campbell had earlier exhorted Pennycuick's sole British regiment, the 24th (Warwickshire) Foot, to go in with the bayonet alone. 'Let it be said,' he told the unit's officers, 'the 24th stormed the guns without firing a shot.' Campbell later apologized for this conceit, explaining that he had long admired the 24th for a similar attack during the Peninsular Wars. But by then the damage had been done.

With Campbell's advice ringing in their ears, the men of the 24th set off at a tremendous clip, with their Colours flying and Pennycuick at their head. Advancing through scrub jungle, they soon lost contact with both flank regiments of Bengal infantry and their artillery support. Undeterred, they pressed on and, with 150 yards still to go, Pennycuick ordered them to charge a Sikh battery of twelve guns. Private Henry Plumb recalled:

When we first took up the charge they was pouring long shot and shell into our line, and as we neared this awful battery they poured grape into us . . . It was then that our fellows got mowed down in sections. Still gallantly on did the Brigade advance, closing as the poor fellows fell. We had to charge through jungle, brushwood, and every other impediment . . . At last the grand struggle for the capture of the guns took place, hand to hand it was carried on, the enemy's artillery standing to their

★ Twenty-four men were killed and sixteen wounded. Both Unett and Sisted survived their wounds and, on their return to Britain, were presented to the queen.

guns gallantly, sword in hand, the infantry skewering them with their bayonets, and others firing at them . . . At length the whole of the Artillery were annihilated.

Yet by attacking without support the 24th gave the Sikhs time to recover. While Sikh horsemen took the British survivors in the flank, a Sikh infantry regiment, hidden from view by the jungle, fired a volley and charged from the front. It was too much for the shattered and by now leaderless regiment. Pennycuick and Colonel Robert Brookes, the 24th's commanding officer, had both been hit during the final charge; moreover, the regiment's Colours had disappeared from view. With no one to rally them, the men of the 24th fled and took their supporting regiments, just now reaching the Sikh position, with them. 'Our brigade retired in disorder,' admitted Private Plumb, 'the cavalry at our heels, cutting every poor fellow that was wounded or exhausted with running to the rear. We had no support, not so much as a gun or a dragoon. Awful indeed was the slaughter in our Regiment.' The headlong flight stopped only when the survivors reached the relative safety of Chilianwalla.

In just a matter of minutes the 24th had lost more than half its strength of 1,050 men, including thirteen officers and 271 men killed and ten officers and 280 men wounded.* The Regimental Colour was brought to safety by a private; the Queen's Colour was lost on the battlefield, the ultimate disgrace, though there is no evidence that the Sikhs recovered it. The death of Brigadier-General Pennycuick was particularly poignant. Shortly after being hit by grapeshot, just fifty yards from the guns, he asked two sergeants and a private to take him to the rear. He was bleeding profusely from a large hole in the chest, and they could see there was no hope, but they made the attempt anyway. He was probably

---

* The lack of dash shown by the supporting native regiments was reflected in their comparatively light casualties: three officers and 201 men in the 25th Native Infantry and just four officers and seventy-five men in the 45th. Both regiments lost their Colours.

dead by the time the retreating 24th swept past, prompting his bearers to drop him as they joined the headlong flight. He had a son in the regiment, however, seventeen-year-old Ensign Alick Pennycuick, who survived the retreat only to hear that his father had been abandoned. He at once set out to recover the corpse and, having located it, was promptly shot in the back and killed. 'Poor Boy,' wrote one officer, 'he was the favourite of all who knew him, warm, generous and kind-hearted, strikingly intelligent & gentlemanlike.' The two bodies, father's and son's, were later found side by side.

The destruction of Pennycuick's brigade tore a huge hole in the British line. Threatened with disaster, Gough ordered his reserve brigade, under Penny, to fill the gap. But in the confusion it lost its way and ended up supporting Brigadier-General Godby's brigade on the right of the British line. Fortunately, and fittingly, the setback on the left was redeemed by the man who was partly responsible for it: Colin Campbell. Advancing with the 61st (South Gloucestershire) Foot of Hoggan's brigade, through jungle less dense than that faced by the 24th, he was on hand as the regiment charged and took a Sikh battery. And, unlike the 24th, it was supported on its left by a field battery and the 46th Native Infantry, which reached the Sikh position soon after. But the sepoy regiment on the right of the 61st had had its flank uncovered by the repulse of Pennycuick's brigade, and it, in turn, was driven back by Sikh infantry. This exposed the flank of the 61st, and, to meet the threat, Campbell wheeled the two right-hand companies. Their volley fire blunted the Sikh advance and prevented the pursuit of the beaten sepoys. 'But for that manoeuvre,' wrote Sir Charles Napier, 'I do not see how the 61st could have escaped the fate of the 24th Regiment. The destruction of the last separated the wings of the army and the change of front and advance made by the 61st and 46th [Native Infantry] united them again.'

Though slightly wounded, Campbell remained in control and ordered the rest of the 61st and the 46th to wheel to the right. Then, having beaten off two more attacks by infantry and cavalry, these regiments began to roll up the Sikh line from the left, retaking the battery the 24th had captured earlier. Eventually they met up with the left brigade of Gilbert's division, which was advancing from the opposite direction. Its British regiment, the 29th Foot, had also captured a Sikh battery, with sepoys from the 30th and 56th Native Infantry in support.

Not all was well, however, on the extreme right of the British line, where Brigadier-General Alexander Pope's cavalry brigade was tasked with protecting Gilbert's open flank. As it advanced through the jungle, it too lost its way by veering to the left and masking the supporting artillery. Realizing his mistake, Pope gave the order to wheel right, in order to give the guns a line of fire. As the brigade started to carry out this manoeuvre, a large body of Sikh horsemen appeared in front. The commander of the 14th Light Dragoons urged Pope to charge, but Pope was wounded before he could respond. Instead an unidentified officer shouted, 'Threes about!'* The result was a shambles: as the brigade turned to the rear, the Sikh horse attacked and set off a chain reaction of panicked flight. Dalhousie wrote later with ill-concealed contempt:

These miserable creatures, the whole 4 regiments, halted, turned about, and *galloped to the rear* as hard as they could ride. They galloped *over our own Artillery*, broke the harness, and were followed by the Goorchurras [irregular Sikh horse], who cut to pieces nearly every man of the battery and took 3 guns. The 14th and 9th [Lancers] galloped on till they rode amongst the field-hospital, and upset the surgeons who were operating on the wounded.

An assistant surgeon recalled: 'The Surgeon & myself were giving directions to have our appliances brought up from a short distance behind. We had scarcely given our directions, the Brigade had not been gone two minutes, when to my utter confusion the whole Brigade came tearing back in the wildest disorder & before I could spring into my saddle I was surrounded by those who were fleetest

---

* When advancing in column, British cavalry rode three abreast. The order 'threes about' was an instruction to reverse direction.

in flight. I enquired the cause, could get no answer, & as those behind the foremost were coming on in mass, I called upon our Surgeon.' The flight was finally stopped by a pistol-wielding chaplain who was assisting the surgeons. Gough later regretted he could not 'make him a Brevet Bishop'.

The disgraceful flight of Pope's horsemen, and the loss of three horse artillery guns, had left the right wing of Gilbert's division hopelessly exposed. Gilbert compensated by ordering the sepoy regiment on the right of Godby's brigade to halt and form square. But now the 2nd Bengal European Regiment, advancing in the centre of Godby's brigade, was vulnerable to an attack from the right. Lance-Corporal George Carter recorded:

We couldn't see the enemy for bushes yet they kept up a hot fire of round shot & musketry as we went up to their position which they soon abandoned. Soon after this a large body of Sikhs moved down on the right flank of the Brigade & as we were the right infantry regiment of the Army, our Co. No. 1 wheeled back & formed a face to the right so as to hinder the enemy from breaking our flank. We fired by files rapidly as the Sikhs were near. They skirted round & got between us & the baggage . . . Some of the sepoys of the Brigade were now seen going about in disorder but re-formed on us, and we got the order to face to the right-about & having shifted the supernumerary rank, we – rear rank in front – charged the mass of the enemy & utterly routed them.

All through the action, according to Carter, invaluable assistance was provided by Captain Michael Dawes's field battery, which 'poured in grape & canister at every favourable opportunity'. Dawes also assisted Penny's brigade when it fetched up in the wrong place and was attacked by Sikhs from three different directions. But even he could not prevent the wholesale murder by Sikh irregulars of British soldiers who had been wounded in the advance. Many were members of the 2nd Europeans, and their comrades, on learning of this, resolved not to take prisoners. Nor did they, and one of the more horrific features of this brutal battle was the general unwillingness to show quarter.

By now the British were in possession of most of the enemy batteries, causing the bulk of the Sikh Army to withdraw from the jungle on to the hills beyond. Gough's inclination was to hold his ground and to continue the attack in the morning. But he was persuaded by a number of his senior officers, including Campbell, to withdraw his exhausted troops to Chilianwalla, where there was water. This movement had unfortunate consequences, however, because it enabled the Sikhs to return during the night and carry away all but twelve of their captured guns. Nor would the weather – incessant rain for the next three or four days – allow Gough to continue the fight. When it improved, the Sikhs were securely ensconced in their old position, and Gough resolved, once again, to wait for reinforcements from Multan.

British losses were almost identical to those sustained at Ferozeshah in the previous war: 2,375 in all, 650 of them fatal. But the medical back-up was now much improved, and amputees had the consolation of a pain-free operation under anaesthetic, the first time it had been used in the field. One witness mentioned chloroform but, as that substance had only made its debut in Europe ten months earlier, the more likely candidate is ether.

Despite the terrible cost, Gough considered Chilianwalla a success and said as much in his official dispatch. A mortified Dalhousie did not agree. 'We have gained a victory,' he wrote privately, 'but like that of the ancients, it is such a one that "another such would ruin us".' He added:

I grieve to say much gloom prevails in the army. One and all, generals of Division, officers, soldiers, sepoys, publicly attribute this great loss and small result to the total incompetence of the C.-in-C., and justly so.* They have totally lost confidence in him, and I do not know what would be the result of his taking them into another action at present. I view

---

* Field Marshal Lord Wolseley, who spoke to a number of those present, would later characterize Chilianwalla as 'that unfortunate battle where British courage was a more distinguishing feature than either the strategical or tactical ability of the general commanding' (Wolseley, *The Story of a Soldier's Life*, I, 12).

the position, I hope, firmly, but I do not deceive myself; it is a grave one ... Except the Cavalry on the right, the troops behaved on the whole admirably well. In any other hands I should have no anxiety. In the hands of Lord Gough, I feel no confidence against disaster.

But Dalhousie did not see how he could sack Gough. 'Her Majesty's Government and the Chief of Staff have thought proper to keep Lord Gough at the head of their army,' he informed the duke of Wellington, who had been serving his second stint as British commander-in-chief since 1842, 'and he has gained me a victory, such as it is. I cannot take the command even practically out of his hands.'

With Gough content to wait for the Multan troops, Sher Singh felt compelled to take the initiative. On 14 February, his army swelled to 50,000 men and fifty-nine guns by the arrival of his father's troops and the Afghan horse, the Sikh general struck camp and marched south-east towards the Chenab River and the road to Lahore. But, with British troops in possession of the Chenab crossings, he chose to take up a defensive position near the walled city of Gujerat, six miles short of the river. Meanwhile Gough had at last discovered Sher's departure and set off in cautious pursuit. He was joined en route by the Multan Contingent, which had covered an impressive 235 miles in eighteen days, fifty in the last forty-eight hours. On the 20th Gough's enlarged army reached Sadiwal, just three miles from the Sikh position. Crescent shaped, with infantry interspersed with artillery, it was flanked by two nullahs: the right one dry, the left one marshy and difficult for cavalry to cross. On each side of the wet nullah a body of cavalry was placed; but the majority of Sikh riders, supported by the Afghan horse, were to the right of the dry nullah. Ahead of the main line of infantry, which had not had time to dig in, were two fortified villages. The ground in front of them was well cultivated, chiefly young corn and sugar cane.

Gough attacked the following morning. Reinforced by the Multan force, he now had 25,000 troops and ninety-six guns. He advanced with three infantry divisions and the Bombay Contingent in line, and two infantry brigades on each flank. Roughly half his army – Whish, Gilbert and two cavalry brigades – was squashed between the two nullahs. Campbell and the rest of the cavalry were on the far side of the dry nullah, facing the Sikh right. It was a beautifully clear day, and as the British soldiers moved forward they could make out the city of Gujerat and beyond it, away in the distance, the white peaks of the Himalayas.

Even before the British had got within range, the Sikh gunners opened fire, giving away their positions. Gough halted his infantry and sent forward his guns. For the next hour and a half they engaged the Sikh artillery and gradually got the upper hand. During this time an attempt by Sikh horse to turn the British right was foiled by a combination of cavalry and horse artillery. With most of the Sikh batteries out of action, Gough ordered the infantry advance to resume. Both fortified villages were stormed and taken, with Bara Kalra, the bigger of the two, offering the stiffest resistance. A private of the 32nd Foot, who walked the ground later, wrote:

In and around the village of Burra-Kalra . . . was literally covered with the dead and dying of the enemy. This place was the key of the enemy's position. It was carried in the most spirited style by the 2nd Europeans, 31st and 70th Regiments of Native Infantry which drove the enemy from their cover with great slaughter. I only saw one European amongst the dead; at least a part of one. He was a sergeant of the 2nd Europeans; his cap, grog bottle, and his head was all we saw. There was a letter in the cap, but I could not make any of it out, for it was saturated with blood.

Despite losing the two villages, the Sikhs put in a number of counter-attacks, the largest down the line of the dry nullah, but all were broken up by artillery fire. Campbell's troops, meanwhile, had hardly fired a shot. Most of the fighting on the far side of the dry nullah was done by British cavalry. First the 3rd Light Dragoons spiked a battery of Sikh guns, having cleverly drawn them into the 60th (King's Royal) Rifles' killing zone; then the Sind Horse, supported by a squadron of the 3rd and another from the 9th Lancers, charged and dispersed a much bigger body of Sikh and Afghan cavalry, capturing four standards in the process. Corporal Pearman wrote:

The battle was now at its highest, and the air had become filled with shot, shell and smoke. Trumpets were sounding, drums beating, bugles sounding, colonels and other officers hollering, when all of a sudden came the order for the 3rd Light Dragoons to charge. I could see the 9th Lancers and the black cavalry [Sind Horse] doing the same. But we did not get much at them this time, as they made a quick movement back into their line. We got among some of their horse and killed a few. My horse ran against one of theirs and knocked him down. It hurt my leg very much as it struck his horse's shoulder. I put my sword into the man and went on with the rest.

By 12.30 p.m. the whole Sikh line was in retreat, and the battle was effectively over. The pursuit continued until nightfall, however, with the irregular cavalry harrying the beaten Sikhs for more than fifteen miles. Again no quarter was given. 'We overtook numbers of their infantry,' wrote an officer of the 9th Lancers, 'who were running for their lives – every man of course was shot. I never saw such butchery and murder! It is almost too horrible to commit to paper . . . But besides all this *ground* shooting, there was a good deal of *tree* shooting. Every tree that was standing was well searched, and two or three Sikhs were found concealing in almost every tree we passed – this afforded great sport for our men, who were firing up at them, as at so many rooks . . . Down they would come like a bird, head downward, and bleeding most profusely.' The fight cost the Sikhs more than 3,000 men, fifty-three guns, and their whole camp and stores. British casualties were just ninety-six killed and 670 wounded, making Gujerat the cheapest, yet most decisive, victory of both Sikh Wars.

Why, given their numerical superiority, did the Sikhs not put up a better fight? The chief reason is surely because the British, for the first time in either war, had more artillery (including no less than eighteen heavy guns); but also because the best Sikh regiments had been decimated at Chilianwalla, and those that remained lacked the training, discipline and equipment to compete with British infantry. That earlier battle had knocked the stuffing out of the Sikh Army, and morale was never as high again. But Gough's solid generalship should not be underestimated: his tight battle formation, with strength in depth, was highly effective, as was his decision to allow his superior artillery to do most of the fighting. The gunners' relatively high proportion of casualties – eighty-six as opposed to fifty at Chilianwalla – is evidence of that.

Most of the Sikh Army withdrew intact to the north. But, harried by Muslim villagers and short on supplies, it was in no condition to fight the pursuing British force under General Gilbert. On 14 March, Sher Singh and the remnants of the Khalsa surrendered to Gilbert at Rawalpindi. Some of the older soldiers, as they threw down their *tulwars*★ in disgust, exclaimed: 'This day Ranjeet Singh has died!' A delighted Dalhousie informed the queen: 'Your Majesty may well imagine the pride with which British Officers looked on such a scene, and witnessed this absolute subjection and humiliation of so powerful an enemy.'

There was, however, still the small matter of the Afghans, who had taken advantage of the war to occupy Peshawar. On 15 March, Gilbert continued his march north, crossing the Indus on the 19th. That same day the Afghans evacuated Peshawar and withdrew through the Khyber Pass, enabling Gilbert to reoccupy the city without a fight on 21 March. The Second Sikh War was over. All that remained was the political settlement.

The preference of the recently knighted Sir Henry Lawrence, who returned to Lahore in January 1849, was to leave the Sikhs a measure of independence: such leniency, he thought, would guarantee their lasting friendship and provide a bulwark against Afghan or Russian aggression. But Dalhousie had long favoured annexation, and he sent Henry Elliot, his foreign secretary, to Lahore to make the necessary arrangements. On 29 March, in the throne room at Lahore Fort, Elliot placed before the ten-year-old

---

★ Curved and extremely sharp Indian swords introduced by the Mughals.

Maharaja Dalip Singh a letter of abdication. Its terms included the resignation 'for himself, his heirs, his successors, all right, title and claim to the sovereignty of the Punjab or to any sovereign power whatsoever, the confiscation of all state property, and the surrender of the Koh-i-Noor Diamond'.

At 186 carats the Koh-i-Nor ('Mountain of Light') Diamond was one of the largest ever discovered. Originally the property of the Mughal emperors, it was acquired by Nadir Shah of Persia when he sacked Delhi in 1739, and later fell into the hands of the Persian general Ahmad Shah, the founder of the Durani dynasty of Afghan amirs. After the deposition of Shah Shuja, Ahmad's descendant, in 1812, the diamond was surrendered to Ranjit Singh in return for material support. None was provided.

To compensate for his abdication and the loss of the diamond, Dalip Singh would receive a pension of 'not less than four and not more than five lakhs of rupees' and permission to live where he chose as long as it was not in the Punjab. With his mother absent – she had been exiled to Chunar in northern India at the start of the rebellion – and the remaining members of his regency council urging him to sign, the young maharaja had little choice. That same day, wrote Dalhousie, 'the British colours were hoisted on the Citadel of Lahore, and the Punjab, every inch of it, was proclaimed to be a portion of the British Empire in India.'

Dalip Singh had done the British no wrong, yet he had been deprived of his throne. Dalhousie explained why in a letter to the HEIC's secret committee on 7 April 1849: 'I cannot permit myself to be turned aside from fulfilling the duty which I owe to the security and prosperity of millions of British subjects by a feeling of misplaced and mistimed compassion for the sake of a child. We must resolve on the entire subject of the Sikh people and of its extinction as an independent state.' Dalip later complained to *The Times* that the annexation of his country had been in direct contravention of the terms of the Treaty of Bhairowal that had authorized British rule during his minority. 'His Lordship', he wrote, 'sold almost all my personal, as well as my private property . . . and distributed the proceeds, amounting as prize money among those very troops who had come to put down a rebellion against my authority.'

Dalhousie later told a friend that he had made up his mind to annex the Punjab as early as September 1848 and informed the 'home authorities' accordingly. Yet they gave him 'no *definite* instructions of any kind whatever'. What he did in March 1849, therefore, he did on his own responsibility. 'I know it to be just, politic, and necessary,' he wrote; 'my conscience tells me the work is one I can pray God to bless; and I shall await the decision of my country with perfect tranquillity.' He would not be disappointed.

The queen was at Osborne House when a letter from Lord John Russell informed her of the latest developments in India. She replied on 26 May that she 'quite approves the annexation of the Punjab, and is pleased to find that the Government concur in this view'. She also sanctioned Dalhousie's elevation to marquess – 'almost the only thing that can be offered him as a reward for his services' – and that of Gough to a viscount. The latter honour was highly controversial. Dalhousie's forthright criticism of Gough during the early stages of the war, particularly the costly 'victory' at Chilianwalla, had prompted Russell's government to select a new commander-in-chief: Sir Charles Napier. The queen was pleased with the choice, noting in a letter to her uncle Leopold that Napier was 'so well versed in Indian tactics that we may look with safety to the future *after* his arrival'. In the event, news of Gough's replacement reached India only after he had partially redeemed himself by his crushing victory at Gujerat, and after he had himself resigned on 'general grounds'. Dalhousie felt sorry for Gough, but thought the 'Government could hardly have done otherwise'.

On 3 May 1849 the new British masters of Lahore Fort were ushered in to the treasure house by the hereditary keeper. One of those present wrote to a cousin:

I wish you could see it, the vast quantities of gold and silver; the jewels not yet to be valued, so many, and so rich – and the Koh-i-noor, far beyond what I had imagined. Runjeet's golden chair of state; his silver pavilion; Shah Soojah's ditto; relics of the Prophet; the Khalgi plume of the last Sikh guru, the sword of the Persian hero Rustum and, perhaps above all, the immense collection of magnificent Cashmere shawls, rooms full of them, heaped in bales.

Dr John Login, the British superintendent of the fort, estimated the value of the jewels alone at almost £1m – and that did not include the Koh-i-Nor, which was, quite literally, priceless. Soon after acquiring the diamond, Ranjit Singh had asked Shah Shuja's wife its value. 'If a strong man were to throw four stones,' she replied, 'one north, one south, one east, one west, and a fifth stone up into the air, and if the space between them were to be filled with gold, all would not equal the value of the Koh-i-noor.' Shuja's answer was briefer. Its value, he said, was 'good fortune, for whoever possessed it had conquered their enemies'.

Lord Dalhousie justified the confiscation of the Lahore crown property on two grounds: 'One, that means of mischief hereafter might not be left to the Maharajah. Two, that of the great debt which is due to this Government, something of the expenses of the war may be diminished by the amount of this property.' The huge diamond, however, would not be part of the war reparations. Instead it was to be presented to Queen Victoria as a 'token' of the maharaja's submission. 'The Koh-i-Noor', Dalhousie wrote to a friend, 'has become in the lapse of ages a sort of historical emblem of the conquest of India. It has now found its proper resting place.'

So precious did Dalhousie regard the diamond that he decided to carry it himself on the first leg of its journey to Britain. On 7 December 1849, the last day of his state visit to Lahore, he followed Dr Login into the treasure house and gazed in wonder as the gleaming jewel was removed from the British-made Chubb safe that had been its home for many years. Handed the gem, he put it into a small silk bag that was fastened to a double-stitched money-belt, itself secured by two chains to his waist and neck. With the diamond safely stowed in this bizarre harness, he signed a letter of receipt in the presence of Login, Elliot and the three

British members of the new Punjab executive. He then left for Bombay by *dak* – an enclosed carriage relayed by men or horses – and, on arrival in early February, deposited the diamond in the city treasury. There it remained for two months while the Royal Navy arranged its transport to England. Finally, on 6 April 1850, it departed Bombay in great secrecy aboard the steam sloop HMS *Medea*.

Dalip, meanwhile, had also left the Punjab. Following a failed kidnap attempt by Sikh extremists, who had planned to use Dalip as a rebel figurehead, Dalhousie moved the maharaja and his small court to Fatehgarh in northern India. There, when he was not indulging his passion for falconry, Dalip spent much time studying the Bible. Though delighted, Dalhousie was keen to avoid any hint of proselytizing. He wrote in March 1851:

My little friend Duleep has taken us all aback lately by declaring his resolution to become a Christian. The pundits,* he says, tell him humbug – he has had the Bible read to him, and he believes the Sahib's religion. Politically we could desire nothing better, for it destroys his possible influence for ever. But I should be glad if it had been deferred, since at present it may be represented to have been brought about by tampering with the mind of a child. This is not the case – it is his own free act, and apparently his firm resolution.

Dalip was keen to formalize his conversion. But the directors of the HEIC, ever anxious not to offend their subjects' religious sensibilities, refused to authorize his baptism for more than two years. Only when they were convinced that his conversion was voluntary, and his religious instruction complete, did they drop their objections. The ceremony was conducted by an archdeacon at Dalip's house in Fatehgarh on 8 March 1853. After it, Dalip symbolically severed his ties to Sikhism by cutting his long hair. Dalhousie was ecstatic. 'I am convinced', he wrote, 'that if ever the shadow of the hand of God was made visible to mortal sight

---

* *pandit*: Learned Hindu Brahman.

. . . it has been visible here in the turning of this boy's heart from darkness to light. This is the first Indian prince of the many who have succumbed to our power, or who have acknowledged it, that has adopted the faith of the stranger. Who shall say to what it may not lead?' As it happened, no other Indian prince – former or ruling – would convert to Christianity during Dalhousie's lifetime.

As a reward for his conversion, Dalip was allowed to visit Europe 'and all its wonders'. It had long been the plan to get him out of India. Chaperoned by Dr and Mrs Login, he left Calcutta on the P & O steamer SS *Hindustan* in April 1854 and, after a brief stop in Egypt to see the Pyramids, reached Southampton a month later. In London he stayed at Claridge's, whence he would regularly sally forth into the busy Mayfair streets, a colourful spectacle in his egret-plumed turban, cashmere tunic and pearl necklace. The memory of the two Sikh Wars was still fresh, and, though he was only fifteen, his presence in the capital attracted huge interest.

Queen Victoria was particularly impressed when she met the young maharaja at Buckingham Palace in July. She wrote in her journal: 'He is 16 and extremely handsome and speaks English perfectly, and has a pretty, graceful and dignified manner. He was beautifully dressed and covered with diamonds. The 'Koh-i-Noor' belonged to and was once worn by him. I always feel much for these poor deposed Indian princes.'

Now thirty-five, and already the mother of eight children,* the queen began to take a maternal interest in Dalip's welfare, no doubt prompted by feelings of guilt at the way he had been usurped. But she had ever admired male beauty, and Dalip's 'strik-ing good looks' were plain for all to see. He was 'small, lithe, and very handsome', observed an American diplomat, with eyes 'large, black and liquid' beneath a turban 'literally flashing with diamonds'.

Dalip's sixteenth birthday fell on 6 September 1854. It was a day of double celebration, because, according to the Treaty of Bhairowal, he had now reached his majority and was entitled to

---

* Victoria (born 1840), Albert Edward ('Bertie', 1841), Alice (1843), Alfred (1844), Helena (1846), Louise (1848), Arthur (1950) and Leopold (1853).

the sizeable pension promised at the time of his abdication. But no extra money was forthcoming, because, on Dalhousie's advice, the HEIC directors had decided to postpone his majority for another two years. Dalip was furious. Yet even the queen was less supportive than he would have liked. The best way to deal with dispossessed princes, she told Dalhousie in October 1854, was not to give them a lifelong pension (which would expire with their death) but rather a property 'which would enable them and their descendants to live respectably'. She added: 'It strikes the Queen that the more kindly we treat Indian Princes, whom *we* have *conquered*, and the more consideration we show for their birth and former grandeur, the more we shall attach Indian Princes and Governments to us, and the more ready will they be to come under our rule.'

As the dispute over money rumbled on, the queen arranged for her young protégé's likeness to be painted by the famous German portraitist Franz Winterhalter. The result was magnificent, portraying as it did a beautiful, almost girlish youth in a martial pose. Clad in the gorgeous dress of the East, Dalip wears a string of pearls around his neck (with a miniature of the queen on the fifth row), two huge gold earrings and an enormous turban encrusted with emeralds. In his right hand he holds the distinctive curved tulwar of his homeland, and in the background can be seen – the result of a little artistic licence – the domes and minarets of Lahore. The numerous sittings, which involved Dalip posing on a wooden platform for up to two hours at a time, took place in the White Drawing Room at Buckingham Palace. The queen attended a number of them, and during one she asked the now Lady Login whether she thought the maharaja would like to see the Koh-i-Nor diamond again. The answer was yes. 'I should like to have it in my power', said Dalip when questioned while riding the following day, 'to place it myself in Her Majesty's hand.'

Much had happened to the diamond since its arrival in Britain in 1850. Its first and only public appearance had been on the queen's breast at the opening of the Great Exhibition of 1851, the huge trade and cultural fair devised by Prince Albert and held in the custom-built Crystal Palace in Hyde Park. A year later, at the queen's direction, the diamond was recut in the multifaceted Dutch style by the royal jeweller Garrard's using steam-powered tools; this reduced its size from 186 carats to 106. Since then it has been kept with the rest of the Crown Jewels in the Tower of London.

On hearing that Dalip wished to see it again, the queen had the diamond brought to his next sitting at Buckingham Palace by an escort of halberd-wielding yeoman warders. Taking it from its casket, she handed it to the startled maharaja. Did he think it 'improved', she asked, and would he have recognized it? For a full fifteen minutes he was too overcome by emotion to reply. It was smaller than he remembered but, thanks to its many facets, much brighter. As he paced up and down, within easy reach of an open window, some courtiers feared he would throw it out. Instead, and at last, he approached the queen, bowed and handed it back. 'It is to me, Ma'am,' he said without a trace of irony, 'the greatest pleasure thus to have the opportunity, as a loyal subject, of myself tendering to my Sovereign – the Koh-i-Noor.'★

★ In 1936 the Koh-i-Nor diamond was incorporated into the coronation crown worn by George VI's consort, Queen Elizabeth, later the Queen Mother. It remains part of the Crown Jewels.

# 6. Burma

On 10 February 1850 Victoria and Albert celebrated ten years of marriage at Windsor Castle. 'Our beloved wedding day,' wrote the queen in her journal, 'when my heart is always very full of gratitude to God, for the great happiness that came into my life, & for that perfect & best of husbands. How well every hour of this day is present to my mind! We wished one another tenderly joy & gave each other souvenirs.'

The queen was pregnant again,* a condition she never enjoyed, but did not let it spoil her day. Instead she invited her long-forgiven mother to join her and Albert for breakfast, and after lunch they took their five children for a walk; later they had them presented during dinner, the three girls 'very pretty . . . in lace dresses over yellow, with little wreaths of ivy, the Boys, in their full Highland dress'. The eldest, nine-year-old Princess Victoria ('Pussy'), was tall, bright and attractive. But her brother Albert Edward ('Bertie'), the heir to the throne, was physically puny and academically slow – and suffered by the comparison. At six the queen had described him as 'more backward' than his elder sister, but with signs of 'improvement'. Three years later she recorded: 'There is much good in him, he has such affectionate feelings, great truthfulness & great simplicity of character' – but he was still failing badly at his lessons. In general, however, it was a happy childhood, with both parents involved: Albert was not above horseplay, while the queen loved nothing better than a family activity and would, for example, help the children tend their individual garden plots at Osborne with specially initialled miniature tools ('P.o.W.', 'Pss. R.', 'Pss. A.', etc.).

Contrary to all expectations, Albert's political 'influence' had

---

* Prince Arthur was born on 1 May 1850 and named after his godfather, the duke of Wellington.

grown steadily during the early years of his marriage. At first, to protect him from criticism, the queen felt he should have no share in government. 'The Prince is indolent,' observed an approving Lord Melbourne, '& it would be better if he was more so, for in his position we want no activity.' But within three months, perhaps appreciating Albert's potential value as a non-partisan political adviser, the prime minister was urging the queen to let her husband see state papers and to discuss with him 'any subject she pleased'. As her first pregnancy progressed, the queen was only too happy to transfer much of the day-to-day business of government to Albert, whose influence grew accordingly. Even before his twenty-first birthday,★ 26 August 1840, parliament registered its confidence in the young prince by appointing him regent in the event of Victoria's death.

By 1841 Albert had completely restructured the queen's working day: they breakfasted at nine, went for a walk and then settled down to read and reply to official correspondence. Work over, they drew or etched together. Lunch was at two, and in the afternoon Victoria, often with Albert present, met one or more of her ministers. While it was still light, the royal couple would go for a drive in the pony phaeton, Albert at the reins. Dinner, usually with guests, was eaten at 8 p.m. Before or after dinner one read to the other, Albert choosing 'serious' books, the queen preferring fiction. By ignoring the excesses of the previous royal generation, not to mention the upper classes, Victoria and Albert were setting a very middle-class model of domestic bliss. But some guests found their company stultifyingly formal, with Lord Melbourne accusing the prince of being 'extremely strait-laced and a great stickler for morality, whereas she was rather the other way'. It was Albert, agreed the duke of Wellington, who 'insisted on spotless character (the Queen not caring a straw about it)'.

A measure of the prince's growing importance was the role he played during the summer of 1841 in heading off a repetition of the 'Bedchamber crisis' of two years earlier. Anticipating the fall

★ The legal majority in England.

of the Whigs, the prince came to an agreement with Sir Robert Peel, Melbourne's likely replacement, that the queen would relinquish her three most politically visible ladies, but that the new offers of appointment would come from her and not the prime minister. Once in office, Peel returned the favour, during the queen's lying-in with her second child, by sending Albert nightly reports of parliamentary debates and cabinet discussions. This close relationship between prince and prime minister continued for the duration of the Tory government, and explains why Albert was as sorry as the queen to see Peel go. There was just one remaining obstacle to Albert's authority: Baroness Lehzen, the queen's confidante and former tutor, who controlled much of the day-to-day running of the royal household. By forcing the queen to choose between them, Albert easily won the day, and a tearful Lehzen retired to Germany with a generous pension in September 1842. With Lehzen gone, the prince set about filling in the gaps in the young queen's education: she knew much about art and music, still more about history and political theory, but little of foreign literature and philosophy, and virtually nothing of science and technology (subjects particularly dear to her husband's heart). Albert encouraged her to read more widely. More importantly, he helped to define her constitutional role by encouraging her to adopt what she later called 'the obvious but up to that time much neglected doctrine that it is the paramount duty of a constituutional monarch to maintain a position of neutrality towards the leaders of the party on both sides'. The row caused by his own ill-judged support for Peel's repeal of the Corn Laws in 1846 simply confirmed his belief that the crown had to be seen to be above party – or even intra-party – politics.

Albert was also making his influence felt in the military sphere. This was a direct result of his successful effort to heal the rift between the queen and the duke of Wellington by asking the latter to act as proxy godfather* at the christening of their first child. As

---

* The actual godfather, Albert's elder brother Ernest, was too ill to attend the ceremony.

commander-in-chief, the duke showed his gratitude by encouraging Albert to make recommendations for the army – some of which were acted upon. In 1842, for example, Wellington adopted the prince's design for a new military helmet – the 'Albert Pattern' shako of 1842 – which was worn until 1855. The satirists had a field day, with *Punch* describing Albert's tall and unwieldy helmet as a 'cross between a muff, a coalscuttle, and a slop-pail'. In January 1844, after a colonel in the 55th Regiment was mortally wounded by his subaltern brother-in-law, the prince demanded that duelling in the military had to end, as it had in Austria, and that henceforth 'affairs of honour' would be satisfied by recourse to the law. Later that year, partly as a result of the prince's pressure, Wellington amended the Articles of War to make it an offence punishable by cashiering for any officer to send or to accept a challenge, or, if aware of a duel, not to take active steps to prevent it. Within a few years military duels were a thing of the past.

In 1847 Albert further impressed the aged commander-in-chief by submitting a memorandum suggesting, amongst other things, the creation of a regular field camp for home-based soldiers and a plan to use railways to concentrate troops in the event of a foreign – presumably French – invasion. The former idea was shelved on the grounds of expense and a fear that it would panic the populace;★ but the latter was looked into, with the South Eastern Railway calculating that by halving existing services 30,000 men could be moved forty miles in three days. So impressed was the duke with the prince's abilities that in 1850 he took the extraordinary step of recommending him as his successor. This was his response to the proposal by Lord John Russell, the prime minister, that the offices of the adjutant-general and quartermaster-general be merged to create a chief of staff. Wellington feared that such a post would make the commander-in-chief redundant, and was prepared to sanction the scheme only if Albert was nominated as his successor, since a chief of staff would release the prince from many of the

★ It eventually came to fruition, a year after Wellington's death, with the holding of a field camp at Chobham in the summer of 1853.

more mundane duties. But it was Albert who scuppered the plan, telling Wellington in April 1850 that it was a 'tempting idea' that he 'must discard'. His chief objection, apart from the inevitable charge of gross nepotism, was that any military controversy would reflect badly on the queen.

When the duke finally died at the age of eighty-four, on 14 September 1852, he was succeeded as commander-in-chief by Albert's personal choice: Lord Hardinge, the former governor-general of India. Hardinge became, if anything, even closer to the prince than his predecessor had been. But the queen found it hard to get over the death of her third close adviser in almost as many years: Lord Melbourne in 1848, Sir Robert Peel in 1850 (the result of a fall from a horse) and now Wellington. 'His loss,' she wrote to her uncle Leopold, 'though it could not have been long delayed, is irreparable!' She added:

He was the pride and the *bon genie*, as it were, of this country! He was the GREATEST man this country ever produced, and the most *devoted* and *loyal* subject, and the staunchest supporter the Crown ever had. He was to us a true, kind friend and most valuable adviser. To think that all this is gone; that this great and immortal man belongs now to History and no longer to the present, is a truth which we cannot realise. We shall soon stand sadly alone; [the earl of] Aberdeen is almost the only personal friend of that kind we have left.

The duke's death hit the country hard. A million and a half people attended his state funeral on 18 November, weeping and raising their hats in silent salute as the funeral procession made its way from Chelsea Hospital to St Paul's Cathedral. An element of farce entered the proceedings on Pall Mall when the elaborate six-wheeled funeral car, twenty-one feet long and eighteen tons in weight, sank in the mud and would move again only when sixty men had been roped in to pull. Worse was to follow as the mechanism for lowering the coffin to the bier at the west door of St Paul's failed for more than an hour. But it was the look of the car, a design overseen by Prince Albert, which attracted the greatest criticism. Greville thought it 'tawdry, cumbrous and vulgar', and Lady de Ros was positively lost for words: 'The car! Oh, so frightful! I can't describe it. I must leave it to the *Morning Post.*'

For British soldiers serving abroad, the news of the Iron Duke's death was particularly poignant. A young ensign by the name of Garnet Wolseley was nearing Calcutta aboard an East Indiaman when he heard the ominous sound of minute guns being fired from Fort William. He wrote later:

I can remember as it might have been yesterday the shock, the thrill I experienced . . . when a voice from the first boat alongside cried out, 'The Duke of Wellington is dead.' As we had speculated upon whom it could be who had passed away, strange to say, the great Duke's name had occurred to none. From earliest childhood we had been so accustomed to hear him referred to as the greatest of living men, that my generation had grown up to regard him as an Immortal, and as a national institution. Every voice was hushed, and in a moment all was silence on deck . . .

Our national influence abroad, as well as our security at home, was felt to be no longer what it had been whilst our great captain and pilot lived. There was no one who could take his place in the Councils of our Sovereign . . . Wellington was dead. And all on that deck who heard the news as it was called out, felt England was no longer what she had been.

The prime minister at the time of Wellington's death was the earl of Derby, formerly Lord Stanley,★ whose minority Tory government had replaced Lord John Russell's Whigs the previous February. Russell's government had been tottering for some time and was finally brought down by one of its own: the third Viscount Palmerston. Born Henry John Temple in 1784, the son of an Irish peer who was not eligible to sit in the House of Lords, Palmerston had become a Tory MP at the age of twenty-two, a cabinet

★ Lord Stanley became the fourteenth earl of Derby on the death of his father on 30 June 1851.

minister at twenty-four and by 1850, having crossed the floor, had
served a total of fourteen years as foreign secretary under three
Whig prime ministers: Lords Grey and Melbourne, and now Lord
John Russell. His guiding mantra in foreign policy was to regard
constitutional states as Britain's natural allies. He tended to support nations struggling for independence, which in turn brought
accusations of meddling from absolutist states like tsarist Russia
and imperial Austria. During the year of revolutions in 1848,* for
example, he encouraged liberals throughout Italy to rebel against
their autocratic rulers: Austria in the north and the kingdom of
Naples in the south.

But it was his high-handed action towards Greece in 1850 that
brought matters to a head. The so-called 'Don Pacifico Affair'
centred around a Gibraltar-born Portuguese Jew, David Pacifico,
who demanded compensation after his house in Athens was pillaged by a mob. Palmerston backed his unsubstantiated claims
and, seeing the issue as the last straw after years of Greek hostility
towards Britain, advised the Greek government to pay all outstanding debts to British subjects. When it refused, he ordered the
Royal Navy to blockade Greek ports without consulting either his
colleagues or the French and Russian governments, co-guarantors
with Britain of Greek independence. He then agreed a settlement
to the crisis with France without notifying the British minister at
Athens, who, meanwhile, had authorized warships to renew the
blockade. The French were outraged and, when Palmerston failed
to censure the minister's conduct, withdrew their ambassador from
London.

Victoria and Albert had long disagreed with Palmerston's heavy-
handed foreign policy, particularly his hostility towards France.
They were no less disapproving of his scandalous private life, which
had included a succession of mistresses and a tribe of bastards
(thus earning him the nickname 'Lord Cupid'). He had brought a

---

* Only one brought about a permanent change of government: in France,
where revolutionaries overthrew King Louis-Philippe and instituted the Second
Republic.

measure of respectability to his life in 1839 by taking as his second wife Lady Cowper, his long-time mistress and the sister of the prime minister. But he was still a philanderer, and that same year, while a guest at Windsor Castle, he tried to seduce one of the queen's ladies-in-waiting.* She woke to find the 55-year-old foreign secretary, primed for action, bearing down on her bed – and screamed. He made a hasty exit, and the following morning wrote an apology, which was accepted. But the queen got to hear of the incident, and, despite Melbourne's insistence that his foreign secretary had never made unwelcome advances, she was unable to forgive Palmerston.

Nor could she forgive his apparent duplicity during the Don Pacifico Affair. At one stage during the crisis he agreed to lighten the tone of a letter to the British minister at Athens in accordance with her and Russell's advice. But he failed to act on his promise, and the letter was sent unaltered. 'This must not happen again,' Victoria fumed. '[The Queen] cannot allow a servant of the Crown and her Minister to act contrary to her orders, and this without her knowledge.' So angry was the queen that, at an audience with Russell on 2 March 1850, she demanded that Palmerston be moved from the Foreign Office. Russell's reply was that he was 'most anxious' not to hurt Palmerston's feelings for fear he would defect to either the Radicals or the Protectionists, both of whom 'would be ready to receive him as their Leader'. Yet he realized that the queen's distrust of Palmerston 'was a serious impediment to the carrying on of the Government'. The solution, he said, was for himself to move to the House of Lords, Palmerston to become leader of the House of Commons, and foreign affairs to be 'entrusted to other hands'. Victoria and Albert approved of the plan, but it never gained Palmerston's assent. He was determined to cling to office and, with that aim in view, made one of the greatest speeches in British parliamentary history.

* The explanation suggested later by George Anson, Prince Albert's personal secretary, was that Palmerston had made an assignation with another lady and had gone to the wrong bedchamber.

The occasion was the debate that followed a Radical motion approving his foreign policy in late June. A Tory motion censuring his actions towards Greece had earlier been carried by the House of Lords, but it was the Commons vote that would decide the government's fate. Day after day, leading British statesmen on all sides of the House – Disraeli, Gladstone, Cobden and Peel★ – rose to condemn his handling of the Don Pacifico Affair. He responded on 25 June with a masterful speech lasting almost five hours. In it he accused his detractors of abetting foreign conspiracy and 'domestic intrigue', and set out the principles that had guided British foreign policy since the death of Canning in 1827. His stirring finale, which was calculated to appeal to any man who held himself a patriot, did much to secure a government majority of forty-six: 'As the Roman, in days of old, held himself free from indignity, when he could say "*Civis Romanus sum*", so also a British subject, in whatever land he may be, shall feel confident that the watchful eye and the strong arm of England will protect him against injustice and wrong.'

So Palmerston survived, thanks to his mastery of the Commons and the popularity of his 'gunboat diplomacy' in the country at large. But Victoria and Albert were not about to let his indiscretions pass unnoticed. On 12 August, '*to prevent any mistake for the future*', the queen sent Lord John Russell a memorandum that purported to come from her but was actually drafted by Albert and his close adviser Baron Stockmar. It explained what the queen '*expects from her Foreign Secretary*':

(1) That he will distinctly state what he proposes in a given case, in order that the Queen may know as distinctly to *what* she has given her Royal sanction.

(2) Having *once given* her sanction to a measure, that it be not arbitrarily altered or modified by the Minister; such an act she must consider as

---

★ It was the last speech that Peel made in parliament. The day after the debate ended, he was badly injured in a fall from his horse, breaking his collarbone and a number of ribs. Four days later, on 2 July 1850, he died.

failing in sincerity towards the Crown, and justly to be visited by the exercise of her Constitutional right of dismissing that Minister. She expects to be kept informed of what passes between him and the Foreign Ministers before important decisions are taken . . . to receive the Foreign Despatches in good time, and to have the drafts for her approval sent to her in sufficient time to make herself acquainted with their contents before they must be sent off.

When shown the letter, Palmerston made all the right noises. He promised Russell he would 'attend to the directions which it contains' and admitted that pressure of business had sometimes caused an unnecessary delay in the sending of dispatches to the queen. He would solve the problem by reverting to the 'old system' whereby copies were made of all important dispatches as soon as they reached the Foreign Office. Yet he failed to learn from the Don Pacifico Affair and continued to regard foreign policy as a personal, rather than as a collective, responsibility. In October 1851 he invited Lajos Kossuth, the champion of Hungarian independence, to the Foreign Office – a meeting that would have infuriated Austria if it had taken place. It never did, thanks to the combined opposition of the queen and the cabinet. Palmerston got his own back by listening with tacit approval to an address by Kossuth's supporters that was violently critical of the emperors of both Austria and Russia. Still Russell refused to sack him, fearing the political consequences. But he had no other option when, in early December 1851, Palmerston recognized Louis-Napoleon's *coup d'état* in France (which made him, in effect, president for life)★ without consulting the cabinet. A delighted Victoria wrote to her uncle Leopold:

I have the greatest pleasure in announcing to you a piece of news which I know will give you as much satisfaction and relief as it does to us, and will do to the *whole* of the world. *Lord Palmerston is no longer Foreign*

★ A year later, Louis-Napoleon declared the Second Empire and became Napoleon III.

*Secretary* – and Lord Granville is already named his successor!! . . . Lord Granville will, I think, do extremely well, and his extreme honesty and trustworthiness will make him *invaluable* to us, and to the Government, and to Europe.

But Granville would not be around for long. In February 1852 Palmerston had his revenge on Russell by helping to defeat a government bill for the creation of a local militia.* Russell resigned and Lord Derby formed a minority Tory government, with Disraeli accepting the cabinet post that Palmerston declined: chancellor of the exchequer. But it was generally assumed that a government based on the narrow issue of protectionism could not last long; and so it proved.

Even as these political skirmishes were being fought out in London, yet another war was brewing on the fringe of empire. Not in India this time but in neighbouring Burma, an inaccessible land of thick jungles, mountains and fast-flowing rivers that lay to the south-east of Calcutta, across the Bay of Bengal.

Though mentioned by the Greek geographer Ptolemy in the second century AD, Burma remained largely closed to the outside world for much of the next millennium. Most foreign contact was with India, from where the Burmese assimilated the Buddhist religion but little else; they remained stoically immune, for example, to the Indian caste system. In the late thirteenth century the Burmese kingdom of Pagan was overrun by the Mongol hordes of Kublai Khan and the country fragmented into a patchwork of states ruled by the Shan princes from the eastern plateau. The Shan were still in power when the first European, a Venetian traveller and writer named Niccolò de' Conti, visited Burma in 1435. It was not until the early seventeenth century, however, that the English and Dutch East India companies established trade links with the Toungu Dynasty of King Thalun. But foreign trade

* Palmerston preferred a national militia and carried a motion to leave the word 'local' out of the bill's title.

ceased entirely in 1755 with the overthrow of the Toungus by a Burmese resistance leader who called himself Alaungpaya ('Embryo Buddha'). For the next fifty years King Alaungpaya and his successors terrorized the region, launching one war after another from their capital of Ava on the Irrawaddy River. Siam – modern Thailand – was overrun in 1767, though never brought properly under control, and a number of Chinese invasions from Yunnan Province were successfully repulsed. But it was the conquest in 1785 of the coastal kingdom of Arakan, which lay between Ava and British India, that set the Burmese on a collision course with the HEIC. Thousands of Arakan rebels fled across the border to British-controlled Chittagong, which they used as a base for raids. Protests from Ava were ignored, and frequent border incidents – such as the pursuit of 'bandits' into Chittagong by Burmese troops in 1795 – continued to sour Anglo-Burmese relations.

Tensions rose further in 1819, when the Burmese conquered the border states of Assam and Manipur, causing a fresh flood of refugees into east Bengal. In September 1823 a small British garrison was ejected from the island of Shahpuri near the Chittagong border; four months later the Burmese invaded Cachar, which was under British protection – and these further encroachments were the final straw for the HEIC. War was declared on 5 March 1824 by William Amherst, the governor-general, citing the Burmese government's 'mischievous aggression'. But even the Calcutta pessimists cannot have expected the fighting to last for two years, costing the British £13m and the lives of almost 15,000 men. Stout Burmese resistance, the swampy terrain, bad weather and poor logistics all played their part; but the biggest killer by far was sickness and disease. Of the 3,115 European fatalities, for example, only 150 died in battle. Despite the huge butcher's bill, the British eventually managed to fight their way to within four miles of the Burmese capital, prompting King Bagyidaw to sue for peace. By the terms of the subsequent treaty, he ceded Arakan, Assam and Tenasserim to the HEIC; he also promised to respect the independence of Manipur and Cachar, and to open up Burmese ports to British trade.

While Bagyidaw ruled, relations between Ava and Calcutta remained cordial. But in 1837 the king was overthrown by his brother Tharawaddy, who then denounced the earlier peace treaty and expelled the British resident. Tharawaddy's son and successor, Pagan Min, was just as Anglophobic as his father, and his subordinates followed his lead. In 1851, tired of reports that the Burmese governor of Rangoon was harassing British merchants and trading captains, Lord Dalhousie demanded redress. Pagan Min made a show of contrition by recalling the governor to Ava; but his replacement was hardly an improvement. He deliberately insulted the British flag, and, in response, the commodore of the nearest British squadron seized a Burmese ship and blockaded the Irrawaddy Delta. On 15 March 1852 Dalhousie issued the Burmese government with an ultimatum: stop interfering with British shipping and trade or face the consequences. When no reply was received, Dalhousie dispatched an expeditionary force. This war, unlike the previous one, was more about 'face' than regional security. 'We can't afford', explained Dalhousie, 'to be shown to the door anywhere in the East.'

Compared to the earlier conflict, this one was a model of British organization and efficiency. The initial British force of two brigades – furnished by the Bengal and Madras armies – was commanded by Major-General Sir Henry Godwin, 'an old man in a wig', who had fought in the first war as a regimental commander. Before leaving India, Godwin put this experience to good use by training his Bengal troops in the art of bombarding and storming stockades, the preferred mode of Burmese defence. British weapons had also improved, with the percussion musket far superior to the assortment of outdated firearms possessed by the Burmese; and, unlike the 1824 campaign, which had deliberately been launched during the monsoon when the rivers were in flood, Godwin timed his expedition to arrive at the Irrawaddy Delta in April, a good six weeks before the rains began.

Godwin's greatest advantage over the previous campaign, however, was the use of steam-powered transports and gunboats to navigate the Irrawaddy. The first successful trial of a steamboat, the tug *Charlotte Dundas*, had taken place on the Forth and Clyde Canal in 1802. But steam-towing was abandoned for fear of injuring the banks of the canal, and it was not until 1812 that Henry Bell's *Comet* began to operate on the Clyde as a commercial paddle-steamer. Yet it took some time to convert the Royal Navy to the idea of steam. This was partly because a steamer's paddles were thought to be vulnerable to enemy fire and did not leave enough room for a full broadside of guns. In 1840, by which time the British merchant fleet had no fewer than 720 large seagoing steamships, the Royal Navy had none. But all this changed with the launch of the first iron-hulled, propeller-driven ship, the SS *Great Britain* by Isambard Kingdom Brunel, in 1843. Within two years the Royal Navy had introduced the world's first steam battle-ship, HMS *Ajax*, and four years after that, in 1849, a screw-propeller battleship, HMS *Agamemnon*. France finished its own screw-propeller battleship, *Napoleon*, just three months before *Agamemnon* was launched, and it was the potential threat to Britain's naval supremacy from another country's steam-powered fleet that had prompted the Royal Navy to act. From 1851 to 1871, when HMS *Devastation* became the world's first mastless warship, all new British warships had sails *and* screw propellers. The best of the hybrids was HMS *Warrior*, the first iron-hulled battleship,★ launched in 1860. Displacing nearly 9,200 tons, with iron masts and retractable funnels for a full spread of canvas, she was the fastest, most powerful warship afloat.

In 1852, however, a much smaller steam-powered vessel gave Britain's armed forces a crucial tactical edge: the gunboat. Under 200 feet long, with pivot-mounted guns and a crew of around thirty, its greatest asset was its manoeuvrability. A two-mast sailing rig gave it speed and agility in open sea, while its steam engine allowed it to chug up navigable rivers, deep into hostile territory. 'The gunboat', writes one naval historian, 'made the Royal Navy for the first time a power on land as well as at sea. Without the

---

★ The French had already launched their own iron warship, the *Gloire*, but it had a wooden hull clad with iron plates. The *Warrior* was made entirely of iron.

gunboat, the navy could never have fulfilled its role as global policeman, intervening at the request of British officials and merchants virtually anywhere in the world.' At no time was the gunboat more effective than during the Second Burma War of 1852–3.

The fighting began in earnest on 5 April 1852 when a British amphibious assault, with gunboats to the fore, captured Martaban on the Rangoon River; a week later, in a battle that raged for three days, Godwin's combined force of 6,000 men stormed and took the fortified settlement of Rangoon itself. British casualties were light: just seventeen killed and 132 wounded. Many more died of sickness and disease during the following month of relative inactivity, as Godwin waited for reinforcements and supplies. By mid May he was ready to continue his advance, this time up the Negrais River to Bassein. This strongpoint, styled the 'Key of Burma', was captured in less than an hour, underlining once again Godwin's facility for combined sea and land operations. After a half-hearted, and only partially successful, expedition to assist anti-government rebels in the southern Burmese province of Pegu, Godwin turned his attention to the lower Irrawaddy Valley. Gunboats reached Prome in early July and found it undefended. But Godwin, short on men, decided not to garrison it until the arrival of extra troops from India.

One of the regiments selected to reinforce Godwin in Burma was the 38th Bengal Native Infantry, full of veterans who had fought in the Afghan and Sikh Wars, and based at Calcutta. Only six of the seventy-four Bengal infantry regiments had been recruited for general service outside India. The 38th was not amongst them, and, in such cases, it was usual to ask the sepoys to volunteer. This was in deference to the Bengal infantry's large proportion of high-caste sepoys, who, theoretically, would become outcasts if they travelled over the 'black water'. At first the men of the 38th said they 'were not unwilling to go' to Burma if their officers accompanied them. But their attitude hardened when Colonel Burney told his company commanders to 'assemble their men, call their roll, ask each man to volunteer, & if he declined *to cause him to state the reason why he declined*'. Company after company refused to comply, because, Dalhousie later explained to the commander-in-chief, 'the sepoys looked on this as compulsion, which practically it was.' Matters came to a head on 17 March 1852, when, depressed by rumours that they would be put on ships by force, they disobeyed repeated orders to return to their lines before finally submitting.

The court of inquiry put most of the blame on Burney and censured his attempt to pressurize the men by asking them to state their reasons for not volunteering. He was transferred to another regiment, and the 38th was posted to Dacca, a notoriously unhealthy station in east Bengal, where it would replace the 47th, which was also under orders for Burma. 'Oh! So they are fond of walking, are they?' Dalhousie is said to have remarked. 'They shall walk to Dacca then, and die there like dogs.' And so they did. By October 1852, according to the wife of a 38th officer, 'there was only Colonel Finnis, Lieutenant Castle and one of our fine men who stood at muster. The rest of the 600 who were stationed there . . . were either dead or dying in hospital.'

Most historians have explained the 'mutiny' of the 38th as an attempt by sepoys to protect their high-caste status. Yet, in this instance, as in a similar mutiny during the previous Burma War,★ it could be argued that the sepoys were simply looking for an excuse not to serve in Burma. Despite Burney's pressure and the inevitable rumours, the sepoys were never actually ordered to embark on ships. There was, moreover, a long tradition of Bengal sepoys volunteering for action outside British India: 7,000 had served against the French in Mauritius and Java in 1811; more recently, the 38th itself had fought in Afghanistan, despite the

★ In November 1825, at Barrackpore near Calcutta, the 47th Native Infantry was decimated by European fire after it had refused orders to march to Burma. In the opinion of Sir John Kaye, the great nineteenth-century historian, the cause of the mutiny was the sepoys' eagerness 'to find a pretext for refusing to march on such hazardous service' (Malleson (ed.), *Kaye and Malleson's History of the Indian Mutiny*, I, 193).

dread most high-caste sepoys had of crossing the Indus, because, in the words of Sitaram Pandy (himself a volunteer), 'the very act means loss of caste.' There was also the example set by the Bombay Army: a quarter of its sepoys were high-caste men from northern India, yet they had never objected to foreign service and, in 1856–7, would cross the sea to fight in Persia without demur. In theory, all three presidency armies were recruited on the basis that their sepoys would march where they were directed, 'whether within or beyond the Company's territories'. But the various interpretations of this rule were very different, as a senior Bengal official explained in 1852:

In Bengal, except for general service regiments, men enlist upon the understanding that they are not sent by sea for service in foreign parts; but the sepoys of the Madras and Bombay armies enlist upon the understanding that they will go wherever they are sent. At the same time, it is the practice at Madras to apprise the sepoys of a regiment ordered on foreign service, that if any are unwilling to follow their colours their places will be supplied in volunteers.

Even Bombay sepoys expected to be consulted before serving outside their presidency, but it was purely a formality. 'They have never objected to go on general service, to go abroad, or anywhere,' stated a Bombay colonel in 1858. The obvious conclusion is that caste was pandered to in Bengal but not in Bombay. There were, for example, many instances of Bengal sepoys avoiding manual labour, because it was demeaning to their caste. After the Battle of Chilianwalla in the Second Sikh War, most of the entrenching work was done by European troops, because Bengal sepoys declined (and were allowed to do duty as a covering party instead). At the siege of Multan, so General Dundas informed the Bombay government, the Bengal sepoys refused to work in the trenches. The officer commanding the Bengal sappers at Multan later rejected this charge but on spurious grounds. For, as Colonel John Hill, commandant of the Bombay Sappers, later testified, the Bengal troops did indeed 'march to the trenches and took the pickaxes and shovels in their hands, but they did not work'. In the Bombay Army, by comparison, Hill had never known caste to interfere with the performance of duty.

In 1853 a Madras correspondent to the *United Service Magazine* observed that it was only natural for the Bengal sepoy to take advantage of the fact that his officer hesitated every time he ordered him to undertake a duty that might transgress his caste. Four years later, with the Indian Mutiny under way, the same magazine aired the argument that caste issues had furnished the sepoy with a 'pretext under the cloak of which he can further his own ends'.

All that lay in the future. In 1852 Dalhousie's priority was to get enough troops to Burma to finish the war. Most of the reinforcements – including the 67th Native Infantry, the 38th's substitute – arrived in Rangoon in early September. Later that month Godwin headed up the Irrawaddy with part of the Bengal Contingent, capturing Prome without a fight on 9 October. But, having discovered that the main Burmese Army, 18,000 strong, was dug in ten miles to the east, Godwin chose discretion and returned to Rangoon, leaving the commander at Prome with orders to act on the defensive.

In November, Godwin led a second – and this time successful – expedition to capture the town of Pegu. Once back in Rangoon, however, he received word that the tiny British garrison at Pegu was under siege. Two relieving forces were hastily dispatched, one by water (which Godwin accompanied) and one by land. Not surprisingly, the flotilla arrived first, and, on 17 December, Godwin's force of 1,200 men was able to outflank the besieging army and force it to retreat. Two days later, the pursuit was broken off because of a lack of supplies, and Godwin withdrew to Pegu, where he was met by the land column, which had just arrived after an uneventful march through seventy miles of hilly jungle.

It was gradually dawning on Godwin that his lack of land transport was hamstringing his attempts to bring the enemy to a decisive battle. As things stood, his troops could never venture far from their waterborne supply line, which made it easy for the

Burmese to fight a hit-and-run style of guerrilla warfare. Constant attacks, lack of sleep and inadequate provisions were beginning to take their toll on British morale. Further pressure was heaped on the British commander by Dalhousie's premature announcement on 20 December 1852 that the HEIC had annexed Pegu Province. It had yet to be pacified, let alone annexed, and to this end Godwin sent another land column into the province, 2,000 strong, under the experienced Brigadier-General S. W. Steel. With transport provided by 120 elephants and 300 bullock carts, Steel's march was a leisurely one, his troops finally reaching Toungu in the extreme south of the province in late February 1853.

Godwin, meanwhile, had returned to Prome, where on 5 January he received some very welcome news: King Pagan Min had been overthrown in a palace coup, and the main Burmese Army had withdrawn to Ava to share in the spoils. In late January, advancing cautiously upriver, Godwin met emissaries from the new king, Mindon, who, they said, was willing to negotiate. The sticking point, however, was Mindon's refusal to cede Pegu. As negotiations continued, the last major operation of the war took place downriver near Donabyu, where the local chief, Myat-Toon, had long been a thorn in the British side. The first attempt to penetrate the narrow creek that led to the chief's stronghold was beaten back on 17 January. A second more powerful expedition was launched in early February, but it too was forced to retire, with the loss of two naval guns and eighty men, including its fatally wounded commander, Captain Granville Loch, R.N. With the honour of the British military at stake, Brigadier-General Sir John Cheape was given the task of capturing the stronghold. He chose to attack by land but lost his way in the jungle and was forced to return to the Irrawaddy. On 7 March, his column increased to 1,100 men and four guns, he set off again with a week's supplies and assurances that his destination was within three marches. It was not. Harassed by the enemy and slowed by endless river crossings, Cheape made tortuous progress, and on 12 March, with provisions running short, he put the men on half-rations and sent the bullock carts back for more supplies. The convoy returned on the 16th, and two days later, leaving his sick and wounded with a small escort, Cheape continued his advance. Early on 19 March his advance guard at last discovered Myat-Toon's formidable stockade.

The officer leading the vanguard was Garnet Wolseley, the young ensign of the 80th Foot who had been so shocked by Wellington's death a few months earlier. Born near Dublin in 1833, the scion of an ancient but hard-up Anglo-Irish family that traced its Saxon descent to pre-Conquest times, Wolseley was a studious and fiercely ambitious officer who had spent much of the voyage out to India learning Hindustani and reading military history. He had been in the army for only a year, the recipient of a commission without purchase in recognition of his late father's many years of distinguished service. Like many of his poorer colleagues, he 'looked forward to an Indian career where high pay enabled the infantry officer to live without assistance from home'. Yet he also hoped to emulate the military feats of his forebears, notably Brigadier-General William Wolseley, his great-great-great uncle, who had raised his own regiment of horse★ and served with William III in Ireland, and his grandfather, who had fought in the Seven Years War with the 1st (Royal) Dragoons before becoming a parson.

Even at this early stage of his career, Wolseley was fiercely critical of anything that did not meet his exacting standards. The 'great bulk' of officers he met in India and Burma were, he wrote later, 'lacking in good breeding, and all seemed badly educated'. Only a small proportion, like him, took their 'profession seriously, studied hard at all military sciences, and spent many of those deadly midday hours of the Indian summers reading military history and the lives of the great commanders'. As for British uniforms, he regarded them as 'entirely unsuited for campaigning in a tropical climate'. He wrote:

The Queen's Army took an idiotic pride in dressing in India as nearly as possible in the same clothing they wore at home. Upon this occasion,

★ Later known as the 6th (Inniskilling) Dragoons.

the only difference was in the trousers, which were of ordinary Indian drill dyed blue, and that round our regulation forage cap we wore a few yards of puggaree* of a similar colour. We wore our ordinary cloth shell jackets buttoned up to the chin, and the usual white buckskin gloves. Could any costume short of steel armour be more absurd in such a latitude?

The army's only concession to the climate was to allow soldiers to remove their stiff leather stocks, but most of the veterans 'clung to theirs, asserting that the stock protected the back of the neck against the sun, and kept them cool'. The Burmese soldier, by contrast, was simply dressed in a short cotton jacket, loin cloth and 'small pugree twisted through his long hair'. His weapons consisted of a *dah*, or hiltless sword, and a variety of outdated muskets. 'A cloth fastened round him contains his rice,' wrote Wolseley, 'and the pot to boil it in is usually slung to the barrel of his ill-kept firelock, together with the mat which forms his bed. A few bananas and a little native tobacco constitute his luxuries.' Broad-shouldered, muscular, hardy and brave, the Burmese should have made ideal soldiers. What they lacked, in Wolseley's opinion, was discipline. 'They revolt against restraint,' he wrote later, 'and if punished for any offence against discipline they desert, and once in their dense forests they are hard to find. They stand being shot at well when behind stockaded defences, but they dislike leaving them, even though a favourable opportunity presents itself, when they might easily inflict great loss upon their enemy.'

This, then, was the foe that Wolseley came up against for the first time – his baptism of fire – on 19 March 1853. Accompanying him on point duty were four privates of the 80th, all recruits in their teens. As they crept along a narrow path, with dense jungle on each side, they could hear the sound of trees being felled for the Burmese to strengthen their defences. Then, as the path turned sharply to the left, the sight of an enemy stockade came into view, about a hundred yards distant on the far side of a large creek: they

---

* A light turban or thin scarf worn round a hat.

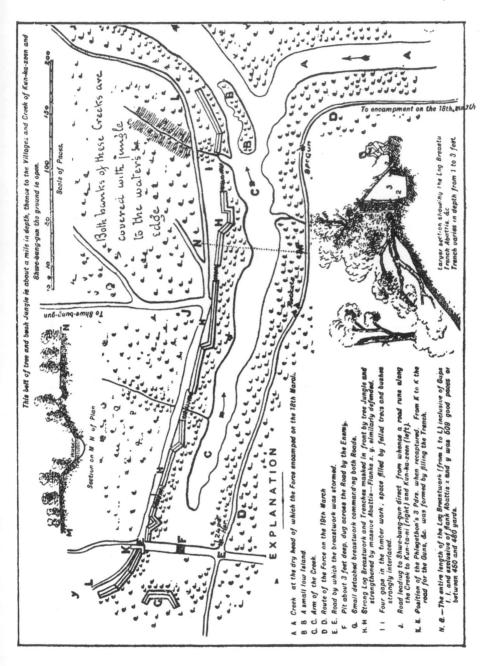

*Plan of the Assault on Myat-Toon's Stronghold: 19 March 1853*
*(from Wolseley's autobiography, 1903)*

had found Myat-Toon's stronghold. With no pickets thrown out, the Burmese were quite unaware of the British presence. Speaking in whispers, Wolseley sent word back to the main force and a short while later received orders to continue his advance – he was 'to move slowly and be careful not to show [himself]'. He had almost reached the point at which a road forded the creek when the Burmese spotted the approaching column and opened fire along the length of their stockade. He recalled:

The whiz of bullets and the sound of their thud into the stems of trees about us at once added enlivenment to the position. Their fire was too high, and it was not until we began to form up to our right, facing the enemy, that I saw any one fall near me, but before the place was taken all the four boys with whom I started in the morning were hit. The detachments of British troops were now withdrawn into the jungle and formed into line facing the enemy's works; our two guns, which had been far behind, were now brought up and into action.

Detachments from three regiments – Britons, Sikhs and sepoys – were ordered to advance up the road and storm the stockade. But the sepoys had gone through the horror of the previous expedition and refused to break cover. 'They seemed in an abject funk', remembered Wolseley, 'and I believe could not be got on by their gallant officers. As we passed over them, our men abused them in strong terms, which they seemed in no way to resent.'

The Sikhs were bolder and advanced shoulder to shoulder with the British troops, but had some of the fight knocked out of them when their popular commander was shot in the head and badly wounded. Before long the troops were all mixed together, and, confronted by a withering fire from front and flank, the advance stalled. Volunteers were called for to lead a storming party, and Wolseley and Lieutenant Allan Johnson, another officer destined for high rank, stepped forward. With the two officers in the lead, the mixed detachment tore down the road towards the stockade's main gate as the Burmese opened up with everything they had, including the two British naval guns that had been lost during the previous expedition. Though out front, and in mortal danger, Wolseley felt something akin to exhilaration as he waved his sword and cheered the men on. Suddenly, not far from the stockade, the ground gave way beneath him, and he fell heavily into a pit disguised with earth and brushwood, a wooden stake almost knocking him unconscious. Gathering his senses, he scrambled out of the far side of the pit and, to his horror, found himself alone, just thirty yards from the enemy stockade. The rest of the storming party had melted away. With bullets kicking up the ground around him, he jumped back into the pit, but it quickly occurred to him that, having dropped his pistol, he would fall easy prey to the first Burmese sally. His only chance was to run for it, and, choosing the moment after a heavy Burmese volley, he set off. Every lung-busting stride brought the anticipation of a bullet in the back. But not one found its mark, and he soon reached the safety of the ragged British line, still angry at being deserted. 'Had a formed company with its officers been there,' he wrote later, 'the whole thing would have been over in a very few minutes.' Instead the storming party was a mixture of volunteers, many of them raw recruits.

By now Brigadier-General Cheape had appeared on the scene and, seeing the difficulty of the approach, ordered the 24-pounder howitzer to be brought forward. He also ordered up his remaining troops and called for a fresh storming party. Wolseley again volunteered, saying he knew the way, and was joined by a young Madras lieutenant called James Taylor. Having warned Taylor about the pit, Wolseley collected as many 80th men as he could before setting off at the run. He could see numbers of the Burmese above their stockade, urging the British on with shouts and gesticulations. Once again he experienced the thrill of the charge as adrenalin coursed through his veins. 'The feeling is catching,' he wrote; 'it flies through a mob of soldiers and makes them, whilst the fit is on them, absolutely reckless of all consequences. The blood seems to boil, the brain to be on fire.'

Never again in his long and illustrious career would he experience 'the same unalloyed and elevating satisfaction'. But it could not last. Having safely skirted the pit, he saw Taylor tumble head over heels. A few paces on he too fell heavily, shot in the left thigh by a bullet from a gingall, a heavy musket fired from a rest. As he clamped his left hand on the wound, blood squirted in jets through the fingers of his pipe-clayed gloves. But the seriousness of the wound did not stop him from urging his men on, including one sergeant who stopped to help him. 'In a few minutes,' recalled Wolseley, 'he and those he led – for he was then in command – had clambered up the roughly-constructed stockade and the garrison bolted. Some more men coming up from the rear carried poor Taylor and put him beside me, where he bled to death. He too was shot through the thigh, the bullet in his case cutting the femoral artery. Mine was a remarkable escape. A doctor soon arrived on the scene and put on a tourniquet, which hurt me, but allowed me to be moved.'

Wolseley was evacuated back to Donabyu in a naval pinnace, and from there to Prome on a flat boat towed by a steamer. By the time he reached England, in late 1853, he could walk again. His 'gallantry in leading the storming party' was mentioned in dispatches and would probably have merited the Victoria Cross if that medal had then existed.

The size of Myat-Toon's garrison was later estimated at 4,000 men, one man for every four yards of stockade. Most fled with their chief, leaving behind a huge stockpile of weapons and food, which the British destroyed. Cheape then retraced his steps to Donabyu, arriving on the 24th. His total casualties were not light – 130 killed and wounded, with a further hundred succumbing to cholera – but just about acceptable, considering the difficulties of the climate and the terrain. The fight near Donabyu was the last serious action of the war. After much negotiation, King Mindon agreed to cede Pegu, and hostilities ceased on 30 June 1853.

# 7. The 'sick man' of Europe

Back in Britain, the public's attention was focused not on war but on domestic politics. In the summer of 1852, in an attempt to win an outright majority in the Commons, Lord Derby called a general election. The Conservatives gained a few extra seats but were still in a minority.* Everything hinged on Disraeli's first budget: too protectionist and it would alienate the Peelites; not protectionist enough and his own supporters would rebel. He opted, as he was bound to, for a compromise: a budget of compensation rather than of protection.

His problem, according to Disraeli's biographer Robert Blake, 'was to satisfy the "interests" that deemed themselves to have been damaged by free trade, and at the same time to avoid reuniting against him the whole of the opposition in the House of Commons'. These 'interests' were the landed, sugar and shipping lobbies, and Disraeli included three measures specifically for their benefit: a reduction of the malt tax; the privilege of refining colonial sugar in bond; and the reduction or abolition of certain shipping dues. But to pay for this he made the error of doubling the highly unpopular House Tax while at the same time halving the exemption limit to houses of £10 rateable value. He also altered the Income Tax – reintroduced, after a lapse of twenty-six years, by Peel in 1842 – by reducing the levy of seven pence on earned income by a quarter, and by lowering the exemption limit from £150 for all forms of income to £100 for earned income and £50 for unearned income.

On 3 December, in a speech spanning five hours, Disraeli

---

* The party breakdown in the House of Commons after the 1852 election was: Tories (Derbyites) 286; Radicals 150; Whigs 120; Irish 50; Peelites 30 (*Victoria Letters 1*, II, 412).

announced the details to a flabbergasted house. Lord Macaulay, not himself the most succinct of orators, commented: 'I could have said the whole as clearly, or more clearly in two.' A week later an acrimonious four-day debate began in which Disraeli's opponents attacked almost every measure. 'Disraeli's enemies', wrote Blake, 'had little difficulty in showing that the boons which he had conferred with one hand upon the middle-class householder in the form of earned income relief were neatly removed with his other when he imposed the house tax and lowered the income-tax exemption limit.' Finally, as the debate was about to wind up in the early hours of 17 December, with the chamber lit by flickering gaslight and a violent thunderstorm raging outside, William Gladstone, the Shadow chancellor, rose to his feet. Displaying that mastery of financial detail that would make him one of the greatest chancellors in history, he dismantled Disraeli's budget piece by piece. When the division was taken at 4 a.m., the whole opposition voted against the budget, and it was defeated by 305 votes to 286.

Derby resigned the following day, leaving the queen in a dilemma. Barring a second general election, the only alternative to a Tory government was a coalition, and this depended on the Peelites joining forces with the Whigs and the Radicals. They were happy to do so, Lord Aberdeen told the queen, but their price was steep: six of the thirteen cabinet seats, including Aberdeen as prime minister and Gladstone as chancellor of the exchequer. Incredibly the other opposition parties agreed, with six Whigs also appointed to the cabinet – amongst them Russell and Palmerston as foreign and home secretaries respectively – and the remaining seat going to a Radical, Sir William Molesworth. The queen had accepted Aberdeen's argument that Palmerston would probably side with the Conservatives if he was left out of government. Her only stipulation was that he be kept out of the Foreign Office. In its final form the cabinet contained no fewer than four past, present or future prime ministers – Russell, Aberdeen, Palmerston and Gladstone – and was rightly known as the ministry of 'all the talents'.

Overall the queen was delighted. 'Our Government is very

satisfactorily settled,' she informed her uncle Leopold on New Year's Eve. 'To have my faithful friend Aberdeen as Prime Minister is a great happiness and comfort for me personally.'

But, even as Aberdeen was forming his government, discussions were taking place in St Petersburg, capital of tsarist Russia, that were destined to plunge Europe into its first Continental war for almost forty years. They centred on the diplomatic conundrum known as the 'Eastern Question': what was to be done with the ramshackle and corrupt Ottoman Empire? At its height, in the early seventeenth century, the empire had included not only modern Turkey but the whole of the Balkan Peninsula, the central Hungarian plain, the Ukraine, the shores of the Black Sea, the Arab lands of the Middle East and most of the African shore of the Mediterranean. In the eighteenth century Austria 'liberated' Hungary, and the Russians advanced south round both sides of the Black Sea, reaching the Danube Delta in the west and the Caucasus Mountains in the east. Successive sultans also relinquished control of outlying provinces in the Balkans and North Africa: Serbia and Egypt were largely autonomous, while Greece was given independence in 1829.

Yet the Muslim-dominated Ottoman Empire still contained more than 13 million Orthodox Christians who looked to Russia as their protector. Ostensibly to protect their rights, Nicholas I, the Russian tsar, had fought a victorious war against the Turks in 1828–9, receiving generous territorial concessions in the subsequent Treaty of Adrianople. Fearful of Russian ambitions, Britain brokered the Straits Convention in 1841, which closed the Dardanelles and the Bosporus to all foreign warships while Turkey was at peace. This allowed Russia freedom of manoeuvre in the Black Sea and Britain peace of mind that its quickest route to India and the Far East, via the Suez Isthmus, would not be at the mercy of the Russian fleet.

In June 1844 Tsar Nicholas arrived in London to discuss the 'Eastern Question' with Peel and his foreign secretary, Aberdeen. 'Turkey is a dying man,' he told them, yet it was important to prevent its early collapse because of the danger that a single foreign power, particularly France, would come to dominate the strategic capital of Constantinople. The British were largely in agreement, and a month later Aberdeen and the Russian foreign minister, Count Nesselrode, signed a joint memorandum affirming the desire of both powers to preserve the Ottoman Empire for as long as possible; if it was in danger of collapsing, they would discuss 'the establishment of a new order of things to replace that which exists today'. So secret was the agreement that it was not even discussed in cabinet and was kept not in the Foreign Office but in Aberdeen's private possession.

This delicate balance was upset, however, by the overthrow of King Louis-Philippe of France and the election of Louis-Napoleon – nephew of the man who had invaded Russia in 1812 – to the presidency of the Second Republic in 1848. Two years later, to whip up clerical support at home, Louis-Napoleon began to promote Roman Catholic rights to the Palestinian Holy Places of the Ottoman Empire, notably the Holy Sepulchre in Jerusalem and the Church of the Nativity in Bethlehem. Tsar Nicholas suspected a hidden agenda, and his fears increased after Louis-Napoleon's successful coup of December 1851 made him a virtual dictator. (A year later all pretence was removed when the Second Empire was proclaimed and he became Napoleon III.)

In February 1852 Sultan Abd-el-Mejid bowed to French pressure by confirming a 1740 treaty between the two countries that had given Roman Catholics, and not Orthodox Christians, 'sovereign authority' in the Holy Land. But Russia's forceful response, citing a later agreement in 1757, prompted the sultan to revoke the earlier concession and to ratify instead the privileges of the Orthodox Church.★ Outraged by this *volte face*, Louis-Napoleon upped the ante in the summer of 1852 by sending the steam-

---

★ A generic term for the family of Christian Churches originating in the East (and including the national churches of Greece, Russia, etc.) that, until recently, recognized the headship of the patriarch of Constantinople and that separated from the Western Church around the eleventh century.

powered warship *Charlemagne* through the Dardanelles, a show of force that contravened the Straits Convention, and infuriated Russia and Britain. Yet this French example of gunboat diplomacy seemed to work. In early December the sultan announced that the Roman Catholic Church would, after all, have supreme authority over the Holy Places. To underline this he ordered Orthodox monks to hand over to their Latin counterparts the keys to the main door and grotto of the Church of the Nativity in Bethlehem. As Aberdeen was forming his coalition government, Latin monks were placing a silver star engraved with the arms of France in the sanctuary of the Church of the Nativity.

Outmanoeuvred by France, but encouraged by reports of clan unrest along Turkey's north-west frontier, Tsar Nicholas suggested to Nesselrode that the time had come to draw up partition plans for the Ottoman Empire. Nesselrode warned that Britain would not cooperate, but Nicholas was unconvinced. On 9 January 1853, in an audience with the British ambassador, Sir Hamilton Seymour, he spoke of the 'close alliance which ought always to exist' between their two countries, adding that if they were on good terms 'what anyone else thought mattered little'. Asked for reassurances about Turkey, Nicholas replied ominously: 'We have a sick man on our hands, a man who is seriously ill; it will be . . . a great misfortune if he escapes us one of these days, especially before all the necessary arrangements are made.'

Over the next three months, in conversation with Seymour, Nicholas kept returning to the same theme: the Ottoman Empire was dying, and it was necessary to come to an agreement over its partition. His preference was for Serbia, Bulgaria and the Danubian principalities (Moldavia and Wallachia) to become independent states under Russian protection; in return Britain could have Egypt and Crete, which would protect her route to India and the Far East. While not overtly hostile to these suggestions, Aberdeen's government refused to sanction any action that would precipitate Turkey's collapse, particularly as Nicholas had hinted that it might lead to Russia 'temporarily' occupying Constantinople.

Convinced – wrongly as it turned out – that he had bought

Britain off, Nicholas now turned to deal with France. In late February he sent the sexagenarian Prince Alexander Menshikov, chief of the Naval Staff, to Constantinople to demand not only that the guardianship of the Holy Places should be returned to the Orthodox Church but also that the Russian tsar be recognized as the protector of all the Orthodox Christians living within the Ottoman Empire. If the sultan was worried about French hostility, Menshikov added, the tsar was willing to offer him a secret defensive alliance. When the French ambassador and the British chargé d'affaires★ learnt of these demands, they decided on a show of strength and summoned squadrons from their Mediterranean fleets. But only French ships appeared. Fearful of provoking Russia, the British cabinet cancelled the order, though the decision was not unanimous. Russell — who had remained in the cabinet despite relinquishing the Foreign Office to Clarendon earlier that month — was convinced that the tsar was bent on destroying Turkey and that it was essential to resist him; Palmerston agreed. But the hawks were outnumbered by doves — led by Aberdeen and Gladstone — and Russell was, in any case, preoccupied with the issue of parliamentary reform.

Before Russell's departure from the Foreign Office, however, he had asked the experienced diplomat Lord Stratford de Redcliffe (the former Sir Stratford Canning) to return to Constantinople as British ambassador. Stratford, who had served four previous stints as ambassador, had forgotten more about Turkish affairs than most men would ever know. Shortly after his return on 5 April, he persuaded Menshikov to accept a compromise on the guardianship of the Holy Places. However, backed by the French, Austrian and Prussian ambassadors, he also persuaded the sultan not to recognize the tsar as protector of his Christian subjects. It would have been tantamount, he said, to ceding sovereignty over the sultan's Balkan and Danubian provinces.

Menshikov left Constantinople in disgust on 21 May. Now was

★ The British ambassador, Lord Stratford de Redcliffe, was on extended leave that was expected to be permanent.

the time, Palmerston urged Clarendon, for a show of strength. Anything less would simply encourage the Russians. Stratford agreed. Everything depended, he said, on the cabinet 'looking the crisis in the face'. But none of Palmerston's colleagues, not even Russell, appreciated the gravity of the situation. While they dithered, the Russians acted. On 31 May they delivered an ultimatum to Turkey: if their demands were not met within eight days they would invade the Danubian principalities. Stung to react, the British cabinet at last ordered its fleet to sail from Malta to the mouth of the Dardanelles. France promised additional naval support. But it was too late. Russian troops crossed the River Pruth into Moldavia on 22 June. Palmerston urged Aberdeen to send the fleet up to the Bosporus and even, if necessary, into the Black Sea itself. But Aberdeen refused: until Russia declared war, such an action would contravene the Straits Convention. It was, railed Palmerston, like 'waiting timidly and submissively at the back door while Russia is violently, threateningly, and arrogantly forcing her way into the house'.

In Constantinople, meanwhile, Stratford advised the sultan not to respond to Russian aggression. This gave the Russians pause for thought, and they halted on the Danube while representatives of the other major powers – Austria, Prussia, France and Britain – met in Vienna to seek a solution. The outcome, the 'Vienna Note' of 31 July, sought to guarantee joint Franco-Russian supervision of the sultan's Christian subjects. The tsar agreed to sign. But the note was unacceptable to Turkey, because it contained a clause that gave both France and Russia the right to approve any change in Ottoman policy towards its Christians: a clear violation of its sovereignty. The official British position was that Turkey should sign. But unofficially Stratford let the Turkish government know that it would be unwise to give in to the Russians. It was clear too that neither the British nor the French would stand by while Russia took Constantinople. Thus emboldened, the sultan demanded amendments to the note that would have given his government a greater say in the protection of the Christian religion within its borders.

Russia refused, and within a few weeks a Berlin newspaper was quoting Nesselrode as saying that he interpreted the Vienna Note as allowing Russia not only to advise on Turkish policy towards Orthodox Christians but also to interfere directly on behalf of their rights and privileges. This went beyond the demands that Menshikov had made earlier in the year, and even the doves in the British cabinet were now convinced that Russia was not interested in a reasonable settlement. A final attempt at a compromise was made by Count Buol-Schavenstein, the Austrian foreign minister, but his note was rejected by Turkey on 20 September. Four days later Clarendon told Stratford that 'the only likelihood now is war.' In the same dispatch he authorized the British ambassador to summon the British fleet to Constantinople. The French followed suit.

Victoria and Albert were strongly supportive of their government's position. In a joint memorandum to Lord Aberdeen, the prince wrote:

It is evident that Russia has hitherto attempted to deceive us in pretending that she did not aim at the acquisition of any *new* Right, but required only a satisfaction of honour and a *re*-acknowledgement of the Rights she already possessed by Treaty; that she *does intend* and for the first time lays bare that intention, to acquire *new* Rights of interference which the Porte [Ottoman government] does *not* wish to concede and cannot concede, and which the European Powers have repeatedly declared she *ought not* to concede.

Such a concession would, the prince added, 'make foreigners of 10,000,000 of the subjects of the Porte, or depose the Sultan as their sovereign, putting the Emperor of Russia in his place'.

But the royal couple's hope that war could still be avoided was dashed by the news, on 4 October, that Turkey had delivered an ultimatum to Russia to quit the principalities within a fortnight. It was tantamount to a declaration of war. Once again the British cabinet was divided as to its response: Palmerston and Russell wanted the immediate authorization of naval operations against

Russia; Gladstone argued for a diplomatic solution. The other members were somewhere in between, and, inevitably, they adopted a compromise: Stratford was to be given authority to order British ships into the Black Sea in the event of Russia attacking Turkey or its fleet leaving the Crimean port of Sevastopol. As one or other was bound to happen, it was like offering Turkey a formal alliance. It was no longer a question of if Britain went to war but when.

Victoria and Albert were at Balmoral and did not hear of the cabinet's decision until 10 October. They were horrified. 'It was evident', wrote the prince in a memorandum, 'that Lord Aberdeen was, against his better judgment, consenting to a course of policy which he inwardly condemned, that his desire to maintain unity at the Cabinet led to concessions which by degrees altered the whole character of his policy.' The queen, moreover, was extremely unhappy that the cabinet had made this momentous decision to go to war without her 'previous concurrence or even the means for her to judge of the propriety or impropriety of the course to be adopted'. And if Aberdeen failed to keep his cabinet together, added Albert, 'the Queen would be left without an efficient Government, and a war on her hands.' Such a position was 'morally and constitutionally' wrong.

Part of the problem, of course, was of the queen's own making: she chose to spend much of her time away from London, at either Osborne or Balmoral, and some issues were so urgent that the government could not always afford the time it took to consult her. Yet her physical absence was also a boon in that it provided the cabinet with an excuse for making controversial decisions without her or Albert's interference. The queen suspected as much, and, when Clarendon attempted to explain himself, she sent a ferocious reply:

We have taken on ourselves in conjunction with France all the risks of a European war, without having bound Turkey to any conditions with respect to provoking it. The hundred and twenty fanatical Turks constituting the Divan [parliament] at Constantinople are left sole judges of the line of policy to be pursued, and made cognizant at the same time of the fact that England and France have bound themselves to defend the Turkish Territory! This is entrusting them with a power which Parliament has been jealous to confide even to the hands of the British Crown.

So serious did the royal couple regard the situation that they cut short their stay in Scotland and rushed back to Windsor Castle, where they summoned Aberdeen on 15 October. He gave them a lengthy review of the government's foreign policy, adding his suspicions that Stratford had played a double game at Constantinople. He also acknowledged the 'disadvantage of the course adopted by the Cabinet, which left the Turks at liberty to do as they pleased', but it had been the only way to appease Russell and Palmerston. 'Had he known what the queen's opinion was,' recorded Albert, 'he might have been more firm, feeling himself supported by the Crown, but he had imagined from her letters that there was more animosity against Russia and leaning to war in her mind.' Yet even now Aberdeen 'saw reason for hope that a peaceable settlement could be obtained'.

It was wishful thinking. On 28 October, with its government's ultimatum long expired, the Turkish Army crossed the Danube into Wallachia and began to drive the Russians back towards the Moldavian border. Palmerston wanted the British fleet to sail into the Black Sea to protect the right flank of the advancing Turkish troops. But Aberdeen, ever hopeful, sent him a bizarre memorandum from Prince Albert suggesting that, instead of forcing the Russians to withdraw from the Danubian principalities, a better solution might be to force the Turks to withdraw from Europe. If that was the case, replied Palmerston tartly, then Britain had better change sides. He added: 'Peace is an Excellent thing, and War is a great Misfortune. But there are Many things More valuable than Peace, and many Things Much worse than war. The maintenance of the Ottoman Empire belongs to the First Class, The Occupation of Turkey by Russia belongs to the Second.'

Public opinion was beginning to agree. When Aberdeen first

took office, the arch-enemy had been Napoleon III. The fear of a French invasion, 'under the banner of the Pope', was so great that parliament had readily agreed to huge service estimates for the improvement of coastal defences. But now Tsar Nicholas was the bogey man, and, urged on by pro-Palmerston papers like the *Morning Chronicle* and the *Morning Post*, the British people scorned Aberdeen's irresolution and demanded action.

Still Aberdeen held back from direct involvement, but all this changed on 30 November, when a Russian naval squadron demonstrated the destructive power of explosive shells against wooden hulls by sinking a convoy of Turkish supply ships – seven frigates, two corvettes, two transports and two small steamers – in the Black Sea port of Sinope. Four thousand Turkish sailors died in the explosions, fires and sea. When news of the 'massacre' reached Britain on 12 December, all sections of the press were outraged. 'The English people are resolved', declared *The Times*, 'that Russia shall not dictate conditions to Europe, or convert the Black Sea, with all the various interests encompassing its shores, into a Russian lake.' Yet there was also a growing belief that had Palmerston been directing policy, British ships would have kept the Russians at bay. 'To stop the unprofitable contest by striking down the aggressor with a blow', wrote the *Morning Chronicle* on 20 December, 'is as plain a duty towards humanity as it was to send succour to Sinope.'

Amidst all the drama, Palmerston resigned: not because of the war, he insisted, but because Russell was about to introduce a Reform Bill he could not support. This did not prevent the press and public from speculating on the real reason: disgust with the government's foreign policy and a lack of support from the crown. It was a clever ploy by Palmerston. If he had gone because of the war, he would have taken Russell with him. By resigning over reform, he identified himself to the electorate as the only minister prepared to make a stand against a variety of government policies. If the war went badly, he was in the ideal position to pick up the pieces.

On 22 December, stung by the British press into action, the cabinet finally responded to Sinope by sending the fleet into the Black Sea with instructions to 'invite' any Russian ship it met to return to Sevastopol. France made a similar move. But, with public opinion strongly in favour of war, many ministers were convinced the government could not survive without Palmerston and so persuaded Aberdeen to ask him to reconsider. The clincher was Aberdeen's assertion that Russell's Reform Bill was open to amendment. This was enough for Palmerston, and he rejoined the cabinet safe in the knowledge that many would interpret his u-turn as a response to the harder line the government was taking against Russia.

Even the queen was coming round to Palmerston's method of dealing with international bullies: that is, standing up to them. The advantage of his mode of proceeding, she told Clarendon, was that it 'threatened steps which it was hoped would not become necessary, whilst those hitherto taken, started on the principle of not needlessly offending Russia by threats, obliging us at the same time to take the very steps which we refused to threaten'. She stopped short of admitting that a firmer line from the start might have prevented war; but she did seem to accept that if Palmerston had been listened to in the first place, and the fleet sent into the Black Sea earlier, the Sinope massacre could have been avoided.

Few Britons, soldiers least of all, were now in any doubt that war was imminent. 'War with Russia at this time was the principal topic of conversation, at Mess, in stables,' recorded Sergeant-Major George Loy Smith of the 11th Hussars. 'In fact everywhere when we met and had an opportunity of discussing the subject.' So powerful was Russophobia that sections of the press began to attack Prince Albert for his apparently pro-Russian stance, accusing him of causing Palmerston's resignation and generally interfering in state affairs that were not his business. A *Punch* cartoon, the most reliable reflection of popular opinion, depicted the prince skating, in defiance of warning, over thin ice. But Aberdeen was quick to assure the queen that, though the position of consort was not 'provided for by the Constitution', he for one had always considered it 'an estimable blessing that your Majesty should possess so able, so zealous, and so disinterested an adviser'. He promised to defend the prince in parliament when it reconvened at the end of January 1854 – and was as good as his word. He spoke in the Lords, Russell in the Commons. Their assertion of the prince's right to advise the queen was concurred in by the leaders of the Opposition in both houses.

By then Napoleon III had written to Tsar Nicholas on behalf of the French and British governments, offering to renew negotiations and to withdraw all ships from the Black Sea if he withdrew from the Danubian principalities. But he also warned that if his proposal was rejected, Britain and France would declare war. The tsar's scornful reply was that France would find Russia every bit as inhospitable as it had in 1812, the last time a Napoleon invaded its soil. He followed this up, in early February, by withdrawing his ambassadors from Paris and London. 'I still say that war is not inevitable,' wrote an out-of-touch Aberdeen to his foreign secretary. 'Unless, indeed, we are determined to have it; which, for all I know, may be the case.' It was. On 9 February, as a precaution, the duke of Newcastle under Lyme, secretary for war and the colonies, issued orders for 10,000 troops to be transported by steamship to Malta, from where they could be quickly deployed in the defence of Constantinople.

On 27 February, four days after the first ships had sailed from the south coast, the British and French governments sent Russia a joint ultimatum to evacuate the Danubian principalities by April or face war. Next morning the men of the 3rd (Scots Fusilier) Guards, resplendent in tall bearskins with the regimental band at their head, marched in slow time out of their barracks in Birdcage Walk and made their way through cheering crowds lining the Mall to the forecourt of Buckingham Palace. A young guards officer, Lieutenant the Honourable Hugh Annesley, recorded:

The Regiment halted in line, the officers came to the front, the colours were lowered, and the whole presented arms. Her Majesty, the Prince, and the Royal children, appeared on the balcony and acknowledged the salute, then the Colonel turned to the men, waved his sword, and a thousand voices gave three hearty hurrahs for their Majesties, waving their bearskin caps in the air and by every gesture manifesting the most intense enthusiasm and loyalty. Her Majesty appeared much affected, and bowed and smiled most graciously on her gallant third Regiment of Guards.

'It was', the queen told her uncle Leopold, 'a *touching and beautiful* sight; many sorrowing friends were there, and one saw the shake of many a hand. My best wishes and prayers will be with them all.'

 With their band playing 'O Where, and O Where is my Highland Laddie Gone?', the guardsmen left Buckingham Palace and marched in extended column towards Waterloo Station and trains for Portsmouth. Exactly a month later, with no response to its ultimatum, the British government declared war on Russia. France had done so a day earlier. The first general European war for forty years had begun.

'No nation', wrote Garnet Wolseley, 'was ever committed to a great foreign war for which it was so unprepared.' There is much truth in this. In the wake of the Napoleonic Wars, military spending had been cut to the bone, with the army budget falling from £43m in 1815 to just £8m at the time of Victoria's accession. During the same period the size of the army shrank from a wartime peak of 250,000 men to just 109,000; and of that number more than half were garrisoned abroad. One of the reasons why the duke of Wellington refused to consider any measure of army reform was his belief that it would give the Treasury an excuse to make further cuts. But the consequence for the army was an ossified administration, with the Horse Guards, War Office, Board of Ordnance and Treasury all possessing responsibilities that overlapped each other. The secretary of state for war, who also had joint responsibility for the colonies, decided important questions of military policy. Yet financial matters were the work of a separate minister, the secretary-at-war, whose functions were never clearly defined. The commander-in-chief, meanwhile, had control over the army in matters of discipline, appointments and promotion; but not over the militia, yeomanry or volunteers, nor the artillery and engineers, who came, respectively, under the authority of

the home secretary and the master-general of the ordnance. The
master-general also had the task of supplying the army with firearms, ammunition and greatcoats; the Treasury provided transport
and supplies, in the form of the Commissariat Department. And
there were other competing authorities: an Army Medical Department, an Audit Office, a Paymaster-General's Department and
a Board of General Officers for the Inspection of Clothing. Two
royal commissions, in 1833 and 1837, had reported in favour of
placing the Ordnance Department under the direct supervision of
the commander-in-chief and of consolidating the work of the
most important departments under the direction of a board, with
a civilian minister as chairman. But Wellington objected, and
nothing was done.

The 25,000-strong British expeditionary force that eventually
took the field in 1854 was a hotchpotch of semi-independent
departments that well reflected this administrative chaos. And
thanks to the disbandment in 1833 of the Royal Wagon Train,
which had served Wellington so well, it had no means of moving
its supplies. Wolseley recalled:

Almost all the Civil departments which feed an army in the field, and
administer to its daily wants, had long since been abolished on so-called
economical grounds, and everything that could be done by contract was
so done . . . We had then no military transport of any kind: and yet our
Cabinet did not hesitate to declare war with one of the very greatest
military nations in the world!

The one saving grace was that the constant sabre-rattling by the
French in the 1840s and early 1850s had led to an increase in both
military budgets and the size of the army. By 1854 it had grown
to 153,000, with roughly a third available for home defence. Yet
it still had difficulties putting together the modest expeditionary
force that was sent to assist the Turks. Wolseley wrote:

Every ordnance storehouse in Great Britain was ransacked in order to
collect guns and harness and ammunition wagons for the ten batteries of

horse and field artillery sent to the East for the war. We had, however, some weak battalions of excellent foot soldiers, and a few attenuated regiments of cavalry, the men of both arms being dressed and accoutred for the show. We had no reserves of any kind, and in order to make up to their regulation field strength the thirty battalions of the Foot Guards and the Line . . . sent to Bulgaria in 1854, the few battalions left at home were drained of their best men.

The invasion scares of the early 1850s had also prompted some minor army reforms. In the summer of 1853, prompted by Prince Albert, Hardinge held large-scale manoeuvres at Chobham Camp in Surrey. The intention was to train individual units to operate at brigade and divisional levels, an obvious necessity in the event of a French invasion. But the actual field days were not a success, with units getting jumbled together and moving in the wrong direction. 'This Army is a shambles,' commented one artillery officer. Nor was the Chobham experiment of any value to the Commissariat Department, because the men never slept away from the camp, horses and carts were hired by the day, and supplies delivered by London contractors.

Of more immediate value were the alterations that Hardinge had begun to make to uniforms. Criticism of the top-heavy shako and tight-fitting coatee worn by British infantrymen had begun in the late 1820s. Minor improvements were made to these items in the 1840s, but it was not until two generals of royal blood, the duke of Cambridge and Lord Frederick Fitzclarence,* entered the lists that real change became possible. Both supported the replacement of the coatee and leather stock with a frock coat that provided better protection from the elements and was easier to wear. But because the frock coat was bigger and therefore more expensive than the coatee, it was bound to reduce the profits that many commanding officers made from 'off-reckonings', the fixed

---

* Both were grandsons of George III and first cousins of the queen. But Fitzclarence, the son of the duke of Clarence (later William IV) and the actress Dora Jordan, was born on the wrong side of the blanket.

sum they were paid annually to clothe their regiments. This obstacle was finally removed in June 1854, when the provision of clothing by regimental colonels was abolished in favour of a contract system. Within a year, the coatee had been superseded by a double-breasted tunic (a modified version of the frock coat) and the 'Albert Pattern' shako by a lower shako.

Important changes that *were* in place by the outbreak of war with Russia included an increase in the number of field guns (another of Prince Albert's suggestions) and the adoption of the Enfield rifled musket as standard army issue. Only three years earlier, in 1851, the British Army had replaced its percussion musket with a French-designed rifle: the Minié. Rifles had been used by British troops for skirmishing and sniping since the late eighteenth century. But, while more accurate, they were slower to load than smooth-bore muskets, because their bullets needed to be tight-fitting enough to engage the rifled grooves. This conundrum was solved in the 1840s by two French officers, Henri-Gustave Delvigne and Claude-Étienne Minié, who developed an elongated bullet with a hollow base that expanded on ignition to take the rifling. As it was Minié who had perfected the design, it became known by his name alone. In 1851, after tests, the British government bought the design and began to adapt its smooth-bore muskets. The result was a heavy, powerful rifle musket – .702 inches in calibre and with a 39-inch barrel – that was accurate up to 500 yards and sighted at almost twice that distance. But it was never generally issued to the British Army, because in 1853 it was superseded by the handier Enfield rifle musket with its smaller .577 bore. Thanks to production difficulties, however, most of the troops sent to fight Russia in 1854 were equipped with either Miniés or the old percussion musket.★ Even those with Miniés had little idea how best to utilize their increased range and accuracy. The recently promoted Lieutenant Garnet Wolseley, recovered from his wound and posted to the 90th (Perthshire) Light Infantry in Dublin, recalled:

★ The majority had Miniés: only one of the four infantry divisions sent to the Crimea, the 4th, was still equipped with smooth-bore muskets.

In the early spring of 1854 the new Minié rifle was given to us. Months were spent in teaching the men how to aim with it, and we were ordered to send an officer to one of the newly opened schools of musketry [at Hythe] to learn the theory and practice of rifle shooting. No one cared much about going there, and it was thought an excellent joke when a one-armed officer was selected for that purpose ... We were all too thoroughly ignorant of war and of tactics to comprehend the complete change the rifle was soon to make in the fate of battles, and even in our mode of fighting. All soldiers knew that the Duke of Wellington had to the last resisted the introduction of the rifle musket, and there could be no appeal from his decision. He believed in the volley delivered at close quarters, and quickly followed by the bayonet charge, in which the superiority of the British soldier was instantly apparent.

Part of the reason why the army had failed to adapt its strategy and tactics to deal with the realities of a modern European war was because it did not expect to fight one. 'The army thought small,' writes Hew Strachan in his book on post-Waterloo army reform, 'because it fought small: the problems had been re-solved to meet the demands of imperial garrisoning and home policing, and were therefore adapted to the level of the regiment.' He adds:

After 1815 the empire became the army's *raison d'être*. Here lay the likelihood of immediate employment, and therefore here too lay the argument for attracting parliamentary funds. Furthermore, Cobden not-withstanding, military involvement in the empire had at least some popular appeal. Radicals were pleased to see the military forsake their aid to the domestic civil power. The colonial reformers, the advocates of emigration and systematic colonization, gave the Whigs ... a case for advocating military efficiency. And finally the soldier overseas became a Christian missionary and the harbinger of British civilization.

He also became a military jack of all trades with experience of many varieties of warfare: he had met the Sikhs in battles re-

markably similar to those of the Napoleonic era; he had fought
in the mountains of Afghanistan, and in the bush of Kaffraria and
New Zealand; and he had campaigned in the cold of Canada and
in the heat of Sind. He had learnt many lessons – such as the value
of mounted infantry, of massed heavy artillery and of looser infantry formations – but few of them were applicable to a European
war.

The general selected to command the expeditionary force was
hardly more suitable for the task than his troops. Ideally the government needed a man with seniority, combat experience and diplomacy – he would, after all, be expected to cooperate with both
the Turks and the French. One man who possessed all three
attributes was the commander-in-chief, Lord Hardinge, but he
was now almost seventy, and, age apart, it was inconceivable for
the army's senior officer to lead such an expedition. With Sir
Charles Napier having died the previous August, by far the most
experienced general available was Viscount Gough: but he had
blotted his copybook in the Punjab and was, in any case, approaching his seventy-fifth birthday. So the government plumped for a
compromise candidate: Lord Raglan.

Born Lord Fitzroy James Henry Somerset in 1788, the youngest
son of the fifth duke of Beaufort, Raglan was still a fifteen-year-old
schoolboy when his father bought him a commission in a cavalry
regiment. In 1808, at the outbreak of the Peninsular Wars, he was
appointed aide-de-camp to the British commander in Portugal, Sir
Arthur Wellesley, later the duke of Wellington. So began a close
personal and professional relationship that lasted more than forty
years. Wellesley found young Somerset to be unflappable, tactful,
industrious and discreet – the ideal staff officer – which is why,
in December 1810, he made him his military secretary. Already
Somerset had proved himself in battle, serving with the Black
Watch at Vimeiro, Talavera and Busaco. But the post of military
secretary was hardly less dangerous, and Somerset, by then a 23-
year-old colonel, played a distinguished role in the bloody storming
of Badajoz in 1812. Two years later his ties to his chief were

strengthened when he married the Iron Duke's vivacious niece, the Honourable Emily Wellesley-Pole.★

At Waterloo in 1815, Napoleon's final defeat, Somerset was still serving as Wellington's military secretary, his right arm; and it was to cost him his own when a musket ball smashed his right elbow, leaving the surgeon no option but to amputate above the joint. With typical stoicism he endured the excruciating pain of the anaesthetic-free operation in silence. Only as his severed limb was tossed aside did he pipe up: 'Hey, bring my arm back. There's a ring my wife gave me on the finger.'

After Waterloo he continued as the duke's secretary, accompanying him on a number of diplomatic missions before being sent to Spain on one of his own in 1823. Four years later, when Wellington became commander-in-chief for the first time, Somerset was appointed military secretary to the Horse Guards and remained in the post until his promotion to master-general of the ordnance in 1852. Also offered a peerage, he was tempted to refuse on the grounds of poverty. But the queen smoothed matters by anonymously paying his peer's expenses of £500, and so, in late 1852, Somerset became the first Baron Raglan.

In almost fifty years of service, Raglan had never commanded a formation larger than a battalion, even in peacetime, and now, aged sixty-five, he was expected to command an army. In his favour was his long association with the Iron Duke: surely, the argument went, some of Wellington's genius must have rubbed off on to him. But just as important was Raglan's fluency in French and his reputation as a man of tact and diplomacy. Hardinge referred to all these qualities when he recommended Raglan to the duke of Newcastle in February 1854. 'He possesses great professional experience under the Duke,' wrote Hardinge, 'and he has for this service personal qualifications most desirable in a chief who has to co-operate with a French force. His temper and manners

---

★ They had four children: Charlotte (born in 1815); Arthur (born in 1816 and killed at Ferozeshah during the First Sikh War); Richard (born in 1817 and later the second Baron Raglan); Cecilia (born in 1823).

are conciliatory, and he would command the respect of Foreigners and the confidence of our own force.'

Newcastle was unsure, citing Raglan's lack of 'experience of the personnel of the army' and want of recent service. But he was overruled by the queen and the rest of the cabinet, and Raglan was officially appointed on 21 February. A hard-working, fearless officer who cared deeply about the welfare of his men, Raglan would prove hugely popular with officers and ordinary soldiers alike. But he was used to acting on orders, not giving them, and this fatal flaw in a commander would be exposed to the full before his death the following year.

If Raglan had his deficiencies, then so too did many of his senior officers. Of his six divisional generals, only two had commanded brigades in action, and only one, the 35-year-old duke of Cambridge, was under sixty. The pockmarked duke had never been to war and, not surprisingly, had his cousin the queen to thank for his selection. The pick of the divisional generals was Sir George de Lacy Evans, sixty-seven, who had seen action in the Peninsular Wars, India and America, and who had been knighted for commanding the British Legion in Spain during the Carlist Wars of the 1830s. But even he had devoted much of his time since to politics as a Radical MP.

It was typical of the class bias of the British officer corps that Sir Colin Campbell, now sixty-one, the most experienced officer available to Raglan, was given only the Highland Brigade to command. At Chilianwalla, after a shaky start, he had led a division with distinction. But that was India, where many of the smarter officers refused to serve because of its distance from home and hostile climate. Back in Britain, hampered by a lack of money and social connections, he was just one of many capable brigadier-generals.

The appointment of the 54-year-old earl of Lucan to command the Cavalry Division, however, was a classic example of how money and influence carried more weight than merit and experience. Within ten years of joining an infantry regiment as a sixteen-year-old ensign, Lucan had – by a series of exchanges, switches to half-pay and purchases (the last of which was reputed to have been for the astronomical sum of £25,000) – risen to the rank of lieutenant-colonel of the 17th Lancers. A notorious martinet whose ceaseless drills and inspections had turned the 17th into one of the smartest yet most disgruntled regiments in the British Army, his sole experience of war had been *with* the Russians during their victory over the Turks in 1828. He left the 17th for half-pay in 1837, and since that time his only skirmishes had been with the oppressed tenants of his huge Irish estates.

As if Lucan's appointment was not bad enough, Hardinge compounded the problem by giving one of the earl's two brigades of cavalry – the Light Brigade – to his despised brother-in-law, James Thomas Brudenell, the seventh earl of Cardigan. The popular image of Cardigan today (propagated most recently by the Flashman novels) is that of the archetypal early-Victorian army officer: a poorly trained amateur with too much money and too few brains, as likely to be found aboard a woman as a horse. There is, of course, some truth in this. Cardigan, like Lucan, was a vain, arrogant snob who had used his family's fortune to gain rapid promotion and the command of a crack cavalry regiment by the age of thirty-four. Relieved of his command in 1834 for persecuting a fellow officer, he was given a second chance two years later thanks to his father's connections at court. But he refused to mend his ways, and his overbearing manner caused constant friction with the officers of his new regiment, the 11th Hussars. One feud ended in a duel in which Cardigan wounded his opponent and was later tried by his peers for intent to murder. He was acquitted on a technicality, but scandal continued to dog his career: two courts martial, two court appearances for adultery, blackballed by the leading military club, debates in parliament about his conduct.

History has condemned Cardigan as an unfeeling disciplinarian, and to his troopers he was certainly a hard taskmaster. But he did not insist on rigid discipline out of sadistic pleasure but rather because he believed it was the best way to ensure efficiency. At the same time he never shirked his own responsibilities, was always conscious of the welfare of his men, and in return was respected and even admired. The steadiness of the Light Brigade in the Crimea was thanks, at least in part, to his tireless preoccupation with drill. But he had done little to merit the command: he had no experience of war and, more importantly, had not been on speaking terms with Lucan since the latter abandoned his wife, Anne, Cardigan's youngest sister, in the 1840s. Incredibly Raglan, who knew Cardigan socially and was well aware of the feud, was told about the appointments only after the event. He at once 'protested strongly to Hardinge about placing in such close professional proximity two such irreconcilable men whose antipathy for each other was well known'. His objections were overruled.

Just about the only area of the expeditionary force over which Raglan had the final say was his personal staff – and even this was indicative of a flaw in the system. Good staff work, as the Prussians had discovered, was the key to any army's success, but in Britain an independent staff college did not then exist. Instead the Senior Department of the Royal Military College, Sandhurst, was the only place an officer could gain theoretical experience of staff work. Yet few well-connected officers aspired to such training, and only fifteen of the 221 staff officers assigned to the expeditionary force had studied at the Senior Department. Influence, rather than ability, was the key to gaining such appointments. Raglan's two senior staff officers – Lord de Ros (quartermaster-general*) and Sir James Estcourt (adjutant-general) – had neither experience nor qualifications. His four aides-de-camp, or personal staff officers, were all nephews.

At a time when the officers of the Royal Navy were becoming ever more professional and technically proficient, thanks to the introduction of entrance exams and a gunnery school at Portsmouth, most of their army counterparts were little more than gentleman amateurs. This was largely because the army's purchase system gave little scope for enterprising men to study their profession. Most officers were drawn from a social class educated in the literary tradition of the public schools. 'Few of them', writes

* A post that combined the duties of a modern chief of staff and quartermaster.

one historian, 'were fitted by temperament for this type of education, and the unchanging round of Greek, Latin, and formal mathematics left the majority with a distaste for any effort or discipline of the mind. They were content to be gentlemen, and to leave the technical questions to those who were not gentlemen.'

Infantry and cavalry officers did not require any formal training, with only around a fifth of new commissions going to graduates of the Junior Department at Sandhurst, an optional rather than a mandatory requirement. Examinations for first commissions had been introduced in 1849, it is true, but they simply assessed 'the elementary principles of a liberal education', as opposed to specific military knowledge, and were not difficult to pass. (Nor, especially, were the examinations for the rank of captain, introduced a year later.) Even gunner and sapper officers – all of whom had to pass through the Royal Military Academy, Woolwich – lacked adequate scientific training.*

Of course there were men who took their profession seriously: ambitious young officers like Garnet Wolseley, Evelyn Wood and Fred Roberts, all commissioned in the early 1850s and all future field marshals, became as adept in the theory as the practice of war. But attitudes took time to change. Even Wolseley was prepared to admit in 1854 that he and his fellow regimental officers were 'thoroughly ignorant of war and of tactics'. A decade later and a guards officer was lamenting the 'want of scientific knowledge in our officers'. They would 'often fight bravely and sacrifice a lot of men', he explained, 'for simple want of knowledge of principles to know when and how to retire'. The creation of a permanent Staff College and the abolition of the purchase system, in 1858 and 1871 respectively, were both attempts to create a better-educated, more professional army officer corps. Yet their benefits would take many years to realize, and, during Victoria's reign at least, the prejudice against 'intellectual' officers was never entirely removed.

★

---

* Particularly sappers, the supposed cream of the officer corps, who received little practical training.

On 21 March 1854, a week before the formal declaration of war, Lieutenant-General Sir George Brown, commanding the Light Division, left London on board the hired steamer *Golden Fleece* with a battalion of riflemen and W. H. Russell of *The Times*. A stocky and forthright Irishman who had made his name covering Irish politics, Russell had been assured by his editor, the legendary J. T. Delane, that the war would be over by the summer. He did not return for two years, by which time his candid reports had made him a household name. He is generally thought of as the first war correspondent; in fact that particular laurel goes to C. L. Grüneisen, who, in the 1830s, reported on the Carlist Wars for the *Morning Post*. But Russell was undoubtedly the most famous and influential of the early correspondents, men prepared to risk their lives to sate the British public's growing appetite for news. Two factors made war reporting viable: improvements in communications, particularly steamships and the telegraph, which hugely reduced the time-lag between the event taking place and the article being published; and the gradual reduction of newspaper tax, from a penny in 1836 to its abolition in 1855, leading to a huge increase in the circulation of British newspapers. Yet even Russell himself, as he set off for Turkey in March 1854, can never have dreamt of the enormous political and military influence that he and his fellow war correspondents were destined to wield.

General Brown's task was to prepare the forward British base at Boulahar on the Gallipoli Peninsula. Arriving on 6 April, Brown discovered scanty cover, little water and rudimentary sanitation. Moreover the base was poorly sited in a strategic sense, as it was a long way from Constantinople and even further from the battle-front in northern Bulgaria. It was decided, therefore, to establish a new base at Scutari, opposite Constantinople, on the Asian shore of the Bosporus.

Raglan reached Scutari on 28 April, having met Napoleon III in Paris en route, and set up his headquarters in a small hut between a line of cypress trees and the beach. Marshal Armand-Jacques Leroy de Saint-Arnaud, the 55-year-old French commander, preferred a villa at Yenikov on the European side of the Bosporus. A short dapper man, Saint-Arnaud had made his name by brutally suppressing a twenty-year-long revolt in the French colony of Algeria. He later supported Napoleon III's coup, receiving as his reward the post of war minister. He owed his latest appointment, at least in part, to his excellent command of English, learnt during the two years he spent in London as a dancing and fencing master in the 1820s. But the British were unimpressed by Saint-Arnaud's selection. 'He is a regular charlatan,' wrote Clarendon, 'and Napoleon I would never have sent such a man to command for France far away from home at such a time.'

No sooner had Saint-Arnaud reached Constantinople than he began to lobby for the command of all Turkish field forces. He was stymied by Raglan and Stratford, who insisted that the three allies should act in concert – but under separate commands. There the matter rested. On 18 May, however, Raglan and Saint-Arnaud did agree to a request from the Turkish commander, Omar Pasha, to move their troops up to the Black Sea port of Varna, from where they could help to raise the Russian siege of the river fortress of Silistria on the Lower Danube. By late June the British and French armies were occupying sprawling camps in picturesque, rolling countryside to the west of Varna. Their presence, however, was largely redundant. On 2 June, fearing Russian control of the Lower Danube, Austria had called on Russia to evacuate the principalities. To back up the threat, Austrian troops began to mass on her Transylvanian frontier. Faced with Turkish, British and French armies in front, Austria on their right flank, and allied naval control of the Black Sea, the Russians decided to end the siege of Silistria and to withdraw from the principalities.

When the news reached London that Constantinople was safe, the British cabinet turned its attention towards the great Russian naval base of Sevastopol in the Crimea. Ever since Sinope, the hawks had regarded it as the primary military objective – and none more so than Sir James Graham, first lord of the Admiralty, who told Clarendon in March 1854 that his heart was set on the port's capture and destruction: '[The] Eye tooth of the Bear must be drawn.'

Clarendon himself had told the House of Lords on 31 March that Britain was going to war 'to check and repel the unjust aggression of Russia'. What better way to do this, the hawks argued, than to neutralize the centre of her naval power in the Black Sea? And with troops now available for such an operation, there was no excuse not to. Much of the press agreed, with *The Times* declaring on 15 June: 'The taking of Sebastopol and the occupation of the Crimea are objects which would repay all the costs of the present war and would permanently settle in our favour the principal questions of the day.'

It was long believed that the final decision to attack Sevastopol was taken at the famous post-dinner cabinet meeting of 28 June, at Lord John Russell's Richmond home, when the balmy summer air and the lateness of the hour caused a number of ministers to doze off. In fact the doves had already been won over, and the meeting was simply to approve the wording of Newcastle's dispatch to Raglan. It instructed him 'to concert measures for the siege of Sebastopol, unless, with the information in your possession . . . you should be decidedly of the opinion that it could not be undertaken with a reasonable prospect of success'. Yet the suggestion that Raglan should use his own judgement was flatly contradicted by a later passage that stated that there could be 'no prospect of a safe and honourable peace' until Sevastopol had been captured; and any delay, moreover, would be dangerous because the retreating Russian troops could be 'poured into the Crimea'.

Too sensitive to be sent by telegraph, the dispatch did not reach Raglan until 16 July. He was less than enthusiastic about his new objective – and with good reason. He lacked intelligence about the strength of Sevastopol's defences, the terrain and the number of Russian troops in the Crimea. Winter came early in the Crimea, and his army was not equipped for cold-weather fighting. It would be forced to rely on lengthy maritime lines of communication. On the 17th he expressed his doubts to Sir George Brown, his senior divisional commander, who sympathized but warned him that any hesitation might lead to his recall. This decided Raglan, and on 18 July he held a council of war with the French to discuss not the wisdom of the operation but the ways and means of making it possible. Again a number of misgivings were expressed by both sides, but Saint-Arnaud had also received orders from his government to attack Sevastopol, and it was eventually agreed to bow to the political will and prepare for an invasion. On 21 July, General Brown and General François-Certain Canrobert left Varna on a steam-driven warship to reconnoitre the coast above Sevastopol for a suitable landing site.

The strongest protest that Raglan was prepared to make was to inform Newcastle that his task was 'of a most serious character, and the information we have upon the Crimea generally and upon Sevastopol, is as imperfect as it was when I left England'. Should he have done more? Probably. While it was not his place to interfere in politics, he was bound to emphasize the serious military hazards that lay ahead. Whether that would have made any difference, however, given the strength of Russophobia in Britain at that time, is another matter.

What made the situation even more galling for Raglan was that, privately at least, he was strongly sympathetic to Russia's cause, as he admitted in a letter of 4 August to his sister-in-law:

My information is that the Emperor is dying and wants peace. He cannot like his trade to be annihilated and his two fleets shut up in cages, but the Western Powers want to strike a blow which if successful will probably make peace more difficult, for the Czar will not, or I should say, dare not, cannot, make [a] peace which would be humiliating to his country. After all he is right in the main . . . There is not an officer in the British Army who will not cry aloud when he gets home that the Turkish Emp[ire] is the most atrocious that ever existed. It's [*sic*] atrocity surpasses all description.

By then, a more pressing reason to abandon the tightly packed and poorly sanitized camps around Varna had arisen: cholera. Prevalent throughout southern Europe that summer, the disease first appeared in the French camp on 19 July and quickly spread to the British. 'The cholera is amongst us!' wrote Fanny Duberly, the wife of the 8th Hussars' paymaster. 'It is not in *our* camp, but it is in that of the Light Division, and sixteen men have died of it this day in the Rifles.' The allies tried to alleviate the problem by shifting camp – but to no avail. By the time they embarked from Varna, in early September, more than 10,000 lives – or 15 per cent of the total force – had been lost to cholera, fever and dysentery. Two thirds of the dead were French.

Brown and Canrobert returned from their reconnaissance on 28 July, having selected the River Katcha, seven miles north of Sevastopol, as the landing site. But the expedition was delayed by a further month while Raglan obtained more intelligence, supplies were arranged, and flat-bottomed landing craft were constructed. The embarkations finally began in late August, and by 6 September the first wave was complete, with 24,000 French, 23,000 British and 5,000 Turkish troops crammed aboard a variety of vessels.★ In order to make room for the soldiers, many essentials were left behind, including tents, medical equipment, baggage animals and spare horses. The British heavy cavalry was also ordered to remain at Varna, as were army wives, though a number of them – Mrs Duberly included – were smuggled on to ships. Cholera provided a little extra space as scores of new corpses were tipped overboard and left to bob in the water.

★ A further 6,000 French, 1,000 British (the Heavy Brigade of cavalry) and 2,000 Turkish would follow in the second wave a few days later, bringing the total invasion force up to 61,000 men.

# 8. Crimea

The huge allied invasion force at last got under way during the morning of 7 September 1854. 'Six hundred sail of all kinds,' wrote a British cavalryman. 'English, French, and Turkish, including men-of-war of all sizes, from the huge three-decker to the tiny gun-boat; steam transports of the heaviest tonnage, sailing ships of all sizes laden with troops, horses, munitions of war, and stores of all kinds that could be got together.' The following day, at a conference on board the French flagship *Ville de Paris* – attended by neither Raglan, who was unable to board the ship with only one arm, nor Saint-Arnaud, who was ill in bed – it was agreed that the initial choice of landing site was too close to Sevastopol, and that Raglan should go and see for himself. He set off in his steam-driven flagship *Caradoc* on 9 September – accompanied by three warships and a gaggle of allied generals and admirals – and arrived off the Crimean coast the following morning. Little attention was paid to the flotilla as it steamed past Sevastopol and along the northern shoreline. After much toing and froing, the allied commanders selected as the new landing site a low-lying stretch of beach, forty miles north of Sevastopol, known ominously as Calamita Bay. It was a sound choice: big enough to accommodate both armies, its left flank protected by a salt marsh, and far enough away from Sevastopol to reduce the chances of an opposed landing. Its chief drawback was that it lay at least two marches from the allied objective: time in which the Russians could strengthen their defences and prepare a counter-stroke. Surprise had been sacrificed for safety – a cautious strategy that rarely saves lives.

The landings began on 14 September in fine weather and were, as anticipated, unopposed. 'For nearly a mile', wrote Sergeant-Major Loy Smith of the 11th Hussars, 'flat-bottomed boats filled with armed men – our Light Division being first – were being towed by sailors rowing in other boats. We saw them leap cheerily on to the beach.' Prince Menshikov, the Russian commander, had more than 45,000 troops in the vicinity of Sevastopol, with more on the way; yet so confident was he that the allies would not land in any force so late in the season that he sent barely a squadron of Cossacks to observe their activities. The Cossacks were soon driven away by Minié bullets, though it took a further four days to complete the disembarkation of all the allied soldiers, horses, equipment and supplies. With hardly any cavalry, the French had room to bring along their tents and transport; the British had neither, though they did have plenty of horses, and so spent considerable sums purchasing 350 wagons from the local Tartar population. Even that number was insufficient.

At 9 a.m. on 19 September, with their bands playing and Colours flying, the allies began their advance on Sevastopol. The carnival atmosphere did not last long. With many British soldiers still weakened by illness, Raglan had given permission for knapsacks to be left on the ships.★ But each soldier still carried his rifle, 'fifty rounds of ammunition, three days' rations, greatcoat and blanket in which was rolled a pair of boots, socks and forage cap'. Under a burning sun, and with water at a premium, even this light load was too much for some. 'I never saw such a scene,' wrote Lord George Paget of the 4th Light Dragoons. 'An occasional shako and mess-tin lying on the ground first bore evidence that the troops in our front had begun to get fatigued . . . Ere a mile or two was passed the stragglers were lying thick on the ground, and it is no exaggeration to say that the last two miles resembled a battle-field! Men and accoutrements of all sorts lying in such numbers . . .'

After a march of eight miles, the allies reached the River Bulganak and many broke ranks to slake their thirst. On high ground beyond the river, Raglan could make out the distinctive outline of Cossacks – with their bulky coats, sheepskin caps, fifteen-foot-long

---

★ The knapsacks were returned to Scutari and not reunited with their owners for many months.

lances and shaggy ponies – and sent Lord Cardigan and four
squadrons of cavalry forward to investigate. Advancing up the hill,
Cardigan came upon a large mixed body of Cossacks and regular
Russian cavalry, and was eager to charge. But he was prevented
from doing so by his hated brother-in-law and superior, Lord
Lucan, who had ridden forward to take command. It was just as
well, because, unbeknownst to Cardigan, a further 6,000 Russians
of all arms were hidden beyond the next rise. Raglan could see
them, having crested the previous hill, and at once sent Brigadier-
General Richard Airey, his new quartermaster-general,* to order
the cavalry to retire. Airey was accompanied by his aide-de-camp
Captain Louis Nolan, a brilliant horseman and noted theorist on
cavalry remounts and tactics, who recorded the 'animated controversy' between Cardigan and Lucan as to what to do next. Airey's
arrival, however, put a stop to all that, and the cavalry withdrew
by alternate squadrons as Russian horse artillery opened fire, killing
seven horses and wounding six men. Raglan responded by sending
forward his own horse artillery, and, having sustained a number of
casualties, the Russian force moved back to the entrenched position above the Alma River, five miles distant, where Menshikov
had chosen to make his stand.

That evening, as the allied armies bivouacked for the night on
the ridges above the Bulganak, Saint-Arnaud rode over to Raglan's
temporary headquarters in a post house on the Sevastopol Road.
In possession of reports from French warships that the Russians
had taken up a strong position at the Alma, Saint-Arnaud suggested
a pincer attack: his troops would climb the high ground on the
left, nearest the river mouth, while the British made an oblique
attack on the Russian right that, if successful, would wheel round
the Russians and cut off their retreat. Raglan agreed.

Next morning the advance was delayed while the strong British
flank guard was realigned with the rest of the army. It finally got
under way at 10.30 a.m., with the allied armies covering a three-

---

* Airey had replaced Lord de Ros, who was suffering from a combination of
nervous exhaustion and sunburn, shortly before the army left Varna.

mile front: British on the left; French on the right, nearest the sea, with the Turks behind. The allies marched in columns of divisions, with artillery in between and the Light Brigade protecting the left flank and rear. Shortly before midday, as the ground started to fall away towards the Alma, they came in sight of the Russian position. It was, recalled Sergeant-Major Loy Smith, 'one of the most magnificent sights that ever man beheld . . . We were now in full view of the Russian Army that crowned the opposite heights of the Alma, their lance points, swords and bayonets glistening in the sun – it was a lovely day.' Between the two forces lay the River Alma, two or three small villages and a gently sloping plain.

Menshikov's position, defended by 39,000 men and ninety-six guns, was later described by Sir John Burgoyne, Raglan's chief engineer, as 'very strong by nature'. On its left, opposite the French, the Alma was overlooked by rocky cliffs that could only be negotiated by a few steep goat tracks. So certain was Menshikov that these 400-foot-high cliffs could not be scaled that he posted just a single regiment to guard them. The cliffs ended, two and a half miles inland, at a feature known as the Telegraph Hill, upon which was posted the bulk of the Russian left. Adjacent to it, across a wide amphitheatre bisected by the post road to Sevastopol, was the 'salient pinnacle' of Kourgané Hill, the 'key of the position' (in Burgoyne's opinion). To protect its upper slopes the Russians had built a hundred-yard-long breastwork – defended by infantry, twelve heavy guns and a number of field batteries – known as the Greater Redoubt. A smaller entrenched battery of eight guns and more infantry, dubbed the Lesser Redoubt, was a little to its left rear. A further five regiments of infantry from the Borodino Corps guarded the pass that led to Sevastopol. Confident in his army's ability to defeat the allies, Menshikov had invited a party of Sevastopol's most prominent citizens to watch the battle from an improvised grandstand on Telegraph Hill. There they sat, smartly dressed men and women, with glasses of champagne in one hand and opera glasses in the other, eager for the fight to begin.

With the Russian Army in sight, Raglan and Saint-Arnaud met

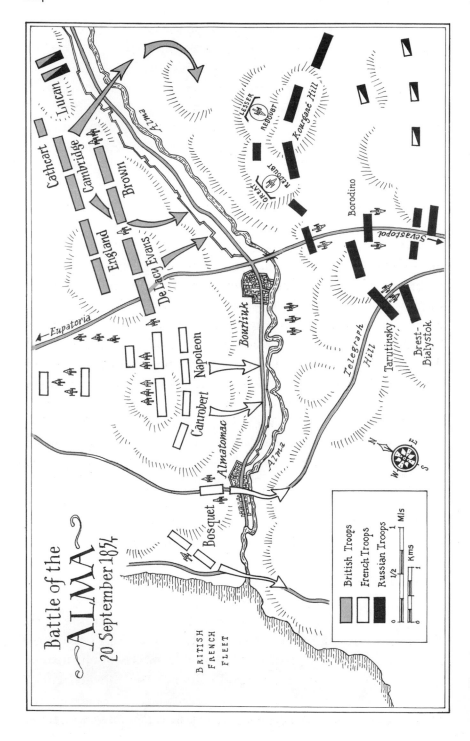

Battle of the
ALMA
20 September 1854

British Troops
French Troops
Russian Troops

Cathcart
Lucan
Cambridge
Brown
England
De Lacy Evans

Eupatoria

Napoleon
Canrobert
Almatamac
Bosquet

BRITISH
FRENCH
FLEET

Bourliuk

Alma

LESSER
REDOUBT
GREAT
REDOUBT
Kourgane Hill

Borodino

Sevastopol

Telegraph Hill
Tarutinsky
Brest-
Bialystok

Mls
Kms

N
E
W
S

on a small rise in front of their troops to review the plan of attack. The French commander agreed to assault both the cliffs and Telegraph Hill. But Raglan, having surveyed the Russian defences with his specially adapted field glasses,★ decided against a flank attack, because he felt it would exhaust his infantry and leave them vulnerable to the numerically superior Russian cavalry. Instead he would make a frontal attack on Kourgané Hill once the French had engaged the Russians on the right. It was hardly the most imaginative tactic and would rely heavily, as ever, on British discipline and skill at close-quarter fighting. The role of the cavalry was confined to flank guard.

At 1 p.m. the armies moved forward until they were within a mile of the river. While the French continued their advance, the British deployed from columns into line and lay down in gently sloping land, dotted with vineyards, to wait. Already they were within range of the Russian guns on Kourgané Hill. A private in the 7th (Royal) Fusiliers recalled: 'As soon as the enemy's round shot came hopping along, we simply did the polite – opened out and allowed them to pass on . . . As we kept advancing, we had to move our pins to get out of their way. Presently they began to pitch their shot and shell right amongst us, and our men began to fall.'

The French troops, meanwhile, had made good progress on the extreme right. Having scaled the heights in two places, General Pierre-François Bosquet's division of colonial troops drove back the lone Russian regiment with their accurate Minié fire. Menshikov responded by ordering a strong mixed force to the threatened sector. But it was too late: the French were already on the plateau. How long they would remain there, however, depended on the success of the attack on Telegraph Hill by the two neighbouring French divisions under Generals Canrobert and Prince Napoleon, the emperor's cousin. At first neither division could make much headway against the heavily defended hill, and they were soon pinned down in the vineyards below the Russian position. At 3 p.m. Saint-Arnaud sent Raglan a desperate plea for help. If it

---

★ They had been fitted with a gunstock to enable him to use them one-handed.

was not immediately forthcoming, the message added, the French might be forced to withdraw. Raglan at once ordered the 10,000 men of his leading divisions to advance.

Faced by a storm of artillery fire from the heights beyond, the two lead divisions★ struggled towards the river. A major of the 33rd (Duke of Wellington's) Foot 'had to pass through a Vineyard with my men, & so dreadful & so *perfect* was the range of their guns, fully ¾ of a mile off, that the men fell about me like leaves, & my charger w[oul]d not move (without being shoved on behind) to cross the river with balls splashing about'. The Russians had set fire to the village of Bourliuk on the Sevastopol Road, forcing the 2nd Division to narrow its front as it skirted round it. Regiments became jumbled together, particularly at the junction between the two divisions where the 95th (Derbyshire) Foot and 7th Fusiliers collided. But, thanks to the efforts of several determined brigade commanders, notably Sir William Codrington of the Light Division, the leading troops crossed the river in open order and formed up in two continuous lines for the attack up the hill. Codrington recalled:

The fire [was] heavy . . . and the officers scarcely able to get the men away from those heaps into the proper formation: I was in front a good deal for example and to lead them on; and in this manner we gradually got up to the entrenchment whilst a heavy column of [Russian] infantry was coming down on the Brigade in column . . . The men remaining somewhat in these heaps, I rode forward towards the battery taking off my cap and leading them as well as I could to the front. Many brave fellows came on, but not much in regularity.

Foremost in this attack by Codrington's brigade was the flank regiment, the 7th Fusiliers, which used its Miniés at 500 yards to inflict heavy casualties on the Kazansky Regiment in the Greater Redoubt. But, as the 7th closed, it suffered its own losses. Lieuten-

---

★ De Lacy Evans's 2nd Division on the right; Brown's Light Division on the left.

ant F. E. Appleyard, who was carrying the Regimental Colour, recorded:

We were busy in a broken line blazing into a Russian column, on their left of the Battery – facing which the 23rd Royal Welch Fusiliers, on our immediate left, had fourteen officers bowled over, of whom eight were killed outright – [when] I received a bullet, a large conical one, near the right collar-bone, which sent me head over heels. After going through Private Barstow's chest, it passed through my rolled blanket, sash, tunic, brace, shirt, jersey, and lodged just under the skin thoroughly spent. Billy Monk, my Captain, was shot through the heart within a few paces of the Russian column.

As the leading elements of the brigade approached the Greater Redoubt, the Russian defenders began to withdraw. General D. A. Kvitsinsky, commanding at Kourgané Hill, recalled:

The mass of English troops, notwithstanding our devastating fire of shot and shell that had made bloody furrows through their ranks, closed up once more and, with new forces, protected by swarms of skirmishing riflemen and supported by a battery firing from behind the smoking ruins of Bourliuk, crossed the river and drove back the brave Kazansky [Regiment], forcing our field battery to limber up and depart.

One gun was on the point of being ridden away when Captain Edward Bell of the 23rd Fusiliers ran forward alone and, armed only with a revolver, surprised its driver, who dismounted and fled. Bell returned to the British side of the breastwork, leading the horse team and gun, an act for which he later received the first Victoria Cross won in the Crimea. But Codrington's attempt to push his brigade on from the Greater Redoubt was not successful. Met by fire from a Russian battery and a fresh column of Russian infantry who were counter-attacking down the hill, Codrington's men fled back to the redoubt.

Codrington needed help, but part of the neighbouring brigade had halted at the foot of the hill. What, then, of the 1st Division, which should have been providing close support? It had been halted on the far side of the river by the duke of Cambridge, its inexperienced commander, and continued its advance only when Raglan sent an express order. Even then, Cambridge was unsure whether to press his attack in the face of such fierce opposition and, according to some accounts, even considered a retreat. His mind was made up for him by one of his brigadiers, Sir Colin Campbell, who, seeing the Light Division in difficulty, ordered his Highland Brigade to form up for an attack on the south bank of the river. 'The Duke at this time came up to him,' wrote Lieutenant-Colonel Anthony Sterling, a member of Campbell's staff, 'and C. energetically recommended an immediate advance, saying that "he foresaw disaster unless we did so." The 42nd [Black Watch] was pushed on at once, marching over the 77th [East Middlesex] Regiment, which was lying down. The soldiers of this regiment called out to us, "You are madmen, and will all be killed!"'

By now the Guards Brigade of Cambridge's division had also crossed the river and begun its advance towards the Greater Redoubt. Lieutenant Annesley, the young Scots Guards officer who had taken such a fond leave of the queen, recorded in his journal:

When formed in line, as well as the ground would allow, we got the order to advance; directly our heads were clear of the hill, the bullets came through us, and before us, [and] at about 200 yards distance, we saw the Russian redoubt, a long low bank of earth it seemed. A Russian battalion was in square close behind it on the left, firing on the 23rd Regiment which was in a sort of irregular mass just in my front, and endeavouring to keep up a feeble desultory fire on the enemy.

At this vital moment, with a huge Russian column approaching, an officer of the Light Division ordered his bugler to sound the ceasefire, believing the column to be French. By the time he realized his mistake, the Russians were on them, and, despite Codrington's best efforts, the remnants of the division fled down the hill and into the advancing Scots Guards. 'To my dying day', wrote the colonel of the 2nd Rifle Brigade, 'I shall never forget following them down the hill. The men were falling fast, and I thought all was lost.'

Half of Annesley's company of guardsmen was swept away by the fleeing horde, but he continued on with the rest. 'I kept on shouting, "Forward Guards",' he wrote, 'and we had got within 30 or 40 yards of the intrenchment, when a musket ball hit me full in the mouth, and I thought it was all over with me.' He and many others were saved by the adjutant, who rode up, revolver in hand, and ordered the guardsmen to retire. Annesley ran for his life – losing his bearskin and sword in a fall – and stopped only when he reached the shelter of the river bank. Despite the severity of his wound – the bullet had gone in his left cheek and out the corner of his mouth, smashing twenty-three teeth and part of his tongue – he survived.

With the Light and 1st Divisions reeling, the battle had reached a critical point for the British. Fortunately the situation was rosier on the 2nd Division's front. Shortly after giving the order to attack, Raglan had ridden forward with his staff to a low rise at the foot of Telegraph Hill, a highly exposed position in the midst of the Russian skirmishing line, from where he could observe at close quarters the progress of his troops. A number of his staff officers and their horses had already been killed and wounded, but Raglan remained miraculously untouched. He was closest to De Lacy Evans's 2nd Division and, when its attack began to falter, he ordered up another brigade in support. But the key to the eventual British success in this sector was the support provided by the artillery of Sir Richard England's 3rd Division. 'Above 20 guns were thus available', wrote De Lacy Evans, '& opened their fire immediately to the right & left, against the retiring & confused masses of the Enemy, which produced a very destructive effect.'

The tireless Codrington, meanwhile, had rallied 300 stragglers at the river bank and was leading them forward to plug the gap left by the routed Scots Guards. Unbeknownst to him, the other two regiments of foot guards – Grenadiers and Coldstreams – already had the situation in hand. As they approached the Greater

Redoubt, the Grenadiers refused★ their left wing, creating a flank from which they engaged a Russian column that was attempting to infiltrate the gap in the British line. The disciplined volley fire from their Miniés tore holes in the Russian ranks. Within minutes the two regiments of guards had retaken the Greater Redoubt and forced the Russians to flee. 'We had merely to pour our fire into immense masses of retiring columns,' remembered one Grenadier officer, 'where nearly every shot told.'

The collapse of the Russian line was due in no small part to the success of Campbell's Highland Brigade in outflanking the Greater Redoubt. Advancing in echelon, with the Black Watch to the fore, they climbed in silence and without firing a shot. 'On crowning the hill,' wrote Colonel Sterling, 'we found a large body of Russians, who vainly tried to stand before us. Our manoeuvre was perfectly decisive as we got on the flank of the Russians in the centre battery, into which we looked from the top of the hill, and I saw the Guards rush in as the Russians abandoned it. The Guards were not moved on quite so soon as our Brigade, and suffered far more, poor fellows.'

With the Highlanders dominating the left of Kourgané Hill, the Guards ensconced in the Greater Redoubt, the 2nd Division advancing up the Sevastopol Road and the French at last in possession of Telegraph Hill, the battle was as good as won. It was 4 p.m. Only now, as Russian troops and civilians streamed away from the battlefield, did the Light Brigade make its appearance, galloping up the hill in column of troops. '[The Russian] dead were lying by scores,' observed Private Albert Mitchell of the 13th Light Dragoons, 'and we could also see that our own poor fellows had suffered terribly. There were Guardsmen, Highlanders and Light Division men in great numbers killed and wounded. We pushed on in haste, expecting to be called into play on the top of the heights.'

At that moment Raglan and his staff made their appearance to

---

★ Wheeled at right angles to the direction of their advance, so forming a protective flank.

a deafening round of cheers and hurrahs as the Highlanders threw their bonnets into the air. Mitchell and his colleagues joined in but were quickly silenced by their troop commander, who told them they had done 'nothing to shout for yet'. There was, however, an opportunity to put that right, with the enemy in headlong retreat. But before Lucan could unleash his men, Adjutant-General Estcourt arrived with orders for the Light Brigade not to pursue, because Raglan was convinced the Russians would make a stand. Instead the cavalry would simply escort two artillery batteries to a position ahead of the main army from where the guns could harry the retreating Russians. Having sited the guns, Lucan and Cardigan each led forward two regiments of cavalry in direct contravention of Raglan's order, capturing a number of Russians in the process. But they were forced to release them when a furious Raglan sent a peremptory order to break off the pursuit. Captain Nolan was aghast. To think, he told Russell, *The Times*'s correspondent, 'that there were one thousand British Cavalry looking on at a beaten enemy retreating – guns, standards, colours, and all, with a wretched horde of Cossacks and cowards who had never struck a blow ready to turn tail at the first trumpet – within a ten minutes' gallop of them, is enough to drive one mad! They ought all of them to be—!'*

Raglan later excused his lack of enterprise by pointing out that the numerically superior Russian cavalry, not yet engaged, was still a threat to his own horse. He also claimed that he had twice asked the French on Telegraph Hill to take the Russians retreating from Kourgané in the flank, but there had been no response.† These were hollow excuses. A bold commander would have used any troops at his disposal to turn a victory into a rout; and yet neither the Light Brigade nor the infantry of the 3rd and 4th Divisions saw action at Alma. It is impossible to imagine any of the great

* Nolan thought Lucan was chiefly to blame for the cavalry's inactivity and dubbed him 'Lord Look-on'.
† Saint-Arnaud explained, in turn, that his infantry were retrieving their knapsacks, which they had left at the river; the sick and wounded needed medical attention; and his gunners were short of ammunition.

commanders in history – from Alexander to Napoleon – acting in such a cautious manner. Only by taking chances are crushing victories won. And the Battle of the Alma could have been a crushing victory; it might even have ended the war. Such was the opinion of Austen Layard, MP, who had been with the army since August. He wrote to a fellow MP:

Lord Raglan & his staff behaved with great courage & were under the heaviest fire, but something more was wanted. Unfortunately the Russians were allowed to retreat unmolested. Had the defeat been followed up, which it might have been as two divisions, the 3rd & 4th, had not been in action & were quite fresh, the Russian army would have been completely destroyed & during the panic we might have taken Sevastopol. Not a deserter or prisoner since taken who does not confirm this.

Though competent, neither Raglan nor Saint-Arnaud had the genius or nerve required to destroy the Russian Army in a single battle. Instead it was allowed to withdraw largely intact to fight another day – with disastrous long-term consequences for the allies.

But that was to come. In the immediate aftermath of the battle, the priority of the allied commanders was to secure their position and treat the wounded. The British bore the brunt of the fighting and so suffered the lion's share of the casualties: 362 killed to just sixty Frenchmen. The Russians lost at least 1,800 killed, with the total number of wounded of all nationalities topping 6,000.★ Unfortunately the British had left their ambulances in Varna, and surgeons had to requisition commissariat wagons to move the wounded. Even those lucky enough to be carried off the battlefield that evening were faced with the grim prospect of being treated by surgeons using unsterilized instruments, followed by a four-day voyage back to the British base hospitals at Scutari, an ordeal that

★ The proportion of dead rose as many of the injured succumbed to their wounds. One historian has estimated the total number of fatalities on all sides at 'over 5,000' (Royle, *Crimea*, 231).

one in four would not survive. Those casualties left on the field, allied and Russian alike, were tormented by thirst. Russell of *The Times* was one of a number of Good Samaritans who responded to their cries by distributing flasks of water. 'We were out for hours among the wounded on the hill-side,' he wrote, 'but all we could do was but the measure of our great helplessness.'

For two whole days the allies remained at the Alma, burying their dead, tending their wounded and replenishing their strength and supplies. Raglan was anxious to press on, but Saint-Arnaud, stricken by an illness that was probably stomach cancer, advised caution. He assumed the Russians would contest both the intervening rivers – the Katcha and the Belbec – and felt that without siege artillery the allies would not be able to capture the formidable Star Fort that guarded the north of Sevastopol Harbour. Far better, he said, to probe the outer defences and give time for reinforcements, including the heavy cavalry, to arrive. Raglan did not agree, but he was under orders to cooperate with the French and had neither the strength of personality nor the will to harangue a sick man.

The march finally resumed on 23 September, and a day later, having crossed the Belbec, Cardigan's cavalry reported an 'impracticable' marsh and a causeway dominated by enemy cannon. This information, added to French fears about the strength of the defences in their path, and their belief that the north side of the harbour had no safe anchorage from which they could be resupplied, led to the joint decision to skirt round Sevastopol, so that it could be attacked from the southern uplands. With panic still gripping the town, it was almost certainly a lost opportunity. But the decision not to pursue Menshikov's beaten army, and instead to waste two days on the Alma, had set the safety-first tone that would be the hallmark of the campaign.

The famous flank march around Sevastopol began on 25 September, with the cavalry leading the way. But Lucan took a wrong turn in dense forest, leaving an unsuspecting Raglan and his staff as the vanguard, an error that nearly cost them their lives. As they debouched from the forest, they came in sight of a powerful

Russian force, the rearguard of Menshikov's army, which, by complete coincidence, was in the process of withdrawing to the north to prevent being bottled up in Sevastopol. Fortunately Airey raised the alarm, and the British commander made his escape, leaving Lucan's cavalry the task of speeding the Russians on their way.

The rest of the march was uneventful, and during the afternoon of the 26th, having bivouacked en route, the British reached the small port of Balaklava. From the north its harbour had the appearance of a lake, being almost entirely landlocked and with high hills obscuring its narrow exit. Yet it was deep and sheltered enough to accommodate the largest battleship. The town itself was on the south-east of the anchorage, its pretty green-tiled villas festooned with flowers and vines. Aside from seventy militiamen, who put up no more than a token resistance, the port was largely deserted: most of its 1,500 inhabitants had already fled the approaching invaders, leaving their homes to be ruthlessly pillaged.

To the north of the town, up a steep gorge, lay a large plain four miles long by three wide. It was divided into two almost equal valleys by an east–west range of hills known as the Causeway Heights. The Worontzov Road, the main route into Sevastopol, ran along part of the heights before dropping down into the north valley and then climbing sharply again up the Sapouné Heights and on to the Chersonese Plateau. It was from this large upland, which could also be reached from the south valley by a rough track known as the Col, that the allies intended to invest Sevastopol.

Having entered the north valley through a gap in the Fedioukine Hills, Raglan's troops had then crossed over the Causeway Heights into the southern part of the plain, where they spent the night of the 26th. The south valley was well cultivated and dotted with cottages surrounded by vineyards and orchards. It also contained two Tartar villages: Kadikoi, on rising ground above Balaklava; and Kamara, towards its eastern end. The inhabitants of both villages welcomed the British, offering them bread and salt, the traditional gesture of friendship.

The French and the Turks joined the British in the south

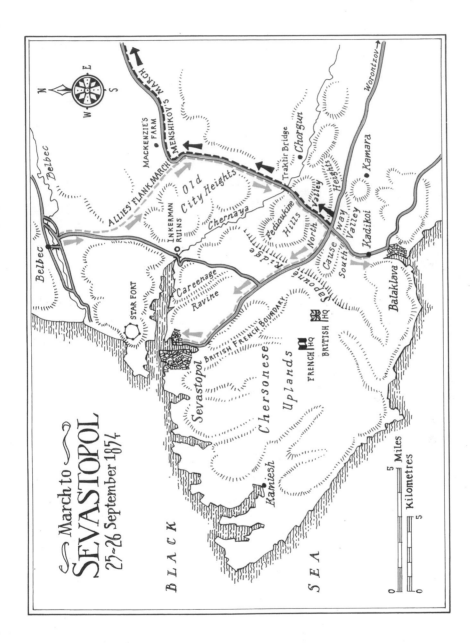

March to SEVASTOPOL 25–26 September 1854

valley on 27 September. The dying Saint-Arnaud* had resigned his command a day earlier, and it was his successor, General Canrobert, who met Raglan on a detached elevation to the south-east of the Causeway Heights (and known thereafter as 'Canrobert's Hill'). A small, effete man with a heavily waxed moustache, Canrobert agreed with Raglan's request for the British to retain Balaklava and form the right of the allied line in front of Sevastopol; the French would occupy the left and be resupplied from two wide bays to the west of Balaklava. But the French general would not agree to an immediate assault. French military thinking was preoccupied with the importance of artillery preparation, and Canrobert was not prepared to sanction an attack until the Russian defences had been sufficiently reduced by bombardment. Raglan's chief engineer concurred, leaving his commander little option but to await the arrival of heavy siege guns.

News of the allied victory at the Alma reached London, via tele-graph from Belgrade, on 1 October. It was at once relayed to Victoria and Albert, who, as usual, were spending the autumn at Balmoral. Aberdeen wrote separately to congratulate the queen on the 'great intelligence', adding his hope that the 'fall of Sebastopol cannot long be delayed'. His preference was for the 'immediate and entire destruction' of the port's defences, thereby presenting Nicholas I with a fait accompli and preventing him from using the forts as a bargaining chip. The allies could then winter in the Crimea, while peace terms were thrashed out, in 'perfect security'.

   The queen was also looking beyond the fall of Sevastopol, which she now regarded, in common with most of her countrymen, as a foregone conclusion. Yet for her the priority was to build on the success in the Crimea by 'strengthening the alliance of the Euro-pean powers, else it may turn out a sterile victory, and the English blood will have flowed in vain'. The government could do this, she told her foreign secretary on 10 October, by responding posi-

---

* He died en route to Constantinople, and his body was taken back to France for burial.

tively to the tentative advances made by Austria for an offensive/ defensive treaty with Britain. Clarendon took her advice, but ultimately the negotiations bore no fruit.

It was also on the 10th that Raglan's official dispatch of the battle, brought to London by his aide-de-camp Lord Burghersh, was published in *The Times*. Saint-Arnaud's dispatch appeared at the same time in the French press. Apart from acknowledging Raglan's personal bravery, it largely ignored the British contribution and made it seem as if the French troops had won the battle single-handedly. Lord Cowley, the British ambassador, complained to the French foreign minister that such a one-sided report would harm allied relations.

Having spoken to Burghersh, the queen confessed to mixed feelings. 'We have received', she wrote to her uncle Leopold, 'all the *most* interesting and *gratifying* details of the *splendid* and decisive victory of the Alma. Alas! . . . Our loss was a heavy one – many have fallen and many are wounded, but my noble Troops behaved with a *courage* and *desperation* which was beautiful to behold . . . Lord Raglan's behaviour was worthy of the old Duke's – such coolness in the midst of the hottest fire.'

But the plaudits were about to turn to groans as the harsh reality of Britain's inadequate war preparation was brought home to the public in a *Times* report of 12 October. It highlighted the lack of medical facilities and was written not by Russell, who had filed a confused account of the battle, but by Thomas Chenery, an Etonian barrister, who was reporting for *The Times* from Constantinople. No decent provision had been made, wrote Chenery, 'for the proper care of the wounded' at Scutari. There were 'not sufficient surgeons', 'no dressers and nurses' and, worst of all, 'not even linen to make bandages for the wounded'. The French, on the other hand, had 'numerous surgeons' and a plentiful supply of nurses from the Sisters of Charity.

At the suggestion of *The Times*'s editor, a fund was established to provide the soldiers with 'creature comforts'. Money began to pour in, as it did to a separate scheme to assist sick and injured soldiers that had been proposed by Sir Robert Peel, the late prime

minister's son. It eventually raised £25,462 for medicines by public
subscription. But that figure was dwarfed by the £1m donated
to the Prince Albert-inspired Patriotic Fund to provide for the
widows and orphans of the dead. The queen did her bit by sub-
scribing to the various funds and by knitting – and encouraging
her daughters and ladies to knit – scarves, gloves and other winter
clothing for her troops in the Crimea; later she would tour hospitals
to visit the returning sick and wounded.

A more hands-on approach was taken by Florence Nightingale,
the beautiful, raven-haired daughter of a wealthy Hampshire
family, who in 1837, at the age of seventeen, had received what
she believed was a 'call' from God to nurse the sick. Nursing
was not then a respectable profession for a lower-class girl, let
alone a lady: most female nurses were either nuns or ill-educated
helpers of dubious moral character and frequently drunk. Yet
Nightingale eventually overcame her parents' objections, and in
1853, having gained some nursing experience in Germany, became
director of a small London hospital for 'Sick Gentlewomen in
Distressed Circumstances'. It was from her Harley Street office, on
12 October 1854, that the 34-year-old Nightingale responded to
a letter in *The Times* from a wounded soldier who wanted to know
why the British had no equivalent of the French Sisters of Charity.
Writing to her friend Mrs Sidney Herbert, the wife of the secretary-
at-war, she offered to create a nursing service to help the Crimean
wounded. By coincidence, Sidney Herbert had already written to
ask her to go out to the Crimea as head of the army's nursing
department. She accepted, and within days her appointment as
superintendent of the Female Nursing Establishment in Turkey,
with a preliminary budget of £1,000, had been approved by the
cabinet.

She left Britain on 21 October, taking with her thirty-eight
nurses. Most came from religious nursing orders and were fairly
typical of their profession: illiterate, hard-drinking and of doubtful
morals. So worried was Nightingale about this motley crew's
future behaviour that, before departing, she specifically prohibited
drunken and licentious behaviour. After an exhausting journey,

the party reached Scutari on 4 November and was taken straight to the dilapidated former Turkish Army barracks that was serving as the main British hospital. Nightingale was horrified. The huge building was broken down, filthy and largely devoid of furniture and sanitation. But worst of all was the overcrowding. 'We have four miles of beds', she estimated in a letter home, 'and not eighteen inches apart. All this fresh influx has been laid down between us and the Main Guard in two corridors with a line of beds down each side, just room for one man to step between and four wards.' It was about to get a lot worse, because on 6 November a fresh batch of casualties arrived from the Crimea. The name of the battle they had fought in would reverberate down the years as a byword for British military incompetence: Balaklava.

Stymied in his attempt to mount an immediate assault on Sevastopol, Raglan had hoped to be able to speed up the bombardment by siting his siege batteries without first digging approach trenches. But when he put this idea to his divisional commanders on 7 October, they insisted that without cover the batteries 'could not maintain an advanced position'. Instead they were sited a full three quarters of a mile from the city's defences, too far away to do any serious damage.

While the allies toiled to bring their guns ashore, the Russians were busy strengthening Sevastopol's southern defences. In overall command was the city governor, Admiral V. A. Kornilov; but the creator of the new defensive system was Lieutenant-Colonel Franz Todleben, the enterprising chief engineer. To protect the vulnerable Malakhov Tower in the south-west sector of the city, Todleben built an elaborate network of trenches and redoubts, and armed them with heavy guns from the scuttled Black Sea fleet. Yet at this stage of the siege Kornilov only had 18,000 troops, most of them sailors, to defend the city, and a full-scale allied assault would surely have succeeded.

But it never took place, and every day that passed spelt danger for the vulnerable British right flank: for somewhere to the east, awaiting its moment, was Menshikov's field army. To guard his open flank, Raglan placed his two cavalry brigades* in the south valley, from where they could carry out regular patrols and picquet duty. But Raglan knew that cavalry could not stop a determined infantry attack, and, following a Russian reconnaissance in force on 7 October, he ordered the construction of a chain of redoubts on Canrobert's Hill and the Causeway Heights. They were armed with seven British naval 12-pounders and garrisoned by 1,400 Turkish militiamen. More naval guns and 1,200 Royal Marines were placed on high ground above Balaklava, while Kadikoi was defended by a battery of field guns, a battalion of Turks and the bulk of the 93rd (Sutherland) Highlanders. Placed in overall command of these troops on 14 October was Sir Colin Campbell.

Three days later, at 6.30 a.m., the allies opened a massive bombardment of Sevastopol with 126 guns. The original plan was for the allied navies to fire simultaneously from the sea, but at the last minute the admirals realized they were short of ammunition and postponed their barrage until the afternoon. Even then the allied ships failed to knock out either of Sevastopol's two sea forts, and two Royal Navy vessels were so badly damaged by Russian fire that they had to return to Constantinople for repairs. On land, two lucky Russian hits on French magazines, the first at 10.30 a.m., the second at noon, caused the Gallic guns to fall silent. The British fired on alone, and their shells eventually blew up a Russian magazine and reduced the main redoubt, the Grand Redan, to rubble. But Canrobert refused to authorize an infantry assault, and the British would not attack alone.

On 18 October, having received reports of Russian troop movements beyond the Chernaya River, Raglan rode with his staff to the edge of the Sapouné Ridge to see for himself. But he failed to spot anything suspicious with his improvised field glasses, and, assuming it was a false alarm, returned to the front line to watch the bombardment. He was wrong. That day, near the village of Chorgun, Lieutenant-General Pavel Liprandi completed the

---

* The Heavy Brigade had arrived from Varna on 30 September, but lost more than 220 horses during an exceptionally stormy crossing.

assembly of 25,000 infantry, 3,400 cavalry and seventy-eight guns. His task: to capture Kadikoi and cut off the British supply base of Balaklava. Two days later, and again on the 22nd, he used cavalry to probe the allied position. The attack was planned for the 25th.

As luck would have it, the Turkish commander on the Causeway Heights received word from one of his Tartar spies on 24 October that 28,000 Russian troops had concentrated at Chorgun 'preparatory to an early attack on Balaklava'. The news was at once conveyed via Lucan to Raglan. But the British commander had little faith in spies: a similar report had resulted in an infantry division being marched down from the Chersonese Plateau on the 20th, and back the following day when it proved to be a false alarm. This time he dismissed the warning with the words 'Very well' and a request that 'anything new was to be reported to him.'

His inaction was unfortunate, and not least because the redoubts on the Causeway Heights were incomplete and far from formidable: only the first three were garrisoned with both guns and Turkish militiamen; No. 4 Redoubt had troops but no guns; Nos. 5 and 6 had neither. Nor were the finished redoubts without fault. 'I went into most of them shortly after they were made,' wrote James Blunt, Lucan's interpreter, 'and among other defects I observed that their ditches and parapets were so low, that a horse could easily have leaped over some of them.'

Raglan was having breakfast at his headquarters, a modest farmhouse on the Chersonese Plateau, when he received word on 25 October of a major Russian attack. 'As usual we thought it was one of Lord Lucan's accustomed alarms,' recalled Lieutenant Frederick Maxse, Raglan's naval aide-de-camp. 'Frequently I had said before that Lord Lucan's crying about a wolf attacking his sheep when there was no wolf would cause (as in the olden tale) him to be disbelieved and paid no attention to when the animal was actually on the premises.' Such had been the response to the spy's report a day earlier. Now so unconcerned was Raglan by Lucan's latest message that he decided not to ride the short distance to the Sapouné Heights – which had a commanding view of Balaklava and the two valleys – until he had finished his breakfast.

He and his staff arrived at around 7.30 a.m., just in time to witness the fall of No. 1 Redoubt on Canrobert's Hill. Attacked by an overwhelming force of Russian artillery and infantry, its 600 Turkish defenders had bravely held on for more than an hour and a half, suffering 25 per cent casualties in the process. But, with no relief in sight and the Russians closing in, the survivors fled down the hill towards Balaklava. Soon after, the garrison of No. 2 Redoubt followed suit. Aware now that the attack was serious, Raglan ordered two infantry divisions down to the plain: Cambridge's 1st, which was in reserve, and was directed down the Col into the south valley; and Cathcart's 4th, which was in the siege lines two miles from the ridge, and was ordered to follow the Worontzov Road down into the north valley. Neither would arrive before 10.30 a.m.

Anxious to preserve the cavalry, Raglan ordered Lucan to move his two brigades from the centre of the south valley, where they had already sustained casualties from Russian artillery fire, 'to the left of the second line of redoubts occupied by the Turks'. By this he meant beyond No. 6 Redoubt – as it and No. 5 were known as the 'second line' – where the cavalry would be out of range. It would take the galloper twenty minutes to deliver the order.

Meanwhile the Turkish garrisons of Nos. 3 and 4 Redoubts also fled, much to the disgust of Raglan and his staff. They ran like 'cowardly curs at *first shot*', observed Maxse, 'leaving *our* guns for the Russians to capture'. Private Mitchell of the 13th Light Dragoons was no less dismayed. 'We were much annoyed at seeing the Turks come flying down past us crying, and calling upon "Allah",' he wrote. 'However great their haste, they were very careful of their kettles and pans, for they rattled and clattered as they ran past us.'

Unlike their compatriots on Canrobert's Hill, who escaped without molestation, the survivors from the remaining redoubts were pursued by Cossacks. 'We could hear the yells of the fugitives,' recalled Russell of *The Times*, who had reached the Sapouné Heights before Raglan, 'and had to witness the work of lance, sword, and pistol on the unfortunates.'

Fanny Duberly, the only officer's wife to reach the Crimea, was supervising the striking of her husband's tent in the cavalry camp when she noticed that the crest of the nearest hill was 'covered with running Turks, pursued by mounted Cossacks, who were all making straight for where I stood'. Without ceremony her husband threw her on to her horse, and they galloped off to safety. Minutes later the Cossacks entered the cavalry camp and speared a number of spare horses that were tied up in the lines. They were finally driven off by a troop of light dragoons.

By now Raglan could see that the Turkish battalion supporting Campbell's 93rd Highlanders at Kadikoi was beginning to waver. He could also see a huge force of Russian cavalry and horse artillery advancing up the north valley. Assuming – rightly – that its objective was Kadikoi, he ordered Lucan to send eight squadrons of heavy cavalry 'towards Balaklava to support the Turks'. Accompanied by Lucan himself, the squadrons were still en route when the Russian cavalry made a two-pronged attack on Kadikoi.

The first prong – 400 sabres in all – crossed the Causeway Heights between the second and third redoubts and headed straight for Sir Colin Campbell's position on high ground to the left front of the village. As well as 500 kilted Highlanders of the 93rd, Campbell had 150 assorted soldiers from Balaklava and the remnants of the Turkish battalion. He also had two batteries – one of field artillery and one of naval guns – in support. With his men still lying down behind a slight rise to protect them from artillery fire, Campbell rode along the line shouting, 'Remember, there is no retreat from here. You must die where you stand.'

Then, as the Russian horsemen got nearer, he ordered his men to stand up, in two lines, with his bearded Highlanders in the centre. Spotting their quarry, the Russians charged. 'Gathering speed at every stride,' wrote Russell, 'they dashed on towards that thin red streak topped with a line of steel.* The Turks fired a volley at eight hundred yards and ran. As the Russians came within

---

* Russell's vivid phrase was later altered by Tennyson to the 'thin red line' so beloved of Victorian jingoists.

six hundred yards, down went that line of steel in front, and out rang a rolling volley of Minié musketry.'

Colonel Sterling, an eyewitness a little closer to the action, remembered the Russians sweeping off to their left, 'trying to get round our right flank, and cut in on the Turks'. Campbell's calm response was to wheel one company to the right and order another volley at 250 yards as the artillery supports fired roundshot and grape. We 'peppered them again,' wrote Sterling, 'and sent them back with a flea in their ears'.

Up on the heights, Raglan's staff cheered Campbell and the 93rd for repulsing the Russians without 'condescending to form square' – the approved method of receiving charging cavalry. But the danger was far from over, because the main body of Russian cavalry – 2,000 lancers and hussars under General Rykov – had reached the gap between the fourth and fifth redoubts and was in the process of crossing the slight rise into the south valley.

At that very moment, Brigadier-General James Scarlett and his 800 sabres of heavy cavalry were picking their way through vines and orchards, en route to support Campbell, when one of Scarlett's aides glanced 'towards the ridge on his left, and saw it fretted with lances'. Seconds later, the skyline was framed with the unmistakable outline of Russian cavalry.

Each force was surprised by the appearance of the other, but the Russians had two crucial advantages: the higher ground and superior numbers. It was fortunate, then, that a number of allied guns – including a troop of Lucan's horse artillery, some French guns on the Sapouné Heights and the field battery near Kadikoi – spotted the Russian horsemen as they came over the rise and opened fire. Though wildly inaccurate, this barrage may have caused the Russians to halt, giving Scarlett vital seconds to form his nearest squadrons into line for the charge.

In response, the Russian commander extended his front two ranks into pincer arms that would, he hoped, envelop the much smaller British force. But the manoeuvre took time and gave Scarlett the initiative. No sooner were his leading squadrons clear of the vineyard than he gave the order to charge. 'The enemy

seemed quite astonished,' wrote Lieutenant Richard Temple Godman, a 22-year-old Old Etonian, 'and drew into a walk and then
a halt; as soon as they met, all I saw was swords in the air in every
direction, the pistols going off, and everyone hacking away right
and left.'

The first rider to be swallowed up by the dense Russian mass
was the short-sighted Scarlett, closely followed by his aide, trumpeter and orderly. Despite parrying numerous blows, Scarlett still
received five slight wounds and a dent in his brass helmet; his aide
was wounded fourteen times, including a cut through his cocked
hat that would have killed him but for a silk handkerchief he
was using as padding. The pair were saved by the arrival of the
2nd (Scots Grey) Dragoons and a squadron of 6th (Inniskilling)
Dragoons, the next British troops into action. Moving at little
more than a trot, they drove like a wedge into the main body of
Russians and were soon hemmed in. 'There they were,' observed
Temple Godman, 'fighting back to back in the middle, the great
bearskin caps high above the enemy.'

As the two Russian wings began to close in, the remaining
squadrons came successively into action: first Temple Godman's
5th Dragoon Guards, to the left rear of the Scots Greys; then
the remaining Inniskilling squadron, which took the in-swinging
Russian left wing in the flank; and finally the 4th Dragoon Guards,
which did the same to the Russian right wing. The two attacks on
the Russian flanks were probably decisive, though the 1st (Royal)
Dragoons, sent on by Lucan, also joined the mêlée. 'In five
minutes', wrote Russell, 'the Muscovy horse, beaten out of shape
and formation, disintegrated and pierced by Greys and Inniskillings,
reeling from the shock of the 4th and 5th Dragoon Guards and
Royals, retired in disorder. It was a marvellous sight! There arose
a great shout from the spectators.' A relieved Raglan at once
dispatched an aide with the message: 'Well done the Heavy
Brigade.'

British losses were remarkably light: just eight killed and seventy
wounded. Russian casualties were closer to 300, though most
survived. Temple Godman, who rode over the same ground a day

later, estimated at least forty enemy dead. 'The ground was strewn with swords, broken and whole, trumpets, helmets, carbines, etc.,' he wrote, 'while a quantity of men were scattered all along as far as we pursued.'

Some British riders – Scarlett's aide among them – survived multiple cuts because the Russians had failed to sharpen their curved swords. Others were not so lucky. 'We lost a corporal,' recalled Temple Godman, 'quite hacked to pieces, and one man shot; another must die, his lungs came through his back.' The straighter British swords were designed to cut and thrust, but the troopers found it hard to force their sword points through the thick Russian overcoats. Cutting was more effective. 'The wounds our long straight swords made were terrible,' wrote Temple God-man, 'heads nearly cut off apparently at a stroke, and a great number must have died who got away.'

The Russian cavalry had suffered two significant setbacks in the space of a few minutes. But the damage – in terms of casualties and morale – could have been much greater still if the Light Brigade, stationed on rising ground 500 yards to the west, had taken the retreating Russians in the flank. A number of Cardigan's officers begged him to intervene. 'My lord,' implored one, 'are you not going to charge the flying enemy?'

'No,' replied Cardigan, 'we have orders to remain here.' He was under the impression that his role was strictly defensive; but Lucan later insisted that his orders were for the Light Brigade to attack anything 'within reach'.

The time was now 9.30 a.m. and the complexion of the battle had completely changed. Having failed to take Kadikoi, Rykov's beaten cavalry had withdrawn to the eastern end of the north valley and re-formed behind a Cossack battery of field artillery. Russian infantry had also pulled back from No. 4 Redoubt. But this still left eleven infantry battalions and thirty-two guns occupying the Causeway Heights as far as No. 3 Redoubt; while a further eight battalions, four squadrons and fourteen guns were established on the slopes of the Fedioukine Hills. Despite the setback to his cavalry, Liprandi was strongly entrenched along three sides of the north valley.

Raglan could see all this from his elevated position and was anxious to follow up Scarlett's brilliant success by retaking the Causeway Heights. But there was still no sign of the infantry, and the minutes were ticking by. At 10 a.m. he lost patience and dictated the following order to Lucan: 'Cavalry to advance and take any opportunity to recover the Heights. They will be supported by the infantry which have been ordered. Advance on two fronts.'

Lucan understood his objective, but wrongly assumed that Raglan wanted him to wait for the infantry. It was a reasonable conclusion, given the vague wording of the order, Raglan's previous restraint of the cavalry and the fact that horsemen rarely attacked fixed positions without support. The upshot was that Lucan moved the Light Brigade into the north valley, while the heavies remained on the other side of the ridge. They would then be in a position to advance on two fronts when the infantry arrived.

With a shorter distance to cover, Sir George Cathcart's 4th Division should have arrived first. But its commander had delayed before issuing the necessary orders, his men were tired from their duty in the trenches, and, instead of taking the quicker Worontzov Road, they had marched south-east towards the Col. For all these reasons they were behind Cambridge's 1st Division, which was also taking its time.

The final straw for Raglan was when an eagle-eyed member of his staff spotted the Russians bringing forward gun teams to remove the captured naval 12-pounders from the first two redoubts. Some historians have doubted whether it was possible, even through field glasses, to see such detail from the Sapouné Heights. But Lieutenant Maxse was in no doubt. Out of the first two redoubts, he informed his mother, 'we soon saw them to be dragging our guns'.

Raglan assumed that the Russians were about to withdraw and take the captured guns from the Heights with them. His mentor Wellington had never lost a gun, and he was anxious to retain the same proud record. Turning to Airey at 10.45 a.m., he dictated the fatal order: 'Lord Raglan wishes the cavalry to advance rapidly to the front – follow the enemy and try to prevent the enemy carrying away the guns. Troop Horse Artillery may accompany. French cavalry is on your left. Immediate.'

Having checked the wording of the pencil-written order, Raglan handed it to Captain Nolan, Airey's aide-de-camp, because he was the finest horseman on the staff. It was an unfortunate choice: no officer had more contempt for the cavalry commanders than the quick-tempered Nolan. Even the mild-mannered Raglan cannot have been entirely ignorant of this. Yet, with time of the essence, Nolan was the best galloper available.

Some accounts suggest that as Nolan spurred down the precipitous slope, Raglan shouted: 'Tell Lord Lucan the cavalry is to attack immediately.' But such an instruction would have gone against the sense of Raglan's order: which was not to attack at all hazards but rather to 'follow' the enemy and take any opportunity to recover the guns. Or, as Maxse put it, to do 'what any cavalry should do, hover over an enemy who seems inclined to retreat'.

Within fifteen minutes the flying Nolan had reached the valley floor and located Lucan on rising ground between his two brigades. By now the vanguard of the 1st Division had begun to arrive, but 'instead of being formed for an attack' they were 'mostly sitting or lying down with their arms piled'.

Lucan read the order with understandable alarm. Now he was being asked to try to recover the guns without infantry support. What was Raglan thinking of? To buy time, he stressed the 'uselessness' and 'dangers' of such an operation.

'Lord Raglan's orders', retorted Nolan sharply, 'are that the cavalry should attack immediately.'

If, as seems likely, Nolan used the word 'attack' on his own authority, it was a fatal intervention. The order itself had made no mention of an attack. So did Lord Raglan perhaps have a different objective in mind?

'Attack, sir! Attack what? What guns, sir?'

Waving his hand vaguely westwards in the direction of the redoubts, Nolan said contemptuously: 'There, my lord, is your enemy! There are your guns!'

Lucan later claimed that from his position he could see 'neither enemy nor guns', and that Nolan's gesture was towards 'the further end of the [north] valley'. There, clearly visible to Cardigan and the Light Brigade at least, was the Don Cossack battery of eight guns, the sun glinting off their polished barrels.

At this critical moment, according to James Blunt, who was present, Lucan 'appeared to be surprised and irritated at the im-petuous and disrespectful attitude and tone of Captain Nolan, looked at him sternly but made no answer, and after some hesi-tation proceeded to give orders to Lord Cardigan to charge the enemy with the Light Brigade'.

If Lucan had only questioned Nolan further, he must surely have discovered that his objective was to recover the captured naval guns on the Causeway Heights, rather than seize the battery of guns in the north valley. How he could have achieved that against fixed positions on the Heights is another matter. But he did not continue the conversation, because of the suggestion in Nolan's taunting tone that he and the cavalry were nervous.

Stung into action, Lucan made his final plans: the Light Brigade would lead the attack down the north valley, with the Heavy Brigade in support. For some inexplicable reason he failed to order the two available troops of horse artillery to provide covering fire. Instead he simply sent orders for the cavalry to remount. As Lucan was short of aides, it is likely that he asked Nolan to alert the Light Brigade. According to Private James Wightman of the 17th Lancers, Nolan rode up to Cardigan for a 'momentary talk . . . at the close of which he drew his sword with a flourish, as if greatly excited'. It has been suggested that, on hearing Cardigan's objec-tions to attacking, Nolan taunted him by asking if the Light Brigade was afraid. Cardigan's furious response was that he would have Nolan court-martialled if he lived through the charge.

Instead of returning to Raglan, as was his duty, Nolan rode over to his old friend Captain William Morris, commanding the 17th Lancers, and got his permission to accompany the attack. He placed himself in front of the right squadron.

Cardigan had earlier sent his principal aide-de-camp, Lieutenant

'Fitz' Maxse,★ to warn Lucan that the Light Brigade was in a dangerously exposed position. Now he sent Maxse again to 'say the spot we were ordered to attack was three-quarters of a mile off' and heavily defended. Lucan's response was that 'he could not help it and we must attack.'

To ensure there was no confusion, Lucan rode over to explain the order in person. 'Lord Cardigan,' he said, 'you will attack the Russians in the valley.'

'Certainly, my lord,' replied Cardigan, 'but allow me to point out to you that there is a battery in front, a battery on each flank, and the ground is covered with Russian riflemen.'

'I cannot help that,' was the retort; 'it is Lord Raglan's positive order that the Light Brigade is to attack the enemy.'

Except that it was not. Many years later Lucan claimed that he was holding Airey's pencil-written order when he spoke to Cardigan, and that he gave him 'its contents so far as they concerned him'. He added: 'I would not on oath say that I did not read the order to him.' But in an earlier speech to the House of Lords in March 1855, responding to Raglan's regret that he did not show the order to Cardigan, he said there was 'no more reason' to show it to Cardigan than to Scarlett, 'because it was not intended to be an operation of one, but of both brigades'. Furthermore, in his many written accounts of the encounter, Cardigan makes no mention of Airey's order. If he had read it, or had had it read out to him, would it have made any difference? Possibly. Because Cardigan would have then been in a position to query how such an order could possibly be interpreted to mean an attack down the valley rather than a foray along the Heights. This might, just might, have caused Lucan to seek further clarification from Nolan (or even Raglan). The discord between the two brothers-in-law did not cause the charge of the Light Brigade, but it may have resulted in the loss of the last chance to avert it.

With his fate sealed, Cardigan returned to his position at the

★ The brother of Lieutenant Frederick Maxse, RN, Raglan's naval aide-de-camp.

head of the brigade. Tall, handsome and ramrod straight, wearing the striking blue and gold tunic, cherrypicker trousers and fur busby of his old regiment, the 11th Hussars, he cut a magnificent figure astride his chestnut charger Ronald. Behind him were his staff officers – Maxse and Sir George Wombwell – in their blue coats and cocked hats, themselves a little way ahead of the leading regiments, the 17th Lancers and 13th Light Dragoons, deployed side by side in two lines. Next came the 11th Hussars, one hundred yards further back; and bringing up the rear, the same distance back still, were the 8th Hussars and the 4th Light Dragoons.

'Here goes the last of the Brudenells,'* muttered Cardigan, as he turned to face the massed ranks behind him. 'Sound the advance!' It was 11.10 a.m.

The 676 riders were still at the trot when Captain Nolan surged ahead of the first line and veered to the right, shouting and waving his sword. He may have realized that Cardigan was not going to wheel right to attack the redoubts, and was trying to correct the awful error. Or he may simply have been urging the brigade on. We will never know. With just fifty yards separating him from Cardigan, a shell burst between them. Nolan gave a ghastly shriek, the sword dropped from his raised arm, and his trunk contorted inwards in spasm. This convulsive twitch of his bridle hand caused his horse to turn and gallop back through the interval between the advancing squadrons of 13th Light Dragoons. A fragment of shrapnel had pierced his heart, killing him instantly.

Onward the brigade rode into that terrible crossfire. 'Hell had opened upon us from front and either flank,'† recalled Private Wightman of the 17th,

and it kept open upon us during the minutes – they seemed like hours – which passed while we traversed the mile and a quarter at the end of which was the enemy. The broken and fast-thinning ranks raised rugged

---

* Cardigan's family name was James Thomas Brudenell.
† In truth the Russian batteries on three sides of the valley opened and ceased fire, one after the other, as the Light Brigade rode into and out of range.

peals of wild fierce cheering that only swelled the louder as the shot and
shell from the battery tore gaps through us, and the enfilading musketry
fire from the Infantry in both flanks brought down horses and men . . .
'Close in! close in!' was the constant command of the squadron and
troop officers as the casualties made gaps in the ragged line, but the
order was scarcely needed, for of their own instance, and, as it seemed,
mechanically, men and horses alike sought to regain the touch.

A corporal who rode on the right of the 13th was 'struck by a shot
or shell full in the face, completely smashing it, his blood and
brains spattering us who rode near'. A sergeant of the 17th had his
head taken off by roundshot, 'yet for about thirty yards further the
headless body kept the saddle, the lance at the charge firmly gripped
under the right arm.' Wightman was hit in the right knee and shin
by musket balls, his horse wounded three times in the neck, yet
he refused to fall out. Amidst the cacophony of battle, Cardigan
ordered his trumpeter to sound the gallop, but the man never had
the chance to sound the charge because seconds later he was
unhorsed.

With the front rank just eighty yards from the guns, the Cossacks fired a point-blank salvo of grapeshot that brought down
men and horses in heaps. Five officers were among the dead, but
Cardigan rode on unscathed. Just yards from the bank of white
smoke that masked the Cossack battery, he raised his sword in
the air and turned to shout a final command: 'Steady! Steady!
Close in!'

As a last defiant salvo was fired, the front rank swept into and
around the battery. While some gunners hid under their gun
carriages and limbers, others were sabred and speared as they tried
to tow the guns to safety. In the smoke and confusion, Cardigan
became separated from his men and made his own way back to
the British lines. The remnants of the brigade were rallied by the
surviving officers and led on in a desperate charge against the
massed ranks of Russian cavalrymen beyond.

'It was the maddest thing that was ever done,' wrote a Russian
officer. 'They broke through our lines, took our artillery, and then,

instead of capturing our guns and making off with them, they went for us . . . They dashed in amongst us, shouting, cheering and cursing. I never saw anything like it. They seemed perfectly irresistible, and our fellows were quite demoralized.'

The Russian cavalry fled as far as a viaduct at the far end of the valley, a bottleneck that forced them to turn and face their pursuers. Only then, realizing their vast superiority in numbers, did the hunted become the hunters. Forced back towards the guns, their line of retreat cut off by 500 Russian lancers who had ridden down from both sides of the valley, the survivors appeared doomed. Yet somehow they managed to hack their way out. 'We got by them without, I believe, the loss of a single man,' recalled Lord George Paget. 'How I know not! Had that force been composed of English *ladies*, I don't think one of us could have escaped.'

Some did not. Wightman was with one of the last groups to break out. But he and his comrades lost their way in the smoke, and, instead of retiring up the valley, they veered on to the lower slopes of the Causeway Heights, where they were engaged by Russian infantry. Wightman recalled:

My horse was shot dead, riddled with bullets. One bullet struck me on the forehead, another passed through the top of my shoulder; while struggling out from under my dead horse a Cossack standing over me stabbed me with his lance once in the neck near the jugular, again above the collar bone, several times in the back, and once under the short rib; and when, having regained my feet, I was trying to draw my sword, he sent his lance through the palm of my hand. I believe he would have succeeded in killing me, clumsy as he was, if I had not blinded him for the moment with a handful of sand.

Wightman was taken prisoner. Unable to walk, he was offered a piggy-back by another captive, Private Thomas Fletcher of the 4th Light Dragoons. While being carried, he noticed Fletcher had been shot in the head. 'When I told him of this,' remembered Wightman, 'his only answer was, "Oh, never mind that, it's not

much, I don't think." But it was that much that he died of the
wound a few days later; and here he was, a doomed man himself,
making light of a mortal wound, and carrying a chance comrade
of another regiment on his back.'

When the battered remnants of the Light Brigade formed up
near the same ground they had charged from twenty-five minutes
earlier, only 195 men out of 676 were still mounted. Even with
the return of dismounted stragglers and riderless horses, the losses
were crippling: 107 killed, 187 wounded and around fifty missing
(most of them captured). The number of dead horses, killed or so
badly wounded they had to be shot, was almost 400.

The human casualties would have been even worse had not
two squadrons of French colonial cavalry – Chasseurs d'Afrique –
advanced upon and forced the withdrawal of the Russian battery
on the Fedioukine Heights during the charge. The Heavy Brigade's
support was less effective. Lucan had planned to lead it in a second
wave, but so severe was the Russian fire that he changed his mind.
The brigade was halted opposite No. 3 Redoubt and eventually
withdrawn. In those few minutes the heavies suffered more casualties than they had during their victorious charge.

Raglan, meanwhile, had watched the drama unfold with mounting horror. When it was over, he rode down into the valley to
question Cardigan. 'What do you mean, sir,' he asked, 'by attacking
a battery in front, contrary to all the usages of warfare and the
custom of the service?'

'My lord,' came the plaintive response, 'I hope you will not
blame me, for I received the order to attack from my superior
officer in front of the troops.'

A little later Raglan confronted Lucan. 'You have lost the Light
Brigade,' he said bitterly.

'I at once denied [this],' recalled Lucan, 'as I had only carried
out the orders conveyed to me, written and verbal, by Captain
Nolan. He then said that I was a lieutenant-general, and should,
therefore, have exercised my discretion, and not approving of the
charge, should not have made it.'

Two days later, in his tent, Lucan told Airey that he had given

the order to charge under what he 'considered a most imperi-
ous necessity'. Airey insisted that the order was 'not imperative'.
But Lucan disagreed, and added that he would not 'bear any'
responsibility for the loss of the Light Brigade. 'You may rest
satisfied', soothed Airey, 'you will be pleased with Lord Raglan's
report.'

He was not. In his official dispatch of the battle, dated
28 October, Raglan wrote: 'From some misconception of the
instruction to advance, [Lucan] considered that he was bound to
attack at all hazards.' When Lucan objected to this 'grave charge'
by pointing out that 'so positive and urgent were the orders
delivered by the aide-de-camp' that he had felt it 'imperative' to
obey, Raglan went further. 'There was nothing in that [written]
instruction', he wrote to Newcastle on 16 December, 'which called
upon him to attack at all hazards.' Yet, 'having decided against his
conviction to make the movement', Lucan 'failed to render it as
little perilous as possible':

He was told that the Horse Artillery might accompany the cavalry, yet
he did not bring it up; he was informed that the French cavalry was on
his left, yet he did not invite their cooperation; he had the whole of the
Heavy Cavalry at his disposal, yet he mentions having brought up only
two regiments in support, and he omits all other precautions.

So bitter was the dispute between the British commander and his
cavalry chief that Newcastle felt compelled to recall Lucan. He
arrived back in London in March 1855 determined to clear his
name – but never succeeded in doing so. Did he deserve, however,
to bear the chief responsibility for the loss of the Light Brigade?
Cardigan was not in any doubt, telling his brother-in-law Earl
Howe: '[Lucan] ought to have had the moral courage to disobey
the order till further instructions were issued.'

In truth, all three principals – Raglan, Lucan and Nolan – were
partly responsible for the blunder. Raglan's justification for sending
the cavalry forward – that the Russians were on the point of

withdrawing from the Causeway Heights – was wildly optimistic. Even interpreted accurately, therefore, his final order was both unnecessary and irresponsible. After all, the naval guns had been spiked and could not be fired, the infantry had nearly arrived, and an attack by cavalry along the Causeway Heights was bound to have been costly, if not disastrous. He should, moreover, have taken into account the fact that Lucan's view of the battlefield was much more limited than his and made the order more precise (by mentioning the 'Heights', for example).

Lucan should have insisted on clarification from Nolan. But he allowed his pride to get the better of him and seems to have come to the inexplicable conclusion that Raglan expected him to seize the battery of eight guns in the heavily defended north valley. He also failed to support the Light Brigade with horse artillery and to request the cooperation of the French cavalry.

As for Nolan, so contemptuous was he of Lucan's ability, so desperate for the cavalry to show its worth, that he failed in the one essential duty of a staff galloper: to provide the officer in receipt of the message with the necessary clarification. If the written order was imprecise, then how much more was Nolan's insolent gesture: 'There, my lord, is your enemy! There are your guns!' And he may even have gone further by referring to an 'attack' when Raglan had simply intended a display of force. If so, he bears the chief responsibility for what followed. Such was the opinion – according to Frederick Maxse – of most cavalrymen. Maxse wrote home:

Went down on the plain [after the charge] thinking to enquire after brother & delighted to hear that he had only been very slightly wounded in the foot by a spent 6lb shot, in fact only a contusion. Then rode slowly on towards neutral ground (I mean the ground between our own & enemy). Suddenly on looking to left saw poor Nolan laying dead who ten minutes before I had seen eager & full of life galloping down to Lord Lucan anxious & determined to make him do something with the cavalry (of which he is a member, he was always very indignant at the little they had done in this campaign & bitter against Lord L). All the cavalry lay this disastrous charge on his shoulders & say that he left no option to Lord L to whom they say his tone was almost taunting on delivering the message – if he was to blame he has paid the penalty.*

* Nigel Kingscote agreed. If Nolan had lived, he wrote to Raglan's son on 23 November, he 'would no doubt have been broke by Court Martial' (GRO, Raglan Papers, Box D).

# 9. Stalemate

The Battle of Balaklava, though far from conclusive, was a Russian victory of sorts – their first of the war. Even after the fatal charge, Raglan had been keen to use his infantry to retake the three captured redoubts, but Canrobert dissuaded him by pointing out that troops could not be spared from the siege lines to garrison them.

So the Russians remained ensconced on the Causeway Heights until the end of the year, thereby denying the British the use of the Worontzov Road for transporting supplies between Balaklava and the Chersonese Plateau. In fine weather this was not a problem, as the shorter route via the Col was preferred; but as winter set in, and the makeshift road up the Col disintegrated, it became increasingly difficult to supply the troops at the front.

And yet, as Sergeant-Major Loy Smith of the 11th Hussars was quick to point out, the day could so easily have ended with a great British victory:

We cut their Army completely in two, taking their principal battery and driving their cavalry far to the rear. What more could 670 men do? A glorious affair might have been made of it, had our infantry been pushed along the Causeway Heights with the Heavy Cavalry, and the French infantry with the Chasseurs d'Afrique along the Fedioukine Hills. The enemy was so panic-stricken that I feel convinced that the greater part of this army of 24,000 would have been annihilated or taken prisoners – they having only two small bridges to retreat over: the Traktir and the Aqueduct.

As it was, the allied army was dangerously overstretched. Half of it – 35,000 troops in all – was besieging Sevastopol, the British on the right, the French on the left. The balance, known as the observation army, faced east to guard the vulnerable right flank from an assault by Menshikov's field army: in the centre were the French and the Turks, with the Guards Brigade on the left and Campbell's Highlanders on the right defending Balaklava.

The next blow came not from Menshikov's troops, however, but from Sevastopol itself. On 26 October, taking advantage of the fact that the British siege line stopped short of Sevastopol Bay, six Russian battalions attacked the open right flank of the 2nd Division. In a brief but bloody skirmish known as Little Inkerman, the Russians overcame the British picquets but were eventually stopped by concentrated artillery fire from Home Ridge. Alerted to the danger, Raglan asked the French to supply troops to defend the broken and difficult terrain, including the high ground known as Inkerman Ridge, that lay between his 2nd Division and the River Chernaya. But Canrobert's chief engineer felt it was too remote to be defended adequately, and it was left unguarded.

All sides were desperate for reinforcements, but, with far less distance to travel, the Russians had the advantage. In early November, Menshikov was stiffened by the arrival of two divisions that had fought in the Danubian principalities. He now had a field army of 107,000 men, compared to the allies' 70,000; and, as French engineers had pushed their siege trenches to within 200 yards of Sevastopol's defences,★ there was every incentive to strike sooner rather than later. His plan was to feint attacks from both the Sevastopol garrison and the 22,000 men of Prince Mikhail Gorchakov's army north of Balaklava. The real attack, by 40,000 troops and 135 guns under General P. A. Dannenberg, would be over the same ground assaulted on 26 October. One corps, led by General F. I. Soimonov, would sally forth from the suburbs; the other, under General P. I. Paulov, would use the Inkerman Bridge to advance over the Chernaya. To oppose them, the 2nd Division had just 3,300 troops and twelve guns.

By daylight on 5 November, Soimonov's men had taken

---

★ Unbeknownst to the Russians, a joint allied assault had been scheduled for 7 November.

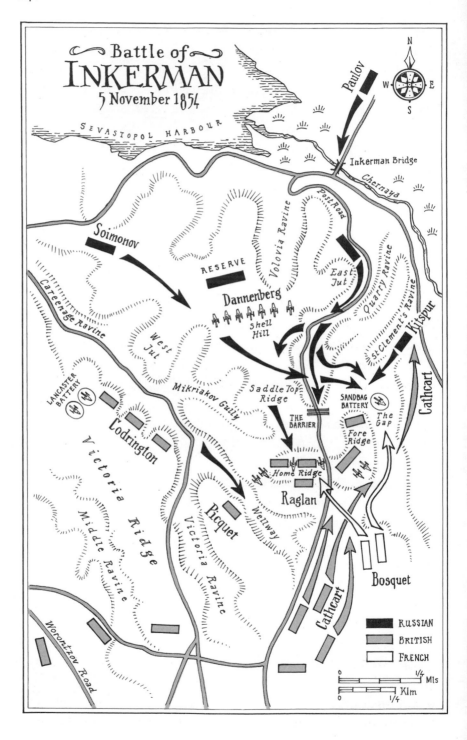

Battle of
INKERMAN
5 November 1854

SEVASTOPOL HARBOUR

Paulov

Inkerman Bridge

Chernaya

Soimonov

Post Road

Volovia Ravine

East Jut

Quarry Ravine

RESERVE

Dannenberg

Shell Hill

St Clement's Ravine

Kitspur

Catcenage Ravine

West Jut

Mikriakov Gully

Saddle Top Ridge

Cathcart

LANCASTER BATTERY

THE BARRIER

SANDBAG BATTERY

The Gap

Codrington

Victoria Ridge

Fore Ridge

Home Ridge

Raglan

Middle Ravine

Picquet

Victoria Ravine

Wellway

Bosquet

Cathcart

Worontzov Road

RUSSIAN
BRITISH
FRENCH

0          1/4  Mls

0          1/4  Klm

advantage of an absent British picquet and thick mist to cross the Careenage Ravine on to Shell Hill, where they sited twenty-two guns. As these guns engaged the main British position on Home Ridge, 1,300 yards to the south, Soimonov's infantry continued its advance across a narrow ridge called Saddle Top Ridge, driving the 2nd Division's picquets before them.

With De Lacy Evans on a ship in Balaklava Harbour, recovering from a fall, the acting divisional commander was Major-General John Pennefather, a foul-mouthed but fearless Irishman who had commanded the 22nd Foot at Miani. Pennefather at once requested urgent reinforcements from the army of observation; and to give these troops time to arrive, he pushed forward his reserves. A company commander of the 55th (Westmoreland) Foot recalled:

We retired gradually before them as they were coming on in Masses of Columns supported by a very powerful artillery and soon had most desperate work, almost hand to hand in the thick brushwood with the guns playing on us in a most fearful way, and ours answering them over our heads, while we were firing musketry into each other at between 15 and 30 paces distance now and then charging and driving them back and then being driven back by superior numbers again.

On their own initiative, Generals Brown and Cathcart ordered up reinforcements from their own divisions. Less helpfully they told General Bosquet, whom they met en route to Home Ridge, that his assistance was not required. The first reinforcements into action were the Irishmen of Brown's 88th (Devil's Own) Foot, instructed by Pennefather to cross the Mikriakov Gully and ascend the Saddle Top Ridge beyond. Captain John Crosse wrote:

The Picquet of the 2nd Div. passed through as we came upon the advancing Russians and an order was given to retire which I thought was for the Picquets and I called out to our men, 'Don't retire, stand your ground', but the men did retire and I found myself close to a knot of 6 Russians who were advancing to attack me . . . I shot four of the Russians, the fifth bayoneted me & fell pulling me down on the top of

him, the sixth then charged on me & [with my sword] I cut down his
firelock on to his hands & he turned back.

Crosse was rescued by a colour sergeant and four men. But the
retreat of his regiment had allowed the Russians to overrun three
of the Light Division's newly arrived guns on the Mikriakov Spur.
With a strong Russian column threatening to outflank the main
position on Home Ridge, the danger was averted by the sudden
appearance of Lieutenant-Colonel Thomas Egerton and 259 men
of the 77th (East Middlesex) Foot, who charged the 1,500 Russians
and drove them all the way back to the foot of Shell Hill. The
main Russian assault on Home Ridge also failed, thanks to the
heroics of the British gun battery and a charge by men of the 49th
(Hertfordshire) Foot. Soimonov himself was amongst the dead.

By now, Paulov's corps had crossed the Chernaya and was
ascending the plateau. As its vanguard emerged from the Quarry
Ravine, it pushed a much smaller British force of the 30th (Cam-
bridgeshire) Foot back from a stone breastwork known as the Main
Picquet Barrier. But the 30th quickly rallied and retook its position.
Meanwhile the left wing of Paulov's corps, spearheaded by the
Taroutine Regiment, had managed to feel its way past the British
right flank, where it found and occupied an empty gun emplace-
ment known as the Sandbag Battery. It too was forced back by
the timely arrival of 500 men of the 41st (Welsh) Foot under
Brigadier-General Henry Adams.

The battle had been under way for less than an hour, and already
15,000 Russians had been repulsed by fewer than 4,000 Britons.
At first the fog had favoured the Russians. But the further they
advanced, the more disorientated they became on ground that was
more familiar to the British. However, Dannenberg still had 20,000
fresh troops, and the majority of his 135 guns were in action. The
British, by contrast, were heavily outnumbered, hungry and short
of ammunition.

Probing for a weakness, Dannenberg sent 10,000 troops against
the British centre and right, which, not counting scattered units,
were defended by just 1,400 men. Fortunately more reinforcements

were beginning to arrive, including part of the Guards Brigade, which the duke of Cambridge himself rushed forward. But they were too late to prevent the Russians from retaking the Sandbag Battery and wounding Brigadier-General Adams in the process. So volunteers were called for, and, led by Colonel the Honourable Henry Percy and Major Sir Charles Russell of the Grenadiers, they stormed and regained the battery.* It was a hollow victory. The battery faced east and, lacking a breastwork, could not be easily defended by infantry; nor could it cover the open ground – known as the Gap – between it and right of the main British position on the ridge. Only as Russian troops continued to appear from the north, on the guardsmen's left flank, did the danger become apparent. An officer of the 95th Foot, sent to support Cambridge's men, recalled:

We were I should think about 60 or 70 yards from the Battery . . . when an exclamation from one of my men drew my attention to the left, and turning round, I saw thro' the mist and smoke a line of the Enemy's skirmishers close to my left flank. I wheeled my company at once to the left and opened fire. At this moment the Duke of Cambridge rode up to me, and not having I suppose noticed the Enemy's skirmishers told me to take care, or that I should fire into the Guards. I pointed out who we had got in front of us, and he then rode on towards the left. Our fire drove the skirmishers, who were quite close to us back, and some of the men . . . began to follow them with the bayonet, but I got them back, and we went on to the Battery, as having both Colours with me, I felt anxious as to their safety.

The fight at the battery continued, with the Russians several times outflanking the position and at one point even entering the left embrasure. But they were driven out, and, shortly after, the garrison was reinforced by a party from the 20th (East Devonshire) Foot. 'They were armed with the Old Brown Bess,' noted Lieuten-

---

* Both officers were later awarded the Victoria Cross for this action, as was Private Anthony Miller of the Grenadiers for saving Russell's life.

ant George Carmichael of the 95th, 'and were able to give their
fire with far greater rapidity, than those armed with the Minié,
which was always difficult to load rapidly.'

At this point Cathcart entered the fray. Most of his 4th Division
troops had been used to bolster the centre and left of Pennefather's
line. Now both Pennefather and Cambridge asked him to use 400
men from his 46th (South Devonshire) Foot and 68th (Durham)
Light Infantry to seal the Gap. Even Airey, on Raglan's behalf,
sent an order for Cathcart to face north. But Cathcart had other
ideas and led his men in a wild counter-attack to the right of the
Sandbag Battery, down the eastern slopes of a feature known as
the Kitspur. Supported by a mixed force from the battery, including
Carmichael, Cathcart drove the Russians before him. Meanwhile
2,000 men of the Russian Iakoutsk Regiment had emerged from
the Quarry Ravine, infiltrated the Gap and were now behind the
British troops in the valley below. Cathcart tried vainly to remedy
the situation. 'He immediately ordered me to get back the Wings
of the 20th and 68th,' wrote Colonel Charles Windham, 'and tried
to show front with the few skirmishers around him and with them
drove back the Enemy twice, but I regret to say he was shot
through the heart.'

Airey had little sympathy. 'Poor Cathcart,' he wrote home, 'so
wild and inconsiderate, was always for performing some action
without reflection or knowledge. What he attempted was quite
wrong & against the orders I had positively given him 5 minutes
before. So sad!'

The survivors scrambled back towards the Sandbag Battery as
best they could, with Carmichael one of the few to reach safety.
Cambridge, meanwhile, had fled the scene of the action with his
ADC. He explained later to Raglan:

I had endeavoured to get our men back but could not manage this as so
many had advanced down the hill with the 4th Division. I saw no men
of the Guards till I rallied them in rear & on the right flank of the 2nd
Division. Here I must record the noble conduct of Assistant Surgeon
Wilson of the 7th Hussars attached to this Division. He was the only

Officer at hand & rallied the few men we could get together & then held the ground to the right for some time preventing the Russians from getting through & enabling a great many of our men otherwise cut off to get back.

In truth it was the timely arrival of the French 6th Regiment – which had been sent on by Bosquet despite Brown and Cathcart's advice – that stemmed the Russian advance on the British right.

Now it was the turn of the British centre to come under pressure. At around 8.30 a.m. the Russians gained a foothold on Home Ridge, capturing three British guns in the process. They were quickly retaken by sixty French Zouaves who had marched to the battlefield on their own initiative, but, in leading the successful charge, Sir George Brown was wounded in the arm and had to be evacuated. Still the Russians made ground, their advance masked by the fire from the ninety guns on Shell Hill. And all the while Raglan, who had arrived on the scene at 7 a.m., was content to let Pennefather direct the fighting. Not that Raglan kept out of danger. He was standing next to Brigadier-General Thomas Strangways, his artillery commander, when the latter lost a leg to shellfire. 'Not a muscle of his (Ld R's) countenance moved,' wrote one of his ADCs, 'tho' 3 were sprawling on the ground close round him.'

It was about now that the remnants of the 30th and 55th Foot were forced back from the centre of Home Ridge by a strong Russian column. All that stood between the Russians and the 2nd Division's camp was the second of the two French regiments that Bosquet had sent forward. 'An immense force supported by numerous artillery drove us to the Camp where a Regt of French were drawn up,' recalled Lieutenant Mark Walker of the 30th.* 'They flinched and also turned then I thought it was all up with our position. Fortunately they rallied and fresh bodies coming up we on the right drove them back with dreadful slaughter.' Amongst

---

* Walker had earlier led the repulse of the Russians at the Barrier, an act of gallantry that earned him the Victoria Cross.

the 'fresh bodies' were Colonel Egerton and the remnants of the 77th who had performed such wonders during the initial Russian attack on the ridge.

Further to the right, 600 men of the 21st (Royal Scots) Fusiliers and 63rd (West Suffolk) Foot pushed a separate Russian column back down the post road and past the Barrier. The victorious Britons eventually retired to the Barrier, where Lieutenant-Colonel Frederick Haines of the 21st organized a spirited defence with stragglers from many units, including the 1st Rifle Brigade and the 68th Foot. On the Home Ridge, meanwhile, two 18-pounders that Raglan had requested two hours earlier finally appeared. One by one the lighter Russian guns on Shell Hill were put out of action or forced to move ground.

At 10 a.m. Bosquet arrived with 2,000 extra troops and twelve heavy guns. The guns helped the British 18-pounders tilt the battle even further in the allies' favour; but the troops were wasted, as Bosquet unwisely led them forward to a position beyond the Gap that was exposed on both flanks. The Russians duly emerged from the ravines on each side, forcing a hurried retreat and almost capturing Bosquet. Yet again the Sandbag Battery changed hands. Bosquet counter-attacked with two battalions of Zouaves and Algerians, accompanied by a handful of British troops. Carmichael of the 95th was amongst them:

I advanced with the [Algerian] Indigenes who charged into the Battery, and drove out the Enemy, a French Officer jumping on the parapet, and waving a tricolour flag for a few minutes. The Indigenes swept down into the ravine, where I did not at first go, thinking it possible that the same incident might happen to them as had befallen us. I went instead to the left to see if there were any troops occupying that ground. I saw none but came across an English Staff Officer mounted . . . He told me that other troops were coming up immediately. Just as we had done speaking, Genl Canrobert with his arm in a sling, Lord Raglan & their staffs rode up to the left of where I was standing, and halted facing Shell Hill. Genl Pennefather came up and was in conversation with Lord Raglan.

It was now 11 a.m., and, having ebbed and flowed all morning, the battle was no longer in the balance. The allies had around 13,000 troops in the field; Dannenberg had more but only 14,000 were fit for battle. His chief priority was to extricate his troops and artillery, and get them back across the Chernaya before they suffered even more casualties. He was helped on his way by the mixed force that Colonel Haines had gathered at the Barrier. With riflemen skirmishing ahead, Haines pushed forward to the base of Shell Hill. He later ascribed the retreat of the Russian guns and the abandonment of eight ammunition wagons to the 'very efficient and enterprising manner' in which the skirmishing was carried out.

By early afternoon the Russians had withdrawn across the Chernaya. Their losses were crippling: 10,729 killed, wounded and captured. Nor were allied casualties insignificant: the British lost 597 killed and 1,860 wounded; the French thirteen killed and 750 wounded. So concentrated was the carnage at the Sandbag Battery that Bosquet dubbed it '*l'abattoir*'.

Raglan was later criticized for not taking a firmer grip on the Battle of Inkerman. But such was the nature of the terrain, not to mention the foggy weather, that overall direction was impossible. Hundreds of isolated actions were fought that day, over rock-strewn ravines and brush-covered slopes, by small groups of officers and men. It was thanks to their individual courage and stubbornness that the allies won the day. But, like Waterloo, it was a 'near run thing'.* Airey wrote to a fellow officer: 'What a fight on the 5th!! Defeat perfect and entire, still touch and go!! If they had succeeded in establishing themselves on our heights we should have gone! Nothing but the sea to fall back upon!'

Even in victory, the outlook was bleak. So shattered were the British regiments that an early assault on Sevastopol was out of the question. It would have to await the arrival of fresh troops, munitions and supplies – and that was unlikely before the New

* The duke of Wellington's actual words were: 'It's been a damned nice thing – the nearest run thing you ever saw in your life.'

Year. In the meantime, lacking shelter and cold weather equipment, the allies would be subjected to the full force of a Crimean winter. Their long ordeal had only just begun.

The first, incomplete accounts of the Battle of Balaklava reached Britain in early November. It was said that four English – and not Turkish – redoubts had been taken and that the Light Brigade had been all but destroyed in a futile charge. Little mention was made, at this stage, of the successful actions fought by Campbell's Highlanders and the Heavy Brigade. Many at home feared that Russian reinforcements from the principalities would further tip the balance.

Not surprisingly, the British government stepped up its efforts to form an alliance with Austria as the surest way to bring the war to a speedy conclusion. It also scrabbled around for reinforcements by asking the Indian government to send what regiments it could.★ Its chief problem, however, was not so much men – though they were in short supply – but transport. The French declared a readiness to send 20,000 extra troops if the British provided ships. But none could be spared. 'We have not a single available steamer,' admitted Clarendon, 'as all must be left in the Baltic until the ice sets in, and the stores, ammunition, and clothing for the Army are going out in sailing vessels.'

A horrified Prince Albert warned Aberdeen on 11 November that the government 'will never be forgiven, and ought never to be forgiven, if it did not strain every nerve to avert the calamity of seeing Lord Raglan succumb from lack of means'. The queen even suggested her steam yacht as a transport, saying it could carry at least a thousand men, but the offer was not taken up.

As the government dithered, the first reports reached Britain of the Battle of Inkerman. Victoria was more relieved than ecstatic. 'We now know', she informed her uncle Leopold on 14 November, 'that there has been a pitched battle on the 6th [*sic*],

---

★ The Indian government eventually sent three regiments: one cavalry and two infantry.

in which we have been victorious over much greater numbers, but with great loss on both sides – the greatest on the Russian. But we know *nothing* more, and now we must live in a suspense which is indeed dreadful.' Four days later, by which time more detailed accounts had been received, the queen wrote to congratulate Raglan on his latest 'glorious, but alas! bloody victory' and to inform him of his promotion to field marshal.* She added: 'These feelings of pride and satisfaction are, however, painfully alloyed by the grievous news of the loss of so many Generals,† and in particular Sir George Cathcart – who was so distinguished and excellent an officer.' Nor did she forget the sacrifices of the ordinary soldiers, whose conduct, she told her uncle, was '*beyond praise*'. Newcastle, in his official response to Raglan's dispatch, wrote:

The Queen desires that your Lordship will receive Her thanks for your conduct throughout this noble and successful struggle, and that you will take measures for making known Her no less warm approval of the services of all officers, non-commissioned officers and soldiers who have so gloriously won by their blood, freely shed, fresh honours for the Army . . . Let not any Private Soldier in those ranks believe that his conduct is unheeded.

Welcome as the queen's praise was, most in the Crimea were more concerned with the practicalities of keeping warm and getting enough to eat. For winter was about to set in, and the British troops, in particular, were woefully ill equipped to cope. A surgeon of the 4th Division recorded on 11 November: 'I find that the men are without camp-kettles, and that each is cooking for himself in his mess tin: frequently he is too tired to cook at all, & therefore some eat their meat in a raw state. I have brought the matter to

---

* Raglan was mortified, telling his staff that he had 'done nothing to deserve it' (Kingscote to Kitty Somerset, 17 Dec. 1854, GRO, Raglan Papers, Box D).
† Besides Cathcart, Brigadier-Generals Strangways and Goldie were killed. Major-Generals Bentinck and Codrington and Brigadier-General Adams were badly wounded, and Sir George Brown was shot through the arm.

the attention of the Brigadier. Heavy rain continues. All doctoring is out of the question, under the present state of affairs.'

Conditions soon got a lot worse. A three-day storm climaxed during the night of 14 November with hurricane-force winds: tents were flattened, horses blown over and equipment scattered. But worst of all the British lost no fewer than twenty-one ships, including the steamship *Prince*, which went down with 40,000 winter uniforms in its hold. For the duke of Cambridge, recuperating from nervous and physical exhaustion aboard the warship *Retribution*, the storm was the final straw. 'I find myself so completely knocked up & shattered in health by this & former exposure to cold & fatigue,' he informed Raglan, 'that I hope you will not object to my going for a short time to Constantinople.' Raglan did not, and Cambridge proceeded to Malta, where he received a letter from his cousin the queen urging him to return to the Crimea. 'The Clubs', she wrote, 'have not been slow in circulating the most shameful lies about you.'

Unfortunately the 'lies' about his conduct in battle were mostly true: years later Cambridge would himself admit that he considered pulling back his division at the Alma (though Campbell managed to dissuade him), and that he was forced to retreat without his command at Inkerman. Though he blamed Cathcart for the latter fiasco, his nerves were shot, and, despite the queen's entreaty, he did not return to the Crimea. Or, as Disraeli put it, 'The Duke's excitement after Inkerman was so great that he had to be sent home lest he should go mad.'

With the siege set to continue into the New Year, and little for the horsemen to do, many senior cavalry officers followed Cambridge home. They included Paget, Cardigan and Lucan (though the latter's return was far from voluntary). The men and horses they left behind, having been moved up on to the Chersonese Plateau, were no better off than the infantry. Lieutenant Temple Godman wrote home:

The winter is setting in and we have just had two days' rain, the misery of which you can hardly realize. The horses up to their fetlocks in mud and slush, through which one must paddle to get at them; the saddles soaked; the tents so crowded that the men have no room in them for their arms, which must therefore lie in the rain. In our tents everything is wet, except what one can wrap up in a waterproof; mud outside, and mud within. The men of course are worse off, most having no change or only one of clothes – of course their clothes get wet in the daytime, and their cloaks, and these they must sleep in as also their boots, for if they pulled them off they would never get them on again.

One of the biggest problems for the overstretched Commissariat Department was how to get enough forage on to the plateau. Its solution was to ask the Light Brigade to send a third of its 330 surviving horses down to Balaklava to collect it. But Cardigan, who did not leave the Crimea until early December, refused to undertake such a duty, because he felt it would interfere with his task to guard the right flank of the army. So nothing was done and when the Light Brigade was finally ordered back down into the south valley in early December its horses were so frail they had to be led. Many were left to die on the plateau, while a further seventeen collapsed and died on the road down. 'I don't think', wrote Temple Godman on 7 December, 'there are six horses in the [Light] brigade that could trot for quarter of a mile. The most miserable starved horse you ever saw on an English common is nothing to the horses here. Our brigade are better, but very bad.'

By the end of November, so overwhelmed was the Commissariat Department, so poor the single road up to the plateau, that many of the supplies that did reach Balaklava were left to rot on the quays. This was in stark contrast to the situation at Kamiesh, the French supply base, where a large hutted town had been built, complete with well-stocked storehouses run by the efficient *intendance* department. French soldiers still suffered but nothing like the British. 'The English', wrote one young French officer, 'will actually exchange their boots for something to eat. In the absence of bread, which we are lacking ourselves, we give them what we can but we never take their money. It's pitiful to see such superb men asking permission to gorge themselves on the dregs in our mess tins.'

With no fuel, inadequate shelter and insufficient food, the British troops fell easy prey to disease. 'I saw *nine* men . . . *lying Dead in one tent* to day, and 15 more dying!' wrote an infantry colonel to the editor of *The Times* on 28 November. 'All cases of Cholera . . . The poor men's backs are never dry, their one suit of rags hang in tatters about them, they go down to the Trenches at night wet to the skin, ly [*sic*] there in water, mud & slush till morning, come back with cramps, go to a crowded Hosp[ita]l Marquee tattered by the storm . . . & die there in agony. This is no romance!'

The medical authorities were overwhelmed. There were still no ambulances to transport the sick to Balaklava, and even at Scutari, where Florence Nightingale and her nurses had begun to make improvements, space was limited and conditions far from ideal. In late December, by which time she had more than 5,000 sick and injured men in her care, Nightingale wrote to Raglan: 'I regret to say that the three last arrivals of men, in number about seven hundred and fifty, have come down in a wretched state of sickness. They complain (upon the passage) only of want of orderlies & of utensils, by which a great amount of avoidable stench results . . . I grieve to find that these men (all landed since the 19th) are more ragged & even destitute of clothing than any of the preceding.'

Gradually Nightingale brought a measure of order out of chaos. She worked day and night, for stretches up to twenty hours, to improve the hospital's sanitation. She organized a washhouse and, with the money she had raised, bought sheets, nightshirts, utensils, towels, soap and screens. Every evening she personally inspected the vast wards, earning herself the affectionate sobriquet 'Lady of the Lamp'. Yet conditions in the Crimea took much longer to improve. Of one consignment of casualties, a surgeon at Scutari wrote in January 1855:

Many were landed dead, several died on the way to the hospitals, and the rest were all in a most pitiable condition; their clothes were begrimed with filth and alvine [of the abdomen] evacuations, their hands & faces blackened with gunpowder & mud etc, and their bodies literally alive with vermin . . . One poor fellow had lost both feet by frost bite: another had lost the fingers of both hands . . . In all these cases the gangrene is far advanced and the whole air of the hospital is tainted with a dreadful stench.

A knock-on effect was felt at Scutari, where the mortality rate was still running at a horrifying 42 per cent in February 1855. By May, thanks chiefly to the work of the Sanitary Commission, which arrived from Britain in March and at once set about purifying the hospitals' water supply, it had fallen to 5.2 per cent.

The most unheralded contribution to the welfare and nursing of soldiers in the Crimea was made by a middle-aged Jamaican called Mary Seacole. Born in 1805, the daughter of a Scottish army officer and the mixed-race keeper of a Kingston boarding house for invalid soldiers, Seacole had acquired a rudimentary medical knowledge during her travels across the Caribbean and Central America.

A widow by the outbreak of the Crimean War – she had been married to Edwin Horatio Seacole, the godson of the late Admiral Nelson – she travelled to London to offer her services as a nurse. But neither the War Office nor Elizabeth Herbert, Nightingale's patron, would grant her an interview, a rejection she put down to the colour of her skin. Undeterred, she made her own way to the seat of war, stopping en route at Scutari, where she was again rebuffed – this time by Nightingale herself. When she finally reached Balaklava, in late January 1855, she began by nursing the sick and wounded as they lay on the quayside. By late spring, on the road inland from Balaklava, she had opened a store known as 'The British Hotel' (a forerunner of the NAAFI), where the troops could buy food and supplies, or just sit and talk in the warm. Her herbal remedies often replaced the medicine prescribed by regimental doctors. During the battles of 1855 she would regularly sally out to tend wounded soldiers of all nationalities, who knew her simply as 'Mother Seacole'.

At great cost to her finances and health, she remained in the

Crimea until the war was over. She was saved from destitution by the fundraising efforts of her many admirers, culminating in a grand military festival over four nights at the Royal Surrey Gardens. She also became the only woman to be awarded the Crimea Medal, not to mention the French Légion d'honneur and its Turkish equivalent. Her memoir, *Wonderful Adventures of Mrs Seacole in Many Lands*, was published in 1857 and became an instant bestseller.

It was only a matter of time before the political consequences of such a drawn-out and poorly managed campaign were felt at home. When parliament reconvened on 12 December 1854, government spokesmen assured MPs that supplies and reinforcements were on their way to the Crimea, and that further steps were being taken to raise troops. A Militia Bill would enable part-time soldiers to transfer to the regular army, while a Foreign Enlistment Bill allowed for the recruitment of non-British soldiers at a cost to the taxpayer of £975 per hundred men. A plan was also put into action to raise a division of Ottoman troops under British officers.

But, with Christmas approaching, and the supply situation in the Crimea showing little sign of improvement, J. T. Delane, the editor of *The Times*, wrote a blistering attack on both the government and the military authorities: 'The noblest Army England ever sent from these shores has been sacrificed to the grossest mismanagement. Incompetence, lethargy, aristocratic hauteur, official indifference, favour, routine, perverseness, and stupidity reign, revel and riot in the camp before Sevastopol, in the harbour at Balaklava, in the hospitals of Scutari, and how much nearer to home we do not venture to say.' A week later he switched his attack to Raglan and his staff. 'There are people', he wrote,

who think it a less happy consummation of affairs that the Commander-in-Chief and his staff should survive alone on the heights of Sebastopol, decorated, ennobled, duly named in despatch after despatch, and ready to return home to enjoy pensions and honours amid the bones of fifty thousand British soldiers, than that the equanimity of office and the good humour of society should be disturbed by a single recall.

Anxious to save his own career, Newcastle joined in the criticism of the British commander. He had heard reports, he wrote to Raglan on 6 January 1855, of 'men in the trenches being on half, and in some instances quarter rations for two or three days together' while there was plenty of food at Balaklava. 'I cannot entirely attribute this state of things if it exists', he added, 'to the badness of the roads, or to the interruption caused by bad weather.'

In this and other letters, Newcastle cited private and unsubstantiated reports from officers serving in the Crimea. Raglan and his staff were understandably furious. 'Did you ever see such villainous articles and letters as that abominable Times publishes?' wrote Captain Nigel Kingscote to Raglan's son in early February.

The latter I really think are concocted in London, if not I blush for a great portion of the British officers are put to shame completely by the men who bear their privations most cheerfully and indeed many officers do. Why they have made such a run against the Staff I cannot for the life of me conceive and no one hits the right nail on the head and which has been the whole cause of our misfortunes, namely the want of transport which as you know is entirely under the Commissariat . . . I have no patience with the Govt, at least with the Duke of Newcastle, and I do not see how he can remain where he is.

Kingscote could not know it yet, but Aberdeen's government had already fallen. On 29 January the House of Commons passed, by a crushing 305 votes to 148, a motion by the Radical MP John Roebuck for the appointment of a select committee to investigate the condition of the army before Sevastopol. Aberdeen and his cabinet at once resigned. More in hope than in expectation, the queen asked Derby to form a new administration. When he was unable to do so, having failed to secure Palmerston's support, the queen turned in desperation to Lansdowne, who also refused, citing age and infirmity, as did Clarendon and a marginalized Russell. Russell had as good as sealed the government's fate by resigning on 23 January, the day Roebuck proposed his motion. He could not see, he told Aberdeen, how the motion was 'to be resisted'.

The only other man who could form a government was Palmerston himself, the people's choice, if not the queen's. 'I had', the queen told her uncle Leopold, '*no* other alternative.' It helped, however, that by the time Palmerston kissed hands on 6 February the queen had persuaded some of the Peelite ex-ministers – including William Gladstone, Sir James Graham and Sidney Herbert – to join the new Whig–Radical government. Other ex-ministers also returned and, apart from Lord Panmure, who replaced the duke of Newcastle as secretary for war, every member of Palmerston's first cabinet had held office under the previous administration.

Palmerston's first task was to persuade the House of Commons that, since the change of government, an investigation into the conduct of the war was no longer necessary. But the House insisted and Palmerston backed down, causing his three Peelite ministers to resign. It was a blessing in disguise. Most MPs, including many of the Peelite rank and file, suspected that Gladstone and the others, far from protecting Aberdeen and Newcastle, were trying to avoid criticism themselves. Even after the resignations many Peelites continued to support Palmerston on the grounds that he was the best man to bring the war to a speedy and satisfactory conclusion.

At his initial cabinet meeting Palmerston began the long overhaul of the army's hopelessly tangled administration by announcing the abolition of the Board of Ordnance and the transfer of its responsibilities to the War Office. The government also implemented existing plans for a Land Transport Corps and the building of a railway from Balaklava to the siege lines. But, even as Palmerston was forming his cabinet, the supply crisis in the Crimea was easing. Nigel Kingscote wrote on 7 February:

Things are very much on the mend. The sickness has received a check. The men have plenty to eat and lots of warm clothing, our only difficulty now being fuel and a want of boots which are hourly expected to make up the great loss of boots in the ill-fated 'Prince' steamer. The French have at last taken some work off our hands but though my Lord begged them to do so two months ago, they never came to the scratch till a fortnight ago.

Balaklava is . . . in very good order, very little confusion, indeed none and in spite of all the lies that are told the Hospital has been & is in excellent order, a little overcrowded but notwithstanding is very clean & sweet.

The French did indeed take over some of the British trenches in mid January, but only after Raglan had threatened to relinquish some of his forward batteries if they did not. By this time the effective strength of the British force had been reduced to just 12,000 men, a quarter of the number of French troops. But British spirits began to lift with the steady improvement in the supply situation, the arrival of reinforcements and the advent of spring. By the end of February the barely passable track up the Col had been replaced by a metalled road. A month later and a light railway was operating between Balaklava and the siege lines. Huts had replaced tents, warm clothing was available, and fresh vegetables and meat were in abundance. 'It is no longer the camp of misery,' wrote one British officer, 'and I could hardly believe my eyes to-day, all looked so happy, so contented, so light-hearted! The poor men lay basking in the warm sun . . . The French stood in wonder and asked if these clean, smart-looking soldiers could be the remnants of the English Army.'

For Raglan, therefore, it was doubly galling to receive Panmure's first dispatch, dated 12 February, accusing him and his staff of neglecting their men, and demanding the recall of Airey and Estcourt. Raglan was also informed that Major-General James Simpson was to be sent out as chief of staff to report on the efficiency of the British headquarters, and that an anonymous source had criticized him for not visiting the troops often enough. In his dignified response of 2 March, Raglan gave a lengthy review of the campaign so far and then turned to the specific charges:

I have visited the camps as frequently as the constant business in which I am engaged, and which occupies me through the day, and a part of the night, will permit; and though I have made no note of those visits, I find from one of my aides-de-camp who keeps a journal, and who frequently, though not always, attends me, that he has accompanied me in my rides above forty times in the last two months.

As for the charge of neglect, he did not 'deserve this reproach', and his staff were 'equally innocent of it'. Airey, he added, was a 'most able, active, and zealous officer', and Estcourt also merited his 'approbation'. He ended by expressing the 'pain' and 'mortification' that Panmure's letter had given rise to.

My Lord, I have passed a life of honour. I have served the Crown for above fifty years; I have the greater portion of that time been connected with the business of the army. I have served under the greatest man of the age more than half my life; have enjoyed his confidence, and have, I am proud to say, been ever regarded by him as a man of truth . . . and yet, having been placed in the most difficult position in which an officer was ever called upon to serve, and having successfully carried out most difficult operations, with the entire approbation of the Queen, which is now my only solace, I am charged with every species of neglect, and the opinion which it was my solemn duty to give of the merits of officers, and the assertions which I have made in support of it, are set at naught, and your Lordship is satisfied that your irresponsible informants are more worthy of credit than I am.

Panmure's reply of 19 March was far from conciliatory. It accused Raglan of failing to furnish the government with 'any details of your arrangements, so as to enable them to support you against those who taxed you with indifference to, and ignorance of, the real condition of your troops'. Panmure concluded: 'Surely I may be permitted to question your judgment without impugning your truth or your honour, both of which, be assured, are as precious in my eyes and in those of your countrymen as they can be in your own.' Fortunately Raglan was saved from the need to defend himself and his staff further by the favourable report upon them that Simpson delivered in April.

Long before then, with the improvement in weather, the allies' thoughts had turned once more to ending the war at a stroke. In late February the French attacked a new system of redoubts that the Russians had constructed at the foot of Inkerman Ridge. But, despite some early successes, they were repulsed, with the loss of 300 men. A week later came news of the death of Tsar Nicholas I from pneumonia and the accession of his son Alexander II. Some of the allied troops were hopeful that the new tsar would seek to end the costly war as quickly as possible. But their hopes were dashed when Alexander announced that he would 'perish rather than surrender'.

Yet, little by little, the allies' position was becoming stronger. In February the Turks strengthened their garrison at Eupatoria with 20,000 troops no longer required in Bulgaria. They soon proved their worth by easily beating off a half-hearted Russian attack on 17 February, a defeat that cost Prince Menshikov his command. He was superseded by Prince Gorchakov, the former commander of Russian troops on the Danube. In early April the Turks were replaced by a French division from Egypt and transferred to the siege of Sevastopol. By now, following negotiations with the French, the Italian kingdom of Piedmont–Sardinia had also joined the allies. The man behind the move was Count Cavour, the ambitious Sardinian prime minister, who was keen to curry Great Power support for his planned unification of Italy. The Sardinian Contingent of 15,000 troops duly arrived in May and, in return for a subsidy of £1m, was placed under British command.

Before then, on 9 April, the allies opened a second massive bombardment of the Russian defences at Sevastopol with no fewer than 500 guns. It continued for ten days, during which time the main Russian positions – the Grand Redan, Malakhov Tower and Flagstaff Bastion – were severely damaged. But still Canrobert refused to sanction an assault, though in truth his hands were tied by his political master, Napoleon III, who was threatening to take over the French effort in the Crimea and wanted neither his thunder stolen nor his strength reduced by unnecessary casualties. It did not help that Napoleon was being told by General Adolphe Niel, his envoy in the Crimea, that the city was too strong to take by direct assault and needed to be invested on all sides. Fortunately for all concerned, Napoleon was eventually dissuaded from travelling to the Crimea by a combination of the British ambassador to Paris and the foreign secretary, Clarendon. Instead he and his wife visited Britain in mid April and were lavishly entertained by Victoria and Albert. The royal quartet got along famously, with the queen mightily impressed by the emperor's 'great qualities'. She wrote: 'He is evidently possessed of indomitable courage, unflinching firmness of purpose, self reliance, perseverance and great secrecy.'

In early April, despairing of a decisive end to the conflict, Napoleon had been keen to accept the latest Austrian-sponsored peace proposal. But, after lobbying from the British ambassador and his own officials, he changed his mind. Palmerston summed up the position of both governments when he told Clarendon: 'We should thank Austria for her office, but her proposals to Russia are too harsh if we decide we want peace at any price, but not harsh enough if we think we can win the war.' Which they did – but it was ultimately down to the commanders in the Crimea.

In late April, Canrobert at last agreed to British proposals for a joint attack on the eastern Crimean port of Kertch, which commanded the entrance to the Sea of Azov and was an important link in the Russian supply chain to Sevastopol. The combined fleet, with 10,000 soldiers on board (three quarters of them French), set off on 3 May. But, just two hours' out from Kertch, the French ships were recalled: Canrobert needed them to carry out Napoleon's latest order to ferry reserves from Constantinople. Too few to go in alone, the British troops also returned.

Raglan was furious and took his revenge by rejecting Canrobert's latest proposal, submitted at a meeting on 9 May, to invest Sevastopol from the north. It was the French commander's last contribution. A week later, humiliated by the loss of British confidence, Canrobert resigned. But, instead of returning to France, Canrobert asked for and received permission to resume command of his original division. His replacement as French commander-in-chief was the recently arrived General Aimable Pélissier. Short, stocky and ill tempered, Pélissier was a no-nonsense engineer who, like Saint-Arnaud, had made his name fighting the Algerians. He at once injected a new urgency into the alliance by dividing his army into two corps and stating his intention to attack Sevastopol at the earliest opportunity. He also revived the Kertch expedition, which, led by the fit-again Sir George Brown, duly captured the vital port on 24 May – but not without controversy. Brown's order to destroy anything that might be useful to the Russian war effort was taken a little too literally, and hundreds of buildings were sacked and burnt, including Kertch's museum with its priceless collection of early Hellenic art. For a time the allied troops – particularly the Turks – were completely out of control, looting homes, killing civilians and raping women. Order was eventually restored, but the damage had been done. Nevertheless, the capture of Kertch cut off a vital supply line to Sevastopol, with the Russians forced to rely henceforth on the overland route.

Emboldened by this success, Pélissier allowed Raglan to talk him into a joint attack on the Russian outer defences at Sevastopol known as the Mamelon Vert and the Quarries. He also agreed that if the initial attack was successful it would be followed by a general assault on the main redoubts: the Grand Redan and the Malakhov Tower. To prepare the ground, the allies opened the third great bombardment of Sevastopol on the afternoon of 6 June 1855. 'The very earth seemed to heave and shake', wrote one British officer, 'from the violent concussion of nearly 600 heavy guns and mortars with which we pounded the Russian works.' The mortars alone continued to fire during the night, but, as soon as it was light, the heavy guns opened up again. By midday most of the guns in the Mamelon, Malakhov and Redan batteries had been knocked out. The plan, however, was not to attack until 6 p.m. to give the assaulting troops the cover of night to secure their gains. The French were marginally first into action and made spectacular early progress. Watching from a battery of Naval Brigade guns was a seventeen-year-old midshipman called Evelyn Wood, who, since

joining the siege the previous October, had committed any number
of gallant acts.* He wrote:

As the signal went up, 25 men jumped out abreast of the trench, and ran
up the slope of the hill towards the Mamelon, from which came but
one cannon-shot. Some Russian sharp-shooters were lying in a trench
half-way up, and firing, killed three or four men, and then ran, they
and the leading Frenchmen crossing the ditch of the Mamelon simultaneously. A Frenchman mounting the parapet waved a Tricolour, and
in four minutes the Russians were driven, from their work. My two
8-inch guns were ready, with fuses accurately set, and we sent several
shells into the retreating Russians before I ceased firing, for fear of hitting
the French following in pursuit.

Within minutes, however, a determined Russian counter-attack
from the Malakhov Tower had not only reclaimed the Mamelon
but penetrated as far as the French trenches. They were quickly
driven out, and, in a supreme effort, the French later retook the
Mamelon and its ninety-three guns. The day's fighting cost them
5,500 casualties.

   The British, meanwhile, had attacked the Russian position
known as the Quarries, a system of trenches on a ridge 450 yards
south-east of the Grand Redan. And, just like the French, they let
their excitement get the better of them by advancing beyond their
objective towards the Grand Redan. They too were repulsed from
the main redoubt but managed to hold on to their original target.
They were assisted by sappers under the command of Captain
Garnet Wolseley, who, having arrived in the Crimea in December
1854 with the 90th Light Infantry, had been transferred to the
engineers. Wolseley's task was to connect the new position with

* The son of an Essex vicar but of good West Country stock (his grandfather,
Sir Matthew 'Alderman' Wood, was lord mayor of London), he dropped out
of Marlborough College at fourteen to join the navy. His acts of gallantry in
the Crimea included bringing up powder through an intense enemy bombardment and extinguishing a fire in the battery magazine. For the latter feat he was
recommended for a Victoria Cross, but it was not approved.

the old British trenches. But when he reached the Quarries, which his old comrades in the 90th had helped to take, he found a 'ridiculously small' British force that was 'entirely inadequate for the double duty of defending the place against the sorties that were sure to try to retake it, and for the formation of a good lodgement there'. The parapet, moreover, was facing the wrong way. So he immediately set his men to work, and, as they toiled through the night, the Russians launched a series of counter-attacks. None succeeded. Yet the operation still cost the British forty officers and 600 men, including the recently promoted Captain Mark Walker of the 3rd Foot, who, with his former regiment, the 30th, had fought so gallantly at Inkerman. Walker was moving up with reserves when his right elbow was smashed by a piece of howitzer shell. Carried back to the General Hospital, he was knocked out with chloroform and his arm amputated above the elbow. 'The loss I have experienced is very great,' reads his shaky, left-handed journal entry for 10 June, 'but I am very thankful that my life has been spared.' His handwriting would improve.

In the brief afterglow of this success, Raglan and his staff found it hard to forgive Canrobert for not authorizing the same attacks three months earlier. 'The deaths of very many men', wrote Nigel Kingscote on 9 June, 'lay with him on account of it.' Yet the coming assault on the main Russian defences was far from a foregone conclusion. The day set for the attack – 18 June 1855 – was deliberate. A great allied victory on the fortieth anniversary of the Battle of Waterloo would not only be a fine tribute to the duke of Wellington, Raglan's mentor, but would also help to heal old wounds by providing an alternative anniversary with which to celebrate Anglo-French unity. But what if the attack failed?

The original plan was for the British to attack the Grand Redan while, on either side, the French assaulted the Malakhov Tower and the Flagstaff Bastion. But shortly before the attack Pélissier decided not to go for the Flagstaff Bastion, which the Russians considered the most vulnerable, and to concentrate instead on the Malakhov and the Point Battery to its left. He also chose to dispense with the two-hour preliminary bombardment in the hope of catching the Russians unawares. The French would now advance at 3 a.m. The British would follow once the French had made sufficient headway.

In the event a mistaken signal caused the right hand of the three French assaulting columns to advance an hour early. Pélissier had no option but to signal the other two to attack, but neither was ready and the operation soon degenerated into a bloody fiasco. Only one column, to the left of the Malakhov, actually penetrated the Russian defences. But its supports were cut down by enfilade fire from the Grand Redan as they raced forward. Raglan felt compelled to act, though he knew the situation was hopeless. 'When I saw how stoutly they were opposed,' he told Panmure, 'I considered it was my duty to assist them by attacking myself . . . If the troops had remained in the trenches, the French would have attributed their non-success to our refusal to participate in the operation.'

Two columns took part in the assault: one from the Quarries; the other from trenches a little to the left. Each was comprised of 400 bayonets, 100 skirmishers, 120 men carrying ladders, sixty carrying wool sacks to lay in the ditches and ten engineers. A further 800 bayonets and a working party of 400 men were in reserve. The assaulters' task: to cross 400 yards of open ground and penetrate the intricate defensive system known as the Grand Redan. It was 'formed of two faces', wrote Evelyn Wood, who rose from his sickbed to join the assault.

. . . each of 70 yards in length, meeting in a salient, the lines of parapet being continued to works on either flank. It stood on a hill 30 feet lower than the 21-gun battery [opposite], but as the ground fell between them, held a commanding position – indeed, looking down into the Quarries, some half-way between it and our 21-gun battery. The parapet at the salient itself was 17 feet high, and on the left face, where I approached it, stood 15 feet above the surface of the ground. The ditch was 11 feet deep, and varied in width from 20 at the salient to 15 feet at the faces. As the work was open in the rear, we could not have held it had we got in, as long as the enemy was still in the Bastion du Mat and Malakoff.

Wood was part of the sixty-strong naval contingent that helped to carry ladders for the right column. No sooner had both columns left the trenches than they were assailed by a storm of cannon fire and musketry the like of which few onlookers, including Raglan, had witnessed before. Wood likened the shower of missiles to a tropical rainstorm that 'swept down the hill, felling our men as a reaping-machine levels standing crops'. Before he had gone a hundred yards, several sailors were hit and he had lost his sword, knocked from his grasp by a musket ball. It was his only weapon. But he continued on and, with half the distance covered, was the only one of seven naval officers still advancing.★ By the time he neared the abatis – a five-foot-high barrier of felled trees – just sixty yards from the Redan's counterscarp, he had with him only two of the ten ladders that had started out. One was being carried by four men, the other by three. Within seconds the four had been reduced to three, prompting Wood to take over from the right rear man. Then the second ladder fell to the ground, 'the men being killed or wounded by a blast of case-shot'. Just twenty-five yards from the abatis his ladder lost another man. 'I had not carried it far,' he recalled,

when the man alongside of me was killed, and then the Ordinary seaman in front, feeling no doubt he was bearing an undue share of the weight, not knowing I was under the ladder, turning his head as far as he could, addressed me as his messmate. 'Come along, Bill; let's get our beggar up first.' Before he recognized me, while his face was still turned backwards, he was killed, and with him tumbled the ladder.

Wood scrambled forward to the abatis, 'under the slight shelter of which a few scattered soldiers were crouching: some were firing, a great many shouting, while on the parapet 15 feet above us stood

★ Captain William Peel, RN, son of the late prime minister and the senior naval officer present, was shot in the arm as he ascended the slope. For this and other gallant actions – including the time he picked up a live shell in a powder magazine and threw it over the parapet – he was awarded the Victoria Cross.

Russians four and in places six deep, firing at, and calling on us sarcastically to walk in'. He looked round and at once saw 'there was no chance of accepting the invitation.' There were places in the abatis, he wrote, 'where a man could have squeezed through the holes made by our shells, but only one at a time, and even then, assuming that he crossed unscathed the open space intervening between the abatis and the ditch, there was still a more formidable obstacle': the height from the bottom of the ditch to the top of the parapet, lined with Russians, was twenty-six feet.

By now the storming party had been reduced to fewer than a hundred men, and Wood knew that without reinforcements the task was hopeless. A number of officers and NCOs did their best to rally the men for a final charge, but all were shot down. Wood was walking along the abatis towards the Malakhov, in the hope of finding a weak spot, when he too was hit, a five-ounce piece of grapeshot smashing his left elbow. 'This sent me screaming to the ground,' he recalled, 'and I rolled some yards down the slope of the hill, where I lay insensible.' He was roused by an Irish corporal who helped him back to the British trenches. From there he was taken by stretcher to the nearest field hospital, where he got into a furious argument with the surgeons who wanted to amputate. Wood eventually got his way, and, under anaesthetic, the grapeshot was removed but not the arm.★

The operation had been a fiasco. Not a single British soldier managed to enter the Redan; the French were no more successful at the Malakhov. And yet the aborted attacks had cost the British more than 1,500 casualties and the French 3,500. Raglan blamed Pélissier, particularly his change of start time and his decision not to attack the Flagstaff Bastion. 'If the attack had been general,' he wrote to Panmure, 'the enemy's troops must have been scattered and there would have been no great mass anywhere and if con-

---

★ Impressed by Wood's gallantry, Raglan sent his own carriage to transport the wounded officer down to the beach at Kazatch, where he joined his ship HMS *Queen*. He also wrote him a letter of recommendation that eventually secured for Wood a commission without purchase in the 13th Light Dragoons.

fusion on their parts had ensued total defeat would have been the consequence.' That may have been wishful thinking, but there is no doubt that the attack was poorly coordinated – the direct result of a divided command structure. Why Pélissier chose to attack on such a narrow front is less clear, but Raglan suspected French indiscipline. 'My impression', he told Panmure, 'is that he is in great apprehension lest his Army should run riot in the event of the successful assault of the Town & should in consequence get into disorder and expose itself to defeat.'

The repulse came at a bad time for Raglan. On the same day as the attack, Roebuck's select committee was presenting its final report to the House of Commons on the mishandling of the army in the Crimea. The overall tone was remarkably restrained. 'An army encamped in a hostile country,' it stated, 'at a distance of 3,000 miles from England, and engaged during a severe winter in besieging a fortress which, from want of numbers, it could not invest, was necessarily placed in a situation where unremitting fatigue and hardship had to be endured.' Such 'unavoidable suffering' was aggravated by 'dilatory and insufficient arrangements for the supply of this army with necessities indispensable to its healthy and effective condition'. In so far as the government was to blame, it was for failing 'to augment the ranks of the army beyond the ordinary recruiting' at the outset of the war; thus the army's numbers were insufficient for the task it was given.

Instead of blaming individuals, the report concentrated on the administrative failings of various military branches, particularly the Commissariat and Medical Departments. The troops, on the other hand, deserved only praise: 'Their heroic valour, and equally heroic patience under sufferings and privations, have given them claims upon their country which will be long remembered and gratefully acknowledged.' But, though Raglan was largely exonerated by the report, the debate that followed saw a renewal of the attacks on his handling of the war. Another disappointment at this time was the news that his pre-war post as master-general of the ordnance had been abolished and its duties transferred to the secretary for war.

These multiple setbacks seem to have affected Raglan's health. On 23 June he was diagnosed as suffering from acute diarrhoea and the death of his good friend Estcourt from cholera the following day can only have depressed his spirits further. He continued to work, but by 26 June was so ill that his doctors confined him to bed. Writing that day to Raglan's daughter Charlotte, Airey tried to sound hopeful. 'I have seen the Doctor a dozen times lately,' he wrote, 'and he assures me it is merely the heat, and if he will consent to lie quiet, on his bed, and not write or do any business, he will be right in a day.'

But he was not. The end came during the evening of 28 June. The headquarters staff was at dinner when Raglan's servant came for the doctor. 'Even then,' wrote one of Raglan's nephews, 'I do not believe the Doctor was much alarmed, but by five the pulse was so low, he told them he was sinking fast. They all went in & the Chaplain followed, read the Service & then a Prayer round his Bed.' Raglan was dead. The following morning, the allied commanders came to pay their respects. Pélissier remained the longest, standing by Raglan's iron campbed 'for upwards of an hour, crying like a child'.

One of Raglan's doctors put his death down not to dysentery or cholera but depression. 'His disease', he wrote many years later, 'may . . . be described as a case of acute mental anguish, producing first great depression, and subsequently complete exhaustion of the heart's action.' Airey had a simpler explanation: Raglan was hounded to death by successive secretaries for war. He explained: 'He died of a broken Heart. Altho' he kept *it hid*, to me his mind was opened, and at night he spoke of nothing, our rooms communicating with each other, but the shameful treatment he had experienced . . . The tone of both [the] Duke of Newcastle and Ld. Panmure, but most especially the latter, was not to be borne.'

The reaction of the British troops to Raglan's death was mixed. Captain Robert Hawley of the 89th Foot wrote: 'The soldiers thought little of him and, though an amiable, good man, he took little pains to ingratiate himself with his officers.' But others thought differently, and it is probably fair to say that the ordinary soldier was much saddened by his death. An artilleryman called Joseph Leggatt may have come closest to the truth when he wrote to his father:

It is thought his having so much on his mind about not taking Sebastopol that it has brought on death sooner than it was expected . . . and the people at Home wanting him to do more than he could do & so much anxiety of mind, & one thing & another. You see yourself it is a very difficult job to have command over so many men, & not taking Sebastopol as soon as he thought he could. It has brought on death. We all wish him everlasting peace, poor fellow. He was a good man to his soldiers in every thing. Sebastopol would have been taken long ago if justice had only been done to him.

Leggatt may be right. If the French had not repeatedly foiled Raglan's plans to take Sevastopol by a *coup de main*, especially in the days after the Alma, the long and costly siege might have been avoided. But Raglan's chief attribute as a diplomat, his equable and convivial temperament, was also his greatest weakness in the field. He may have kept the alliance intact, but he failed to exert sufficient pressure on successive French commanders to act decisively when the time was right. Would another British general have done any better? It is difficult to say. The country did not then have a single outstanding soldier of sufficient rank and experience to take command. Hardinge was too old, Gough too limited and Napier too dead. Even Sir Colin Campbell, arguably the finest soldier of his generation, was essentially cautious in his approach to battle. Given the difficulties of fighting in an alliance, Raglan was probably the best man available. He was not the most imaginative general that Britain has ever produced, but he did get the French out of a fix at the Alma and tried to do so again at the Redan. It was not his fault that his French counterparts, hampered by interference from Napoleon III in Paris, were even more averse to taking risks than he was.

★

Following hard on the heels of the successes of 7 June, the news of the allied repulse on the 18th and Raglan's death ten days later came as quite a shock to the British people. The queen wrote at once to General Simpson, Raglan's chief of staff and temporary replacement, and asked him to pass on to the troops her 'deep and *heartfelt grief* at the irreparable loss of their gallant and excellent Commander'. Yet she also wished to express her 'earnest hope and confident trust that every one will more than ever now do their duty, as they have hitherto so nobly done, and that she may continue to be as proud of her beloved Army as she has been, though their brave Chief, who led them so often to victory and to glory, has been taken from them'. To Lady Raglan she wrote:

Words *cannot* convey *all* I feel at the irreparable loss you have sustained, and I and the Country have, in your noble, gallant, and excellent husband, whose loyalty and devotion to his Sovereign and Country were unbounded . . . We must bow to the will of God; but to be taken away thus, on the eve of the successful result of so much labour, so much suffering, and so much anxiety, is cruel indeed!

The government's chief concern was to find a replacement. With Sir George Brown about to be invalided home, Simpson was the next senior officer and the obvious choice. But in one of his earliest letters to Panmure he made no secret of his misgivings. 'It is quite evident', Panmure told the queen, 'that General Simpson thinks himself unequal to the task of [commanding] the Army & is anxious to be relieved from so weighty a responsibility. With this feeling so strongly expressed, Lord P[almerston] is of the opinion that it would be unjust to the Army to leave it in trembling hands.' The prime minister had, as a result, asked Panmure to discuss an alternative with Hardinge. But none of the candidates was suitable. Lord Seaton was too old, Lord Hardinge was 'physically unfit' and the duke of Cambridge did not have the requisite 'coolness and self possession'. General Ferguson, then at Malta, was considered, as was General Codrington, who was already in the Crimea. But in the end the cabinet decided to stick with

General Simpson as the lesser evil, with Codrington his nominated successor.

They were soon regretting their decision. Simpson's dispatches became ever more pessimistic, with one, towards the end of July, hinting at the possibility of raising the siege during the winter months. The government's reaction was emphatic. 'Under no circumstances whatever', Panmure told the queen, 'will it be consistent with the honor of England and France to withdraw from the heights before Sebastopol unless driven from them.'

Though the British were losing sixty men a day to enemy fire and illness, Russian casualties were far greater. The loss of their supply line through the Sea of Azov had hit them hard, and in mid August they made one final attempt to lift the siege by attacking French and Sardinian positions on the River Chernaya. It was a costly failure, and the end of the siege seemed that bit closer when the defenders of Sevastopol began to construct a pontoon bridge across the harbour – as if planning their escape. Only in Asia Minor, where the Turks were poorly led, had the Russians gained the upper hand by defeating a much larger Ottoman force near Kars in early August. Kars finally fell to the Russians on 16 November.

By the end of August even Simpson was hopeful that Sevastopol might soon be in allied hands. 'General Simpson writes in better spirits as to himself,' the secretary for war informed the queen, 'and Lord Panmure feels easy now that he has in his possession your Majesty's Commission to Major General Sir W. Codrington.'* Part of the reason for Simpson's confidence was the fact that the French had now pushed their approach trenches to within fifteen yards of the Malakhov's ditch. The British had also moved closer, though 200 yards still separated their approach trenches from the Redan. Nevertheless it was felt that a fresh attack must succeed, and the date for the combined assault was fixed for 8 September. With three days to go, the allies began their sixth and final bombardment.

On the 8th the timing of the French attack took the Russians

---

* Codrington had been given a dormant commission to take over as commander-in-chief if anything happened to Simpson.

completely by surprise. Expecting an assault at either dawn or dusk, in line with previous attempts, the Malakhov's garrison was in the process of being relieved when the French troops leapt from their approach trenches at noon. Within ten minutes the seemingly impregnable Malakhov Tower had been taken and a White Ensign hoisted in the Mamelon Vert to signal the start of the British attack. It began well enough, with Ulstermen of the 97th Regiment scrambling across the ditch and up the parapet, some entering the apex of the Redan through its gun embrasures. But, once in, they found it difficult to advance over such a narrow front, their way blocked by a storm of fire from a smaller parapet at the rear of the Redan where a mass of Russian infantry had formed. British reinforcements simply added to the confusion. A captain of the 97th wrote:

Men of other Regts., principally 90th, 3rd and 41st, then came to help us; & the parties got so mixed and jammed together that one could not get a formation for a rush. Just at this time, the enemy driven out of the Malakoff, took us in the flank, and by keeping up a heavy fire killed a great number of men. They profited by this, made a charge, and by their superior numbers drove our men into the angle of the Redan, where from behind 2 Guns, they kept up a vigorous fire for nearly 2 hours, the men of different Regiments being closely packed on the extreme slope of the parapet, and firing over its crest; with a great many on the other side of the ditch who were trying to keep down the fire of the Flanking Batteries, which were causing great havoc amongst the supports, both with grape, and musquetry.

By now the reserves in the poorly constructed approach trenches were also taking heavy casualties from Russian artillery fire. In control of the battle, Codrington knew that it was futile sending more troops to join the mêlée at the apex. So, in a final throw of the dice, he ordered a wing of the 23rd Fusiliers to attempt to outflank the Russian defenders by attacking the Redan's right face. Lieutenant-Colonel Daniel Lysons of the 23rd recalled:

The moment we were out shot, grape and musketry came from the batteries on our left . . . in storms. It was a beautiful sight to see all the rosey faced boys of Officers leading on the men, waving their swords in the air. The men came on splendidly. But when we had passed the crowds clustering on the salient angle, the Russians fired down on our shoulders from the long face. I was knocked over and got into a large shell hole. When I looked round Dyneley was close to me, and Drewe, Corporal Shields and about a dozen men. All the ground behind me was covered with killed and wounded. I desired Drewe, if he could get men enough, to charge across the ditch; and after putting a tight bandage round my leg I crawled to the Salient Angle. The rascals fired at me all the way, and shot off my shirt ornaments . . . I asked an officer of the 2nd Division . . . if possible to reinforce our men at the re-entering angle, and to try with Drewe to get in there. He did so; but the fire [was] too heavy for any thing to live in it. Some of our men were killed on the top of the parapet, where they were found next morning.

As Drewe and the anonymous officer made their futile attempt to cross the parapet, events at the apex were approaching crisis point. Captain Nathaniel Steevens of the 88th recorded:

At last our ammunition became entirely exhausted, and our position became therefore untenable. The enemy, perceiving this, made a sudden rush upon the salient, which caused those in front to fall back, and never shall I forget the frightful scene that consequently ensued: the whole of us, *en masse*, were precipitated into the ditch upon the top of bayonets, ladders, and poor wounded fellows, who writhed in their agony under the crushing weight of us all; and the shouts and cries were fearful.

The Russians now stood upon the parapet, which we had just left, and pelted us with hand-grenades, stones, etc.; under a heavy shower of these missiles I found myself in the ditch, jammed under a ladder, a firelock between my legs with the bayonet through my trousers, while I was trodden upon by numerous feet. With no little difficulty I managed to extricate myself . . . and clamber up the side of the ditch; and then what a gauntlet there was to run!

With Russian fire kicking up the ground around him, Steevens ran until he was out of breath. He walked the rest of the way to the British trenches and, incredibly, arrived unscathed apart from the odd bruise and bayonet nick. Few others were so lucky. No fewer than 250 British soldiers and 150 Russians were later buried in the ditch at the apex of the Redan, close to where they fell. '*Never* had to perform such a disgusting duty,' wrote the British officer in charge of the burial party. 'The bodies were so mangled, and some of the Ruskies had been dead for days. Quite worn out when we at length got home.'

The recriminations began at once. '*There was*', wrote one British brigadier-general, 'a sad *deficiency* of *pluck* & courage in the main bodies of the assaulting columns.' He blamed the high number of young recruits, who, in the campaign so far, had been 'accustomed to look for cover'. But Lieutenant-Colonel Sterling, Campbell's staff officer, thought Codrington was the chief culprit:

There he stood in the advanced trench, with all his Staff, about 250 yards from the angle of the Redan, with his men clustered on its rampart, neither advancing nor retiring for three quarters of an hour. If ever there was a time when a General should have played the part of a grenadier, that was the time. If he had rushed up, he might have failed in getting the men to move on; but he should have tried, and have died there. Could he have got fifty men to go over the parapet, the rest would have followed. England has suffered an indelible disgrace; and this young general, I should suppose, is extinguished.

Sterling's criticism is harsh, and was actuated partly by the anger that Campbell and other generals felt at being superseded by the less senior Codrington. Nor was Codrington's career over: within weeks of the battle he had taken over from Simpson as commander-in-chief. Codrington's own assessment was that the attack was unnecessary: everyone knew that Sevastopol was untenable without the Malakhov – and so it proved.

At 5.30 p.m. on the 8th, once it was clear that the Malakhov was lost, Prince Gorchakov ordered his army to withdraw across the pontoon bridge to the northern side of the city. Before leaving, the rearguard blew up the ammunition stores and sank the remaining ships. When all but the most severely wounded were across, the bridge was destroyed. It was a brilliant operation and, untroubled by allied fire, was achieved without the loss of a single life.

Next day the allies entered the town and were appalled by what they found. 'Never saw I such a scene of misery,' wrote one British surgeon. 'Dead, dying and wounded lay without attendance, shrieking and calling for drink, squalid, starving, dirty and miserable in the extreme. None of the doctors (shame on them) remained behind with them. I gave my brandy and water to them, though I wanted it badly myself.' For some the most poignant sight was the corpse-strewn inside of the Grand Redan, which had twice resisted the best British efforts to capture it. 'I stood in the Redan,' wrote an officer of the Rifle Brigade, 'more humble, more dejected and with a heavier heart than I have yet felt since I left home . . . I looked toward the Malakov, there was the French flag, the Tricolour, planted on its parapet . . . no flag floated on the parapet on which I stood.'

Strictly speaking, the allies had captured only half of the great port of Sevastopol – albeit the important half, containing the main town, harbour and dry docks – but this did nothing to dampen the celebrations in both Britain and France. Victoria and Albert were at Balmoral, having just returned from a highly successful state visit to France, when the news reached them during the evening of 10 September. The queen wrote: 'Albert said that they should go at once and light the bonfire which had been prepared when the false report of the fall of the town arrived last year . . . In a few minutes, Albert and all the gentlemen, in every species of attire, sallied forth, followed by all the servants, and gradually by all the population of the village – keepers, ghillies, workmen – up to the top of the cairn.' The queen woke the young princes, and together they watched the bonfire from the house. Later, as she prepared for bed, 'all the people came down under the windows, the pipers playing, the people singing, firing off guns, and cheering – first for me, then for Albert, the Emperor of the French, and the "downfall of Sevastopol".'

The queen's delight was soon tempered by the knowledge that the war was far from over. The Russians still held the Mackenzie Heights above Sevastopol, and Tsar Alexander II had no intention of suing for peace. Napoleon III, moreover, was anxious to capitalize on the crucial French role in the capture of the port – regarded by many as a rebirth of French military might – by further humbling Russia in the field. Palmerston also felt that further victories were necessary to bring Alexander to heel. 'Russia', he told Clarendon on 9 October, 'has not yet been beat enough to make peace possible at the present moment.' There was also the question of military pride. The fall of Sevastopol had not been celebrated by the ringing of church bells, because Palmerston did not feel the British contribution merited such an honour.

In early October, stung by criticism of his inactivity, Simpson resigned and was eventually replaced by Codrington, who had arrived in the Crimea as a supernumerary major. Many more senior generals were furious at being passed over, though two, Colin Campbell and William Eyre, were given the consolation prize of army corps, the multidivisional formations into which the British force, thanks to a suggestion by Prince Albert, was now divided. The supply problem had also largely been solved, with British soldiers better clothed, fed and housed than a year earlier. And yet the allies, despite two more notable victories over the Russians in October – at Eupatoria and at Fort Kinburn on the confluence of the Rivers Bug and Dnieper – were no closer to striking a knock-out blow.

Public opinion was beginning to turn against the war, particularly in France, where the new foreign secretary, Count Walewski, had long been conducting secret negotiations with the Russians. Napoleon III had come to the conclusion that the presence of so many allied troops in the Crimea was a hindrance to peace, though under pressure from Britain he agreed to let the French Contingent remain until the spring. It was a mistake, because the French lost more soldiers from disease – at least 30,000 – in the last three months of the war than had been killed in almost two years of fighting. The British Army, by contrast, lost relatively few men during this second winter and was actually in a position to assist the French with surplus warm clothing and other supplies.

In January 1856 the allies met in Paris to discuss their objectives for the coming year – but little was achieved beyond a general agreement to continue the war. The key diplomatic breakthrough came in St Petersburg on 15 January, when Alexander, threatened with war by Austria if he did not agree to a new five-point peace plan, finally agreed to sue for peace. Diplomatically isolated and exhausted by war – both financially and militarily – Alexander had run out of options. An armistice was signed in late February, by which time preliminary negotiations had begun in Paris. They lasted until the signing of the Treaty of Paris on 30 March 1856. In all there were twenty-four official sessions and numerous closed-door meetings. The treaty ran to thirty-four articles, and its main provisions were roughly in line with the original Austrian ulti-matum. Russia agreed to the demilitarization of the Black Sea and to return Kars in exchange for territorial concessions in Bessarabia. (She was no longer required to cede the whole of Bessarabia to Moldavia, just the territory covering the mouth of the Danube.) She also agreed to relinquish claims to the Danubian principalities and to drop the right to act as guardian to Turkey's Christians. The Ottoman Empire, meanwhile, agreed to preserve the privileges of its Christian minority.

A couple of months earlier the queen had received news of the forthcoming peace negotiations with a distinct lack of enthusiasm. 'The honour and glory of her dear Army', she informed Clarendon, 'is as *near* her heart as almost anything, and she cannot *bear* the thought that "the failure on the Redan" should be our *last fait d'Armes*, and it would cost her more than words can express to conclude a peace with *this* as the end.' But, with the treaty signed, she felt only relief. 'Much as the Queen disliked the idea of *Peace*,' she wrote to Clarendon on 31 March, 'she has become reconciled to it, by the conviction that France would either not have continued the war, or continued it in such a manner that *no* glory could have been hoped for for us.' Britain, she told her uncle Leopold, had much to thank its foreign secretary for: 'That so *good* a Peace *has* been obtained, and that this country stands in the high position she now does by *having* made peace, but not *yielding* to unworthy and dishonourable terms, is *all* owing to Lord Clarendon, whose difficulties were immense, and who cannot be too highly praised.'

The war had cost the British the lives of almost 21,000 servicemen, only a quarter of whom were killed in action. Such a stark statistic only serves to underpin the traditional view of the conflict as one of incompetence and waste; nor did its conclusion, in the opinion of many commentators, result in positive gains for Britain. One historian writes: 'The treaty left England largely isolated. Russia was, and would be, hostile for decades, and Austria and Prussia had not, as [Prince] Albert put it, laid down their stake. Further, England's sole major-power ally, excepting disintegrating Turkey, was an unstable France only as reliable as its unreliable Emperor.'

But was this the case? Trevor Royle, the author of the best recent book on the conflict, insists that the war did result in important gains for Britain: Russian military power had been 'revealed as a sham', the threat to India had been 'neutralised' and the Royal Navy still controlled the Mediterranean. In so far as these 'limited strategic requirements had been met', he writes, 'the outcome of the Crimean War was far more satisfactory than anyone in the country could have dared to hope at its outset.' Moreover, the territorial integrity of the Ottoman Empire, the ostensible reason for going to war, had been maintained. Nor would Britain, having shown she would fight if she had to, be drawn into another Continental war for a further sixty years.

As for the British Army, the war helped to quicken the pace of reform that Hardinge and Prince Albert had begun in 1852. From October 1854, in an attempt to ensure younger and fitter commanders, promotion to general was no longer on the basis of seniority but on merit; and brevet rank was to be converted to substantive rank at the earliest opportunity, so ensuring younger officers of all ranks. In addition, control of the Commissariat Department was transferred from the Treasury to the War Office, a centralized system was set up to supply the army with uniforms (including the new single-breasted tunic), and the Land Transport Corps was kept in being as the Military Train. Also, thanks to the lobbying of Florence Nightingale, a Royal Sanitary Commission was appointed under the chairmanship of Sidney Herbert in 1857 to investigate the conditions of army barracks and hospitals. It found that the high mortality rate in the army – double that of the civilian population – was explained by insanitary conditions, poor diet and 'enervating mental and bodily effects produced by ennui'. Their recommendations eventually led to a parliamentary grant of £725,000 in 1859 to improve leisure facilities, ventilation, sanitary conditions and waste disposal. But it would take another two years before the Commission on Barracks and Hospitals was able to report that forty-five barracks had replaced their cesspits with proper lavatories. By then a Royal Military Hospital had been built at Netley, near Southampton, and an Army Medical School opened.

But many other inefficient and outdated practices remained: the administration of the army was still divided between two competing agencies, the War Office and the Horse Guards; regiments still spent an inordinately long time in foreign garrisons; commissions were still purchased, though official prices were reduced by a third; soldiers could still be flogged; and canteen contractors still earned exorbitant sums by providing poor-quality food. This was largely thanks to the appointment of the young but conservative duke of Cambridge as the new commander-in-chief of the British Army in the summer of 1856. Despite Cambridge's inadequacies as a field commander, both Victoria and Albert were convinced he would leave his mark at the Horse Guards. And so he did; but not in the way the reform-minded Prince Albert would have liked. Instead he devoted all his considerable energy to blocking fundamental change, and it would take a further decade of various royal commissions and select committees before the wholesale reorganization of the army was begun by the great reforming secretary of state for war, Edward Cardwell.

For Victoria, the Crimean War did not end with the Treaty of Paris. There was still another year of visiting the seriously wounded, laying the foundation stone for the new military hospital, awarding medals and receiving the Crimean heroes and heroines – including Florence Nightingale, who paid a number of visits to Balmoral in September 1856. The queen was enchanted with her ideas to reform military hospitals and wrote to the duke of Cambridge: 'I wish we had her at the War Office.' The previous January, in recognition of Miss Nightingale's 'Christian devotion' to the welfare of the casualties, the queen had sent her a diamond brooch inscribed with the words 'Blessed are the Merciful' and 'Crimea'.

But the emotional high point of the year for the queen was the royal review to welcome the returning troops at Aldershot on 8 July 1856. Victoria and Albert watched from a closed carriage as, in pouring rain, a selection of Crimean regiments formed three sides of a hollow square around them. The rain had stopped, however, by the time an officer and four men from each regiment came forward to greet the queen. 'Tell the others for me', she told them, 'that I have watched anxiously over the difficulties and hardships which they have so nobly borne, that I have mourned deep sorrow for the brave men who have fallen . . . I thank God, that your dangers are over.'

The massed ranks responded with 'God save the Queen!' as bearskins and shakos were hurled into the air.

Later that day, the recently promoted Field Marshal Lord Hardinge presented the queen with the report of a Board of General Officers that had been sitting at Chelsea Hospital to inquire into the failure of army supplies in the Crimea.★ He was discussing the

★ The board was set up at the insistence of senior military figures like Lucan, Airey and Commissary-General James Filder, who had been criticized by an earlier commission headed by Sir John McNeill and Colonel Alexander Tulloch. The report of the board – dubbed the 'Whitewashing Board' – largely exonerated those blamed by the commissioners.

findings with the queen when he staggered and fell. Albert at once helped him to a sofa, from where he tried to continue the conversation. But his right leg and arm had been paralysed by a stroke, and he knew, as he was lifted into his carriage, that his career was over. Two days later he resigned and was replaced by the duke of Cambridge. 'There was', the queen told her uncle Leopold, 'really *no one* who could have been put over him; though in some respects it may be a weakness for the Crown, it is a great strength for the Army.' Hardinge died on 24 September.

To reward the troops for their service in the Crimea, a campaign medal was struck with clasps for the various battles: Alma, Balaklava, Inkerman and Sevastopol. When the medal arrived in the Crimea for distribution in September 1855, one cavalry officer described it as a 'vulgar looking thing' and likened its clasps to decanter labels. 'They call them here "Port", "Sherry", and "Claret".'

The conflict also saw the creation of the first gallantry medals for ordinary servicemen: the Distinguished Conduct Medal for soldiers and the Conspicuous Gallantry Medal for seamen. But both were overshadowed by the institution of the Victoria Cross by royal warrant on 29 January 1856. The original suggestion for a gallantry award open to all ranks was made by the duke of Newcastle during his stint as secretary for war. The idea was enthusiastically endorsed by the queen, who insisted that the medal could be awarded only 'to those Officers or Men who have served Us in the presence of the Enemy and shall then have performed some signal act of valour or devotion to their Country'. But in 1858 this stipulation was extended to include servicemen who showed 'conspicuous courage' in peacetime and civilians who fought alongside troops.

The medal's distinctive design – a Cross Patté\* (from the French for 'with feet' or 'paws') decorated with a crown topped by a lion, and inscribed with the words 'For Valour' – is often attributed to Prince Albert. *The Times*, which thought the medal 'poor looking

---

\* And not a Maltese cross as described in the original warrant.

and mean in the extreme', wrote facetiously: 'The merit of the design, we believe, is due to the same illustrious individual who once invented a hat.' But a recent book on the Victoria Cross is adamant that the designer was H. H. Armstead, a young employee of the London jewellers Hancock's, who still make the medals today. Cast from the bronze cascabels★ of two Russian cannon captured at Sevastopol – hence the dull, gunmetal colour – the medals were originally suspended from two types of ribbon: crimson for the army and dark blue for the navy. Since the formation of the RAF in 1918, however, all awards have come with a crimson ribbon. The tax-free annuity for non-officers has also increased from an initial £10 in 1856 to £1,300 today.

Victoria took a proprietorial interest in everything to do with the award, approving the final design and insisting on the inscription 'For Valour' instead of 'For the Brave'. The latter motto, she argued, might lead to the inference that only those who hold the Victoria Cross 'are deemed brave'. But her suggestion that holders should use BVC (Bearer of the Victoria Cross) after their names rather than VC – on the grounds that 'no one could be called a Victoria Cross' – was not taken up.

★ The large knobs at the rear of the cannon, used for securing ropes. The remaining metal from the cascabels is kept in the Small Arms building of the Royal Logistics Corps at Donnington, Worcestershire. It is said to contain enough for a further eighty-five medals. The cannon themselves stand outside the Rotunda of the Royal Arsenal, Woolwich.

# 10. The Devil's Wind

Britain had barely extricated itself from the war with Russia when it became embroiled in one with Persia, though on a much smaller scale. The two countries had not been on good terms since the aborted siege of Herat in 1838, with Persia finally carrying out its threat to occupy the Afghan city in 1852. A British ultimatum forced the Persian shah Nasr ad-Din to withdraw his troops early the following year, but fresh disagreements gave him an excuse to reinvade Afghanistan in 1856 and install a pro-Persian ruler in Herat. This time he refused to withdraw, and the Indian government, under orders from London, declared war on 1 November 1856.

An expeditionary force of 4,000 British and Indian troops was sent from Bombay to the Persian Gulf, where it captured the port of Bushire on 29 November. Reinforcements arrived in the New Year, and on 8 February the combined force, under the leadership of Major-General Sir James Outram, decisively defeated a much larger Persian force near the village of Kush-ab. Seven hundred Persians were slain; Outram lost just eighty-three killed and wounded. To increase the pressure on the shah, Outram re-embarked half his force in March and took it by sea across the Persian Gulf and up the Shat-el-Arab waterway as far as the town of Mohumra. Unbeknownst to him, the Persians had already signed a peace treaty in Paris on 4 March, promising to withdraw from Herat and renouncing all claims over Afghanistan. They also undertook, at Palmerston's personal insistence, to abolish the slave trade in the Persian Gulf.

The peace treaty was timely because a separate conflict was already under way between Britain and imperial China. Diplomatic relations between China and the West had been poor since an imperial edict of 1757 confined foreign trade to the port of Canton in the south. Foreigners, moreover, were restricted to their trading factories, had no diplomatic representation and were liable to prosecution under the harsh Chinese law. Matters came to a head in the late 1830s, when the Chinese emperor appointed a new commissioner for Canton with orders to stop the illegal British-dominated opium trade. Until 1833 the trade had been monopolized by the HEIC, which grew the drug in India and then shipped it to China, where millions were addicted to smoking it. But that year the Company's trading monopoly with China was ended by the Whig government of Lord Grey, causing an explosion in the volume of opium shipments as merchants from Britain, Portugal and America entered the trade. But, despite the loss of its trading monopoly, the Company still made a fortune from the trade in the form of customs' revenue. By the late 1830s the sheer scale of the operation, and its continued importance to the Indian government, was staggering: opium accounted for 40 per cent of the total value of Indian exports; and the revenue it raised was roughly equivalent, and often superior, to the amount the HEIC had to remit to London to pay the interest on its huge debt. Morality did not come into it. For the Company to remain solvent, the trade simply had to continue. So when the new Chinese commissioner confiscated 20,000 chests of British-owned opium* in March 1839, and later expelled the British communities of Canton and Macao, the British government was bound to respond to pleas for assistance from powerful trading houses like Jardine Matheson & Co.† It did so by dispatching a fleet of gunboats and a tiny expeditionary force of 4,000 troops under Colonel Burrell (later replaced by Major-General Sir Hugh Gough). The combined force reached Hong Kong, where the British community was holed up in ships, in the summer of 1840. Over the course of the next two years it occupied Hong Kong and captured Canton and a number

---

* Worth around £2.5m.

† Anticipating an end to the HEIC's trading monopoly, the company was formed in 1832 by two Scotsmen, Dr William Jardine, a former HEIC naval surgeon, and James Matheson, a Canton-based merchant.

of towns on the Yangtse. Exhausted by constant defeats, the Chinese eventually sued for peace. The First Opium War was over.

By the terms of the Treaty of Nanking (1842), Britain acquired the island of Hong Kong, diplomatic representation, and the right to trade in the ports of Canton, Amoy, Foochow, Ningpo and Shanghai. Further treaties gave other countries, including France and the USA, the same privileges as Britain, including the right to live in special areas, or concessions, where their own laws operated. The opium trade was not legalized, though smuggling continued as before. 'The only real benefit of acquiring Hong Kong as a result of the war of 1841', writes imperial historian Niall Ferguson, 'was that it provided firms like Jardine Matheson with a base for their opium-smuggling operation.'

The spark that ignited the Second Opium War was the boarding of the *Arrow*, a British-registered lorcha,★ by Chinese coastguards at the mouth of the Canton River on 8 October 1856. The lorcha was actually owned by a Chinese merchant who used the Hong Kong registration and the presence of an inexperienced Belfast skipper, 21-year-old Thomas Kennedy, to claim the privileges granted genuine British ships by the Treaty of Nanking. Though it was carrying only rice, not opium, it had previously served as a pirate vessel, and three members of its crew were known pirates. This was the excuse the Chinese authorities used to seize it. Only later did it emerge that its British registration had lapsed.

No sooner had the boat been impounded, its British flag taken down and its Chinese crew arrested than Kennedy reported the loss to Harry Parkes, the 28-year-old acting British consul at Canton. Parkes at once demanded the release of the crew, citing the Supplementary Treaty of 1843 that required the Chinese to ask the British consul's permission before arresting Chinese crew members of British-registered vessels. The coastguard commander refused, saying that one of the crew members was the father of a notorious pirate and the others were required as witnesses. When

★ A hybrid trading vessel with a European-style hull and battened mat lugsails like a junk's.

Parkes persisted, he was slapped. A furious Parkes at once appealed to Ye Mingchen, the local viceroy, who agreed to release all but three of the crew. But he was keeping the vessel, he said, because the crew had admitted it was Chinese built and owned.

Parkes now raised the stakes by suggesting to Sir John Bowring, the British governor of Hong Kong, that they should seize one of the war junks that had commandeered the *Arrow*. Sensing an opportunity to 'carry the city' – by which he meant extending the area in which the British could operate from their cramped 'factories' to Canton proper – Bowring agreed, and on 14 October the British gunboat *Coromandel* boarded a Chinese vessel★ and towed it to Whampoa. By now Bowring was aware that the *Arrow*'s registration had already expired. But he kept this quiet, and instead, on 21 October, issued Ye with an ultimatum: he had twenty-four hours to free all the *Arrow*'s crew, provide a public apology and a promise to respect all British shipping in China. If he did not, force would be used.

Ye's response was to release the rest of the crew; but he would neither apologize nor do more than promise to consult with the British over the arrest of alleged pirates. In a spirit of compromise, he added: 'Hereafter Chinese officers will on no account without reason seize and take into custody the people belonging to foreign lorchas, but when Chinese subjects build for themselves vessels, foreigners should not sell registers to them . . . for it will occasion confusion between native and foreign ships, and render it difficult to distinguish between them.'

Despite the 64-year-old Bowring's reputation as a cultured liberal – he had sat as a Radical MP, edited the *Westminster Review* and published books and papers on politics, economics and European and Oriental poetry – his reaction was typically Palmerstonian. A squadron of the Royal Navy was sent to blockade the river and bombard the city, razing Ye's palace in the process. Ye retaliated with a virtual declaration of war, offering a bounty for British heads that eventually resulted in a number of murders and

★ It turned out to be privately owned.

19. Sir Alexander Burnes, British resident in Kabul, in native dress. He was killed during the attack on his residency on 2 November 1841.

20. Florentia, Lady Sale, the formidable wife of Brigadier-General Sir Robert 'Fighting Bob' Sale. She and her daughter survived the disastrous retreat from Kabul in January 1842; her son-in-law, Captain Sturt, did not.

21. Captain George Lawrence, one of the famous Lawrence brothers and secretary to the murdered British envoy Sir William Macnaghten. Lawrence was taken hostage during the retreat from Kabul and also survived.

22. Akbar Khan, son of the deposed Amir Dost Mohamed, who took control of the rebellion after arriving in Kabul in late November 1841. He shot Macnaghten on 23 December with a double-barrelled pistol that the envoy had given him as a gift.

23. 'The Remnants of an Army' by Lady Elizabeth Butler, depicting the arrival at Jelalabad of Dr William Brydon on 12 January 1842. Brydon was the only European to avoid capture or death during the retreat from Kabul.

24. Lieutenant-General Sir Charles Napier and his Arab charger Red Rover in 1853. Ten years earlier, the eccentric and God-fearing Napier had annexed Sind without government sanction.

25. Lieutenant-General Viscount Gough in 1850, a year after his victory at Gujerat brought the Second Sikh War to a successful conclusion.

26. The 31st Foot charging at the Battle of Mudki, 18 December 1845. Colour lithograph by H. Martens from a sketch by Major G. F. White of the 31st.

27. Charge of the 3rd Light Dragoons at the Battle of Chilianwalla, 13 January 1849.

*(Left)* 28. Dalip Singh, the ex-maharaja of Lahore. The original portrait by Franz Winterhalter was commissioned in 1854 by Queen Victoria, who wrote: 'I always feel much for these poor deposed Indian princes.'

*(Top)* 29. Queen Victoria and Prince Albert at Chobham Camp, 1853.

30. The Scots Guards parade in front of Queen Victoria at Buckingham Palace on 28 February 1854, prior to their embarkation for Turkey. Colour lithograph by E. Walker after G. H. Thomas.

31. 'Alma. Forward 42nd!' Sir Colin Campbell urges the Black Watch onward at the Battle of the Alma, 20 September 1854. Colour lithograph after Robert Gibb.

32. 'Before Sebastopol', watercolour by Lieutenant Henry Wilkinson, November 1854.

33. 'Interior of the Redan', watercolour by William Simpson, September 1855.
Painted from its left looking towards the salient angle.

34. 'The Fall of Sevastopol, 1855' by William Simpson.

35. Thomas Henry Kavanagh being disguised as a native, having volunteered to guide the Lucknow relief force, 9 November 1857. He became only the third civilian to win the Victoria Cross. Oil painting by L. W. Desanges, *c.* 1860.

36. 'Mutinous Sepoys', watercolour by George Franklin Atkinson, 1857–8.

37. Garden of the fabled Summer Palace at Peking, by George Newenham Wright, 1843.

the destruction of British factories. By mid January 1857, with the stand-off continuing, Bowring requested reinforcements from India. 'The gate of China is Canton,' he wrote to Lord Canning, the governor-general, 'and unless we can force an entrance there, I believe the difficulties of obtaining any improved position in China will be almost invincible. The valour of H.M. naval forces [is] not able to take the city.'

On 31 January, even before learning of Bowring's requests, the British cabinet had instructed Canning to send extra troops to Canton. A week later the Royal Navy was ordered to seize the Grand Canal and cut off the food supply to the Chinese capital of Peking. Only when the Chinese emperor granted new concessions – including a permanent British ambassador at the imperial court, and more ports and rivers opened up to British ships – would the siege be lifted.

The home government was not wholly supportive of Bowring's actions. Even the attorney-general, Sir Richard Bethell, was of the opinion that there was no justification for bombarding Canton. But the cabinet had come to the conclusion that it was in Britain's commercial interests both to uphold Bowring's authority and to punish the Chinese authorities for what amounted to state-sponsored murder. The Tory opposition did not agree, and on 24 February a motion of no confidence in the government's policy in China was debated in the House of Lords. The *Arrow* incident, declared Derby, was the 'most despicable cause of war that has ever occurred' because it was not really a British ship and had no right to be registered as such. His speech received a standing ovation, but it was not enough to carry the House in the face of Palmerston's cynical offer of honours and positions to those peers who stood by him. The government won by 146 votes to 110.

But the real test would come in the House of Commons, where a similar motion was introduced by Richard Cobden, the leading Radical. Cobden's argument was simple: Bowring had acted illegally, and the government was doing likewise by supporting him. Most prominent MPs agreed, including Gladstone, Disraeli, Russell and Sir James Graham. Palmerston's defence smacked of desperation. Bowring, he said, was 'a man of the people', while Ye was 'one of the most savage barbarians that ever disgraced a nation'. He accused Cobden of 'an anti-English feeling . . . which I should hardly have expected from the lips of any member of this House. Everything that was English was wrong, and everything that was hostile to England was right.' In a rather pale imitation of his successful '*Civis Romanus sum*' speech, Palmerston warned the Commons not 'to abandon a large community of British subjects at the extreme end of the globe to a set of barbarians'. It was not enough to prevent Cobden's motion from carrying by 263 votes to 247 on 3 March.

Perhaps swayed by Prince Albert – who told him that the heavily pregnant queen★ felt herself 'physically quite unable to go through the anxiety of a Ministerial Crisis and the fruitless attempt to form a new Government out of the heterogeneous elements of which the present opposition is composed' – Palmerston called a general election. He suspected that his gunboat diplomacy would find more favour with the electorate than it had with MPs – and he was right. During the three days of voting that began on 28 March, the Whig–Radical coalition – which even Palmerston was beginning to refer to as the Liberal Party – increased its representation to 367 seats, giving it an overall majority of eighty-five, the largest since 1832. The Conservatives lost thirty-four seats and the Peelites nineteen, reducing their totals to 256 and twenty-six respectively. The Peelites, as a result, were all but spent as a political force.

Even as the election campaign was being fought, Palmerston hardened his stance towards China by appointing the eighth earl of Elgin,† a former governor-general of Canada, as his new envoy.

---

★ Princess Beatrice, the last of Queen Victoria's nine children, was born on 14 April 1857.

† Born James Bruce on 20 July 1811, the son of the famous antiquarian who preserved or vandalized – depending on whether you are British or Greek – the friezes on the crumbling Parthenon in Athens by shipping them to Britain. The Greek government is still demanding the return of the 'Elgin Marbles', which reside in the British Museum.

Elgin's instructions were brief: he was not, under any circumstances, to attempt the reconquest of Canton; instead he was to demand, by direct negotiation with imperial officials in Peking, the establishment of a permanent ambassador at the capital, the opening of new ports to British trade and a Chinese promise to comply with the provisions of the Treaty of Nanking. A sizeable military force would accompany him – under the joint command of Rear-Admiral Sir Michael Seymour and Major-General the Honourable T. Ashburnham – but it was to be used only as a last resort. In the event, unforeseen circumstances would divert the bulk of this force long before it reached China.

Queen Victoria woke early at Buckingham Palace on 26 June 1857, 'full of agitation for the coming great event of the day'. The award of the Victoria Cross had been made retrospective to June 1854, to reward the heroes of the Crimea, and the queen was due to distribute the first sixty-two medals at a review in Hyde Park. It was a significant day in other ways too: Prince Albert would officially become the prince consort, marking the end of the queen's long battle to secure for him a title that was suitably dignified;* and it was the first time she had ever ridden at a great review in London, no mean feat given the birth of her ninth and last child, Princess Beatrice, two months earlier.

It was a beautiful midsummer day, and at 9.30 a.m., wearing 'full uniform', Victoria mounted her horse 'Sunset' in the palace courtyard and, flanked by Prince Albert and her future son-in-law Prince Frederick William of Prussia,† rode, sidesaddle, out of the palace gates and up a crowd-thronged Constitution Hill. 'The road all along was kept clear,' noted Victoria, '& there was no pushing or squeezing. Constant cheering, & noises of every kind, but the horses went beautifully.' In the park itself, 9,000 troops and a

---

* The cabinet made objections to the end, forcing the queen to award the new title by letters patent. It was approved by the Privy Council on 25 June.

† He married the queen's eldest daughter, Vicky, on 25 January 1858. He was twenty-seven; she just seventeen.

battery of artillery were waiting before a specially built pavilion to
receive the royal party. As they approached, the guns fired a royal
salute. Victoria thought the sight 'very fine – the tribunes & stands,
full of spectators, the Royal one being in the centre. After riding
down the Line the ceremony of giving medals began.'

The queen stayed mounted, a bonnet protecting her from the
hot sun, as each name was called and the recipient stepped forward.
Handed the medal from a scarlet-covered table by Lord Panmure,
she bent down and pinned it to the winner's tunic. The first man
to be decorated was Lieutenant Henry Raby of the Naval Brigade,
who, at the Redan on 18 June 1855, had braved a storm of fire to
rescue a soldier shot in both legs. As the queen fastened the medal
to Raby's breast, she accidentally pushed the pin through his tunic
and into his chest. He bore the eye-watering pain in silence, and
Victoria was none the wiser. With the awards complete, the march
past began. 'I never saw finer troops, nor better marching,' wrote
the queen, 'excepting the Life Guards, who did not come by well.'
By noon the queen was back in Buckingham Palace, grateful to
be out of the sun. It had been a 'most proud, gratifying day' – but
it was about to take a turn for the worse.

Since January there had been ominous signs of discontent in
India, chiefly amongst the native troops of the Bengal Army. Two
infantry regiments had been disbanded for mutinous acts relating
to the issue of the new Enfield rifle. But the threat of a major
outbreak was not taken seriously by either the Indian or British
governments, and few anticipated the appalling events at Meerut
on 10 May when the Indian garrison rose, murdered scores of
European officers and civilians, and then marched off to nearby
Delhi to proclaim the aged Bahadur Shah II, king of Delhi and
a descendant of the Mughals, as emperor of India. Swelled by
the local garrison, the mutineers carried out another massacre of
Europeans, Eurasians and Christian Indians in Delhi on 11 May.

This was the depressing news that greeted Victoria on her return
to Buckingham Palace on 26 June. It came in the form of a
letter from Palmerston, who had just received dispatches from the
governor-general of India, Lord Canning, which had taken more

than a month to reach Britain via the Cape of Good Hope mail packet. 'Delhi is in the hands of five insurgent regiments,' Canning had written on 19 May, the day the mail packet left Calcutta, '& has been so since the 11th. Meerut is quiet & safe in possession of European troops of the station. On all sides of Delhi, but especially from the hill stations on the north . . . European troops & irregulars are collecting & when the Europeans are in sufficient strength they will close upon the town & crush the rebels.' Canning then detailed the steps he had taken to procure reinforcements – including those regiments bound for China and those due to return from Persia – and ended with an appeal for more.

In his letter to the queen of 26 June, Palmerston said he had 'no fear' of the mutiny's 'results'. He added: 'The bulk of the European force is stationed on the North-West Frontier, and is, therefore, within comparatively easy reach of Delhi, and about six thousand troops will have returned to Bombay from Persia.' It was nevertheless advisable 'to send off at once' the 8,000 troops already under orders for India. As for the cause of the mutiny, he suspected either the machinations of Hindu priests, who feared that their religion was 'in danger by the progress of civilization in India', or 'some hostile foreign agency', by which he meant the old enemy Russia. He could not have been more wrong on both counts.

Owing to supply problems and the outbreak of the Crimean War, the first 1853-pattern Enfield rifle-muskets, the weapons commonly assumed to have caused the 1857 rebellion, did not reach India until the spring of 1856. Even by May 1857, the start of the mutiny, only 12,000 rifles had arrived in Bengal: some had gone to a British regiment; all the rest were in magazines and musketry depots.

It was, in any case, not the rifles themselves but their cartridges that were to prove so controversial. Cartridges for most muzzle-loading guns took the form of a tube of paper containing a ball and enough gunpowder for a single shot. The approved method of loading was to bite off the top of the cartridge and pour the powder down the barrel. The rest of the cartridge, including the ball, was then forced down the barrel with a ramrod. Because an Enfield rifle bullet needed to be tight-fitting for the grooves to take effect, its paper cartridge was greased to facilitate loading.

As early as 1853, when the first Enfield cartridges were sent to India to test their reaction to the climate, the commander-in-chief had warned that the grease used should not be 'of a nature to offend or interfere with the prejudices of caste'. But his warning was ignored by the Bengal Ordnance Department, which used animal tallow as one of the constituents of the grease without verifying its type.

In January 1857 native infantry regiments all over the Bengal Presidency were ordered to send detachments to one of three musketry depots – Dum-Dum near Calcutta, Ambala in the Cis-Sutlej and Sialkot in the Punjab – for instruction in the care and handling of the new rifle. Not a cartridge had been issued, however, nor a practice shot fired by the time a rumour began to circulate amongst the sepoys at the Dum-Dum Depot that the cartridge grease was offensive to both Hindus and Muslims, and that this was part of a systematic plot by government to convert all Indians to Christianity.

The origin of the rumour was said to have been a conversation between a Brahman sepoy and a low-caste labourer. On being asked to share the water in his *lota*,★ the sepoy responded: 'You will defile it by your touch.'

To which the labourer replied: 'You think much of your caste, but wait a little, the *sahib-logue*† will make you bite cartridges soaked in cow and pork fat, and then where will your caste be?'

Ever sensitive to issues of religion and caste, the military authorities at once ordered that all cartridges at the musketry depots were to be issued free from grease and the sepoys allowed to apply their own mixture. They also conducted an investigation into the composition of the grease and were horrified to discover that 'no extraordinary precaution' had been taken to ensure 'the absence

---

★ Brass drinking vessel used by high-caste Hindus.

† Europeans; *sahib* means European or other superior; *logue* means people.

of any objectionable fat'. While it has never been proved beyond doubt that the cartridge grease contained cow or pig fat, the circumstantial evidence is compelling. Canning himself admitted, in a letter of 7 February, that the grease grievance had 'turned out to be well founded'. Yet he assumed that the order for sepoys to apply their own grease would calm fears. It did not. On 4 February, at Barrackpur near Calcutta, sepoys voiced their fears that even ungreased Enfield cartridges were contaminated. Three weeks later, at nearby Berhampur, men of a different regiment refused to accept blank cartridges for their old muskets because they suspected them of being greased. And on 29 March, again at Barrackpur, an intoxicated sepoy★ wounded two Europeans – an officer and an NCO – in an attempt to incite his regiment to mutiny. 'Come out, you *bhainchutes*,† the Europeans are here,' he is said to have cried. 'From biting these cartridges we shall become infidels!'

The sepoy's comrades decided not to join him; yet they failed to obey orders to apprehend him, and some even attacked the Europeans who tried to do so. Punishment was swift: the sepoy was hanged and his regiment disbanded (as was the Berhampur unit). The reaction of the English-language *Hindoo Patriot* was to indicate a cause far deeper than the so-called cartridge question. '*Months before* a single cartridge was greased with beef-suet or hogslard,' it commented on 2 April, 'we endeavoured to draw public attention to the unsatisfactory state of feeling in the sepoy army . . . [There is] a powder mine in the ranks of the native soldiery that wants but the slightest spark to set in motion gigantic elements of destruction.'

The sepoys' objections, it seems, had switched from the grease on the Enfield cartridge to the paper used for the new cartridge, and finally to the paper on the old musket cartridge. Convinced that agitators were manipulating the cartridge question for their

---

★ Sepoy Mangal Pande. At his trial Pande admitted to having taken *bhang*, an infusion of hemp, and claimed he did not know what he was doing. 'Pandy' became the generic name by which most Europeans referred to the mutineers.
† Sister-violators.

own sinister ends, the Indian government tried to remove any remaining objections by altering the firing drill for both rifles and muskets in early April. Instead of tearing the top of the cartridge with their teeth, sepoys would now do so with their left hand. The first live firing of Enfield rifles, using cartridges greased with *ghi**★* and beeswax, took place at the Ambala Musketry Depot on 17 April. Indian troops had already warned the commander of the depot that any live firing would lead to a mutiny, and a spate of arson attacks seemed to confirm this. The commander wrote to army headquarters on 5 May: 'I know that at present an unusual agitation is pervading the ranks of the entire native army, but what it will result in, I am afraid to say. I can detect the near approach of a storm, I can hear the moaning of the hurricane, but I can't say how, when, or where it will break.' The bloody events at Meerut, five days later, would provide the answer.

As every schoolboy knows (or once knew), the Indian Mutiny, the military and civil rebellion that swept through northern and central India in 1857, was caused by the greased cartridges. Sepoys and civilians were convinced, so the argument goes, that the cartridges were part of a British plot to convert the whole of the subcontinent to Christianity. Such suspicions were believed because the previous quarter century had seen a number of new laws and trends that appeared to undermine Indian religion, caste and custom. For example, as already mentioned, the practice of suttee – whereby Hindu widows would immolate themselves on their husbands' funeral pyres – was outlawed in 1829, and later, in the early 1850s, these widows were allowed to remarry. Another law enabled religious converts to inherit their fathers' property, and in jails the right of prisoners to prepare their own meals – an important privilege for high-caste Hindus – was abolished in favour of group messing.

Many Indians also resented the government's policy of Anglicization, particularly the decision in 1813 to remove the ban on

★ Clarified butter.

Christian missionaries and to spend £10,000 a year educating Indians. The long debate between Anglicizers and Orientalists over the best type of education – English or classical Indian – was finally settled in 1835, when T. B. Macaulay penned his notorious minute recommending the raising up of an English-educated middle class. Missionary activity was no less controversial, though the actual number of Christian converts in northern India was negligible. There were also some proselytizing officers in the Bengal civil service and army – including Colonel Steven Wheler of the 34th – but they were in a tiny minority. General George Anson, the commander-in-chief of India, did not believe the disaffection in 1857 could be 'traced to the preaching of Commanding Officers' because Wheler was an isolated case. Instead, as the *Bengal Hurkaru* put it, the actions of Wheler and men like him were grist to the mill of those who wished 'to win away the allegiance of the sepoys from Government'.

High-caste sepoys, it must be said, were especially susceptible to such misgivings because their stranglehold over recruitment to the Bengal Army was beginning to loosen in the years prior to 1857. In 1815 they had made up four fifths of one newly raised regiment. Yet by 1842 the high-caste proportion of the Bengal Native Infantry had fallen to around 66 per cent. This was the result of a deliberate attempt by Lord William Bentinck, governor-general of India in the early 1830s, to reduce the influence of the high-caste sepoys by enlisting more 'middling' castes and respectable Muslims. Further inroads were made into the high-caste monopoly by the recruitment of Sikhs and Punjabi Muslims after the Second Sikh War and the issue of the General Service Enlistment order in 1856. As mentioned previously, it had hitherto been the practice in the Bengal Army to ask for volunteers when troops were needed for foreign service; this was in deference to its high-caste sepoys, who would, in theory, lose their caste if they crossed the 'black water'. Now all new recruits would be taken for general service. Taken in the context of the previous twenty years, when successive governments had sought to broaden the recruitment base of the Bengal Army, it is possible to understand why, in the words of Sir John Kaye, the general service regulation caused 'the old race of [sepoys] to leap to the conclusion that the English had done with the old Bengal Army, and were about to substitute for it another that would go anywhere and do anything, like coolies and pariahs'.

No less unpopular were the many annexations of princely states during the governor-generalship of Lord Dalhousie (1848–56). Most were justified on the grounds of the pseudo-legalistic 'Doctrine of Lapse' – whereby the HEIC could confiscate the territory of any Indian prince who died without natural issue, and so ride roughshod over Hindu law and custom. The states absorbed into British India on this pretext included Satara in 1848, Sambhalpur in 1849, and Jhansi and Nagpur in 1854. But no annexation aroused more bad feeling among Bengal sepoys than that of Oudh, on the grounds of misrule, in February 1856. This was because a significant proportion of sepoys – as many as three quarters, according to one authority – came from that province. The 'seizing of Oudh filled the minds of the sepoys with distrust', wrote a Bengal soldier who remained loyal, and 'led them to plot against the government'.

The perceived threat to the sepoys' religion posed by the Enfield cartridges is seen by most historians as the last straw. But two questions need to be asked: were the prime motives for mutiny really the preservation of caste and religion, or were grievances particular to the Bengal Army more to blame? And did the sepoys act of their own volition, or was there an element of manipulation both within and without the military? In both cases the latter argument is more compelling.

All armies have generic grievances relating to conditions of service, including pay, promotion, discipline and relations with officers. What set the HEIC Army apart is that it was a volunteer mercenary force officered by men of a different race and religion. Its soldiers' loyalty to its paymasters, therefore, was entirely dependent upon the incentives for service outweighing the disincentives. By 1857 this was no longer the case, mainly because the number and seriousness of the sepoys' grievances were increasing, while the Bengal Army's control over its soldiers was weakening.

So what were these professional grievances? The minor ones included uncomfortable European-style uniforms and equipment, irksome peacetime duties (such as guarding treasuries and government buildings) and poor insanitary barracks. The more serious ones – which played a major part in the outbreak of mutiny – were low pay, a lack of career prospects and deteriorating relations with their European officers.

There was a strong financial incentive to serve the HEIC in the late eighteenth and early nineteenth centuries because it offered regular pay, pensions and other economic benefits like foreign service *batta*, or bounty – perks largely unheard of in princely armies. Yet the basic pay for ordinary sepoys – seven rupees, or fourteen shillings, a month – was the same in 1857 as it had been at the turn of the century. During the same period the cost of living had almost doubled. This was not such a problem while low pay could be offset by booty from successful campaigns. But by the 1850s the internal conquest of India was complete, and the occasional punitive expedition against unruly tribes did not provide the same opportunity to loot as a conventional campaign. Only by serving outside India – an unappealing prospect for a high-caste soldier – could a Bengal sepoy hope to augment his pay. Under the circumstances, an uprising against their colonial masters – and a return to the traditional cycle of war – would have appealed to many.

But money was not the only advantage to be gained from a successful rebellion. Power and prestige were also on offer: incentives that were virtually non-existent in an army where an Indian officer could not even give orders to a European NCO. To allow a veteran subedar* to be 'commanded by a fair-faced beardless Ensign, just arrived from England', wrote Sir Charles Napier, was the 'imposition of conquerors' and 'one which the Native gentlemen feel deeply and silently'. Henry Lawrence agreed, pointing out the danger of this situation in a country that 'above all others, has been accustomed to see military merits rewarded,

* A senior Indian officer, equivalent in rank to a European captain.

and to witness the successive rise of families from the lowest conditions'. The inadequacy of career prospects was particularly acute in the Bengal Army because its system of promotion was based upon length of service rather than upon merit.* This so-called seniority system had three potentially disastrous consequences: it deprived the European commanding officer of an important power to reward, thereby reducing his authority; it frustrated ambitious and talented sepoys, who had to wait in line for promotion; and it produced old, inefficient and often bitter Indian officers who had no worthwhile occupation. These last two groups may hold the key to the uprising. Lawrence believed that, on average, three out of every hundred sepoys were 'dangerously discontented' in 1856 because they felt 'they have that in them which elsewhere would raise them to distinction.' It is highly probable that such men were the instigators of the mutinies in 1857, and that they used the religious and caste implications of the cartridge question to persuade the rank and file to join them in rebellion.

Deteriorating relations with their European officers was another reason for the sepoys to rebel. It had not always been so. In the old days, before the arrival of the *memsahibs*, many officers had Indian mistresses and even wives, which facilitated their grasp of Hindustani and the ease with which they could communicate with their men. But the practice began to die out in the 1820s and 1830s as more European women arrived in India, and it became socially unacceptable to keep a mistress or marry a Eurasian. And, as Europeans increasingly kept their own society, contact between officers and men was reduced to a minimum. Officers 'never, as a general rule, mix or converse with their men', wrote one authority, 'but, on the contrary, too often refuse to listen to their complaints, at the best telling them to go to the adjutant, and not unfrequently, "Go to hell – don't bother me!"'

One final cause of rebellion was the fact that the Bengal Army – in line with the political theory of Utilitarianism prevalent in India at the time – had become increasingly centralized, which, in

---

* In Bombay and Madras the opposite was true.

turn, reduced the power of European colonels to punish and reward their sepoys. They could no longer administer corporal punishment, for example, and were not feared by their men. Some writers have characterized the mutiny as a backlash against the excessive brutality of white officers. Yet the officers lacked the authority to be brutal and, if anything, were too lenient. Discipline suffered, and the sepoys interpreted this as a sign of weakness. 'The principal cause of the rebellion', wrote one Bengal soldier, 'was the feeling of power that the sepoys had, and the little control the sahibs were allowed to exert over them. Naturally, they assumed from this that the *Sirkar*★ must be afraid of them, whereas it only trusted them too well.'

By 1857 the Bengal Army was ripe for mutiny. Its infantry regiments, in particular, contained a significant proportion of malcontents who were seeking an end to British rule. They were, by definition, drawn from a complete cross-section of army ranks. Their aim was to replace their British employers with an Indian government that would, at the very least, provide greater career opportunities and increased pay.

A similar network of conspirators had, according to Sir Charles Napier, coordinated the Punjab mutinies of 1849/50, when Bengal regiments objected to the withdrawal of foreign service batta. 'In all mutinies', wrote Napier, 'some men more daring than others are allowed to take the lead while the more wary prepare to profit when the time suits; a few men in a few corps, a few corps in an army begin; if successful they are joined by their more calculating comrades.' Such cabals were present in most Bengal native regiments in 1857. 'The plot for revolt was not recent,' wrote one colonel, 'although probably known to a select few only in each Regiment.'

It was not just disgruntled soldiers who were plotting to topple the British. Indian civilians were also involved, particularly members of princely families who had lost out during Dalhousie's time: men like Nana Govind Dhondu Pant, better known as Nana Sahib, the adopted son of Baji Rao II, the last peshwa, or chief minister, of the

★ The Indian government.

Maratha Confederacy.★ When Baji Rao died in 1851, Dalhousie refused to grant his huge annual pension and titles to his adopted heir. Nana never forgave the British, and there is evidence that he was plotting rebellion long before the military uprising in 1857. According to an Indian emissary named Sitaram Bawa, Nana was sounding out a host of Indian princes – including the rulers and former rulers of Gwalior, Assam, Jaipur, Jodhpur, Jammu, Baroda, Hyderabad, Kolapur, Satara and Indore – as early as the autumn of 1855. At first nobody replied to his letters, but after the annexation of Oudh the 'answers began to pour in' from both Hindus and Muslims. Among the Nana's first adherents, claimed Sitaram, was Raja Man Singh, the Oudh chieftain who had lost all but three of his villages in the controversial revenue settlement of 1856. Other dispossessed chieftains then joined the conspiracy, as did the leading citizens of Lucknow, the capital of Oudh, and Gulab Singh, the maharaja of Jammu and Kashmir. An agreement was also made with the king of Delhi. The financial assistance provided by many of these influential plotters was used to seduce serving sepoys and disbanded members of the king of Oudh's army alike. 'The military classes were enticed by a promise of restoring old times of licence,' said Sitaram, 'and they all prefer that to a regular form of government.'

But for the conspiracy to transform into open rebellion, the disgruntled elements of the Bengal Army needed an issue controversial enough to win over their fellow sepoys and so tip their general feelings of discontent – over British arrogance, over pay, over poor career prospects – into a readiness to take up arms. It arrived in the form of the Enfield cartridge.

The storm finally broke at the British station of Meerut,† forty-five miles north-east of Delhi, on 10 May 1857. At dawn the day

★ For a time, during the late eighteenth century, the Marathas were the dominant power in western and northern India. The British fought three wars, over forty years, to eclipse them.

† As headquarters of both the Bengal Artillery and a division of the Bengal Army, Meerut was a key military station. Moreover it had, in May 1857, the highest proportion of European to Indian troops of any station in India: 1 : 1¼.

before, eighty-five skirmishers of the 3rd Bengal Light Cavalry had been paraded in front of the whole garrison to hear their sentence for refusing to accept cartridges for loading drill. They had been found guilty of collective disobedience by a general court martial – composed of fifteen Indian officers – and sentenced to between five and ten years' imprisonment with hard labour.

During the trial the court was told that on 24 April the men had repeatedly refused to accept their allocation of three blank cartridges, despite being assured that they contained no grease and were the same smooth-bore type they had been using all season. The men had refused to give a reason for their recalcitrance, according to their colonel, beyond the conviction 'that they would get a bad name; they all said they would take these cartridges if the others did'. But it later emerged that two ringleaders, both Muslim corporals, had organized the strike by warning their fellow skirmishers that the cartridges had been deliberately prepared with beef and pork fat. All had then agreed not to use the cartridges until the entire Bengal Army had accepted them.

One young European officer, however, blamed his colonel for poor leadership. 'The real case', wrote Cornet John MacNabb to his mother,

is that they hate [Colonel Carmichael-] Smyth, and, if almost any other officer had gone down they would have fired them off . . . The men of course had *no* real excuse for not doing what they were ordered, and they knew what these cartridges were made of, as they had fired them off privately in riding school since the 19th N.I. were disbanded, and they would have continued to do so if they had been left alone, instead of being paraded, and addressed, and all that humbug.

The punishment parade of 9 May was a heart-rending occasion. It took two hours to read the sentences, remove the skirmishers' buttons and boots, and shackle their ankles. All the while, according to one British officer, the prisoners were 'loudly calling' on their comrades for help, 'and abusing, in fierce language, now their colonel, now the officers who composed the court-martial, now

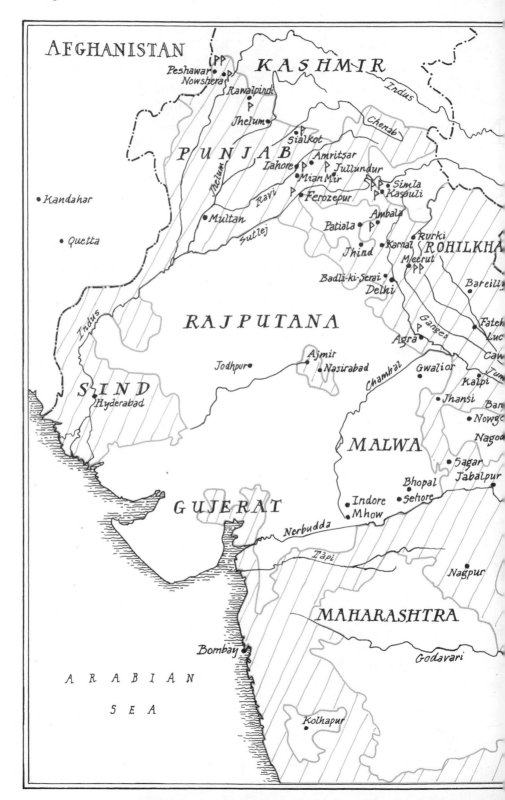

LOCATION OF
MUTINIES
IN
NORTHERN
INDIA
~1857~

INDIA

BAY OF
BENGAL

ARABIAN
SEA

NEPAL

Mt Everest △

Katmandu

Darjeeling

BHUTAN

Brahmaputra

Ghaghra

Sigauli

BIHAR

Dinapore

Ganges

ASSAM

UDH

Benares

Bhagalpur

Berhampur

Dacca

Ilahabad

BENGAL

Raniganj

In Burma PP

BURMA

Barrackpur
Calcutta • Dum-Dum

Chittagong

ORISSA

Sambhalpur

BAY OF

BENGAL

Areas under direct British Rule
Stations of British regiments May 1857

Kilometres  0    200    400
Miles       0    100    200

the Government'. But it would have been madness for the Indian troops to intervene, he added, 'for they would have been swept off the face of the earth by the guns of the artillery and the rifles of her Majesty's 60th Foot [1/60th Rifles], not to speak of the swords of the 6th Dragoon Guards, all of whom were provided with service ammunition, and were so placed as to have the native regiments at their mercy.' That evening, as the prisoners languished in the city jail, Lieutenant Hugh Gough of the 3rd was warned by one of his men that the whole Indian garrison would mutiny the following day and release their comrades. But, when he reported the conversation to Carmichael-Smyth, he was abused for listening to 'idle words'.

At 5 p.m. on 10 May, as predicted, the three Indian regiments rose and began to murder their European officers. They were quickly joined by the rabble from the bazaar, who set upon any Christians they could find. The response of the European troops at Meerut was tardy in the extreme, and by the time they reached the native lines the mutinous troops had already set off for Delhi. Left behind were forty-one white corpses, including those of Cornet MacNabb and the pregnant wife of another British officer who was found with her stomach cut open and her unborn child lying across her chest.

Many historians believe the outbreak was not premeditated and that it began after a cook's boy started a rumour in the bazaar that European troops were coming to disarm their Indian comrades. But this discounts the warning given to Lieutenant Gough the night before, and the fact that the telegraph wire between Delhi and Meerut was cut before the outbreak. The conclusion drawn by the prosecutor of a leading rebel was that the mutiny at Meerut did not occur on 9 May, the day of the punishment parade, because the conspirators needed time to warn the Delhi regiments. Even the hour of mutiny – five o'clock – was evidence of 'cunning and craft' in that the Indian lines were two and a half miles from their European equivalent. The conspirators would have calculated on a lapse of at least one and a half hours before the Europeans could make an appearance. By that time it would be dark and the mutineers long gone – which is exactly what happened.

A short way down the road to Delhi the mutineers stopped and debated their best course of action. Some regard this as proof that the Meerut rising was not pre-planned. Yet the scenario is entirely consistent with the theory that only a small number of sepoys and sowars were part of the conspiracy. Those shouting 'To Delhi!' were almost certainly the ringleaders who had already been in contact with the Delhi troops. Ahsanullah Khan, the king of Delhi's chief physician, later revealed that men of the Delhi garrison told him 'they had leagued with the troops at Meerut' before the mutiny, and that the latter had 'corresponded with the troops in all other places, so that from every cantonment troops would arrive at Delhi'. Even after the outbreak, said Ahsanullah, 'letters were received at Delhi from which it was evident [sepoys all over India] had beforehand made common cause among themselves.'

The first mutineers reached Delhi at 7 a.m. the following morning and made straight for the royal quarters of the Red Fort, where they shouted up to the octogenarian Bahadur Shah II, king of Delhi and grandson of the last Mughal emperor: '*Dohai Badshah!*★ We pray for assistance in the fight for the faith.' The king's response was to instruct his British guard commander, Captain C. R. G. Douglas, to close all the palace and city gates. But it was too late, and Douglas, the commissioner and a handful of other Britons, including two eighteen-year-old girls, were hacked to death by a mob that included royal servants. Shortly after, the mutineers entered the palace and, amidst a clamour of gunshots and shouts, demanded to see the king. A witness recalled:

The officers of the cavalry came forward, mounted as they were, and explained that they had been required to bite cartridges, the use of which deprived Hindus and Mahomedans of their religion, as the cartridges were greased with beef and pork fat, that they accordingly killed the Europeans at Meerut, and had come to claim his protection. The King

★ 'Help, O King!'

replied, 'I did not call for you; you have acted very wickedly.' On this about one or two hundred of the mutinous infantry . . . ascended the steps, and came into the hall, saying, 'that unless you, the King, join us, we are all dead men, and we must in that case just do what we can for ourselves'. The King then seated himself in a chair, and the soldiery, officers and all, came forward one by one, bowed their heads before him, asking him to place his hand on them. The King did so, and each withdrew.

By nightfall the city was in the hands of the mutineers, whose numbers had been swelled by the three Indian regiments of the Delhi garrison. There was no British regiment at Delhi to oppose them, and hundreds of Christians fled towards Meerut and Ambala. But scores did not make it and were either butchered in the city or on the road north by hostile villagers and Gujar tribesmen.

Bahadur Shah was proclaimed emperor of India, and his sons were given command of the various rebel regiments. Yet it seems he was neither aware of the plot to mutiny nor particularly enthusiastic when presented with the fait accompli. He gives the impression of a frightened man, overwhelmed by events and trying desperately to keep in with both the rebels and the British.★ Not that he had any love for the British authorities, who, a few years earlier, had refused either to increase his pension or to recognize his favourite son as his heir. Yet he feared a breakdown of order and was understandably pessimistic about the chances of the rebellion succeeding.

The rebel officers were, in any case, the real power in Delhi. They persuaded the old king to write letters to various Indian rajas, requesting them 'to march at once to Delhi with all their forces to join the King's army, and to repel any attack on the city by the English'. They also forced him to send letters to other Indian regiments, 'promising monthly salaries of thirty rupees to infantry soldiers and fifty to cavalry, if they would join the King's army'.

★ One source suggests that, soon after the rising at Delhi, the king sent a request for help to the lieutenant-governor of the North-Western Provinces at Agra.

# 11. Retribution

Hot weather, long distances and ruptured communications all conspired to slow the government's response to the outbreak of rebellion in India. It was not until 8 June 1857, almost a month later, that a hastily assembled force of 4,000 men* arrived at Delhi from Meerut and the Punjab. It was commanded by Major-General Sir Henry Barnard, who had taken over from General the Honourable George Anson, the commander-in-chief, after the latter succumbed to cholera on 27 May. Having won a crushing victory over the rebels at nearby Badli-ki-Serai on 8 June, Barnard occupied the old military cantonment on a ridge to the north-west of the city. But his plan to take Delhi by *coup de main* was first postponed and then abandoned until the arrival of reinforcements. It was a lost opportunity. Instead of besieging the rebels in the city, Barnard was himself soon besieged on the ridge. And every day that he remained on the defensive, his position became relatively weaker.

The biggest problem for the British was a lack of reliable troops. In the whole of India there were only 45,000 white soldiers (14,000 of them serving in Indian regiments as officers and NCOs), compared to 232,000 Indians. Of the 23,000 British and 136,000 Indian troops in the Bengal Presidency – the epicentre of the rebellion – nearly all the British were concentrated in the recently annexed Punjab. There was only one British regiment in the 700 miles that separated Lucknow from Calcutta. Where the British did have troops – at Agra, Cawnpore and Lucknow – they quickly withdrew behind makeshift defences, having disarmed as many sepoys as possible.

By late June, heartened by the news from Delhi, nearly half the

* Assembled by General Anson, who was at Simla in the hills when the mutiny began, it was made up of British, Sikh, Punjabi and Gurkha regiments.

Indian regiments in the regular Bengal Army had mutinied, partially mutinied or been disbanded.* They had been joined in rebellion by numerous European-officered local and irregular corps, including the whole of the Oudh Irregular Force, the Malwa Contingent, the Bharatpur Legion and most of the Gwalior Contingent. A further thirteen regiments of regular infantry and six of cavalry had been disarmed. In the majority of cases – as if in confirmation of Ahsanullah Khan's claim that it was agreed by the conspirators beforehand – the mutinous corps headed for Delhi. But only a relatively small number of trained Bengal troops, perhaps a couple of thousand in all, had reached the Mughal capital by 16 June, when Barnard postponed his attack on the city for a third time. Over the next ten days, however, the rebels were joined by a further 7,000 men from garrisons as far afield as Nasirabad in Rajputana, Bareilly in Rohilkhand and Jullundur in the Punjab. During the same period Barnard received fewer than a thousand reinforcements. The possibility of a successful assault was becoming ever more distant; and while Delhi remained in the hands of the mutineers, the rebellion continued to spread.

Already large swathes of northern and central India were under rebel control. And, as the sepoys attacked and murdered their officers and families, they were joined by a host of disgruntled civilians. They included: dispossessed rulers like Nana Sahib and the rani of Jhansi; landlords who had had their estates confiscated by the various revenue settlements; disbanded soldiers (particularly from the Oudh Army); Muslim holy men; and petty criminals eager to profit from the breakdown of authority.

In an attempt to suppress the mutiny, every British soldier that arrived at Calcutta was immediately dispatched upcountry: first by railway to Raniganj and then on by bullock cart. But initially these reinforcements were pitifully few and could not prevent the infamous massacre of Wheeler's garrison at Cawnpore in the Doab† on 27 June. Major-General Sir Hugh Wheeler, commanding the

* There were seventy-four regiments of Bengal Native Infantry and ten of Light Cavalry.
† The strip of land between the Ganges and Jumna Rivers.

Cawnpore Division, was the last of a dying breed. Born in Ireland in 1789, he had joined a sepoy regiment at the age of sixteen and had been in India virtually ever since. In that time he had acquired a formidable reputation as a fighting soldier, particularly during the three major campaigns of the 1840s. He was, moreover, an old-style Company officer: the father of mixed race children, fluent in the vernacular, loved by his men, proven in battle – the ideal man to prevent the important garrison of Cawnpore, on the right bank of the Ganges, from falling to the rebels. 'Cawnpore is now the most anxious position,' recorded the governor-general's wife on 21 June 1857, 'but every one speaks alike of Sir Hugh Wheeler and his brave spirit. There is not a better soldier, and all say, if any one can hold it, he will.'

Cawnpore was particularly vulnerable because its 4,000-strong garrison was made up entirely of Indian troops. Even after borrowing fifty soldiers from nearby Lucknow, Wheeler could muster only 400 European men – three quarters of them soldiers, the rest civilians – to protect a further 500 European, Eurasian and Christian women and children. So he took the precaution of building a low mud entrenchment around two disused barracks in the middle of the military cantonment, south of the city. When the Indian troops mutinied in the early hours of 5 June, the men joined the non-combatants in this modest redoubt.

Wheeler was later criticized for choosing such a poor site for his entrenchment (he could have selected the more secure magazine) and for the inadequacy of its three-foot-high mud walls. But he had always assumed that only a temporary refuge was required in the event of a rising, as the mutineers were almost certain to head for Delhi. Which is what would have happened if emissaries of the disgruntled Nana Sahib, who lived at nearby Bithur, had not intervened. Why not overwhelm the weak British garrison first, they suggested, and then proceed to Delhi? The waverers were won over by promises of double-pay, free food and a bonus for destroying the entrenchment.

So on 6 June, having hailed Nana as the new peshwa, the rebels began the siege of Wheeler's entrenchment with a heavy artillery bombardment that continued, with varying degrees of ferocity, for almost three weeks. Attack after rebel attack was beaten off, but the effects of almost constant artillery and sniper fire, not to mention the ravages of disease and lack of food, took their toll. By the time the most determined rebel assault was repulsed on 23 June, the centenary of Robert Clive's victory at Plassey, more than a third of the 900-strong garrison had already perished,* many more were sick and wounded, and the rest were scarcely recognizable as human beings, let alone as members of the pampered, arrogant race that had dominated India for a century. 'Tattered in clothing,' wrote one officer, 'begrimed with dirt, emaciated in countenance, were all without exception . . . Some were sinking into the settled vacancy of look which marked insanity.' No one had washed since the start of the siege, but the rank smell of body odour was nothing compared to the stench from animals that had been shot in the entrenchment and could not be removed, or the torment of flies attracted as a consequence.

With time running out and no relief in sight, Wheeler was persuaded by a conference of surviving senior officers to accept a rebel offer to surrender in return for safe passage down the Ganges. But it was a trap, and during the morning of 27 June, as the garrison struggled to board a fleet of country boats at the Satichaura Ghat, the rebels opened fire from hidden positions, setting alight the boats' thatched roofs. Two boats managed to get away, but both were hunted down and only four European males† avoided the massacre by swimming to safety. The rest of the men were butchered on the river bank and in the boats – General Wheeler amongst them – as were a number of women and children. The shocked and bedraggled survivors – about 125 in all – were led away and later moved to a small, single-storey house on the edge of the city known as the Bibigarh.‡ There they were joined by refugees from

---

* Including Wheeler's son, who was decapitated by a roundshot, leaving his hair and brains smeared on the wall of the general's room.
† Lieutenants Mowbray Thomson and Henry George Delafosse, and Privates Murphy and Sullivan.
‡ A house built for a European's Indian mistress, or *bibi*.

other stations, swelling their numbers to around 200. A Eurasian described the pitiful conditions in which they lived:

It is not easy to describe, but it may be imagined, the misery of so many helpless persons, some wounded, others sick, and all labouring under the greatest agony of heart for the loss of those, so dear to them, who had so recently been killed (perhaps before their own eyes), cooped up night and day in a small low pukka-roofed house, with but four or six very small rooms, and that in the hottest season of the year, without beds or punkahs, for a whole fortnight, watched most carefully on all sides, by a set of unmannerly, brutish, rebellious sepoys.

The Nana had planned to hold the women and children as hostages. But their fate was sealed by the rapid advance of a British relief force under Brigadier-General Henry Havelock. The son of a Wearside shipowner who later lost his money, Havelock was commissioned into the 95th Foot without purchase in 1815 as a reward for his brother's gallant conduct at Waterloo. Eight years later, to save money, he exchanged into the 13th Light Infantry, which was bound for India. But once in India his increasingly radical religious beliefs tended to isolate him from his fellow officers. He had always regarded himself as a 'Christian soldier', and the first troops he had commanded in battle, during the First Burma War, were known as 'Havelock's Saints'. In 1829 he married the daughter of Dr Marshman, the famous Baptist missionary, and thereafter devoted much time to the spiritual welfare of his men, holding religious meetings, preaching sermons and giving Bible lessons.

Regarded warily by his superiors, and lacking the cash to buy promotion, he was still a captain after twenty-three years' service. The logjam was broken by his daring exploits in the First Afghan and Gwalior Wars, which won him a CB and a brevet promotion to lieutenant-colonel. Thereafter his administrative talents secured him a series of high-profile staff appointments and finally, in 1856, his first operational command as a divisional general in Sir James Outram's Persian Expeditionary Force. It was he who masterminded the successful capture of Mohumra on the Euphrates and, having reached Calcutta with the first of the troops from Persia on 17 June, was the obvious choice to command the Cawnpore relief force that was assembling at Allahabad, at the confluence of the Ganges and Jumna Rivers.

Havelock was then sixty-two years old, barely five feet high, with a pinched leathery face, white hair and an old-fashioned beard. And yet he retained an alertness and vigour that inspired confidence. 'General Havelock is not in fashion,' wrote Lady Canning, 'but all the same we believe he will do well. No doubt he is fussy and tiresome, but his little, old, stiff figure looks as active and fit for use as if he were made of steel.'

Havelock reached Allahabad on 30 June and at once assumed command from Colonel James Neill of the 1st Madras European Fusiliers. A tough Scotsman, Neill had helped to disperse mutineers at Benares and later prevented the fort at Allahabad from falling to the rebels by racing ahead of his regiment with a tiny detachment of men. But, since reaching the city on 11 June, he had wasted much time brutally suppressing a local rebellion, and it was not until the 30th, the day of Havelock's arrival, that he at last dispatched a tiny force of 800 men and two guns, under Major Sydenham Renaud, to relieve Cawnpore. A day later came the first news of the massacre and, when it was confirmed on 3 July, Havelock ordered Renaud to halt until he and his Persian veterans – detachments from the 64th (North Staffordshire) Foot and 78th (Seaforth) Highlanders – had caught up. He finally set out from Allahabad on 7 July with a tiny force of 1,185 men and six guns, and, after a series of forced marches, effected a junction with Renaud south of Fatehpur town in the early hours of 12 July.

Later that morning Havelock's combined force – 1,400 Europeans, 560 Indians and eight guns★ – was in the process of setting up camp near the Fatehpur Road when it was attacked by a massive rebel army. Havelock at once pushed forward his guns, under Captain Francis Maude, and those troops of the 64th Foot who were armed with Enfield rifles. Their combined fire drove the

---

★ All smooth-bore, muzzle-loading 9-pounders firing roundshot or canister.

rebels back, in a series of leaps, to a position a mile beyond Fatehpur, where they attempted to make a final stand. By now the British troops were in such a state of exhaustion that Havelock despaired of being able to finish the job. But Maude's guns and the riflemen of the 1st Madras Fusiliers made the difference. 'Their fire', wrote Havelock, 'soon put the enemy to final and irretrievable flight, and my force took up its present position in triumph.' As would become common British practice during the mutiny, his men took no prisoners.

Havelock had routed a numerically superior force, capturing ten guns and two mortars, at a cost of just thirteen casualties. It was a stunning victory and due, in no small part, to the fact that two of his partial regiments – the 1st Madras Fusiliers and 64th Foot – were armed with the new Enfield rifle. Even the columns made up of other units were preceded by skirmishers armed with the Enfield. The rifle was accurate up to 800 yards, and the advantage it gave British troops was as much psychological as tactical. The other key factor was the mobility and accuracy of the British artillery, which was able to provide the advancing infantry with constant close support. The combined effect of the disciplined British cannon and rifle fire was to disrupt the enemy formations before they got anywhere near close-quarter fighting. 'In [the first] ten minutes', wrote Havelock, 'the affair was decided.'

On 14 July, after a day's rest, Havelock's column reached Kolyanpur. The following day the column fought and won two minor engagements* en route to the Pandu Nadi River, twenty-two miles from Cawnpore. On 16 July a sixteen-mile march under a blazing sun brought the column to the village of Maharajpur. There Havelock discovered that the rebels had taken up a strong position two miles ahead at Aherwa, where the Grand Trunk Road forked with the road that led to the military cantonment. 'It was evident that an attack in front would expose the British to a murderous fire from [the Nana's] heavy guns sheltered in his

---

* During the first, Major Renaud was badly wounded in the thigh and died after his leg was amputated below the knee.

entrenchment,' recorded Havelock. 'I resolved therefore to manoeuvre to turn his left.'

He delayed his flanking movement until his lead troops were within range of the rebels' heavy guns, costing him a number of casualties; scores of exhausted and sunstruck soldiers had already fallen out of the ranks, some to be cut down by rebel cavalry. But the manoeuvre was a success, and, at a range of 900 yards, the British cannon opened fire on the rebels' left flank. Screened by riflemen skirmishers, the British regiments attacked in echelon with the 78th Highlanders in the van. Two bayonet charges later and the rebels were driven from the two villages that formed the left and centre of their line. Now the weary Scots were halted, and it was left to the 64th, 84th (York and Lancaster) and Sikhs to race on and take the village of Aherwa and the three guns on the extreme right of the rebel front.

The battle was far from won. A big group of rebels had rallied in a village between the Grand Trunk Road and the Cawnpore Road. With the artillery cattle exhausted and the guns temporarily out of action, Havelock sent in the infantry alone, and they soon cleared the village. But, on re-forming, the infantry columns were amazed to see the whole rebel army drawn up in battle array on each side of an enormous 24-pounder sited on the Cawnpore Road. Havelock at once ordered his troops to lie down, as a rider was dispatched to bring forward the missing artillery. With round-shot from the 24-pounder tearing great gaps in his ranks, however, he could not wait and called on his men, 'who were lying down in line, to leap on their feet' and advance. 'It was irresistible,' he reported. 'The enemy sent round shot into our ranks, until we were within three hundred yards, and then poured in grape with such precision and determination as I have seldom witnessed.'

But, gallantly led by Major Thomas Stirling and Lieutenant Harry Havelock,* the general's son and aide-de-camp, the 64th

---

* For this act, Havelock recommended his son for a VC and it was duly conferred. He did not recommend Stirling because he felt the major had simply been doing his duty. Stirling had to be content with promotion to lieutenant-colonel.

charged and captured the 24-pounder. On seeing this, the rebels 'lost all heart, and after a hurried fire of musketry gave way in total rout'. Only now did four British artillery guns appear to hasten the rebels' departure with a 'heavy cannonade'. Unlike the earlier fight at Fatehpur, this battle was won largely by the bayonet. The relative cost of such a close-quarter fight was heavy: 108 killed and wounded.

That night Havelock's weary troops bivouacked on the battle-field, with the roofless artillery barracks of Wheeler's entrenchment dimly visible in the distance. An elated Havelock slept amongst his troops, a waterproof coat protecting him from the worst of the damp. He had good reason to be pleased. In nine days he and his men had marched 126 miles at the hottest time of the year, won four pitched battles against superior numbers and captured twenty-four guns and mortars. Cawnpore was at last in his grasp.

Next morning, 16 July, Havelock and his men marched the short distance to the Cawnpore cantonment. At its entrance they were met by a filthy, bearded man in chains. He identified himself as Jonah Shepherd, the head clerk of the local Commissariat Department office and the only Eurasian male to survive the siege. He had been captured trying to get through enemy lines and held until the night before, when his jailers fled. He provided the first authentic account of the garrison's treacherous demise, prompting an officer of the Madras Fusiliers to write home: 'The frightful massacre that was reported to have taken place, I am grieved to say, is too true.'

But it was not long before locals revealed the location of an even worse crime: the Bibighar. There, during the late afternoon of 15 July, the 197 captives – all but three of them women and children* – had been murdered in cold blood. The decision to execute them was taken at a council of war convened by Nana Sahib during the afternoon of 15 July, in the wake of Havelock's

* The three men were fugitives from nearby Fatehgarh: two colonels and a magistrate, Robert Thornhill, who also happened to be the son of an HEIC director. The trio were shot.

two victories en route to the Pandu Nadi River. The majority of his advisers were keen to fight it out at Cawnpore (which is what they attempted without success on the 16th). But first they needed to deal with the hostages because 'if they were left alive, they would reveal everything, and thus everyone concerned in the rebellion at Cawnpore would be known.' Nana reluctantly agreed, and the necessary orders were given. As it happened, the captives' sepoy guard refused to take part in the murders, and it was left to a member of Nana's personal bodyguard and four lackeys to carry out the awful deed. This they did with swords, methodically hacking their way through the crowd of screaming women and children. One killer needed two replacement swords before the job was done. It took more than an hour, and even then not all the victims were dead. Some died during the night; at least six – three women and three young boys – were still alive the following morning. They were callously thrown down a nearby well with the bulk of the corpses and left to suffocate.

One of the first of Havelock's column to visit the charnel house on 17 July was Major G. W. P. Bingham of the 64th, who noted in his diary:

The place was literally running ankle deep in blood, ladies' hair torn from their heads was lying about the floor . . . poor little children's shoes lying here and there, gowns and frocks and bonnets belonging to these *poor, poor* creatures scattered everywhere. But to crown all the horrors, after they had been killed, and even some alive, were all thrown down a *deep* well in the compound. I looked down and saw them lying in heaps. I very much fear there are some of my friends included in this most *atrocious fiendish* of murders.

The discovery of the Bibighar made Havelock doubly determined to get to Lucknow – the capital of Oudh, where a large British community of 3,000 souls had been besieged in the residency compound by 20,000 rebels since early July – before an even worse massacre took place. The Indian garrison at Lucknow had first risen and marched away on 30 May, sparking a series of copycat mutinies in stations right across the province. But it was not until late June that the rebels returned to threaten the capital. Sir Henry Lawrence, the inspirational chief commissioner of Oudh, responded by marching his troops out to meet the much larger rebel army on 30 June. It was a mistake. Ambushed near the village of Chinut, Lawrence's Indian troops broke in the face of a massive rebel assault, leaving the British soldiers of the 32nd Foot to fight their way back to the residency as best they could. Casualties included 172 Europeans and 193 Indian soldiers, far more than Lawrence could afford. He himself was mortally wounded on 21 July, the day after the siege of the residency began, by a shell splinter from an 8-inch howitzer. His last request: to 'ask the poor fellows who I exposed at Chinhut to forgive me'.

On 29 July, having laboriously ferried his tiny force of 1,500 men and twelve guns across the Ganges, Havelock began his march on Lucknow. The distance between Cawnpore and the Oudh capital was just sixty miles. But the recently annexed province was teeming with rebels and, having fought and won two battles on the 29th, Havelock came to the reluctant conclusion that he did not have enough men to fight his way through. He had already lost a sixth of his force to battle casualties and illness. He was low on ammunition and had barely enough transport to carry the sick. Then came the news on 31 July that the Bihar Province had risen in revolt and the two regiments he was daily expecting would not be available for at least two months. That day he withdrew towards the Ganges, informing Calcutta that he 'could not . . . move against Lucknow with any prospect of success'. Two further actions were fought against the rebels, both successful, but by 13 August he and his rapidly dwindling column were back in Cawnpore.

In the interim Neill had been meting out his own warped form of justice to rebels suspected of complicity in the Bibighar massacre. He explained in a letter:

Whenever a rebel is caught he is immediately tried, and unless he can prove a defence he is sentenced to be hanged at once; but the chief rebels or ringleaders I first make clean up a certain portion of the pool of blood, still two inches deep, in the shed where the fearful murder and mutilation of women and children took place. To touch blood is most abhorrent to high-caste natives, they think that by doing so they doom their souls to perdition. Let them think so.

The more liberal-minded officials in India, including Lord Canning himself, were appalled at this gratuitous humiliation of high-caste prisoners. But their counterparts in Britain, assailed by exaggerated press accounts of rebel atrocities, were not so squeamish. 'It is rumoured', wrote the president of the Board of Control to Canning, 'that your Government has disapproved of Neill's defilement of the Brahmin mutineers, by making them wash up the blood of their victims, before they were hung. It seems to me a proper characteristic punishment without being brutal or offensive.'

Most Britons in India agreed, particularly those soldiers who had passed through Cawnpore and visited the Bibighar in person. Amongst them was Captain Garnet Wolseley, the veteran of Burma and the Crimea, who was on his way to China when his regiment was diverted to India. He wrote of the Bibighar:

Upon entering those blood-stained rooms, the heart seemed to stop. The horror of the scene was appalling and called up our worst angry passions. The coldest blooded foreigner would have been deeply affected by it, but it awoke in us, the countrymen of these helpless victims, a fiendish craving for the blood of the cowardly brutes who had perpetrated it . . . The walls had been scrawled over as if every man in General Havelock's force who could write had there recorded his vow to God that he would exact punishment in full measure for this crime, which blood alone could expiate . . . Had any English bishop visited that scene of butchery when I saw it, I verily believe that he would have buckled on a sword.

The initial response of Palmerston's government to news of the rebellion was piecemeal at best. At an emergency Commons debate on Monday, 29 June, three days after the news reached Britain, Robert Vernon Smith, president of the Board of Control, told a packed House that 10,000 British troops – mainly reliefs and recruits – were scheduled to sail for India in mid July. A further 4,000 troops requested by the HEIC's court of directors would accompany them. Yet Vernon Smith was keen to downplay the danger. 'Our Indian empire is not "emperilled",' he declared, 'and I hope that in a short time the disaster, dismal as it undoubtedly is, will be effectually suppressed by the force already in the country.'

The queen was not fooled. 'The moment is certainly a very critical one,' she informed Panmure that day, 'and the additional reinforcements now proposed will be much wanted.' Yet not a single infantry regiment would reach the Bengal Presidency from Britain until October.* Part of the reason was the government's insistence on sending the majority of regiments, including the first batch, in sailing ships rather than in steamers. Panmure gave the excuse in parliament that steamers took just as long because they had to keep restocking their coal en route. This was nonsense, and Vernon Smith admitted as much when he wrote to Canning: 'I think it most advisable you should send steamers to tow the sailing vessels from Point de Galle on Madras if you stand in greater need of their accelerated arrival.'

By early August, with no news of Delhi's recapture, the queen complained to Palmerston:

The last accounts from India show so formidable a state of things that the military measures hitherto taken by the Home Government, on whom the salvation of India must depend, appear to the Queen as by no means adequate to the emergency. We have nearly gone to the full extent of our available means, just as we did in the Crimean War, and may be able to obtain successes; but we have not laid in a store of troops, nor formed Reserves which could carry us over a long struggle, or meet unforeseen new calls.

---

\* The 34th (Cumberland) Foot and 3/60th Rifles landed at Calcutta in October 1857. A further nine regiments arrived in November.

Victoria was right. The government was not displaying the urgency the situation in India required, because it continued to under-estimate its seriousness. This was, in part, owing to the desire to avoid the expense of another large-scale conflict, in the wake of the Crimean War. It was also owing to Canning's overly optimistic dispatches. On 5 June, for example, he stated that once Delhi had been recaptured 'the neck of the insurrection will be broken'. A month later he mistakenly informed the queen, in a letter that arrived in early August, of Delhi's recapture by General Barnard. 'Nothing remains in the hands of the insurgents except the Palace or Fort, in which they have all taken refuge.' In fact, as he soon discovered, all of Delhi was still under rebel control, and if any-thing was in danger of falling it was the British position on the ridge. Barnard, moreover, had died of cholera on 5 July and been replaced by the ineffectual Major-General Thomas Reed, who lasted only twelve days in command before he was invalided back to the Punjab. Brigadier-General Archdale Wilson became, there-fore, the fourth commander of the Delhi Field Force in three months. He described the promotion to his wife in the hills as a 'fearful responsibility' and told her: 'knowing as I do my own weakness and incapacity I feel as if I should faint under the burden.'

By now word had reached Britain of Anson's death. Canning recommended Sir Patrick Grant, commander-in-chief of the Madras Army, as his replacement. But the government, the Horse Guards and the queen all preferred the old warhorse Sir Colin Campbell, sixty-four, who was a far more experienced battle-field commander. Never the most daring of generals – and known from his previous stint in the subcontinent as 'Old Kharbadar (Old Careful)' – Campbell was seen as a safe pair of hands. Not everyone was convinced. 'He was utterly devoid of dash,' wrote one Highland officer. 'His whole thoughts were centred on a peerage and he'd risk nothing for fear of losing it, nay more he'd sacrifice all and anybody for its attainment . . . A brave man undoubtedly, but too cautious for India, and too selfish for any place.'

This was a bit harsh. Campbell was generally popular with the men who served under him because they knew he had their best interests at heart. He had a paternalistic reputation, promoting healthy living and discouraging drunkenness. He looked like a concerned grandfather, with his shock of grey curly hair, furrowed brow and goatee. Yet many in India did not approve of his appointment. He had left the subcontinent in 1853 under something of a cloud, after a difficult time as brigade commander at Peshawar, and Canning was amongst those who questioned his return. His objections were brushed aside by Vernon Smith: 'I trust he may prove different when at the head, than what he was when previously known in India.'

Before leaving London, Campbell was summoned to Buckingham Palace so that the queen could thank him for his 'loyalty and patriotic readiness' to serve her in 'so prompt & handsome a manner'. He embarked the same day – 12 July – by mail packet and, travelling via Marseille and the Suez Isthmus, reached Calcutta a month later. The news was bad: a series of fresh outbreaks since June had left much of central India in flames. Recent mutinies had also taken place in the Punjab and in the Benares Division of Bihar Province. At Sasia near Agra, on 5 July, Brigadier-General Thomas Polwhele had been heavily defeated by 4,000 mutineers from Nimach and Kotah. In the wake of this defeat, Agra's entire Christian community was confined to the fort in a virtual state of siege. It was kept there not by the mutineers, who had continued on to Delhi, but by civilian rebels, who had risen in the city and surrounding districts.

Campbell also learnt of the failure of Havelock's first foray into Oudh and, more importantly, of the continued stalemate at Delhi. Soon after Barnard's decision to delay the assault on Delhi in mid June, the rebels had taken the initiative and made almost daily attacks on the ridge. None succeeded, but the position of the British was not improving. By mid July reinforcements from the Punjab had brought the number of British effectives at Delhi to around 6,000; rebel numbers, by the same date, had increased to more than 20,000. Spirits on the ridge finally lifted on 14 August, the day after Campbell reached India, with the arrival of Brigadier-General John Nicholson and his Movable Column.

Nicholson had come a long way since that fatal day on the Khyber in October 1842, when, as a young ensign, he happened upon the mutilated remains of his brother Alexander. At the age of twenty-five in 1848, two years after being appointed political assistant to Sir Henry Lawrence, he was in charge of a frontier province the size of Wales. He had grown into a tall, powerful man whose courage and physical strength were legendary. On one occasion he is said to have ridden alone into a robber village and decapitated the chief, who refused to come quietly, in full view of his men. Some of his Sikh followers were so impressed they formed a religious sect called the 'Nikal Seynis'. Nicholson had them flogged.

When the mutiny began, Nicholson was a deputy commissioner at Peshawar, the most northerly outpost of British India. He and his immediate superior, Herbert Edwardes, were able to keep the turbulent frontier region quiet by acting decisively: first by using British troops at Peshawar on 22 May to disarm their far more numerous Indian comrades; then by appealing to local tribesmen to join them in crushing the sepoy rebellion. The gamble worked, as it did right across the Punjab, because the one race the Sikhs and Pathans hated more than the British was that of high-caste Hindus from northern India. To encourage the others, Edwardes ordered forty mutineers captured by Nicholson to be blown from guns – an old Mughal practice – on 10 June. Another eighty rebels had received the same sentence, but it was commuted by Sir John Lawrence, chief commissioner of the Punjab, who wanted Edwardes to 'temper stern justice with mercy'. He explained: 'Blow away all the rest by all means, but spare boys scarcely out of their childhood, and men who were really loyal and respectful up to the moment when they allowed themselves to be carried away in a panic by the mass.'

A day later, worried that he did not have enough resources to hold the frontier and recapture Delhi, Lawrence suggested withdrawing from the Trans-Indus region and inviting Dost

Mohamed to hold the Vale of Peshawar as an ally.* Edwardes and Nicholson were appalled, and at once drafted a reply: 'It would be a fatal policy to abandon [Peshawar] and retire across the Indus. It is the anchor of the Punjab, and if you take it up the whole ship will drift to sea . . . As to a friendly transfer of Peshawar to the Afghans, Dost Mohammed would not be a mortal Afghan – he would be an angel – if he did not assume our day to be gone in India, and follow after us as an enemy. Europeans cannot retreat – Kabul would come again!' Lawrence ignored this sensible advice and appealed to Canning for permission to withdraw. It was refused in emphatic terms: 'Hold on to Peshawar to the last.'

Edwardes did just that. Nicholson, meanwhile, had left Peshawar on 14 June to take command of the Movable Column of British and irregular troops that had been put together a month earlier to respond to any fresh rebellions in the province. With the appointment went the temporary rank of brigadier-general, not bad for a 34-year-old substantive captain. Nicholson, however, was clearly the man for the job, and his ruthlessness was soon in evidence: disarming Indian regiments before they could mutiny and destroying them when they did. At Trimmu Ghat on the Ravi River, for example, on 16 July, he decimated a mixed rebel force of infantry and cavalry for the loss of just six wounded. Convinced that Nicholson would make the difference at Delhi, where hitherto the commanders had shown a distinct lack of vigour, Lawrence dispatched him and his column from Amritsar on 25 July. His arrival in the British camp on 14 August – bringing the number of British effectives up to 8,000 – was greeted with universal acclaim. Few veterans of the siege were more delighted than a young artillery subaltern called Fred Roberts, the son of Lieutenant-General Sir Abraham Roberts,† who had served with Nicholson on the frontier. He wrote later:

* Dost had signed two treaties with the British: the first, in March 1855, bound the Afghans to be 'friends of our friends and enemies of our enemies' in return for a British promise not to expand to the west; and a second, in January 1857, declaring that he would keep the alliance 'faithfully till death'.
† The brigadier-general who had commanded Shah Shuja's troops during the First Afghan War.

Nicholson impressed me more profoundly than any man I had ever met before, or have ever met since . . . His appearance was distinguished and commanding, with a sense of power about him which to my mind was the result of his having passed so much of his life among the wild and lawless tribesmen, with whom his authority was supreme.

It was not long before the small but fiercely ambitious Roberts was appointed to his hero's staff. But even Nicholson's presence could not persuade General Archdale Wilson to risk an assault until the arrival of a siege train and yet more reinforcements from the Punjab, scheduled for early September.

Campbell's arrival at Calcutta in mid August coincided with the high-water mark of the rebellion. Already more than 60,000 trained troops, two thirds of them regulars, had mutinied. Some had returned quietly to their villages, but many more had materialized from furlough and disbanded regiments to join the revolt. The rebel ranks had been further swelled by tens of thousands of armed civilians.

British commanders had won some important tactical victories. But in a wider, strategic sense the rebels were still in the ascendancy. British garrisons at Delhi, Agra and Lucknow were in a virtual state of siege. Havelock was stalled at Cawnpore, and the revolt in Bihar meant that communications between Calcutta and northern India were intermittent at best. Set-piece battles had not always gone the way of the British. At Chinut, Sasia and elsewhere the rebels had overcome white troops. Yet, with more British troops on the way, and loyal Indian units of the Bombay and Madras Armies advancing into the disaffected areas of central India, time was running out for the rebels.

By the end of August there had been mutinies in Jhansi, Nowgong, Banda, Gwalior, Indore, Mhow, Sagar and Sehore in central India. Large areas of Bundelkhand, Bhopal and the Sagar and Nerbudda Territories were in rebel hands. What helped to prevent the outbreak of rebellion in western and southern India, and enabled the British to gain the upper hand in the central belt, was the hasty departure of the mutineers. In far too many cases they evacuated their stations and headed for the rebel centres of Delhi and Cawnpore, leaving civilian insurgents to oppose a British return. When the sepoys did remain, or entered the region after suffering reverses further north, they showed what redoubtable opponents they could be.

But even trained troops were deficient in three key areas: they lacked a unified chain of command; their officers had no experience of handling large formations; and their muskets were inferior to the British Enfield (though some mutineers are said to have overcome their scruples and used captured Enfields). With this in mind, it is amazing that the rebels won any set-piece battles at all. Their only real hope of defeating the British was by avoiding direct confrontation and waging a guerrilla war, severing lines of communication and appearing where least expected. Had the flame of rebellion spread into western and southern India, some of the ruling princes and significant elements of the Bombay and Madras Armies might have turned against the British. This was still a possibility in August 1857. Yet the aims of most rebels were too localized and disparate. They lacked a leader with the vision to see the wider strategic picture and the military genius to take advantage of it. 'Fortunately for us,' wrote Garnet Wolseley later, 'no great man arose in the upper provinces to take the lead in this Mutiny. Had there been any very able man, amongst the royal family of Delhi, for instance, who had had the sense to head a mutiny at the beginning of 1855, when every soldier we could spare from our ridiculously small army had been sent to the Crimea, our trouble and difficulty would have been increased a hundredfold.'

At the time of Campbell's arrival, however, the fate of British India was still in the balance. With no more reinforcements expected until October, he felt it best to remain in Calcutta and direct operations from there. But his enforced stay with the Cannings at Government House was not entirely fruitless: he arranged supplies for the expected troops, including ammunition, remounts, tents and transport; he established a bullock train between the railhead at Raniganj and Allahabad; and he formed movable columns of 600 men to guard the Grand Trunk Road. He also began to re-form regiments for the heavy fighting still to come. 'The troops which have come in from time to time,' he told Sir John Lawrence, 'have been sent up country by detachments, without regard to the ensemble of regiments. This circumstance, which from the emergency of the case it was, I suppose, impossible to avoid, I am now trying to remedy.'

The royal family was summering at Osborne House, as usual, when a telegram arrived on 22 August with the unwanted news that Delhi was still in rebel hands and both Sir Henry Lawrence and Sir Henry Barnard were dead. Victoria wrote at once to Palmerston, repeating her belief 'that the measures hitherto taken by the Government are not commensurate with the magnitude of the crisis'. She added:

We have given nearly all we have in reinforcements, and if new efforts should become necessary, by the joining of the Madras and Bombay Armies in the revolt, for instance, it will take months to prepare Reserves which ought now to be ready. Ten Battalions of Militia to be called out is quite inadequate; forty, at least, ought to be the number, for these also exist only on paper . . . Financial difficulties don't exist; the 14,000 men sent to India are taken over by the Indian Government, and their expense saved to us; and this appears hardly the moment to make savings on the Army estimates.

Palmerston's rejoinder was that it was always difficult to recruit during harvest-time, and that if 10,000 militiamen 'should be found insufficient, it would be easy afterwards to embody more'. As for the estimates, he said, 'it would be very inconvenient and embarrassing to exceed that amount without some urgent and adequate necessity'. This infuriated the queen, who replied the same day:

The Queen, the House of Lords, the House of Commons, and the Press, all call out for vigorous exertion, and the Government alone take an apologetic line, anxious to do as little as possible, to wait for further news, to reduce as low as possible even what they do grant, and reason as if we had at most *only* to replace what was sent out; whilst if new demands should come upon us, the Reserves which ought now to be decided upon and organized, are only then to be discussed. The Queen can the less reconcile herself to the system of 'letting out a little sail at a time', as Lord Palmerston called it the other day, as she feels convinced that, if vigour and determination to get what will be eventually wanted is shown by the Cabinet, it will pervade the whole Government machinery and attain its object.

Palmerston continued to offer unconvincing excuses, causing Victoria to explode on 25 August: 'The Government incur a fearful responsibility towards their country by their apparent indifference. God grant that no unforeseen European complication fall upon this country – but we are really tempting Providence.'

For some time Victoria had been receiving detailed news from India in the form of monthly letters from her former lady-in-waiting Viscountess Canning. In a letter dated 20 July, for example, Lady Canning informed the queen of the large number of British refugees who were arriving at Calcutta 'almost naked & clothed in rags'. In response the people of Calcutta had spared no effort 'to show them every kindness', throwing open their houses, donating clothes and paying into a public subscription at the rate of £1,000 a day. Far less welcome was a letter of 10 August, detailing the murders of a Major and Mrs Holmes at Sigauli, in the Bihar Province, on 25 July. Lady Canning wrote:

Major Holmes is a fearful story. He raised the 12th Irregulars (cavalry) & loved them as his children. They were doing zealous service, severely punishing offenders, keeping a district quiet, till the moment they hacked him & his wife to pieces & burnt the doctor and his family, all but one child saved by an ayah. Mrs Holmes was the daughter of Lady Sale, widow of Lt. Sturt who was killed in the Cabul retreat. Her child born in that captivity, I am glad to hear, was safe in England.

The queen had met Mrs Holmes, then Alexandrina Sturt, after she and her parents returned to Britain to a hero's welcome in 1844. The cruel irony of surviving the horrific retreat from Kabul, only to be hacked to death by mutineers fifteen years later, was not lost on the appalled monarch. As a mother she was tormented further by the sketchy details she had received of the Cawnpore massacres. 'Poor little scraps of journal,' wrote Lady Canning, 'one by a child, & a letter from a lady to her mother with verses of "Farewell", were picked up in that house where they were murdered. The sight of those rooms makes strong men faint. The bodies were never seen, all were already thrown down a well.'

Victoria's reply, from Balmoral on 8 September, underlines the extent to which she and Albert were affected by events in India. She wrote:

That our thoughts are almost solely occupied with India – & with the fearful state in which everything there is in, that we *feel* as we did during Crimean days, & indeed *far* more anxiety, you will *easily* believe. That my heart *bled* for the horrors that have been committed by people once so gentle (who seem to be seized with some awful mad fanaticism, it is, there cannot be doubt) on my poor country women & those innocent little children, you, dearest Lady Canning, who have shared my sorrows and anxieties for my beloved suffering troops, will comprehend. It haunts me *day* & night. *You* will let *all* who have escaped & suffered, & all who have lost dear ones in so dreadful a manner, *know* of my sympathy – you cannot say too much. A woman & above all a wife & mother can only *too well* enter into the agonies gone into. Of the *massacres* I ask *not* for detail. I cd *not bear* to hear more, but of those who have escaped I *should* like to hear as much about them as you can tell me . . . The distance & the length of time between the mails is *very* trying & must be harrowing to those who have (& *who* has not amongst the gentry & middle classes in England, Gt Britain I should say?) relatives in uncertain & dangerous places?

And yet the queen – unlike some of her subjects in the British press who regarded all Indians as rebels and deserving of punishment –

was able to retain a sense of proportion. She accepted that the retribution of the British 'will be a fearful one, but I hope & trust that our officers & men will show the difference between the Christian and Mussulman & Hindoo by sparing the old men, women & children'. As for the loyal Indian troops, they deserved 'every reward & praise for their position must be very trying & difficult'.

In northern India, meanwhile, Nicholson had brought the capture of Delhi one step closer by soundly defeating a 6,000-strong rebel force under Bakht Khan that was trying to intercept the siege train as it crawled down the Grand Trunk Road from the Punjab. He left the camp with 2,000 men at dawn on 24 August and, after an exhausting march of twenty miles in the burning sun, attacked the main rebel position in a stone enclosure as the sun was beginning to set. His speech to his men echoed Campbell's at the Alma: 'Hold your fire till you are within twenty or thirty yards of the enemy, then pour your volleys into them, give them a bayonet-charge, and the serai is yours.' And so it was, with up to a thousand rebels killed and all but two of their fifteen guns captured.

Wilson received the news with a mixture of admiration and relief. 'Considering that the country was nearly impassable from swamps,' he wrote to his wife, 'I look upon it as one of the most heroic instances of pluck and endurance on record, and [it] does credit as well to Nicholson as to the gallant fellows under him.' Sir John Lawrence was similarly impressed, telling Nicholson that he wished he had 'the power of knighting you on the spot'. But the news he really wanted to hear was of Delhi's fall. 'Every day disaffection and mutiny spread,' Lawrence wrote from Lahore on 29 August. 'Every day adds to the danger of the Native Princes taking part against us.' He also told Wilson that he could expect no more reinforcements from the Punjab. But, even after the arrival of the siege train* on 4 September, bringing the number of

---

* It contained thirty-two howitzers and heavy mortars and more than 100 bullock carts of ammunition.

British effectives to more than 10,000,★ Wilson was loath to order an assault. Fred Roberts wrote later: 'Everyone felt that the time had come for the assault to be made, and Wilson's hesitation caused considerable anxiety. For some unaccountable reason he kept hoping that assistance would come from the south.' And yet everyone knew, added Roberts, that Cawnpore had fallen, Lucknow and Agra were still under siege, and Havelock had failed in his first invasion of Oudh. The responsibility of retaking Delhi was beginning to tell on Wilson, and by early September, wrote Roberts, he was 'quite broken down'.

The matter came to a head at a council of war in Wilson's tent on 7 September. Before the meeting Nicholson had told Roberts: 'Delhi must be taken and it is absolutely essential that this should be done at once; and if Wilson hesitates longer, I intend to propose at today's meeting that he should be superseded.' Fortunately Wilson saw sense at the council and agreed to the plan formulated by his chief engineer, Richard Baird-Smith, to assault the city after a sustained bombardment. His cowardly get-out clause was to insist that Baird-Smith would take the blame if the attack failed. Nicholson was outraged. 'I have seen lots of useless generals,' he wrote to Sir John Lawrence, 'but such an ignorant, croaking obstructive as he is, I have hitherto never met.'

With the forward batteries complete, the bombardment of Delhi's walls began on 12 September. The rebels responded with a storm of mortar, artillery and musket fire that would cost the British more than 300 casualties. But the battering of Delhi's defences continued, and the great attack finally took place at dawn on the 14th. Five columns were involved: three to storm the breaches, one to follow up the initial incursion and one in reserve. The greatest heroics were at the Kashmir Gate, where an eleven-strong party of engineers crept forward with bags of gunpowder to blow the heavy wooden door: two were shot nailing the bags to the door, another two attempting to light them. The second

---

★ 2,000 of them were the maharaja of Jammu's troops and of doubtful quality. A further 3,000 men were in hospital, with the number rising daily.

completed the task, though mortally wounded, and before the dust had settled the assault troops of the 52nd Light (Oxfordshire) Infantry were scrambling towards the gap. Ensign Reginald Wilberforce, the son of the bishop of Oxford, recalled:

I saw my captain, Crosse, go through the gate. It was only large enough to admit one at a time. I was going next when Corporal Taylor pushed me on one side and got second. I came next – third man in. Through the gateway we saw an open square, the sunlight pouring into it, empty. Under the arch of the gateway stood a nine-pounder gun . . . Next to and around the gun lay some dead bodies, the defenders of the Gate . . . [It] was soon thrown open, and our men, Coke's Rifles and the Kumaon Battalion, which formed our assaulting column, poured in after us.

Once in, the stormers raced off towards their various objectives: the 1st and 2nd Columns up the narrow road that followed the ramparts; the 3rd Column towards the famous Jama Masjid mosque in the city centre. But, having passed the Delhi Gate, the men of Nicholson's 1st Column began to meet heavy resistance from rebel guns and snipers. 'As long as we rushed on cheering and never stopping, all went well,' recorded one officer. 'But the check was sad: the men, crouching behind corners, and in the archways which support the ramparts, gradually nursed a panic.' Outside too the supporting column had almost been driven back to its start line, the Jammu troops fleeing in disorder. Someone had to take the initiative, and that man, inevitably, was Nicholson. Calling on the men of the 1st Bengal Fusiliers to follow him, he led the way towards the Burn Bastion, halfway between the Kabul and Lahore Gates. But only a handful followed, and as he turned, sword in hand, to harangue the rest, he was shot and mortally wounded by a sniper.

General Wilson, meanwhile, had set up his headquarters in the ruined church just inside the Kashmir Gate. There he heard of the repulse of the supporting column and, worse, that Nicholson had fallen. 'All this greatly agitated and depressed the General,' recalled Fred Roberts, who was present, 'until at last he began seriously to consider the advisability of leaving the city and falling back on the Ridge.' Wilson rallied momentarily at the news that the support column was holding its ground. But word that the 3rd Column had been forced to retire from the Jama Masjid, that there was no hope for Nicholson, and that British casualties were extremely heavy,★ seemed to 'crush all spirit and energy' out of the British commander. He became more convinced than ever of the need to withdraw and would have 'carried out this fatal measure', wrote Roberts, had it not been for Baird-Smith's determined opposition. The dying Nicholson was just as emphatic. When told of Wilson's wavering, he rose up in bed and roared: 'Thank God I have strength yet to shoot him, if necessary.'

It was not, as it happened, because Wilson accepted the argument that any withdrawal would be a severe blow to British prestige. But in the coming days he could never quite dispel his fear of failure. 'We are now holding what we have taken,' he wrote to his wife on the 15th, 'but nothing more . . . All we can now expect to do, is to get on gradually.' And a day later: 'Our force is too weak for this street fighting, where we have to gain our way inch by inch.' It did not help that many of his British and Sikh troops were drunk and incapable of doing their duty, nor that the rebels defended the city with the desperation of men who could expect no quarter.

The tide finally turned on 19 September, by which time the king and most of the mutineers had already evacuated the city, with the capture of the Burn Bastion. A day later and the Lahore Gate, the Jama Masjid and the Red Fort were all in British hands. The city had been captured, and Sikh troops celebrated by lighting fires in the sacred mosque. Others plundered to their hearts' content, shooting any adult male they found, though most obeyed Wilson's order to spare women and children.

On 21 September, acting on a tip-off, Captain William Hodson and a small force of cavalrymen captured Bahadur Shah and his

---

★ On 14 September the Delhi Field Force lost sixty-nine officers and 1,104 men killed and wounded.

favourite wife at Humayun's tomb on the outskirts of Delhi. A day later Hodson returned to the tomb to arrest two of the king's sons and one grandson, leading lights in the rebel government. As before, Hodson was accompanied by fewer than a hundred troopers of Hodson's Horse, the irregular cavalry regiment he had raised at the start of the rebellion. Guarding the tomb were more than 3,000 of the royal family's armed retainers. Yet Hodson's bold gamble paid off, and, like their father before them, the princes surrendered without a fight. They would soon regret their pusillanimity. On the way back to Delhi, Hodson's cavalcade was stopped by an angry mob. Fearful that his prisoners would escape, Hodson grabbed a carbine and shot them one by one. Wilson refused to condemn the summary executions, telling his wife on 22 September that the princes 'have been most virulent against us' and that 'Hodson, as a Partizan Officer, has not his equal'. But others further afield were not so sure.

With Delhi in British hands, it was as much as Wilson could do to scrape together a mobile column of 2,500 men to pursue the flying rebels and relieve Agra to the south. The six-day battle for Delhi had cost the British almost a thousand killed and 2,845 wounded, more than a third of effectives. Many hundreds more had died of disease and exposure. Yet Wilson knew that the rebel cause had been struck a mortal blow.* 'If Havelock could only relieve Lucknow and move up this way,' he wrote on 22 September, 'the whole rebellion could be put down.' His wish – or at least part of it – was about to be granted.

On 19 September, his force now increased to 3,200 men, Havelock crossed once more into Oudh by the newly completed bridge-of-boats. He had assumed that Major-General Sir James Outram's arrival at Cawnpore on the 15th would result in his supersession. But, in an extraordinary act of generosity, Outram waived his right to military command so that Havelock and his troops could

---

* Wilson's reward for retaking Delhi was a baronetcy and a pension of £1,000 a year. No mention was made, in public at least, of his hesitant – almost defeatist – conduct in the days leading up to and during the assault.

complete the task for which they had 'so long and gloriously fought'. He would accompany the relieving force as a volunteer, he said, and resume his military seniority only once Lucknow had been relieved. In reality, Outram continued to issue orders as 'though he had never resigned in the first place', so that 'no one in the force knew who actually was commanding'.

The seriousness of the Lucknow garrison's position was underlined by a message – written in Greek and hidden in a tiny piece of quill – that had reached Cawnpore by Indian courier a few days earlier. 'I hope to be able to hold on to the 20th–25th,' wrote Lieutenant-Colonel Inglis, the garrison commander. 'I must be frank and tell you that my force is daily diminishing from the enemy's musketry fire and our defences are daily weaker. Should the enemy make any really determined effort to storm this place I shall find it difficult to repulse him.' Since Lawrence's death in early July, the residency compound had been under almost constant bombardment, with one large-scale rebel attack on 10 August only narrowly beaten off. Snipers, shellfire, disease and hunger were claiming more than twenty victims a day, many of them children. So desperate was the situation by late August that Havelock advised the garrison to cut its way out. Inglis declined. His strength was now down to 650 troops, half of them British, and a further 120 sick and wounded, 220 women and 230 children. He had 'no carriage of any description' to transport the non-combatants, a huge stockpile of treasure and thirty guns.

Havelock began his advance from the Ganges on 21 September, outflanking a strong rebel force in the village of Mangalwar and driving it back down the Lucknow Road. The following day, after a long unopposed march of sixteen miles, he reached Banni on the River Sai. Next morning, the 23rd, his advance guard came upon the main rebel position, its left resting on a walled enclosure known as the Alambagh ('Garden of the World') and its centre and right on a chain of hills. Havelock again displayed his tactical dexterity, fixing the rebel centre with one brigade while he moved round its right flank with another. Having driven the enemy from a number of villages, the flanking brigade attacked and took the Alambagh at the point of the bayonet. Outram and the volunteer cavalry finished the job by pursuing the beaten rebels to within sight of Lucknow's domes and minarets.

The final assault on the city, however, was delayed for a further three days, while Havelock rested and reorganized his column. During the morning of 25 September, having left his baggage and wounded in the Alambagh with a guard of 250 men, Havelock continued his advance, placing Neill's 1st Brigade to the fore. It drove the rebels from a succession of gardens and walled enclosures, and then captured the strongly held Charbagh Bridge intact. An officer who crossed over minutes later recalled that 'the dead and dying lay so thick it was impossible to avoid treading on them.'

Havelock knew that the direct route to the residency was heavily defended. So instead he took a more circuitous route to the east. No serious opposition was encountered until the lead troops approached the Kaisarbagh, the principal residence of the kings of Oudh, where a large rebel force and two guns were ensconced. Scores of Havelock's men were hit as they attempted to cross a small bridge. Those who made it were able to cover the others. With the column strung out, the light failing and half a mile still to go to the residency, Havelock and Outram held a council of war. Weakened by a flesh wound, Outram suggested occupying a nearby palace to give the rearguard time to close up. Havelock had other ideas:

I esteemed it to be of such importance to let the beleaguered garrison know that succour was at hand, that with [Outram's] ultimate sanction I directed the main body of the 78th Highlanders and the regiment of Ferozepore to advance. This column rushed on with desperate gallantry led by Sir James Outram and myself and Lieutenants Hudson and Hargood of my staff, through streets of flat-roofed loopholed houses, from which a perpetual fire was kept up, and overcoming every obstacle, established itself within the enclosure of the Residency.

The delighted occupants of the residency were as surprised as the rebels by Havelock's rapid progress. A Mrs Harris recorded:

At dusk, we heard a very sharp fire of musketry close by, and then a tremendous cheering; an instant after, the sound of the bagpipes, then of soldiers running up the road. Our compound and verandah filled with our deliverers, and all of us shaking hands frantically and exchanging fervent 'God bless yous!' with the gallant men and officers of the 78th Highlanders.★ Sir J. Outram and staff were next to come in, and the state of joyful confusion was beyond description. The big, rough, bearded soldiers were seizing little children out of our arms, kissing them with tears running down their cheeks, and thanking God they had come in time to save them from the fate of those at Cawnpore.

The bulk of Havelock's column did not reach the relative safety of the residency until the following day. Amongst those who never made it was Brigadier-General Neill, the scourge of Allahabad and Cawnpore, who was shot as he tried to prevent a battery of artillery from taking a wrong turn; and a large group of wounded who, abandoned by their bearers, were murdered in their litters.

Outram now resumed command. But so expensive had the relief of Lucknow been – 535 casualties on 25/26 September alone – that he did not feel strong enough to withdraw the 1,500 non-combatants to Cawnpore. Instead he would reinforce the original garrison, he informed Sir Colin Campbell by letter on 30 September, and await his own relief. Having already endured a siege of three months, many of the women and children were bitterly disappointed. 'Everyone is depressed,' wrote one widow, 'and all feel that we are in fact *not relieved*. The fighting men we have are too few for our emergency, and too many for the provisions we have in the garrison.'

---

★ A total of seven Victoria Crosses were awarded for gallantry that day, four of them to men of the 78th Highlanders.

## 12. The 'jewel of her Crown'

The news from Delhi and Lucknow was greeted with considerable relief at Government House. It arrived at Calcutta shortly after more troops from the China expedition, including Sir Colin Campbell's beloved 93rd Highlanders. 'He went to see them on board their transport before they arrived,' Canning informed the queen, 'and when . . . asked how he found them, replied that the only thing amiss was that they had become too fat on the voyage, and could not button their coats.'

The rebellion, however, was far from over: the Dinapore mutineers were still at large in Bihar; recent mutinies had taken place in Jabalpur and Nagode in central India; and much of Bundelkhand, Oudh and the North-Western Provinces was still under rebel control. Sir Colin Campbell's priority was to recapture Lucknow, and, to that end, all new troops were dispatched up the Grand Trunk Road by bullock train. Campbell followed on 27 October, by which time a further eight regiments – or parts of them – had arrived from England.

Narrowly avoiding capture by rebels in Bihar, Campbell reached Cawnpore on 3 November, only to be told that Tatya Tope, a lieutenant of Nana Sahib, and 5,000 mutinous troops of the Gwalior Contingent were approaching Kalpi to the south-west. Even Outram felt that Campbell should deal with the Gwalior rebels before liberating Lucknow. But the commander-in-chief did not agree. Lucknow, he felt, was a prize of much greater strategic and symbolic worth. On 9 November, leaving Major-General Charles Windham and 500 troops to guard Cawnpore, he set off to join the main British force, which was camped on a sandy plain between Banni and the Alambagh. The majority were men from the Delhi Movable Column, which, having defeated a rebel army at Agra on 10 October, had received orders from Campbell to

advance into Oudh and make contact with the tiny garrison in the
Alambagh. This was achieved on 5 November, though not without
a scare. 'As we neared the Alambagh,' recalled Fred Roberts, 'the
enemy's guns opened on us from our right, while their Cavalry
threatened us on both flanks. They were easily disposed of, and
we deposited the stores, receiving in exchange a number of sick
and wounded who were to be sent back to Cawnpore.'

By coincidence Captain Garnet Wolseley of the 90th Light
Infantry, who would become Roberts's great rival for the accolade
of Victoria's finest general, was also at the Alambagh on the 5th.
He had arrived a couple of weeks earlier, with a small relief column
of 500 men and four guns, and described the position as

a large three-storied and very substantially built square brick building,
with a tower at each corner, in which there was a staircase. Round it
was a large square garden, whose sides were about four hundred yards
each, the whole enclosed by a thick wall some twelve or more in height.
There was a large two storied gateway opening out upon the road,
beyond which was a pretty little mosque with minarets. At each angle of
the garden was a tower, round the outside of which we had constructed a
bastion with a feeble attempt at an abattis beyond the ditch.

Every day the garrison was bombarded by a battery of huge 32-
pounder guns sited on the edge of Lucknow. Wolseley and the
other young officers urged the commandant, an old major of the
75th (Stirlingshire) Foot,* to let them sally out and destroy
the battery. 'We were then well into the cold weather,' wrote
Wolseley, 'and just before daybreak at that season the sepoy is at
his worst. Almost paralysed with cold, he is nearly torpid and good
for very little. All ranks in those three companies of my regiment
were young, and, as they had but lately served in the batteries
before Sebastopol, they thought little either of the feeble fire from
the battery or of the sepoys who worked it. If permitted to attack
it they would have made short work of both the battery and its

---

* Later the 1st Battalion, Gordon Highlanders.

garrison. But the commandant had been in India almost all his service; he had seen next to nothing of war, and knew little of its ways; besides, the sun had apparently taken all "the go" out of him.'

The morning after his arrival in the main British camp, six miles south-west of the Alambagh, Campbell was at the entrance to his tent when he was approached by a tall Indian in a dishevelled costume who said he was looking for the British commander-in-chief. 'I am Sir Colin Campbell,' came the reply. 'And who are you?'

By way of response, the Indian took off his turban and from its folds produced a letter and a map, both signed by Sir James Outram. The letter explained that the bearer was none other than Thomas Henry Kavanagh of the Bengal Civil Service, a former chief clerk to Sir Henry Lawrence, and that he had volunteered to cross enemy lines to bring Campbell a map of the best route into the residency. As Campbell read the letter, he kept glancing up at his bizarrely attired visitor. 'Is it true?' he asked.

'I hope, sir,' said Kavanagh, 'you do not doubt the authenticity of the note?'

'No! I do not!' came the testy reply. 'But it is surprising. How did you do it?'

Kavanagh pleaded exhaustion and only later, once rested, did he recount his adventures to Campbell and his staff. The day before, aware that Outram had drafted a map to assist Campbell's advance, he had offered to deliver it, because only he had the 'requisite local knowledge' to explain it. At first Outram was against the idea, urging the impossibility of a European getting through the rebel lines. So insistent was Kavanagh, however, that Outram eventually said he could go – but only if his disguise passed muster. That evening, 9 November, Kavanagh returned to Outram's quarters with his face and hands blackened and his body encased in an outlandish costume: white muslin shirt, tight trousers, tight native shoes turned up at the toe, cream turban, yellow silk coat and a yellow chintz sheet thrown round his shoulders; in his hands were clutched a sword and shield. He looked like Ali Baba, but the 'disguise' was enough to fool Outram and his staff, some of whom berated the impertinent 'native' for sitting down without permission. Impressed, Outram hid the plans in Kavanagh's turban, while an officer gave him a double-barrelled pistol to use on himself if he was captured. At 8.30 p.m. he set off with an Indian courier, Kanauji Lal. No one expected them to survive.

The series of scares and travails that the pair experienced during that seemingly endless night would fill a chapter on their own. They lost their way, fell in a canal and were repeatedly questioned by suspicious rebels. But they somehow kept going and, at one point, were even given directions by a squad of sepoys. They finally reached the outer British picquets – and safety – at five in the morning. With dawn approaching, Kavanagh's streaked face and inadequate disguise would not have held up for much longer. He had made it just in time.*

Outram's advice was for Campbell not to enter the city by the same route he and Havelock had taken, because the rebels had destroyed the Charbagh Bridge and were strongly posted in the streets beyond. His recommendation was for Campbell to take an even bigger detour to the east of the city by heading for the Dilkusha hunting lodge and park. From there he could turn north, cross the canal near the Martinière College and advance through the palace area to the residency. 'Outram showed his military acumen in suggesting this route,' recalled Fred Roberts, now on Campbell's staff, 'as our right flank would be covered by the [Gumti] river, and therefore could only be molested by a comparatively distant fire. Sir Colin, appreciating all the advantages pointed out, readily accepted and strictly adhered to this plan of advance, except that, instead of crossing the canal by the bridge, we forded it a little nearer the river.'

On 12 November, Campbell marched his force to the Alambagh, where he deposited his heavy baggage and collected a handful of reinforcements, including Wolseley's company, which was enrolled in a composite battalion of 90th Light Infantry, 84th Foot

* For this extraordinary feat, Kavanagh became only the third civilian to win the VC. The first two, William McDonell and Ross Mangles of the Bengal Civil Service, won theirs at Arrah on 30 July 1857.

and 1st Madras Fusiliers. Two days later, armed with Outram's map and with Kavanagh at his side, Campbell began his advance on Lucknow with a force that now numbered 4,700 men and forty-nine guns and mortars. Wolseley wrote:

We circled, as it were, round the southern and eastern outskirts of Lucknow at a distance of about a mile and a half from the then unfordable canal which there formed the city boundary, until we struck the river Goomtee as it flows below the high ground upon which stands, in imposing grandeur, the palace known as the Dil Koosha . . . A high wall of sun-dried brick surrounded it, through which openings were easily made. As we entered it, several small deer of various sorts ran about, terrified at this unusual invasion; most of them were in the soldiers' camp kettles that evening . . .

Below us, and about three-quarters of a mile north of the Dil Koosha, stood a very large, ugly, and un-Indian looking edifice known as the Martinière College, between which and the city were fine mango gardens. From both it and the Dil Koosha the enemy retired upon our approach, treating us to a few round shot as they did so.

The troops slept that night in the Dilkusha, and most of the 15th was taken up with preparing the final advance: stores were brought forward, and the Dilkusha was turned into a forward base camp with five guns, an infantry regiment and some cavalry to protect it.

Next morning, having feinted an attack over the canal to his left, Campbell's advance guard crossed below a dam on the right and headed straight for the Sikandarbagh, a large fortified garden a mile ahead. But, as it moved down a lane to the right of the building, it was checked by fire from three directions: from the garden, from some barracks to the left, and from the Kaisarbagh and other buildings to the front. The 93rd Highlanders took care of the barracks, but heavy guns were needed to breach the Sikandarbagh. Wolseley helped tow one into position, with the enemy's bullets hammering 'the iron tyre of the wheel I was working at'. He added:

I don't think we were over eighty yards from the corner tower of the place when we hauled the gun into action. The gun opened fire at once, sending great clouds of dust into the air when at each round its heavy shot struck the wall. Close behind me were the 93rd Highlanders, and as soon as the gun had made a sufficiently big hole in the wall, they went gallantly for it, whilst Wylde, with his magnificent regiment of Sikhs, went for the only gateway into the place and quickly burst it open.

There was a narrow staircase on each side of the arched gateway leading to an upper story, well packed with the enemy. Without a moment's hesitation the Sikhs mounted these winding corkscrew-like stairs, and in a few minutes were amidst the enemy, cutting them up with their tulwars and hurling others out of open windows. Few British soldiers would have done this.

With the gateway and the breach as the only exits, the 2,000 rebels inside the Sikandarbagh were caught like rats in a trap. 'Inch by inch,' recalled Fred Roberts, 'they were forced back to the pavilion, and into the space between it and the north wall, where they were all shot or bayoneted. There they lay in a heap as high as my head, a heaving, surging mass of dead and dying inextricably entangled. It was a sickening sight, one of those which even in the excitement of battle and the flush of victory make one feel strongly what a horrible side there is to war.' Given the odds against the original stormers and the desperate nature of the fighting, British casualties were relatively modest: twelve officers and 130 men killed and wounded.

With the Sikandarbagh in British hands, the next objective was a walled mosque called the Shah Najaf. Attack after attack was beaten off, as the infantry failed to find a way past its high walls. Field guns were brought up, but their fire had little effect. In desperation, two 68-pounder guns of Captain William Peel's Naval Brigade were sent so far forward that their crews were sitting ducks. Within minutes the entire crew of one had been killed, and only Able Seaman William Hall, a black Canadian, and his badly wounded officer remained alive at the other. Amidst a storm of musket balls they continued to serve the gun, Hall heaving it back into position and the officer firing it. It was almost nightfall when the mosque was at last taken, two officers having discovered that the shell-shocked defenders were leaving by a back entrance. Hall survived to become the first black recipient of the VC.

Next morning the assault continued, with a delighted Wolseley put in charge of an attack on the mess house of the 32nd Foot, the only British regiment in Lucknow when the mutiny began. He recalled:

I steadied my men and 'whipped them in' at the garden wall as we scrambled over it, and then made for the open doorway of the Mess House itself. It was a fine, strongly built square building, and as I reached the masonry-reveted ditch round it, I rejoiced to find the drawbridge down, and quite passable . . . As I ran across it, no sepoy was to be seen anywhere! I ran to the corresponding door on the opposite side of the house, and could see the enemy as they scuttled quickly away from the bullets some of my men were firing to help them on their way. The garden in that direction seemed fairly full of them.

Having secured the mess house, Wolseley led his company on towards the Moti Mahal* Palace, while another company commander made for the Tara Kothi. They did not know it at the time, but these were the last enemy-held buildings that lay between them and the hard-pressed Lucknow garrison. They broke through the bricked-up entrances of the Moti Mahal using crowbars and picks, and were in the process of clearing the complex room by room when they heard an enormous explosion on the opposite side of the courtyard. Out of the dust and smoke appeared an officer and some British soldiers coming from the direction of the residency. 'To the astonishment of us all,' wrote Wolseley, 'it was Captain Tinling of my regiment with his company behind him. They had sprung a mine to blow down the palace wall to enable them to make a sortie in order to meet our relieving force.' Tinling and his men had taken part in the first relief of Lucknow. Now,

* Literally the 'Pearl Palace', the home of the queen mother.

uniquely, they were relieved in turn by men of their own corps.

Minutes later, in the same square, took place the celebrated meeting between Campbell and the two besieged generals, Outram and Havelock, the latter looking 'ill and worn'. Raising his cap, Campbell shook Outram's hand with the words: 'How do you do, Sir James?' Then, turning to Havelock, he added: 'And how do you do, *Sir* Henry.' It was the first Havelock knew of his knighthood, and it helped to brighten his sickly countenance. But his and Outram's suggestion that Campbell should attack and take the formidable Kaisarbagh Palace, whose guns were at that very moment tearing up the ground around them, was not heeded. Campbell's priority was to rescue the non-combatants and return them safely to Cawnpore. Having already lost 500 men in the assault, he did not consider he had enough left to capture the city.

While the meeting was taking place, Wolseley was congratulated on the achievements of his company by Brigadier-General Adrian Hope. But Hope added a word of caution: 'I advise you to keep out of Sir Colin's way: he is furious with you for pushing on beyond the Mess House, for the capture of which his orders to you alone extended.'

'Rather hard on me,' came the hurt reply. But Wolseley knew the real reason behind Campbell's anger. 'I had', he wrote later, 'upset Sir Colin's little plan for the relief of Lucknow by the 93rd Highlanders.' His beloved 93rd, who had fought so well at Balaklava and in numerous actions during the advance, had been denied the honour of saving the beleaguered garrison by a no account captain from a county regiment. Campbell had 'never been so enraged by any man in his life'. By next morning his mood had softened enough for him to congratulate Wolseley and promise him promotion. But he never forgave him properly and made scant mention of the 90th's feats in his official dispatch.

The withdrawal began on the 19th, and it took a further three days to move all the non-combatants, money, stores and guns from the residency to the Dilkusha. During that time a heavy bombardment was kept up against the Kaisarbagh to convince the rebels an attack was imminent. Secrecy was vital and, to that end, a screened roadway was made from the residency to the Moti Mahal. Thereafter the route was fairly secure, though Wolseley had to remind a number of women that 'although hidden from the enemy's view they had no protection there from his round shot.' He was surprised by their grumpy demeanour. 'Not one of them said a gracious word to the soldiers who had saved them,' he wrote, 'a fact which my men remarked upon. Indeed, poor creatures, they did not make a favourable impression upon any of us, for they seemed cross; they certainly grumbled much at everything and everybody.' Small wonder. They were dirty, unkempt and undernourished. They had lost their homes, their possessions, and some their husbands and children. Many must have regarded their own lives as hardly worth saving.

On 24 November, the day Campbell began to move his force back to the Alambagh, Havelock died of dysentery. He had been sick for some time and knew the end was near. 'I die happy and contented,' he told his son Harry, before expiring in his arms. He was, wrote Campbell in a general order, 'a martyr to duty'.

Three days later, leaving Outram and 4,000 troops to garrison the Alambagh, Campbell retraced his steps to Cawnpore with the balance of his force: 3,000 fit men and a further 1,500 casualties and non-combatants. 'It was a strange procession,' recalled Fred Roberts. 'Everything in the shape of wheeled carriage and laden animals had to keep to the road, which was narrow, and for the greater part of the way raised, for the country at that time of the year was partly under water, and *jhils* were numerous. Thus, the column was about twelve miles in length, so that the head had almost reached the end of the march before the rear could start. Delays were constant and unavoidable, and the time each day's journey occupied, as well as the mode of conveyance – country carts innocent of springs – must have been trying to delicate women and wounded men.'

As the column proceeded in this tortoise-like fashion to Cawnpore, Campbell received the alarming news that Windham's small force had been attacked and driven back into its new entrenchment by Tatya Tope and the Gwalior Contingent on the 26th and

27th. Fearful for Windham's safety, Campbell hurried his column forward, crossing the bridge-of-boats and linking up with the entrenchment on 29 November. For a week he remained on the defensive while the non-combatants were sent down river to Allahabad. Then on 6 December, without warning, he attacked the right of the rebel position and routed it, capturing nineteen guns and the enemy camp intact. The 13,000 rebels fled in two directions: Tatya Tope and the Gwalior Contingent back to Kalpi; Nana Sahib and his remaining troops north to Bithur. For one British officer, the defeat of the Gwalior Contingent was a psychological turning point. 'Our star was in the ascendant,' he wrote, 'and the attitude of the country people showed that they understood which was the winning side.'

'Thank God! Lucknow is safe!' wrote the queen to Lady Canning on 25 December 1857. 'I cannot tell you how truly thankful we all are – & how rejoicing it should have been known just *before* Christmas!'

A month earlier, to her great relief, she had learnt of Delhi's capture and Lucknow's first relief. 'They did not arrive a moment too soon,' Lady Canning had written to her on 11 October, 'for besides scarcity of provisions, one shudders to hear that mines were found, stretching far within the works, ready to be loaded, and another day might have been too late to save that garrison.' At Delhi, she added, 'the soldiers inflicted murderous retribution' and private letters told of an 'immense slaughter of men'. But 'they always spared women and children', just as the queen hoped they would.

The queen replied on 25 November, thanking Lady Canning for the excellent news and commiserating with the deaths of Nicholson and Neill, 'just when they seemed to have overcome their greatest difficulties'. A far more revealing letter was the one she wrote in late September, asking the Cannings to 'ascertain *how far*' the reports of atrocities were 'true'. She was, she explained, not referring to the butchery of women and children, which, 'while very shocking in itself', was all too commonplace in war.

Even British troops had committed crimes during the sacking of Badajoz and San Sebastián in the Peninsular Wars, 'which if published in newspapers wd raise outbursts of horror & indignation'. She meant, instead, reports of 'people having to eat their children's flesh – & other unspeakable & dreadful atrocities which I could not write'. As it turned out, such reports were fictitious, as were those that referred to the wholesale rape of European women.* Yet the very fact that the queen was trying to view the atrocities in context is testament to an impressive breadth of mind. She displayed more of the same in a letter to Lord Canning on 9 November, congratulating him on his policy of moderation in dealing with captured 'rebels'. He had earlier insisted, in a controversial resolution of 31 July, that only those guilty of bloodshed, or from mutinous regiments that had committed atrocities, were liable to summary execution. It was a distinction that earned him the scathing epithet 'Clemency Canning' and the enmity of much of the Indian and British press. Even Palmerston was oddly unsupportive, fearful of inflaming public opinion and still angry at Canning's unauthorized diversion of the China expedition. But the queen had no doubts. 'For the perpetrators of these awful horrors,' she wrote, '*no* punishment can be severe enough &, sad as it is, stern justice must be dealt out to all the guilty ones. But to the native at large, to the peaceable inhabitants, to the many kind & friendly ones who have assisted us, sheltered the fugitives & been faithful and true – these should be shown the greatest kindness. They should know there is no hatred of brown skin.'

Mopping-up operations in India continued well into 1859. But as early as December 1857 – following the recapture of Delhi, the rescue of the Lucknow garrison and the defeat of the Gwalior Contingent – the failure of the rebellion was certain. As British reinforcements poured into the subcontinent, rebel numbers were

---

* A government inquiry reported in December 1857 that there was no definite proof that any European women had been raped, though some Eurasians were taken as concubines.

being steadily eroded by battle casualties, illness and desertions. Of the three main centres of residence – Delhi, Cawnpore and Lucknow – only the last remained in rebel hands, and it had twice been penetrated by British columns. Large parts of central India, the North-Western Provinces, Bihar and Oudh were, it is true, still outside British control. But the rebels had neither an army nor a commander capable of defeating the British in the field. The interesting question now was not whether the British would reconquer India, but when and what form the subsequent political settlement would take.

The next stage of the reconquest began with Sir Colin Campbell's victory over the forces of the rebel nawab of Farrukhabad* at Khudaganj, north of Cawnpore, on 2 January 1858. An easy success against demoralized opponents, the battle is chiefly remembered for providing Fred Roberts with the opportunity to win a Victoria Cross. Like many ambitious officers without money or influence, he knew that the cross was a shortcut to promotion. For months he had been telling his family, in letters home, of his determination to win one. His chance came during the cavalry pursuit with the 5th Punjab Cavalry and he grabbed it with both hands. He wrote:

The chase continued for nearly five miles, until daylight began to fail and we . . . overtook a batch of mutineers, who faced about and fired into the squadron at close quarters. I saw Younghusband fall, but I could not go to his assistance, as at that moment one of his *sowars* was in dire peril from a sepoy who was attacking him with his fixed bayonet, and had I not helped the man and disposed of his opponent, he must have been killed. The next moment I descried in the distance two sepoys making off with a standard, which I determined must be captured, so I rode after the rebels and overtook them, and while wrenching the staff out of the hands of one of them, whom I cut down, the other put his

---

* Part of the nawab's forces were under the command of General Bakht Khan, the former rebel commander-in-chief at Delhi, who had fled to Fatehgarh after the fall of Delhi.

musket close to my body and fired; fortunately for me it missed fire, and I carried off the standard.

These two acts of outrageous bravery were deserving of a VC. But the almost suicidal nature of the second – unnecessary – act underlines just how desperate Roberts was to make his name. All things being equal, he would have died that day, and history would never have heard of Field Marshal Earl Roberts of Kandahar, arguably the greatest soldier of the Victorian period. But he was preserved, like so many others in war, by a fluke of fate, and a promising career was well on its way.

For a month Campbell remained at Fatehgarh to keep the rebels guessing. All the while more British troops were concentrating at Cawnpore for the reconquest of Oudh. The campaign finally began in mid February with a triple-pronged invasion by Campbell's main force of 10,000 men, a smaller column under Major-General Thomas Franks and an army of 8,000 Gurkhas commanded by Jung Bahadur, the prime minister and effective ruler of Nepal. By 21 March, after much bitter fighting, Lucknow was in British hands. But errors by the plodding Campbell allowed the bulk of the rebel defenders to escape, and Oudh and neighbouring Rohilkhand would not be properly pacified for a further twelve months. Meanwhile the unacclimatized British troops would pay the price, with more than a thousand dying of sunstroke, fatigue and disease in May 1858 alone. During the same period only a hundred were killed in action. Yet Campbell could afford these losses, because, by April 1858, there were almost 100,000 British soldiers in India, supported by a similar number of 'loyal' Indian troops, particularly Gurkhas, Sikhs and Punjabi Muslims.* The number of mutineers (as opposed to armed civilians), even at the outset of the rebellion, was never more than 60,000.

While Campbell and his subordinate commanders toiled in Oudh and Rohilkhand – not helped by Canning's divisive 'Oudh

---

* The so-called 'martial races' that would dominate the reconstructed Bengal Army for the remainder of the century.

Proclamation', which dispossessed the vast majority of the province's feudal landholders — another British general was cutting a swathe through rebel-controlled central India. His name was Major-General Sir Hugh Rose, the experienced soldier and diplomat who had acted as British liaison officer at French headquarters during the Crimean War. Rose had not served in the subcontinent before, and many old hands thought it a mistake to give him command of the newly constituted Central India Field Force in January 1858, soon after he had reached Bombay. At first Rose did nothing to dispel these doubts, making a mess of his first two minor engagements. But he soon became conditioned to the climate and terrain, relieving the British garrison at Sagar on 3 February and soundly defeating the rebel raja of Shahgarh a month later.

On 21 March, Rose's tiny force came in sight of the walls of Jhansi, the scene of a brutal massacre of British civilians in June the previous year. The town was defended by 10,000 armed civilians and a further 1,500 mutineers, all owing allegiance to the delectable rani of Jhansi, the thirty-year-old widow of the late maharaja, who was hoping to regain the former principality for her son. For months after the outbreak at Jhansi, she had denied any involvement in the massacre and protested her loyalty to the British. Only as Rose approached her city did she finally declare herself for the rebels, organizing the defence with extraordinary vigour and determination.

With just 3,000 men of his own, Rose was loath to risk an assault and, at first, preferred negotiations. But they came to nothing, and a preliminary bombardment was opened on 25 March. Six days later, as Rose made his final preparations for an attack, a mighty cheer erupted from the city. Tatya Tope had crossed the nearby Betwa River with 22,000 men, including the redoubtable Gwalior Contingent, and had lit a huge bonfire to signal his arrival. Rose was in a quandary: if he confronted Tatya with the whole of his force, the Jhansi garrison might take him in the rear; but if he detached too small a force, it ran the risk of being defeated. He compromised, taking just 1,200 men (only 500 of whom were British) to oppose Tatya on 1 April. The risk paid off, because the untrained Tatya arranged his army in two huge, widely spaced lines. Rose used accurate artillery fire and flanking attacks by cavalry and light guns to deal with the first line; the second simply fled, with Tatya leading the way. The rebels lost eighteen guns and 1,500 men, many of them during the ruthless cavalry pursuit. British casualties were under a hundred.

Two days later, the British stormed and eventually took the city and fort, with up to 3,000 Indians killed, many of them unarmed civilians. The rani was not amongst them. She had taken advantage of a British ruse to lure her out of the fort by removing an adjacent picquet. But the plan to apprehend her went awry, and she escaped on horseback with her young son and fifty followers.

Rose followed, and on 22 May, having repulsed a determined rebel attack on his camp, captured the stronghold of Kalpi. The rani had led one assault in person, and was about to overrun a British artillery position when Rose himself appeared with reinforcements. Thus did the two opposing commanders come within yards of each other during the battle, though neither was aware of it. Again the rani escaped and, with the remnants of the rebel army, headed west to the principality of Gwalior. There she and her fellow rebel leaders – Tatya Tope, the nawab of Banda and Rao Sahib, a nephew of Nana Sahib – incited the 8,000-strong Gwalior Army to rise and join the rebellion, forcing the pro-British maharaja to flee.

Rose, meanwhile, had resigned his command in protest at Campbell's decision to downgrade the Central India Field Force to a mere division. But he changed his mind after hearing the news from Gwalior – much to Campbell's fury – and made preparations for one last campaign. He reached the outskirts of Gwalior city on 16 June, after a 'rapid march of unparalleled hardships', and in a cavalry skirmish a day later the rani of Jhansi was killed. According to one eyewitness, she 'boldly attacked one of the 8th [Hussars] in their advance, was unhorsed and wounded', probably by a sabre cut. She then tried to shoot her assailant with her pistol, but missed and was herself dispatched with a carbine. Because she was 'dressed as a sowar' – in a red jacket, red trousers and a white turban – the trooper never realized that he had 'cut off one of the mainstays of the mutiny'. Little wonder that the rani is still revered in the subcontinent today as 'the Indian Joan of Arc'.

On 19 June, Rose captured Gwalior after a five-hour battle, and the surviving rebels fled west into Rajputana. Tatya Tope remained at large for a further seven months, living off the land and using guerrilla tactics to evade the countless British columns sent to destroy him. When he did stand and fight, at Rajgarh in September 1858, he was badly defeated and lost all his guns. Thereafter he kept on the move, travelling as far south as Nagpur Province before returning north to Rajputana. His luck ran out on 7 April 1859, when he was betrayed by a fellow rebel in return for an amnesty. Arrested by the British, Tatya was convicted of rebellion and hanged.

One young cavalry officer who tried and failed to apprehend Tatya Tope was the former sailor Evelyn Wood. Having recovered from the serious wound to his arm at the Redan, Wood had made good on Raglan's promise by asking for and receiving an army commission without purchase. Pneumonia prevented him from returning to the Crimea in early 1856 to join his new regiment, the 13th Light Dragoons. But the outbreak of the mutiny promised a fresh opportunity of glory, as well as relief from his debts, and he was quick to exchange into the 17th Lancers when he learnt that his own regiment would not be involved. The 17th landed at Bombay in late December 1857 but, much to Wood's chagrin, spent the first half of the following year on garrison duty. In August 1858 he was transferred to a squadron of Indian light cavalry and fought with it at Rajgarh. But it was during a minor skirmish with Tatya's men a couple of months later, at Sindhora in central India, that Wood was to win the VC he felt he had been unfairly deprived of in the Crimea. Spotting a group of a dozen rebels, he gave the order to charge. But only one of his Indian troopers followed him, and even he withdrew after firing his carbine. Wood was left to attack the group alone, and, incredibly, he survived long enough for his faithful orderly and some British cavalry to intervene. With the odds now even, Wood selected his quarry:

My man stood 50 yards from where the group had dispersed when I rode amongst them, and with his right foot placed on an antbear heap, awaited me with fixed bayonet. I approached in at a smart canter, with elbows close to my sides to protect the lungs, and the point of my sword low down under the horse's forearm. I guided the horse so as to take the point of the bayonet on its chest, but the Sepoy when he saw that I was 'riding home' wavered, and attempted to club his musket. As he swung it, butt uppermost, over his head, the point of his bayonet caught in the cummerbund which he wore over his coatee. This delayed him for a second, and my sword entering under the left armpit went through him up to the hilt, the butt of the musket falling over my shoulder, but without hurting me seriously, as my horse stopped. As the Sepoy dropped off the point of my sword, I galloped after the others.

Since the very start of the mutiny it had been obvious to everyone in British politics that the HEIC was an anachronism that could no longer be trusted to govern India. Yet the ministry that oversaw the transfer of government from the Company to the crown was not Palmerston's, which fell in March 1858 after the defeat of an anti-terrorist measure, but that of Lord Derby's minority Conservatives. Palmerston had set things in motion by introducing the first India Bill to the House of Commons in February 1858. But, on assuming power, Derby introduced one of his own, and, after various amendments, it finally became law in early August 1858. The Board of Control and the Court of Directors were abolished and replaced with a secretary of state and an advisory council of fifteen members. The governor-general was henceforth known as the viceroy, the queen's representative in India, though he would continue to be assisted by a supreme council. On 1 September the Court of Directors held its last meeting in Leadenhall Street, though the Company would retain a shadowy legal existence until it was finally wound up in 1874.

Queen Victoria's 'Proclamation', the formal announcement of the transfer of authority from the Company to the crown, was read out across India on 1 November 1858. It ensured stability by confirming all offices held under the HEIC and guaranteed all existing treaties with independent princes. It also denied any further territorial ambitions and promised religious freedom. 'We declare it our Royal will and pleasure', it stated, 'that none be in anywise favoured, none molested or disquieted, by reason of their religious faith or observances, but that all shall alike enjoy the equal and impartial protection of the law.' And, in an attempt to end the fighting, it offered an unconditional pardon to all rebels who were prepared to return peacefully to their homes. The only exceptions were those who had 'taken part in the murder of British subjects' and those who had knowingly harboured murderers or 'acted as leaders or instigators in revolt'.

Though not responsible for drafting the proclamation, Victoria made minor changes and was particularly insistent that the passage on religious freedom was as emphatic as possible. She wrote to Lord Canning, the first viceroy:

It is a source of great satisfaction and pride to her to feel herself in direct communication with that enormous Empire which is so bright a jewel of her Crown, and which she would wish to see happy, contented, and peaceful. May the publication of her Proclamation be the beginning of a new era, and may it draw a veil over the sad and bloody past! The Queen rejoices to hear that her Viceroy approves this passage about Religion. She strongly insisted upon it. She trusts also that the certainty of the Amnesty remaining open till the 1st January may not be productive of serious evil.

Far from it. Many minor rebels were tired of fighting and gladly accepted the amnesty. Those who did not – the hard core – were targeted by Sir Colin Campbell, now Lord Clyde, in his final Oudh campaign, which began in November 1858. By early 1859 his plan to herd the remaining rebels across the Nepal border had largely succeeded: amongst their leaders were Birjis Qadir, the boy 'king' of Oudh, Khan Bahadur Khan, the 'nawab' of Bareilly, and Nana Sahib, the infamous 'butcher of Cawnpore'. Penned into the fever-infested forests of the Nepal Terai, most of the rebels died of starvation and disease; others were captured by Jung Bahadur's troops and handed over to the British for trial. Nana almost certainly suffered the former fate in 1859, though 'sightings' of the notorious rebel continued until 1895. The last was made by a young British officer in a remote station in Gujerat. 'Have arrested the Nana Sahib,' he informed Calcutta. 'Wire Instructions.' The response was immediate and emphatic: 'Release at once.'

The great rebellion officially ended on 8 July 1859 with the declaration throughout India of a 'State of Peace'. A special day of thanksgiving and prayer was held three weeks later, with the viceroy proclaiming: 'War is at an end. Rebellion is put down . . . Peaceful pursuits everywhere have been resumed.' Canning's reward for saving India was a GCB and an earldom. Neither was particularly welcome: he resented the fact that Sir John Lawrence had received his GCB first and, with no children, saw little point in a step in the peerage. Much against his will he continued as viceroy until March 1862, introducing a series of measures designed to make the British Raj more inclusive. In 1861, for example, he enlarged the legislative council to make room for non-official Indian members. He also encouraged the founding of universities in Calcutta, Madras and Bombay, and gave grants to private colleges. Such initiatives were designed to create a 'Westernized' Indian middle class that would cooperate rather than confront. So successful were these educational reforms that by the mid 1880s there were 8,000 Indians with degrees and a further half million had graduated from secondary schools. Yet the plan ultimately backfired in that it was this English-speaking elite – Gandhi, Nehru and others – that would spearhead the campaign for independence.

Canning's other post-mutiny initiatives included the introduction of a penal code and the acceleration of railway building. But the most important reform of his viceregal administration was that of the Indian Army. Prompted by the recommendations of the Peel Commission – set up in London in July 1858 to advise on the reorganization of the army – Canning's government introduced a number of changes to prevent any further uprisings: increasing the ratio of European to Indian troops from the pre-mutiny level of

1:7 to 1:2; concentrating all artillery in European hands; and brigad-
ing every two Indian regiments with at least one European, so that
no major station was left without a European presence. But it also
tackled the fundamental cause of the mutiny by making significant
improvements to the army's conditions of service: creating a Staff
Corps from which all European officers were selected for lucrative
regimental duty; increasing the power of commanding officers to
punish and reward, including the replacement of seniority with
merit as the dominant principle of promotion; switching to an
'irregular' system of regiments whereby Indian officers had greater
responsibility; increasing pay for Indian infantry officers and all
cavalrymen; replacing uncomfortable European-style uniforms
with those more suited to the Indian climate; and, crucially, shifting
the recruitment base of the Bengal Army from high-caste Hindus★
to Sikhs, Dogras, Pathans, Gurkhas and other 'martial races'. So
successful were these reforms that until independence in 1947 there
was just one mutiny involving sepoy violence: that of the 5th Light
Infantry at Singapore during the First World War. Otherwise,
despite the occasional 'industrial action', the army stayed faithful
to its colonial masters to the end.

In November 1861, just four months before Canning was due
to return home, his wife died suddenly of jungle fever. A heart-
broken Lord Canning handed over the viceroyalty to Lord Elgin
in March 1862 and arrived back in London a month later. But the
burden of six years as head of the Indian government had taken its
toll, and he died on 17 June at the age of fifty. Within a year Elgin
had followed Canning to the grave. He was succeeded by Sir John
Lawrence, the 'hero of the Punjab', who sought to centralize
authority further by monopolizing financial control and by blocking the creation of executive councils for his lieutenant-governors.
He was also keen to prevent the Indianization of the higher civil
service, which had been open to all since 1853, and was so successful that only one Indian entered the service before 1871. His rule
was typically paternalistic: he tried to lighten the fiscal burden on

---

★ The rebel regiments had already been disbanded.

the peasantry by limiting government spending, lowering the salt tax and taxing the middle classes; he also set in motion an ambitious programme of railway and canal building, and did much to promote public health, prison reform and primary education.

He had become increasingly convinced that British rule in India was part of God's purpose. 'We have not been elected or placed in power by the people,' he wrote, 'but are here through our moral superiority, by the force of circumstances and by the will of Providence.' Such views were entirely in line with the subtle post-mutiny shift in the British perception of empire from civilizing mission to godly duty.

In India itself, the British became preoccupied with personal security and the very survival of the Raj. No longer was the inevitable progress of Christian and Western civilization taken for granted; gone was the old, easy indulgence of racial and cultural differences that had eased relations between rulers and ruled. In their place came an even more rigid segregation and a widespread British fear of renewed rebellion and atrocity. Such was the siege-like mentality of a man like Brigadier-General Reginald Dyer, the 'Butcher of Amritsar', who had lived and worked with Indians all his life, and yet who was capable of ordering his troops to open fire on an unarmed, if illegal, political gathering in the Jallianwala Bagh in 1919, killing and wounding more than 1,500, including a baby of six weeks. He explained: 'If I fired I must fire with good effect, a small amount of firing would have been a criminal act of folly. I had the choice of neglecting to do my duty, of suppressing a mutiny or of becoming responsible for all future bloodshed . . . It was no longer just a question of dispersing the crowd but of producing a sufficient moral effect, from a military point of view, not only on those who were present but more specially throughout the Punjab.' Dyer's use of the word 'mutiny' was not meant to indicate a contemporary military insurrection, but rather his belief that in 1919 the British faced a repeat of the 1857 rebellion. Many Britons agreed, hailing Dyer as the saviour of India. But not Lloyd George's coalition government, with Winston Churchill, the secretary for war, condemning Dyer for inflicting a 'massacre upon a particular crowd of people, with the intention of terrorizing not merely the rest of the crowd, but the whole district or country'. By abandoning the principle of minimum force, said Churchill, Dyer had laid himself open to the charge of 'frightfulness'. He added: 'We have to make it absolutely clear, some way or other, that this is not the British way of doing business.' Gandhi and his fellow political activists were not convinced, and, in the words of one historian, Dyer's actions made it 'impossible for the British to leave India in 1947 with honour and with the affection or respect of their Indian subjects'. Such was the long-term legacy of the 1857 rebellion.

# 13. China

Lord Elgin received the first sketchy reports of unrest in India as he steamed around the southern tip of Ceylon in late May 1857. But it was not until he docked at Singapore Harbour on 3 June that the full seriousness of the insurrection was brought home to him by two letters from his old Oxford classmate Lord Canning. They gave a brief summary of the risings at Meerut and Delhi, and begged Elgin to divert the troops assigned to his China expedition. 'If you send me troops,' Canning promised, 'they shall not be kept one hour more than is absolutely needed.'

With the telegraph line ending at Alexandria, and at least a month needed to get a message back to London, Elgin had no time to consult his superiors. Instead, on his own authority, he at once dispatched the 1,700 troops that had already reached Singapore to Calcutta. More would follow. But Elgin can never have imagined that events in India would delay his own mission by almost a year.

He continued on to China with just one ship, the frigate HMS *Shannon*, arriving in Hong Kong on 2 July. Over the next few weeks he was pressed by local officials and traders alike to order an attack on Canton. But Elgin had no authorization from London for such a drastic step, and preferred to negotiate from a position of strength: which meant the backing of the military force diverted to India. To find out exactly how long Canning might need his troops, he sailed for Calcutta, arriving in mid August. But the emergency was still at its height, and, having received a promise of troops by the end of the year, he returned to China aboard the steamship *Ava* on 20 September. The *Shannon* remained behind, its company of 408 sailors and marines, and ten 68-pounder guns, having been formed into the Naval Brigade, which, under its captain, William Peel, VC,* would perform so well during the Second Relief and later capture of Lucknow.

Soon after returning to Hong Kong, Elgin was joined by the French envoy Baron Gros, who had been sent by Napoleon III to demand reparations for the execution of a French Catholic missionary a year earlier. Elgin was still keen to negotiate with the Peking government; Gros favoured an assault on the imperial capital. But the local officials – Bowring and Parkes – preferred an attack on Canton, and, crucially, they were now backed by Clarendon, the foreign secretary. The necessary British firepower arrived at Canton in December in the form of 2,000 soldiers from Calcutta; they were supported by an even more powerful French fleet. Both envoys now submitted ultimata: Gros wanted the missionary's murderer(s) brought to justice, reparations and per-mission for Frenchmen to operate anywhere in Canton; Elgin demanded compliance with the Treaty of Nanking, a permanent British ambassador in Peking, and unspecified reparations for loss of life and property following the (unnamed) *Arrow* incident.

Ye Mingchen, the local viceroy, tried to stall for time but in late December, having run out of patience, the two envoys authorized a joint attack. The bombardment began on the 27th, and within two days the city had fallen: the British shouldered the bulk of the fighting, losing a hundred men killed and wounded, the French just thirty-three. Chinese casualties were closer to 450. Despite Elgin's best efforts, the victorious troops proceeded to strip the city bare. 'My difficulty', noted Elgin in his diary, 'has been to prevent the wretched Cantonese from being plundered and bullied. There is a [Hindi] word called "loot" which gives unfortunately a venial character to what would, in common English, be styled robbery. Add to this that there is no flogging in the French Army, so that it is impossible to punish men committing this class of offences.' Not that Elgin himself was above plundering the city treasury of fifty-two boxes of silver, sixty-eight boxes of gold

* Peel was knighted for his service during the mutiny but died of cholera at Cawnpore in April 1858.

ingots and the equivalent in taels of half a million pounds. This freelance booty was put aboard HMS *Calcutta* and sent to India in lieu of official reparations.

Ye was arrested and deported to Calcutta. In his stead the allies appointed his deputy, Pih-kwei, and an advisory council of Parkes and two allied officers. But the imperial government refused to accept this new status quo, or indeed to bow to the allies' other demands, and in April 1858 Elgin and Gros sailed north to the mouth of the Peiho,★ the river that led to Peking, in a show of naval force. At first the local governor refused to negotiate. But in early May, after consulting Peking, he offered certain concessions: to open more treaty ports, to grant religious freedom to Christians and to pay reparations for European property destroyed in Canton. The sticking point was the establishment of permanent foreign embassies in the capital. The Chinese government would not hear of it; the allies would not leave without it.

On 20 May 1858, to put pressure on Peking, a fleet of allied gunboats attacked and took the five Taku mud forts at the mouth of the Peiho. By now Palmerston's Whig government had been replaced by Derby's Conservatives, who, a year earlier, had so strongly opposed Elgin's mission. But once in power they were loath to anger public opinion by ordering a withdrawal from China; instead, Derby congratulated Elgin on capturing the Taku forts in a dispatch the latter described as 'giving me latitude to do anything I choose, if only I will finish the affair'. Thus emboldened, the foreign envoys sent a force of eight gunboats up the Peiho towards Tientsin,† just thirty miles from Peking. Their unopposed arrival in late May forced the 26-year-old Emperor Hsien Feng to seek terms.

After much negotiation, the Treaty of Tientsin was signed by Elgin and the two imperial commissioners on 3 July 1858. Representatives of imperial Russia and the United States had already concluded separate treaties; Gros would do likewise a day later.

★ Or Po Hai, as it is known today.
† Modern Tianjin.

But Elgin's treaty was easily the most stringent, and its terms included: the payment of £5m in war reparations; the opening up of China to Christian missionaries; eleven more ports opened to foreign trade; Europeans free to travel anywhere in China; and, most importantly, a permanent British ambassador in Peking. No mention was made in the treaty, nor had it been during the negotiations, of Clarendon's wish for the opium trade to be legalized. This was partly because Clarendon was no longer foreign secretary, and partly because Elgin assumed the Chinese would never agree.

The terms of the treaty were generally well received in Britain, with *The Times* describing Elgin's work as 'manly and consistent'. But it was one thing getting the Chinese commissioners to sign the treaty and quite another for their imperial master to ratify it. The Second China War may have finished, but a third was just around the corner.

On his way back from Tientsin, Elgin stopped off at Shanghai to negotiate a tariff agreement with a new pair of Chinese commissioners. At first all went well, with the commissioners agreeing to a 5 per cent tariff on standard imports and 8 per cent on opium, a tax that represented a de facto legalization of the drug. Elgin sweetened the deal by allowing additional taxes to be levied on opium as it made its way inland. But both treaties were then thrown into doubt when the commissioners reneged on the clause that allowed a permanent diplomatic presence in Peking, arguing that it had been agreed to only under duress. The commissioners went on to hint that such a concession would cause the government a serious loss of face and might even topple the Ch'ing Dynasty, leaving the way open for the Taiping rebels★ and any other dis-

★ The Taiping Rebellion raged for fourteen years (1850–64) and affected, at one time or another, sixteen of China's eighteen provinces. It was led by Hung Hsiu Ch'uan, a failed scholar, whose guiding dogma was a potent mix of Evangelical Christianity and primitive communism. Hung declared himself 'Heavenly King' of a new 'Kingdom of Heavenly Peace' and, having defeated a number of imperial armies, established his capital at Nanking, where he outlawed opium- and tobacco-smoking, alcohol, gambling, ancestor worship,

affected group that wished to seize power. Elgin could see the sense of this argument, and promised to consult his government.

In the event, Derby's ministry was not prepared to drop the Peking embassy, and Elgin's brother Frederick Bruce was sent back to China to ratify the whole treaty and take up the post of ambassador. He reached the mouth of the Peiho with sixteen warships in mid June 1859 and discovered that the Chinese had repaired the Taku forts and constructed three booms across the river. When the Peking government refused to remove the booms, Bruce ordered his naval commander, Rear-Admiral James Hope, to breach them by force. But the attempt on 25 June was an unmitigated disaster, with six gunboats 'sunk or stranded' and more than 500 casualties, including the admiral and two of his captains. Most of the losses were suffered during a failed attempt to storm one of the forts, with the attackers shot down in their hundreds as they struggled through the thick mud.

The British blamed the Emperor Hsien Feng. But in truth Hsien was a weak-willed drug addict who had little time for the day-to-day business of government, preferring to spend it in bed with his favourite concubine, Tzu-hsi. The daughter of a Manchu banner captain, Tzu-hsi was just seventeen when she and her cousin Sakota were chosen with twenty-six other Manchu beauties to share the young emperor's bed on his accession in 1851. Though Sakota became empress consort, Tzu-hsi quickly established herself as the imperial favourite, a position she cemented after giving birth to the emperor's only son, Mu-Tsung, in 1856. Thereafter she was known as empress of the Western Palace, while Sakota was empress of the Eastern Palace. But Tzu-hsi was the real power behind the throne, and, when Hsien Feng died in 1861, she overthrew the regency council and became the effective ruler of China for almost half a century. She was an opium addict like the emperor, and it was said she stuck strictly to a maintenance dose that prevented both mental impairment and physical withdrawal. She was shrewd,

prostitution and polygamy. Nanking was finally captured by imperial troops in 1864, prompting Hung to commit suicide.

ruthless and a fierce xenophobe, and as such a prime mover in Peking's policy of resistance during the late 1850s.

By the time news of the repulse at the Taku forts reached Britain, 75-year-old Lord Palmerston had returned to power. At the beginning of the year, in a cynical attempt to curry favour with its Radical allies, Derby's Conservative government had introduced a limited parliamentary Reform Bill, promising the redistribution of seventy-five seats, a £10 household franchise in the counties, and votes for men with various other property and professional qualifications. But this was too progressive for many Tories and not progressive enough for the Radicals, who regarded the 'fancy franchises' as a naked attempt to increase the Conservative vote. The Bill was defeated on a Whig amendment to reduce the household franchise to £6, but, instead of resigning, Derby called a general election. Of the relatively small number of seats contested – 158 – the Conservatives gained twenty-six: enough to keep them in power, if not to give them an outright majority.

The election had been contested amidst the opening salvos of a European war that would ultimately lead to Italian unification. It was fought between Piedmont and France, on the one hand, and the Austrian Empire on the other. Austria had long dominated northern Italy and still controlled the wealthy provinces of Lombardy and Venice. The Kingdom of Piedmont's far-sighted prime minister, Count Cavour, saw the defeat of Austria as the necessary precursor to Italian independence, and, crucially, he had gained the support of Napoleon III. Fearing the spread of French influence, Derby's Conservatives were cautiously pro-Austrian. Not so the various Opposition factions, including the Whigs, who regarded French involvement as a price worth paying for Italian liberty. On 6 June, the day before the opening of the new parliament and two days after the Austrians had suffered their second serious defeat, at the Battle of Magenta, the Opposition met in Willis's Rooms in St James's to plot a new broad-based alliance. It had the support of the Whigs, the Radicals, the Irish Nationalists and the remaining Peelites, and would henceforth be known as the Liberal Party.

Four days later the Liberals proposed a vote of no confidence in the government, which was carried by thirteen votes. Derby at once resigned and, after Russell had refused to serve under Granville, Palmerston became prime minister with Russell as his foreign secretary. Gladstone completed his lengthy move from the Conservative to the Liberal Party by accepting the chancellorship of the exchequer, and was joined in the cabinet by his fellow Peelites, Sidney Herbert and the duke of Newcastle, who became war and colonial secretaries respectively.

On 20 June, the day Palmerston completed his cabinet, the French and Piedmontese again defeated the Austrians at Solferino, a bloody battle that left more than 40,000 dead and wounded on the field. A rich Swiss observer, Henri Dunant, was so appalled by the carnage that he returned home to found the International Red Cross. Just as sickened, and also worried by the build-up of Prussian troops on his Rhenish frontier, Napoleon III persuaded the Piedmontese to end the war.★ By the terms of the Treaty of Villafranca, Piedmont gained Lombardy but not Venice: too little for Palmerston, who regarded Venice as necessary for any viable buffer state in northern Italy; and too much for Queen Victoria, who saw a dangerous precedent in a brother monarch being asked to give up territory that had been guaranteed by the Treaty of Vienna in 1815. Neither can have envisaged the domino effect that would see the whole of Italy united under Piedmont's leadership by 1870.

With the war over, Palmerston could concentrate on events in China. Outraged as he was by the repulse at the Taku forts, he was far too quick to swallow Admiral Hope's face-saving assertion that the Chinese defenders were assisted by their nominal Russian allies – which was not the case. Yet, either way, British prestige had received a severe blow, and he demanded revenge. 'We must in some way or other make the Chinese repent of the outrage,' he

---

★ In return for its support, France was ceded the Piedmontese provinces of Nice and Savoy, which remain French to this day. An appalled Palmerston concluded that Napoleon III had entered the war only for territorial gain.

informed the Foreign Office. 'We might send a military-naval force to attack and occupy Peking.' This was the course of action recommended by Frederick Bruce, biding his time in Shanghai, and of Palmerston's cabinet only Gladstone disagreed on the grounds of expense. The other voice of caution was that of Lord Elgin, Bruce's brother, who had joined the government as post-master-general on his return to Britain. Any foreign occupation of Peking, he warned, might topple the Ch'ing Dynasty and leave the anti-capitalist Taiping rebels as masters of China. 'If you humiliate the Emperor beyond measure,' he advised a fellow cabinet member, 'you imperil the most lucrative trade you have in the world.' By which he meant opium.

Palmerston was not convinced, but he agreed to Elgin's suggestion that the Chinese should be given thirty days to apologize for the action at the Taku forts, pay unspecified reparations and promise to ratify the Treaty of Tientsin. The instructions reached Bruce at Shanghai in January 1860, but he put off delivering the ultimatum for a further two months, because Elgin's sanction, a blockade of the Peiho River, would not have the desired effect until the annual rice shipments began in the spring. It made little difference. The ultimatum was speedily rejected, and in April, when the news reached Britain, Elgin was once again sent out to China to take charge. He and Baron Gros, who would head the new French mission, were given an extraordinary degree of latitude. 'It is the opinion of H.M. Government', wrote Foreign Secretary Russell on 17 April, 'that . . . the Plenipotentiaries should be the sole judges of all matters pertaining to negotiations – when they should commence, when break off, what terms to be accepted, what refused.' The decision on whether to risk an advance on the Chinese capital was to be left to Elgin and Gros in consultation with their military commanders. But Palmerston himself did not believe an occupation of Peking would lead to the overthrow of the Ch'ing Dynasty, an opinion borne out by events.

By the time Elgin reached Shanghai on 29 June 1860, sizeable allied forces had already set up their forward bases on each side of the gulf that protected the mouth of the Peiho: 13,000 British and

Indian troops at Tahlien Bay, on the east side, and 6,500 French at Chefu, to the west. Command of the British Contingent, the bulk of which had come from India, was in the hands of Lieutenant-General Sir Hope Grant. Born in 1808 into a talented family of Scottish gentry – his brother Sir Francis Grant was the celebrated portraitist and president of the Royal Academy – he had been educated in Switzerland and was an expert cellist. But at the age of eighteen he exchanged his cello for a sword and joined the 9th Lancers. His military career had not always gone smoothly: he was commanding the 9th the day it broke and ran at Chilianwalla, though he did his best to rally it; far more illustrious was his service during the First China War, the First Sikh War and, most recently, the Indian Mutiny, when he was present during the siege of Delhi and later commanded Campbell's cavalry. Lieutenant-Colonel Garnet Wolseley, on Grant's staff as a deputy assistant quartermaster-general, had a particularly high opinion of his chief's ability. 'He was', he wrote later, 'the best of men and the bravest of soldiers.'

Fred Roberts had served under Grant, that 'dear old fellow', during the mutiny and was extremely disappointed not to be assigned to his staff for the China expedition. The reason was his recent marriage to Nora Bews. 'If Roberts had not been a newly-married man,' Lord Clyde (formerly Sir Colin Campbell) told Mrs Roberts at dinner in Government House, 'I would have sent him.'

Her indignant reply: 'I am afraid I cannot be very grateful to you for making my husband feel I am ruining his career by standing in the way of his being sent on service. You have done your best to make him regret his marriage.'

An astonished Clyde responded: 'Well, I'll be hanged if I can understand you women! I have done the very thing I thought you would like, and have only succeeded in making you angry. I will never try to help a woman again!'

According to Wolseley, Clyde had tried to get Sir William Mansfield, his former chief of staff, appointed as expedition commander. But Mansfield was known to be an irascible character with very poor eyesight and the duke of Cambridge preferred Grant. It was a wise choice. He was popular with men and officers alike, even-tempered and 'possessed keen, bright views upon war in all its many phases'. If he spoke a little hurriedly, and sometimes had a problem putting his ideas into words, his 'military instinct, mellowed by war's experience, invariably prompted him correctly'. He was fiercely religious, 'but detested priestly dogmas and the sophisms of theology'. Best of all he looked the part, with his tall, manly bearing and magnificent set of mutton-chop whiskers.

On Elgin's staff when he joined Grant at Tahlien Bay in early July was a young diplomat called the Honourable William de Norman, cousin of the marquess of Northampton, who had originally come out to China with Frederick Bruce. When it became clear that Bruce would not be accompanying his brother to Peking, de Norman asked for leave and joined Elgin's staff as an extra attaché. He described Tahlien Bay in his diary:

We came in sight of the high land on both sides of the entrance into Ta-lien-wan at an early hour in the morning . . . The climate is very agreeable, cool in the morning & evening, & a breeze to modify the heat of mid-day . . . The houses of the villagers are of stone, joined with a coarse mortar or mud & the roofs are thatched with straw or with sea weed. The windows are large and made of oiled paper & lattice work. Most houses have a courtyard, a pig stye, or some such small building attached to it. The people are Chinese colonists from Shan-tung . . . In this bay are now 192 ships, of which 46 are men of war & 14 troop ships.

British preparations for the Chinese expedition could not have been more different from those for the Crimea. Medical facilities were excellent and a battalion of the Military Train was in charge of transport, having assembled horses, asses, pack-mules, bullocks and drivers from as far afield as Bombay and Manila. These beasts of burden were supplemented by a large corps of 2,500 Chinese coolies that had been raised in Hong Kong. Wolseley remembered them as 'plucky, cheery and very strong carriers' but also 'great rascals and difficult to keep in any order'.

The British fighting troops comprised two infantry divisions, a cavalry brigade and a small siege train: 13,000 men in total. Each division was made up of two infantry brigades, each containing two British and one Indian infantry regiment, a company of Royal Engineers and two batteries of Royal Artillery. The cavalry brigade included one British and two Indian regiments, and a battery of horse artillery.

British infantrymen were still equipped with the Enfield rifle, though Indian troops had to make do with percussion muskets (a precaution against any further uprisings). The only major technological advance had been in the field of artillery, where, as recently as the Indian Mutiny, cannons were cast-iron or bronze, muzzle-loading and with smooth-bore barrels that fired roundshot, canister or shell. This all changed in 1859 with the introduction of the Armstrong gun. Developed by William G. Armstrong,* a Tyneside civil engineer, the gun was not only rifled but breech-loading, and had a range of up to five miles. It was made of wrought-iron, with its barrel reinforced by hoops and layers of shrunken metal, and much lighter than a conventional artillery piece: a standard Armstrong 12-pounder, of the type used in China, needed only a six-horse team, instead of the eight required by the old 9-pounder. It was also incredibly versatile and fired a shell that could be fused to air-burst as shrapnel, explode on impact, after penetrating a wall or shortly after leaving the barrel, much like case-shot. And the Armstrong could fire more accurately at two miles than a smooth-bore gun could at a quarter of the distance. Yet, despite its advantages, it was expensive to produce and sometimes difficult to load, and would not long survive the campaign.† Of the eight batteries of artillery that served in China, only two were equipped with Armstrongs: one of field artillery (12-pounders) and one of horse artillery (9-pounders). Another three field batteries used the

---

* Armstrong was knighted in 1859 and made engineer-in-chief of Rifled Ordnance.
† After trials in the late 1860s, there was a reversion to muzzle-loaders with rifled barrels. It was not until 1885 that a rifled breech-loader was again introduced.

standard 6- and 9-pounder smooth-bore cannon, while the remaining three heavy (or siege) batteries were armed with eight-inch guns, mortars and howitzers, and some 32-pounders.

Overall it was a formidable force, not least because of the quality of its senior officers and staff. Grant's two divisional commanders – Major-Generals Sir John Michel and Sir Robert Napier – had both distinguished themselves during the Indian Mutiny: Michel as the commander of an independent column in central India and Napier as Campbell's chief engineer. Napier had also done well during both Sikh Wars and was destined, in 1868, to command one of the most hazardous, and yet ultimately successful, expeditions of the Victorian period: to rescue British hostages held by the mad King Theodore of Abyssinia in his mountain fortress of Magdala. He learnt valuable lessons for that campaign during the preparation for the China expedition, when he was given the task of organizing the equipment and embarkation of the Bengal Contingent. So successful was he that the contingent arrived in China 'in excellent condition and fit for immediate service after a three-month voyage'.

Other talented senior officers included Colonel 'Jock' Mackenzie, Grant's quartermaster-general, Captain Robert Biddulph, his military secretary, Wolseley himself and Brigadier-General Thomas Pattle, the cavalry commander. Under Pattle were two of India's finest cavalrymen, Major Dighton Probyn, VC, and Lieutenant Walter Fane. Most of these men were experienced warriors, having fought in either the Crimea or the Indian Mutiny, or both, and a greater contrast with the force that set off to fight the Russians in 1854 is hard to imagine.

On reaching Tahlien Bay on 11 July, Elgin was told that General Charles Cousin-Montauban, the French commander, had yet to agree a date for the joint attack on the Taku forts. Montauban did not want to commit himself until he had procured enough mules to transport his field guns, but had assured Grant that he would make up his mind by 20 July. The original plan, agreed at Shanghai, had been for the French to land south of the Taku forts and the

British to the north. Major Edward Greathed, Napier's ADC, explained:

The eastern coast of the Gulf of [Pechili] on which the Taku & Peiho forts are situated is most unfavourable for the landing of troops. It is a vast mud flat on which the tide recedes upwards of two miles from the high water mark, so soft and tenacious as to be entirely impracticable for the passage of horses and wheeled carriages, and only traversable by men with great difficulty at high water when the mud is somewhat hardened under the water which covers it to the depth of a few inches. The only points at which the landing of troops is possible is at the mouth of the Peiho river, or of the smaller Pehtang and Chi-ho rivers which fall into the gulf, the former twelve miles to the north, the latter fourteen miles to the south of the Peiho mouth. That river has much larger volume and depth of water, but its channel was so obstructed with booms and stakes, commanded and flanked by the forts on either side as to make a landing there difficult and dangerous to the last degree.

General Montauban had therefore decided to land at the Chi-ho, while Grant preferred the Pehtang further north. But, after a reconnaissance of the Chi-ho by the French Navy on 19 July, Montauban changed his mind and said he wanted to disembark at the same point as Grant. Wolseley commented: 'We suspicious Britishers imagined they had begun to think that their army was too small to operate far away from us.'

Grant's army finally set sail for Pehtang on 26 July and was joined en route by the smaller French force. Wolseley described the combined fleet of 206 vessels – men-of-war, gunboats and transports – as a 'magnificent spectacle, never to be forgotten'. He added:

It was no mere naval review intended to amuse Cowes yachtsmen; it was an actual fighting reality; a man-of-war fleet convoying a huge collection of transports that carried an army of about 20,000 soldiers, with all their horses, guns, fighting material and food, for the invasion of a great and ancient, though little understood, empire. The distant

Chinese capital, the far-famed Pekin, the city of mystery and of fable to all the yellow race, was our hoped-for destination.

Having anchored close in to the Pehtang River on 31 July, they began the landings a day later. Greathed recalled:

On the 1st August [one British and one French brigade] were embarked in a fleet of gunboats, each containing 150 troops on its decks and in boats in tow. The flotilla steamed with the high tide in the Pehtang river and anchored at a distance of 2000 yards from the two snug-looking forts constructed for the defence of the town . . . [which] adjoins the fort on the right bank. A vigorous resistance was expected, the forts appeared to be armed, the operation of landing was certain to be long and difficult; and the gunboats were anchored in a position likely to tempt the Chinamen to try their range. But to our surprise no resistance was offered and the troops being disembarked at high tide as near to dry land as the boats could arrive, waded upwards for a mile or more knee deep in water and mud, and formed up without opposition on what could only by custom and comparison be termed dry land.

The landings took place on the south bank of the river, about a mile below the forts. The first Briton ashore was Brigadier-General William Sutton, 'an old campaigner famous for his swearing propensities, and famous as a great game shot in South Africa'. Wolseley, who was present, would never forget the sight of Sutton as he struggled barefooted through the knee-deep mud, his trousers, boots and sword slung over one shoulder. 'Picture a somewhat fierce and ugly bandy-legged little man thus accoutred in a big white helmet,' he wrote, 'clothed in a dirty jacket of red serge, below which a very short slate-coloured flannel shirt extended a few inches, cursing and swearing loudly "all round" at everybody and everything as he led his brigade through the hateful mire. I remember many funny scenes in my soldiering days, but I never laughed more than I did at this amusing "disembarkation" of the first brigade that landed in northern China.'

That evening, as the advance troops bivouacked on a muddy

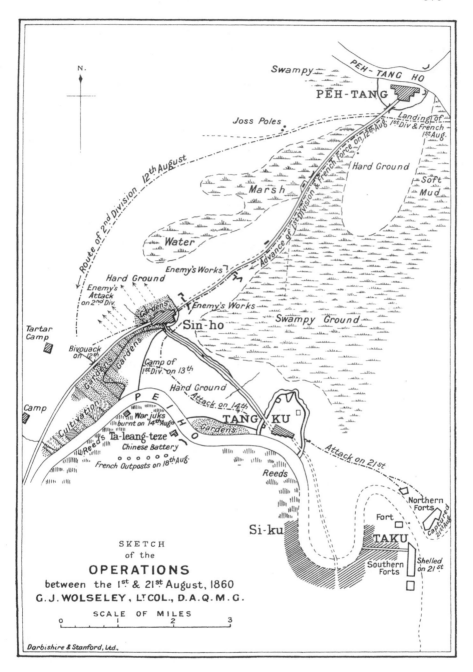

N.

Swampy

PEH-TANG HO

PEH-TANG

Joss Poles

Landing of 1st Div & French 1st Aug.

Hard Ground

Route of 2nd Division 12th August

Advance of 1st Division & French Force on 12th Aug.

Soft Mud

Marsh

Water

Enemy's Works

Hard Ground

Enemy's Attack on 2nd Div.

Enemy's Works

Swampy Ground

Gardens

Sin-ho

Tartar Camp

Bivouack on 12th

Camp of 1st Div. on 13th

Cultivation  Gardens

Hard Ground

Attack on 14th

Camp

P E I H O

War juks burnt on 14th Aug.

TANG KU

Reed's Ta-leang-teze

Gardens

Chinese Battery

Attack on 21st

French Outposts on 18th Aug.

Reeds

Northern Forts

Captured 21st Aug.

Fort

Si-ku

TAKU

Southern Forts

Shelled on 21st

SKETCH
of the

**OPERATIONS**

between the 1st & 21st August, 1860

G. J. WOLSELEY, Lt COL., D.A.Q.M.G.

SCALE  OF  MILES

0       1       2       3

Darbishire & Stanford, Ltd.,

causeway that connected Pehtang with the high ground north of the Peiho, Harry Parkes and a staff officer broke into the nearby fort, which a friendly local had assured them was deserted. They found mocked-up wooden guns and 'no trace of recent occupation', though the entrance was mined with enormous shells 'fitted with percussion locks'.

The Chinese guide told Parkes that the local people 'suffered much from the Tartar patrols that frequently visited them'. By 'Tartars' he meant the Manchu and Mongol cavalrymen who made up the bulk of the imperial army. Originally from Manchuria, to the north-east of China proper, the Ch'ing emperors had been ruling China since their successful invasion had toppled the Ming Dynasty in the mid seventeenth century. Their forces were divided into eight hereditary armies, or banners, with each bannerman entitled to rations and equipment at the emperor's expense. These bannermen dominated the imperial cavalry, infantry and artillery, with ethnic Chinese chiefly employed as garrison troops under 'the Green Standard'. But even the bannermen, with their outdated weapons and tactics, were no match for a modern European army. A contemporary wrote:

The principal drill in which the troops, both Mandshoo [*sic*] and Chinese, are exercised, is shooting with the bow, both when mounted and dismounted; a portion of them are practised in discharging firearms without locks or ramrods; and a minor portion in loading and firing cannon. The dress of the troops does not differ essentially from that of the people at large, excepting in the [surcoat] . . . which is of a similar colour to the standard under which a soldier serves . . . Even in time of war, the addition of an iron helmet, a wadded frock, and a bamboo shield, renders his appearance still more anti-martial. The horseman is rapid in his movements, and advances to the attack with much impetuosity – at least, when no enemy is before him. But his little, slender horse, with his short, quick step, wants the qualities of a charger.

At daybreak on the 2nd, the allies took possession of a near-deserted Pehtang, and the landings continued. 'The beach was a busy scene,' wrote Greathed, 'especially at high water when the gunboats arrived from the fleet in rapid succession and landed cargoes of troops, horses, guns, Chinese coolies, transport ponies, medical comforts, hospital stores, tents, litters, ammunition, or provisions.' Over the next few days the rain 'fell in torrents' and gradually reduced the unmetalled roads in Pehtang to a quagmire. They were repaired 'for want of better materials with flour, baskets, wardrobes, old hats, broomsticks, tables, china cups, joss paper, beer bottles, chairs, straw mats, books, lanterns, corn, chaff and oil cake, being chiefly the contents of the houses, turned out of windows to make room for the troops'. But the incessant trampling of men, horses and store carts soon reduced this ballast to a sticky, dangerous mess, and it was 'a question whether it was most perilous to walk or ride'.

Sir Hope Grant had set up his headquarters in the fort, and it was from its ramparts, on the 3rd, that a large force of enemy cavalry was spotted further down the causeway. An allied force of 2,000 infantrymen was sent to reconnoitre, and, after an exhausting march of four miles, it was fired on by Tartar matchlockmen secreted behind some sand hills. The French at once deployed on a narrow strip of hard ground and drove the Tartar back to their main entrenchments, which covered the village of Senho, eight miles from Pehtang. The Chinese commander-in-chief, Prince Sang-kol-in-sen,★ had made little attempt to impede the progress of the allied troops along the causeway, neglecting even to destroy the single bridge. 'This valuable reconnaissance showed us', wrote Greathed, 'that our position was perfectly safe against attack and that there was no occasion for us to advance against the enemy until we had landed all our troops.'

But, with fresh water scarce and an increasing number of his men falling sick, Grant was anxious to get on with the job. Frustratingly he again had to wait for the French, who 'were slow in their disembarkation of both men and stores, through want of necessary

★ Dubbed 'Sam Collinson' by the British troops, he had won renown for his victories over the Taiping rebels.

appliances'. Harry Parkes wrote of his allies: 'They act in every respect like a drag on the coach. They use our stores, get in our way at all points and retard all our movements.' To be fair, the French had had to transport the majority of their force all the way from France, and had much less experience of small expeditions than the British. But many Britons remembered with shame the unfavourable comparison their army had made with its French counterpart in the Crimea, and were delighted now that the boot was on the other foot.

Much to Napier's irritation, Grant had given warning that Michel's 1st Division would lead the advance on Senho, with the 2nd Division in reserve. But he altered his plans after a second reconnaissance – by Wolseley on 9 August – discovered a way to outflank the left of the Chinese position by using firm ground to the right of the causeway. This line of attack was now assigned to Napier's 2nd Division and the Cavalry Brigade, while the 1st Division and the French force moved up the line of the causeway. Obstructive as ever, Montauban tried to persuade Grant to delay his attack until the ground had dried a little. But Grant was firm, and the day set for the advance was the 'Glorious Twelfth'.★

With the furthest distance to cover, Napier's men and the cavalry set off at 4 a.m. But so heavy was the going, with gun wagons sinking axle-deep in the mud, that it took six hours to cover just four miles. Napier recorded: 'I advanced by brigades in line of contiguous columns at quarter distance, my front covered by an advanced guard of 200 men, 3rd Buffs and Milward's Battery, under Lieut.-Colonel Sargent; the cavalry was formed on my right.'

About a mile from Senho, with the main enemy position in sight, Napier ordered Captain Milward's battery of 12-pounder Armstrongs to fire on a large force of Tartar cavalry. It was the first time Armstrongs had been used in anger, and, according to Napier, 'the range and accuracy of their fire excited the admiration of the force.' An artillery officer recorded: 'The first gun was fired, at 10.40 a.m., at a range of 1200 yards. The first shot was bad, the

★ The opening of the grouse-shooting season.

elevation was too great ... The second shell burst right in the midst of the largest group, and half-a-dozen saddles were instantly empty. For upwards of ten minutes the battery made magnificent practice. The Tartars found the place too hot for them; so after some wavering, they took the desperate resolution of attempting to turn both flanks of the English and get into their rear.'

On Napier's front, a large body of cavalry 'streamed out in a long line through a passage across the marsh which separated us, and forming with great regularity and quickness enveloped my force in a great circle of skirmishers'. Napier recorded:

As soon as the enemy's movements were clearly defined, I sent to Brigadier Pattle, commanding the Cavalry, directing him to detach a troop to protect my right rear, and to take the opportunity to charge, which the enemy so boldly offered him. I then had the satisfaction of seeing the admirable charge of my Cavalry, by which the Tartar horde in front of them was driven from the field in disorder ... About this time Stirling's half battery [of horse artillery], which being unable to follow the movements of Cavalry in such heavy ground, had been left with an escort of thirty of Fane's Horse under Lieutenant MacGregor, was charged by a body of Tartar Cavalry of very superior numbers. Lieut. MacGregor gallantly led his small party against the enemy, and defeated them; many Tartars being killed, and Lieut. MacGregor and many of his men severely wounded.

While this action was being fought, a separate body of Tartar cavalry approached to within 450 yards of the Buffs on Napier's left front, 'apparently regardless of the fire from two of Milward's guns ... and of Rotton's rockets'. The 4th Brigade, under Brigadier-General Reeves, was also attacked by horsemen who seemed oblivious to its 'steady fire'. But within minutes, recalled Napier, the 'courageous endurance of the enemy began to give way, and they fled'. The Indian and British cavalry pursued for five miles but found it difficult to overtake the fitter Chinese horses.

Meanwhile the 1st Division and the French had used artillery fire to drive the Tartar infantry from their entrenchments astride the Causeway. The two forces met at the western end of Senho village, where an uncharacteristically gung-ho Montauban urged Napier to attack the fortified village of Tangku, two miles to the south-east on the bank of the River Peiho. The two villages were linked by a narrow causeway with a ditch on each side, but Montauban's scouts had spotted a patch of ground between the causeway and the Peiho that was reasonably firm. This was where the French general wanted to advance. But Grant refused. Until the canals that separated the causeway from the firm ground had been bridged, he argued, the only possible access was along a single narrow road commanded by the enemy's guns. To avoid unnecessary casualties, it was better to wait. Montauban was furious and ordered his own troops to engage the Tartars in front of Tangku. But after a brief exchange of artillery fire, during which the Tartars gave as good as they got, he broke off the action and returned to Senho.

That same day, during the attack on Senho, an atrocity took place that would outrage Victorian Britain. A small party of Chinese coolies, under an Irish sergeant of the 44th Foot★ and a private of the Buffs, was bringing up supplies of rum when it was surrounded and captured by Tartar horsemen. Bound and taken before the Tartar commander, Prince Sang-kol-in-sen, they were ordered to kow-tow, the traditional Chinese act of obeisance whereby the supplicant kneels and bows his head to the ground nine times. The only captive to refuse was an old sweat called Private John Moyse, a Scotsman serving in the Buffs. He had earlier helped himself to his unit's rum ration, and his recalcitrance was due in no small part to the fact that he was drunk. Prince Sang's brutal response was to have him beheaded on the spot. Only later, when the sergeant and the rest of the party were released, did Moyse's fate become known.† Impressed by the dead private's

---

★ The regiment wiped out during the retreat from Kabul in 1842.

† Wolseley, for one, was unconvinced by the Irish sergeant's version of events and preferred to believe a Chinese coolie, who insisted that Moyse 'had died from the effects of drink' (Wolseley, II, 48).

refusal to bow to the enemy – though blissfully ignorant of his age, nationality and the real reason for his stand – *The Times* published the following poem in his honour:

> Let dusky Indians whine and kneel,
> An English lad must die.
> And thus with eyes that would not shrink,
> With knee to man unbent,
> Unfaltering on its dreadful brink,
> To his red grave he went.

The verse was written by Sir Francis Doyle, professor of poetry at Oxford, who probably heard the story from Lord Elgin, a contemporary at Eton and Christ Church, where they both took Firsts in Classics in 1832. His reference to 'dusky Indians' is because some reports insisted Moyse's fellow captives were not coolies but Sikhs; but no mention is made of the Irish sergeant, who, presumably, was tapping the ground like a woodpecker. Quite what Gladstone, the pacifist chancellor of the exchequer, made of his best man's poem is not recorded. But he can hardly have approved of the jingoistic lines:

> Last night among his fellow roughs,
> He jested, quaff'd and swore;
> A drunken private of the Buffs,
> Who never look'd before.
> Today, beneath his foeman's frown,
> He stands in Elgin's place,
> Ambassador from Britain's crown
> And type of all her race.

The allies spent the day after Moyse's death bridging the canals and ascertaining that all the Tartar cavalry had withdrawn south of the Peiho. The only enemy troops still north of the river were those at Tangku and in the Taku forts a couple of miles beyond. At daybreak on the 14th the allies' thirty-six guns opened fire on

Tangku from a distance of 900 yards, while the 1st Division and the French attacked across the hard ground between the Peiho and the causeway. The Chinese artillery was quickly silenced, and by the time a party of 2/60th Rifles entered the entrenchment, having discovered a dam across the ditch close to the Peiho, the defenders were in full retreat. They left behind a couple of dozen dead; allied casualties were just fifteen wounded.

Nobody expected the four Taku forts to crack so easily. On each side of the Peiho was a principal fort and a detached fort, with the former closer to the mouth of the river than the latter. Grant quickly saw that the detached northern fort was the key to the position, in that it overlooked both the principal northern fort and the corresponding detached fort on the southern bank. Its capture would render the other forts untenable, and Grant was determined to concentrate his force against it. Montauban disagreed, arguing that 'all military science' demanded a simultaneous attack on the southern bank. But, after a bridge-of-boats had been thrown across the Peiho at Senho, and scouts had discovered the unsuitability of the terrain for an attack on the southern forts, he gave in and agreed to join Grant's assault.

By the night of 20 August the allies' preparations were complete: a road had been constructed over the two miles of ground that separated Tangku from the detached northern fort, so as to take advantage of the shelter offered by the numerous canals that intersected it; those canals had been bridged; and batteries, containing twenty-three guns, had been thrown up to the north of the detached fort. The fort's defenders were mostly ethnic Chinese, and they too had been hard at work improving their defences and adjusting their gun positions to point inland. The result was by no means contemptible: to gain entry to the fort, the allies would have to cross, in turn, a deep dry ditch, an open space blocked by an abatis, a moat, twenty feet of ground bristling with sharpened bamboo stakes, a second moat, another staked space, and finally a thick wall of unburnt brick with embrasures for artillery. A causeway led through all these obstacles to the gate, but the bridge over the first moat had been destroyed, and the drawbridge over the second raised.

The allied batteries opened fire on the two northern forts at dawn on the 21st, and were immediately answered by all the guns the Chinese could bring to bear, including two naval 32-pounders they had recovered from sunken British gunboats the previous year. At around 6 a.m., by which time a number of Chinese guns had already been disabled, a huge explosion rocked the detached fort. An eight-inch mortar shell had scored a direct hit on the fort's magazine, causing a 'tall black pillar of smoke and rubbish' to shoot up into the air and then burst like a rocket shell, 'scattering around in all directions a shower of earth, planks and other wooden debris'. For a few moments the firing on both sides ceased, 'the common opinion being that all further resistance there was at an end'. But then the Chinese guns started up once more, and the unequal duel continued, until a shell from a British gunboat blew up the magazine in the principal northern fort.

At 7 a.m., with the guns in the detached fort all but silenced, Sir Hope Grant ordered Napier to begin the assault. He duly advanced his skirmishers to within 300 yards of the fort while field batteries were established 150 yards further back, the intention being to breach the wall to the left of the main gate. But the light field guns made little impact on the solid rampart, and, as an eight-inch gun was being brought up, the skirmishers were pushed even further forward, establishing a position on the 'edge of the outermost of the two wet ditches which surround the fort'.

Now the two attacking columns were sent forward – French on the right, British on the left – with the British preceded by a party of Royal Marines carrying a small pontoon bridge. But so heavy was the Chinese defensive fire, from muskets and gingalls, that most of the marines were hit and the bridge badly damaged long before it could reach the ditch. The much smaller French column – 500 men to the British column's 2,500 – had more success by sending Chinese coolies into the centre of the ditch and using them as piers for their scaling ladders. The French were followed over these improvised bridges by a number of British soldiers, though most were forced to swim the ditch.

By now the causeway leading to the fort gate was 'covered with killed and wounded', and the second moat with its raised drawbridge still had to be negotiated. The obstacle was overcome by the daring of Major Augustus Anson of Grant's staff, the winner of a VC during the Indian Mutiny, who swam the moat and then scaled one of the side posts of the drawbridge, sword in mouth, before cutting the rope. Down came the drawbridge with a crash and over it raced the waiting British troops.

The French had also managed to negotiate the inner moat and, recalled a watching Garnet Wolseley, a 'considerable number of officers and private soldiers of both nations were soon gathered together under the steep outer slope of the parapet that enclosed the face of the fort we were attacking'. The French were concentrated against the angle of the fort closest to the river, and relatively safe from flanking fire. Their first few efforts to scale the wall were unsuccessful, their ladders either pushed back or hauled into the fort. 'At last', wrote Wolseley, 'a French soldier reached the top, and, bounding upon the parapet, tricolor in hand, he had just time to wave it and to hear it greeted by his comrades with a wild huzzah before he fell.'

In the British sector, meanwhile, Napier had moved two howitzers and two 9-pounder guns to within eighty yards of the rampart, 'which firing over the heads of the men on the berm,★ cut away the parapet at the points where the defence was most obstinate'. A partial breach was created, and the men of the 44th and 67th (South Hampshire) Foot made every effort to enter it. But, as with the French, all initial efforts failed. 'All the time', recalled a watching British rifleman, 'the guns were crashing, and the enemy were hurling vases of lime, stinkpots, cold shot, stones, and anything else on which they could lay their Celestial hands, while the air, thick with battle-smoke, resounded with the heathens' yells and

★ The narrow ledge between the ditch of a fortification and the base of its parapet.

noises.' Twice Lieutenant Robert Rogers of the 44th tried and failed to enter the breach. On the third attempt he was assisted by a Lieutenant Edmund Lenon of the 67th, who provided him with a step by driving the point of his sword into a crevice in the wall. Rogers made it through the gap and was closely followed by Lenon and a Private John McDougall of the 44th. At about the same time the French finally entered the embrasure at their angle, the signal for the troops of both nations to pour into the place. 'But foot by foot,' reported Napier, 'the brave garrison disputed the ground, and as there was no means of exit, other than by dropping over the works and crawling over the defensive obstacles of ditches, stakes, and abattis, the loss of the enemy when they were ultimately driven out of the works was very severe, both from the rifles of our infantry, who crowded the cavalier, and from the guns moved round to the left, which swept their line of retreat on the further northern fort.'

The honour of capturing the cavalier, or central redoubt, was left to Ensign John Chaplin of the 67th, who, Queen's Colour in hand, led the charge up the long ramp. He was shot three times and badly wounded, but the desperate defenders were soon overwhelmed by hordes of allied infantry. Chaplin was later awarded the Victoria Cross, as were Rogers, Lenon and McDougall, the first three in the fort, and Lieutenant Nathaniel Burslem and Private Thomas Lane of the 67th. The final VC recipient was Andrew Fitzgibbon, a fifteen-year-old hospital apprentice,* who twice crossed open ground to tend wounded men, and was himself badly injured during the second attempt.

By 8.30 a.m. the detached northern fort was in allied hands. Its guns were now turned on the principal northern fort while fresh infantry was brought up for a second assault. But, as Hope Grant had calculated, it was not necessary. After a short bombardment, white flags appeared in all three remaining forts to signal the surrender of their garrisons, though the allies did not take possession of the southern forts until the following day.

---

* At fifteen years and three months, Fitzgibbon is the joint youngest winner of the VC.

In the detached northern fort, the scene of the hardest fighting, Wolseley estimated there were 400 'dead and dying Chinamen', including two generals, out of a total garrison of 500. Some of the dead artillerymen had portfires attached to their wrists, prompting speculation that they had been tied to their guns to prevent their running away. In the larger fort were discovered 'about 2,000 Chinese soldiers who divested themselves of their military regalia in an attempt to appear harmless'. None the less 'they expected to be killed', recalled Wolseley, 'and were astonished when we told them they might go free.' Total allied casualties at the Taku forts were 201 British and 159 French, but just thirty-four killed (seventeen on each side). A measure of the ferocity of the Chinese defensive fire is the fact that Napier, a divisional general, had his field glass shot out of his hand, his sword hilt broken by a shell splinter, and his coat ventilated by three bullets. He escaped unhurt.

Later that day Harry Parkes opened negotiations with Hang-Fu, the provincial governor, who agreed to an allied advance as far as Tientsin, thirty miles upstream, where further talks would be held. With the mouth of the Peiho clear of obstacles, four gunboats set off for Tientsin on the 22nd, carrying Parkes and two of Elgin's assistants, Henry Loch and Thomas Wade. Most of the allied force followed, with Elgin and Gros reaching Tientsin by boat on 24 August. There they were met by Hang-Fu and two other peace commissioners appointed by the Manchu court: the moderate Hang-ki and Kweilang, who had drawn up the original Treaty of Tientsin.

Emboldened by successive military victories, the allies' terms were harsh: the complete ratification of the Treaty of Tientsin, 'particularly with regard to the [ambassador's] residence at Peking'; an apology for the Taku battle a year earlier; the opening of Tientsin to foreign trade; the payment of an indemnity of £3m, an eighth of which was to be paid within two months; and the Taku forts and Canton to remain in allied hands until all the money had been handed over.

At first − according to William de Norman − the Chinese commissioners 'demurred at the hardship of paying 1 million [taels]

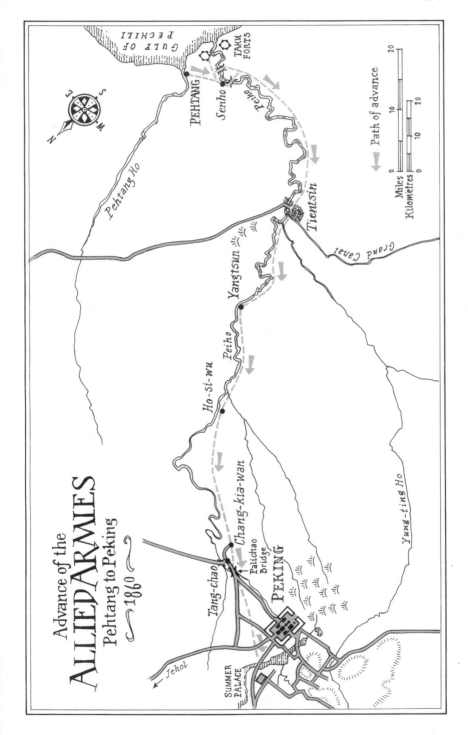

Advance of the
ALLIED ARMIES
Pehtang to Peking
1860

GULF OF PECHILI

TAKU FORTS

PEHTANG

Senho

Peiho

Pehtang Ho

TIENTSIN

Grand Canal

Yangtsun

Ho-si-wu

Peiho

Chang-kia-wan

Tung-chao

Palichiao Bridge

PEKING

SUMMER PALACE

Jehol

Yung-ting Ho

Path of advance

Miles
Kilometres

in two months, but eventually acceded to everything' and 'promised a reception at Peking, where the ratifications were to be exchanged'. With Napier and the last of the allied troops reaching Tientsin on 5 September, a grand review was scheduled for the 8th to celebrate the new agreement. But it was never held, because at the last minute the Chinese commissioners insisted they did not have the necessary authority to sign such a deal. Elgin saw it for the ruse it was: an attempt to stall negotiations until the onset of winter made any further military action impossible. Yet, in his opinion, the ruse had backfired. 'The blockheads have gone on negotiating with me just long enough to enable Grant to bring all his army up to this point,' he wrote in his diary on 8 September. 'Here we are with our base established in the heart of the country, in a capital climate, with abundance around us, our army in excellent health, and these stupid people give me a snub which obliges me to break with them.'

On 9 September, having told the Chinese commissioners that he would resume negotiations at the walled city of Tang-chao, just four miles from Peking, Elgin ordered the march to continue. Two days later the allied envoys received a letter announcing that Emperor Hsien Feng had appointed two new commissioners: Tsai Yuen, prince of Ei and the emperor's cousin; and Muyin, president of the Board of War. Both were known as hardliners, though the letter announcing their appointment was conciliatory enough, promising to concede 'everything' but begging the allies not to advance as far as Tang-chao for fear of alarming the people. Grant was sympathetic to this request, because he was having trouble supplying his troops. But Elgin thought the soldiers far too pampered – noting with disgust their refusal to drink their daily ration of rum unless it was iced – and insisted that the advance would continue.

Parkes and Wade were sent ahead, and on 14 September they met the new envoys at Tang-chao. The prince of Ei was later described by Wade as a 'tall dignified man with an intelligent countenance, though a somewhat unpleasant eye'; Muyin he thought 'softer and more wily in his manner, but also intelligent'.

After exhaustive negotiations lasting eight hours, the commissioners signed a letter agreeing to all the allies' demands. It was also arranged that Elgin and Gros would proceed to Tang-chao with a thousand men to sign the agreement in person, and then carry on to Peking to ratify the Treaty of Tientsin. Meanwhile the majority of the allied troops would not advance further than Chang-kia-wan, four miles short of Tang-chao.

Elgin and Gros were happy with these arrangements, and on 17 September – the day the troops reached Matow, just ten miles from Chang-kia-wan – Parkes was sent ahead to arrange the envoys' accommodation in Tang-chao. He was accompanied by Loch, de Norman, Thomas Bowlby of *The Times* and an escort of Fane's Horse commanded by Lieutenant Robert Anderson. Two other staff officers went with them: Lieutenant-Colonel Beauchamp Walker, whose job it was to inspect the proposed camping ground, and a Mr Thompson of the Commissariat Department, who was on the lookout for supplies. The party was well received in Tang-chao, but Parkes felt uneasy when the commissioners objected to a number of points that had already been conceded. After five hours of talks, the commissioners again gave way, and the party spent the night in the city.

The following morning Walker, Thompson and the two diplomats went to inspect the camping ground while the others remained in Tang-chao with the bulk of the escort, 'pending the return' of Parkes and Loch, 'who had yet to find a suitable residence for Lord Elgin'. En route the Britons passed large numbers of Tartar horsemen heading in the direction of the allied army and, on reaching the proposed campsite, 'discovered it to be entirely commanded by the position which the Tartar Forces supported by a numerous Artillery were then taking up'. Suspecting a trap, Parkes sent Loch to warn Grant, while he himself returned to Tang-chao to protest. Walker, Thompson and a tiny escort of five dragoons and four Sikh troopers were left in the Tartar camp to await Parkes's return.

Loch located the allied army a couple of miles from the proposed camping ground. Having informed Grant of the danger ahead, he volunteered to return and gather up the rest of his party. Grant gave his permission and added: 'I will send Wolseley with you.'

At which point Captain L. Brabazon, also on Grant's staff, interjected: 'Colonel Wolseley has not yet come up, sir; may I go instead?' Grant gave his permission, and the pair rode off, Brabazon never to return.

Parkes, meanwhile, had reached Tang-chao, where he was told by a belligerent prince of Ei that peace could not be guaranteed until the allies had given a satisfactory response to the objections he had raised the day before. Realizing that the hawks had gained the ascendancy and that further talk was futile, Parkes gathered up de Norman, Bowlby and the rest of the escort, and set off to rejoin Grant. On the way they were joined by Loch and Brabazon. But, before the British riders had gone much further, they were surrounded by Tartar cavalry and told they would need Prince Sang's permission to proceed. So Parkes, Loch and a single Sikh sowar set off to speak to him and found the short, fat, acne-ridden general on the edge of a maize field, surrounded by infantry-men who raised their weapons aggressively as the foreigners approached. Parkes at once went on the offensive, pointing out that he was travelling under a flag of truce and demanding freedom of passage. But Prince Sang angrily refused, insisting that Parkes was personally responsible for all of China's recent woes. On his signal, Parkes was dragged from his horse and ordered to kow-tow. When Parkes refused, his head was slammed repeatedly into the ground. The humiliation over, all three were bound and sent into Peking on carts.

Sang also sent troops to secure the rest of the party. As they approached, some of the Sikhs suggested cutting their way out. But Lieutenant Anderson said no, it would compromise the others. So they surrendered without a fight, and they too were escorted to Peking.

Colonel Walker's party had better luck. Sir Hope Grant wrote:

Suddenly we heard a heavy fire of matchlocks and gingals, and a number of horsemen were seen galloping furiously towards us. They turned out to be Colonel Walker and his party. They soon reached us, and told us their story. They had been detained by the enemy, but were civilly treated, when a French officer rode up and began a dispute with some Tartars about a mule he was riding. At last he drew a pistol and fired it, when his mule was immediately shot, and he himself murdered. Colonel Walker rode to his assistance, but his sword was struck out of his hand; and though it was restored to him by a Chinese officer, fresh efforts were made to wrest it from him, and in his endeavours to retain it, his fingers were so badly cut that his hand was disabled. Then finding that the only hope of safety was to force their way out, he shouted to his party to ride for their lives. All charged through the enemy and made their escape – viz., Colonel Walker, Mr Thompson of the commissariat, one sowar, and four Dragoon Guards, one of whom was shot through the leg. Mr Thompson received several spear wounds in the back; and one horse was shot through the body, but managed to convey its rider back in safety.

Outraged by this act of Manchu aggression, Grant and Montauban ordered an immediate attack, and their combined force of 3,500 troops soon dispersed the much larger Tartar Army, capturing eighty guns in the process. Captain R. H. R. Rowley, RA, recalled:

The French went off to the right, supported by Desborough's battery and a squadron of horse, and the 99th [(Lanarkshire) Foot] and Marines. Sir John Mitchell [*sic*] went to the left to turn the right of the enemy's position with Probyn's Horse, 2nd Queens and Stirling's half battery. Our battery, the 1st Punjab Infantry and a squadron of K.D.G.s formed the centre, where Sir Hope Grant commanded in person. We opened fire on a strong body of cavalry, who fired at us with gingalls. We drove them back; but we were at once time enfiladed from an entrenchment and had a gun leader's leg broken by a round shot. Several of the Punjab Infantry were wounded at the same time. However we pushed on and by 2 p.m. the entrenchments were in our hands.

Next morning Thomas Wade was sent forward under a flag of truce to demand the prisoners' release. But he was given short shrift by the prince of Ei, and, on the way back, he and his escort were fired at by Tartar troops encamped near Tang-chao. That evening, during dinner in his Chang-kia-wan headquarters, Grant told Elgin that the time for diplomacy was over. Elgin agreed: 'We must have one more fight.'

That fight took place on 21 September when the allies attacked the Chinese Army's new position in front of the Yang-Liang Canal, the waterway that connected the Peiho and Peking. The canal was spanned by two bridges: one of marble, called Palichao, and another of wood, a mile to the west. The intention was for the French, on the right, to take the marble bridge, the British the wooden one. Meanwhile the cavalry would make a wide sweep to the left and drive the enemy's right on to his centre between the two bridges. In the event, the Tartar cavalry took the initiative by attempting to turn the British left flank, but they were met by the much heavier British and Indian cavalry. Wolseley recorded:

They were mounted on small ponies, our men on great troop horses . . . The Tartar cavalry had, however, cunningly halted behind a wide ditch to receive the charge, and delivered a volley when our horsemen reached it. At that period our irregular cavalry always rode with short, standing martingales,★ which prevented their horses from jumping freely. Many accordingly went head over heels into that ditch, their riders being unable to pull them up in time. Not so, however, the King's Dragoon Guards whose horses having free heads, jumped or scrambled over safely. They were soon well in amongst the Tartars, riding over men and ponies, and knocking both down like so many ninepins. But Probyn's and Fane's sharp-sworded Sikhs, Pathans and Punjaubee Mussulmans soon followed and showed splendidly, fighting side by side with the big sturdy Dragoon Guardsmen. In a few minutes riderless Tartar ponies were to be seen galloping in all directions.

★ A strap or arrangement of straps fastened at one end to the noseband, and at the other to the girth, to prevent a horse from rearing or throwing back its head.

Captain Rowley and his battery of Armstrongs passed over the same ground shortly afterwards and found it 'strewn with dead Tartars, who had received tremendous sabre cuts'. They un-limbered as yet more Tartar horsemen approached, but three rounds were enough to drive them off. Camp after neatly laid-out military camp was burnt by the British troops as they advanced towards the canal. Swarms of Chinese peasants 'helped at this work, and crowds were soon to be seen staggering to their homes as fast as they could under the weight of the loot they had collected'.

The French faced the stiffest resistance from detachments of the elite Imperial Guard, dug in around the Palichao Bridge. Attack after attack was repulsed, but the Manchu general was twice wounded in the desperate fighting. In retaliation he ordered two prisoners – Captain Brabazon, who had been separated from the rest of the British captives, and a French abbé called Duluc – to be brought on to the bridge and beheaded.★ The French eventually took their bridge, as had the British further west, and the pursuit of the beaten Chinese Army continued to within six miles of Peking.

The defeat at last prompted Emperor Hsien Feng to leave Peking for the relative safety of Jehol, eighty miles to the north. He had been considering flight for some days, suggesting at one stage the face-saving option of leading his troops out of the city before heading north on a hunting expedition. Tzu-hsi had dissuaded him, but now, with the barbarians literally at the gates, there was nothing to be gained by staying. So he departed, and with him went Tzu-hsi, his concubines and court officials. In his stead he left his brother Prince Kung, the highest mandarin in the land, and the moderate Hang-ki to conduct negotiations with the allies. Both seemed keen to end hostilities, and on 22 September, under a flag of truce, Kung told Elgin that the emperor was prepared to come to terms if the allies agreed to restore the Taku forts and

★ Wolseley had once again cheated death: but for his tardy arrival at Grant's headquarters on the 18th, he, and not Brabazon, would have lost his head.

leave China. Elgin's response was that discussions could not even begin until all the prisoners had been released. Unless that happened quickly, he warned, the allies would storm Peking.

This was easier said than done, because Grant was unwilling to risk an attack on Peking's formidable walls – forty feet high and sixty thick – without his heavy siege guns and the remainder of his troops, notably Napier's 2nd Division, which had been left at Tientsin. It would take at least a fortnight to bring them forward, and Elgin, in any case, was reluctant to authorize an assault in case it brought about the downfall of the Ch'ing Dynasty. Yet not a single prisoner had been released by the time the siege guns and extra troops arrived in early October, and Elgin's only option was to order an advance. Wolseley wrote:

October 6 saw us again on the march, and in the evening we bivouacked inside the ramparts from which Sang-ko-lin-sin and his army had just retreated. But in the close country we had just passed through, not only the French but our own cavalry also had 'lost touch' with us. The latter had been ordered to make a wide sweep to our right and take up a position on the main road running from Pekin northwards to [Jehol], by which we expected the enemy to retreat. During the day Sir Hope Grant had sent to tell General Montauban that he understood Sang-ko-lin-sin had fallen back upon Yuen-ming-Yuen, and that consequently he would push for that place. It was thought advisable, however, to wait until our cavalry had rejoined us before we did so.

The Yuen-ming-Yuen* was the centrepiece of the emperor's fabled Summer Palace. A more accurate description would have been Summer Palaces, because, as well as the principal palace, the great walled park contained more than 200 summer houses and pavilions in its eighty square miles of exquisitely landscaped gardens and artificial lakes. Within those buildings were housed countless treasures, the pick of Chinese art and civilization, not to mention many centuries of tribute from barbarian states, including a

---

* Literal translation: 'The Enclosed and Beautiful Garden'.

Baroque audience chamber designed by Jesuit missionaries in the seventeenth century.

The allies had agreed in advance to preserve this unique cultural jewel. But by the time Elgin, Grant and his staff reached the Yuenming-Yuen during the afternoon of 7 October, the French were busy stripping it. Wolseley recalled:

General Montauban met Sir Hope at the door and begged him not to allow his staff to enter, and he at once assenting told us to stay outside. I was amused at this, because at that very moment there was a string of French soldiers going in empty-handed and another coming out laden with loot of all sorts and kinds. Many were dressed in the richly embroidered gowns of women, and almost all wore fine Chinese hats instead of the French kepi.

As Wolseley waited outside, chatting to a French general, he was much amused by the way the looters presented the general 'with a gift of something curious as they saluted him in passing out of the palace gates'. Eventually one of the looters, a gunner, handed Wolseley what appeared to be a tiny framed picture, saying: '*Mon camarade, voici un petit cadeau pour vous.*' Wolseley thanked him and put it in his pocket. Only later did he discover that it was 'an extremely good French enamel of a man in a flowing wig, evidently one of the many fine presents sent by Louis XIV to the Emperor of China'.

Elgin and Grant, meanwhile, had accompanied Montauban into the main palace. Grant recalled: 'It was pitiful to see the way in which everything was being robbed. Only one room in the Palace was untouched. General de Montauban informed me he had reserved any valuables it might contain for equal division between the English and French.' But in the absence of any British troops the arrangement quickly broke down, and, a day later, Grant authorized a free-for-all. Wolseley wrote:

For some days afterwards the looting was continued, and a large number of our officers secured a good deal, but neither the non-commissioned officers nor the privates – being in camp several miles away – had the chance of obtaining anything. This Sir Hope Grant thought unfair, so he issued a general order directing all our officers who had obtained any loot to send it forthwith to prize agents, whom he named, in order that it might be sold by public auction, and the sum thus obtained distributed forthwith amongst the army.

One of the British officers who visited the Summer Palace on 8 October was a 27-year-old captain of engineers called Charles Gordon. The son of an artillery general, Gordon was a zealous Christian who had proved himself an enterprising, intelligent and courageous officer during the trench warfare of the Crimean War. Soon to win worldwide acclaim – and the sobriquet 'Chinese' Gordon – for his skilful command of Chinese irregulars in the war against the Taiping rebels, he would meet a grisly if glorious end at the epic siege of Khartoum in 1885. But in October 1860 he was a little-known, if well-regarded, engineer who was horrified by the gratuitous destruction of the Summer Palace. He wrote in a letter:

You would scarcely conceive the magnificence of this residence or the tremendous devastation the French have committed. The Throne room was lined with ebony carved in a marvellous way. There were huge mirrors of all kinds, clocks, watches, musical boxes with puppets on them, magnificent china of every description, heaps and heaps of silks of all colours, embroidery and as much splendour and civilization as you would see at Windsor. Carved ivory screens, coral ditto, large amount of treasure, etc.; and the French have smashed everything in the most wanton way.

Gordon secured a few choice items. But he and other British officers were forced to hand over their loot to the prize agents. The public auction was held on 11 October and eventually netted around £50,000. Grant and his two divisional commanders were due the largest shares, but they generously returned them to the pot. Even so, the individual amounts – £3 for privates and £50 for field officers – were small beer compared to the riches the French made off with. They were allowed to keep their plunder, and one officer later sold a pearl necklace in Hong Kong for £3,000; even privates made a small fortune. The French, wrote Major Greathed, 'take the broadest view of the question of "halves" '.

Years later Montauban (by then the Comte de Palikao) was questioned by a French government inquiry into the looting of the Summer Palace. He blamed the British. 'I had sentries posted', he told the inquiry, 'and directed two officers with two companies of marine infantry to protect the palace from depredation and to allow nothing to be moved until the arrival of the English commanders. Thus there would be no pillage. Nothing had been touched in the Palace when the English arrived.' This was a bare-faced lie, but there was no one to contradict it. On his return to France, Montauban is said to have presented the Empress Eugénie with a pearl necklace worth many thousands of pounds. To assuage his guilt he had given Hope Grant half of a pair of gold and jade sceptres as a gift for Queen Victoria; the other half was intended for Napoleon III.

The issue of plunder, however, was a much lower priority than the fate of the prisoners. On 7 October, Wade met Hang-ki beneath the walls of Peking, the Chinese commissioner having been lowered in a basket so that the city gates did not have to be opened. Wade offered a deal: release the prisoners immediately, put a gate of the city in the allies' hands and depute competent persons to conclude a peace; in return the allied troops would be kept out of the city and 'the lives and property of the inhabitants' would be 'respected'. Prince Kung responded the following day by releasing Parkes, Loch and the Sikh orderly with whom they had been captured. Compared to the other prisoners, these three had been relatively well treated. Released from their tight bonds after the first eight hours, they were put in separate cells in Peking's common jail. Loch remembered:

I found myself in the presence of, and surrounded by, as savage a lot of half-naked demons as I had ever beheld; they were nearly all the lowest class of criminals, imprisoned for murder and the most serious offences (they were kindly disposed to the Englishmen all the same). On one side of the room, running the whole length, was a wooden bench extending about eight feet from the wall, sloping a little towards it; this was the sleeping place; chains hung down from several of the beams, reaching nearly to the bench, with the use of which I was soon to be made practically acquainted.

Chains were placed round his hands, neck and feet, and at night were connected to the beam. He was only able to lie flat on his back, 'and even that was painful with my elbows pinioned'. By day he could move around the cell, his fellow prisoners helping to carry his chains. But the jailers were 'harsh and rude' and the food allowance 'scanty'. Parkes also received kindness from the thieves and murderers who shared his cell, but he was repeatedly interrogated and threatened with execution. All this changed on 29 September when Parkes and Loch were released from their chains and transferred to a temple near the Antung Gate, where they were given a change of clothes and food from a nearby restaurant. The reason: Parkes had agreed to write to Elgin, asking for 'hostilities to be temporarily suspended to give opportunity for negotiation'. Of course Elgin refused the request, insisting instead on the release of all prisoners before talks could begin. But he was relieved to know the prisoners were still alive.

Prince Kung ordered the first batch of prisoners – including Parkes, Loch and a French savant – to be handed over on 8 October, because he knew an assault on Peking was imminent. It was not a moment too soon for the British diplomats, as on that very day, in retaliation for the looting of the Summer Palace, the emperor had signed their death warrants. But for many of the other prisoners, kept in far harsher conditions, it was already too late.

Kung had been given until noon on 13 October to release the remaining prisoners, open the Antung Gate and surrender the city. If he failed to do so, the allies' heavy guns would open fire. With a day to spare, a French soldier and ten Sikhs of Fane's Horse, the remnants of Parkes's escort, were given up. The story they told of their horrific confinement – first in the courtyard of the Summer Palace, then in the Board of Punishments in Peking – was beyond belief. Major Greathed recorded:

Their hands and feet tied together behind their backs they were thrown on their chests and kept in the open air, exposed to the cold at night and the still considerable heat by day, without food or water for three days and nights. From the first their bands were wetted to tighten them and if they attempted to turn around to rest themselves they were cruelly kicked and beaten. On the third day poor [Lieutenant] Anderson's fingers and nails burst from the pressure of the cords which were not even then released. The wrist bones became visible, mortification ensued, the victim became delirious and happily unconscious of the horror of his position this gallant soldier died.

During his sufferings his men made efforts to approach him and gnaw his cords, but they were savagely kicked away by his inhuman jailers. The condition was duly ameliorated after the lapse of three days by the bonds on the hands and feet being exchanged for heavy chains and irons. But from this time they were regularly tho' most scantily and miserably fed.

Poor Bowlby died on the 5th day in the same way, then De Norman and several of the men. All appear to have kept noble heart and to have cheered and encouraged each other, but no less than thirteen sank under the horror of their captivity.

Of the thirty-nine French and British captives, only nineteen were released alive. So infuriated were some Sikh cavalrymen by the barbaric treatment of their comrades that they abducted two Chinese civilians at random and subjected them to the same roped torture. The Chinamen were only saved, close to death, by the intervention of British officers. But the blood of the whole allied force was well and truly up, and it was lucky for the inhabitants of Peking that Prince Kung surrendered the city before the 13 October deadline. Wolseley, who was in the main breaching battery as noon approached, recalled:

I took my place by the right-hand gun, where the captain of artillery in command stood, like myself, watch in hand, awaiting what was to be a noon of dire import not only to the inhabitants, but also to the fortunes of the Chinese reigning family. Up to within ten minutes of the time named, no sign of surrender was made by the enemy. Our embrasures were then unmasked, the guns were deliberately sponged, loaded, run out, and then laid upon the wall where we meant to batter it. I held my breath; I was not happy feeling we were playing at a 'game of brag', for I knew too well that with the number of rounds we had with us no effective breach could be hoped for.

But the Chinese did not know this, and, with just ten minutes to go, the gates swung open and in marched Lord Elgin with 500 men. 'In a few minutes', recorded Captain Rowley, 'the English flag waved over the wall. Desborough's battery were sent in and the guns placed in position to sweep the streets, the horses remaining outside. I rode down to the gate and saw huge crowds of people who were being kept in order by mandarins' whips. We encamped for the night near the Temple of the Earth.'*

Over the next few days, the corpses of most of the dead prisoners were delivered to the allies in rough coffins. Only Brabazon and the French abbé were unaccounted for, their bodies having been thrown into the Yang-Liang Canal and never recovered. The Protestant dead – including de Norman, Bowlby, Anderson and a dragoon called Phipps – were buried in the Russian Orthodox Cemetery on 17 October. The French conducted a separate Catholic funeral service a day later.

Elgin was tormented by the thought that lives could have been saved if Grant had not been so cautious. 'None of this would have happened,' he informed his wife, 'if we had moved with celerity and not been scared by bugbears.' Yet it had happened, and for many days he anguished over how best to punish those responsible. He eventually decided, and not without regret, to burn the mag-

---

* Built by the Ming Dynasty and known as the Di Tan, where the emperors worshipped the Earth God.

nificent Summer Palace. Such an act would serve, he told Prince Kung, 'as a lasting mark of the abhorrence of our Government at the violation of the law of nations which had been committed'.

The destruction was carried out by British troops on 18/19 October, a light northerly wind carrying to Peking 'dense clouds of smoke from this conflagration' and covering its streets with 'a shower of burnt embers, which must have been to all classes silent evidences of our work of retribution'. Both Wolseley and Loch thought that the burning of the Summer Palace 'hastened the final settlement of affairs and strengthened our ambassador's position'. Certainly Prince Kung was quick to pay the additional indemnity of £100,000 that Elgin intended to distribute among the families of the dead. Kung also agreed to Elgin's earlier demands, and on 24 October, in the heart of the Forbidden City,* the 1858 Treaty of Tientsin was finally ratified.

Prior to the ceremony, Wolseley inspected the venue for bombs. But he 'could find nothing suspicious, and felt that it would be difficult to blow up Lord Elgin without killing Prince Kung also'. Security was tight, nevertheless, with British soldiers lining the route to the Forbidden City and a strong guard surrounding the sedan chair† that carried the British envoy.

Waiting to receive Elgin in the Hall of Audience was Prince Kung, 'surrounded by Imperial officers of State'. Wolseley recorded: 'Prince Kung was a nice-looking, yellow-faced Tartar, of middle height and good features . . . He looked a gentleman amidst the crowd of bilious, bloated, small-pox-marked faces of the mandarins around him.' As well as ratifying the earlier treaty, Kung and Elgin signed a separate convention that declared Tientsin a free port, transferred the territory of Kowloon (opposite Hong Kong) to the British and fixed the war indemnity at £3m. Until it was paid, British troops would remain at Tientsin. With the

* A city within a city, made up of a series of courtyards within courtyards, the middle one containing the emperor's palace.

† To emphasize his status as the representative of a sovereign, Elgin's sedan chair was carried by eight porters. In China, only the emperor was entitled to eight porters.

paperwork complete, Elgin expressed a hope that the two nations would remain on good terms. Kung replied that 'he had been himself about to utter the self same words'. He then admitted that 'affairs had hitherto been greatly mismanaged', adding that things would improve now that the imperial government was exclusively 'in his hands'. A day later he and Gros ratified the earlier Franco-Chinese treaty.

The allies began their withdrawal to the coast in early November, leaving a strong force in temporary occupation of Tientsin and the Taku forts. The campaign had been extraordinarily successful, achieving all its military and diplomatic objectives, and more, with minimum casualties and hardly any cost to the British and French taxpayer. In recognition of this, Elgin was appointed Canning's successor as viceroy of India, Montauban became Comte de Palikao (after the bridge his men so gallantly captured) and Grant received the GCB. Grant also received the thanks of Sidney Herbert, the war secretary, who wrote: 'The public here are, I think, very pleased with the way everything has been done in China – firmness, temper, skill, success . . . a first-rate general, a capital staff, an excellent commissariat, and a good medical department are four things the English public are especially pleased to see, and the more so when all are got together.'

Napier provided a less rose-tinted assessment of the allied campaign in a letter to a friend:

I most sincerely hope that this is the last Gallic alliance that we shall have – it has been a most unfortunate one, and has hampered us in every way . . . I found Montauban very civil and Divisional Generals very friendly . . . Their staff is in many respects better than ours, their system better; their soldiers as material infinitely inferior . . . The more I see of the two armies, the more I admire the French administration and our superb material, which would, if made the most of, walk over the armies of any other people whom I have seen and trample them in the dust, though we have much to learn before our soldiers will be prepared to do all that they are capable of.

Napier was right. Even in the wake of the post-Crimea reforms, the British Army had serious flaws. Its main task of policing the empire left it permanently overstretched, with no reserve for emergencies like the Crimean War; its administration, though improved, was still tangled and inefficient; and its officers were still selected on the basis of influence and privilege, rather than merit. Most of these problems were tackled, not entirely successfully, by the Cardwell reforms of the early 1870s. But to take advantage of such weaknesses in 1860 would have required a foe less technologically and tactically inferior to the British than the Chinese.

It is ironic that Elgin, the son of the self-styled 'saviour' of the Parthenon friezes, was the man who gave the order to destroy the Summer Palace, one of the wonders of the world. Castigated by the world's press, he defended himself in a letter to Russell, the foreign secretary: 'It was necessary to discover some act of retribution and punishment, without attacking Peking, and in such a manner as to make the blow fall on the Emperor who was clearly responsible for the crime committed [the murder of the prisoners] without, however, so terrifying his brother [Prince Kung] whom he had left behind to represent him, as to drive him from the field . . . The destruction of the Yuen-ming-yuen Palace . . . seemed to me to be the only combination which fulfilled these conditions.'

Palmerston agreed. 'It was absolutely necessary', he wrote to Herbert, 'to stamp by such permanent record our indignation at the treachery and brutality of these Tartars, for Chinese they are not.'

Bar a few Radical MPs, most of his fellow Britons thought the same; but not, curiously enough, Queen Victoria and Prince Albert, who were appalled for different reasons.★ Victoria was against the burning of royal residences in principle, in case the

★ Indignant she may have been, but Victoria had enough of a sense of humour to name a Pekinese lapdog, found in the Summer Palace and later presented to her by one of her officers, 'Lootie'. She was also happy to accept, from Sir Hope Grant himself, the jade-and-gold sceptre and three huge enamelled bowls that had been filched from the same doomed residence.

practice proved catching, while Albert feared the emperor's humiliation would topple the Ch'ing Dynasty and usher in the anti-capitalist Taipings, with all the dire consequences that would have for British commerce. In the event the Manchus survived – thanks in part to Tzu-hsi's cunning and 'Chinese' Gordon's military expertise – and Britain's profitable, if morally indefensible, trade with China continued well into the twentieth century.

Within four years of the war ending, China drew seven eighths of its imports from the British Empire, an annual trade worth more than £100,000. And it continued to grow, with the quantity of opium chests expanding from 58,000 in 1859 to 105,000 in 1879, and the import of British textiles quadrupling over the same period. The Chinese responded by growing their own opium, causing British imports to level off. Yet the number of Chinese addicts continued to increase, with *The Times* estimating in 1888 that seven in every ten adult males were users. Two years later the trade itself was legalized, a policy reversed in 1906, as use of the drug permeated every level of society. Only the over-sixties were exempt. The reason: the Dowager Empress Tzu-hsi was herself an addict.

# Epilogue
## 'Oh, yes, this is death!'

With far more dramatic events closer to home during the summer of 1860 – notably the invasion of the Two Kingdoms of Sicily by General Giuseppe Garibaldi's Redshirts – the war in China passed largely unnoticed in Britain. The queen herself made no reference to the conflict in her journal, though she was sent regular updates by the Foreign Office. Only when it had been successfully concluded did she express, in a letter to Lord John Russell, her satisfaction at the 'excellent telegraphic news' and her deep grief 'over the cruel sufferings & deaths of the poor prisoners & especially of poor W. de Norman'.

The royal couple still took a keen interest in all things military, with the queen firing the new Whitworth steel rifle at the National Rifle Association's annual competition at Wimbledon Common in July 1860,★ and Albert writing regularly to the government on issues as diverse as the Fortifications Bill (which he supported, though he suspected Gladstone did not) and the desirability of a Naval Reserve. On 6 August, while the invasion of China was under way, they both attended a grand review of 22,000 volunteer troops in Edinburgh. 'The French', wrote Albert to his old mentor Baron Stockmar, 'are as much out of humour at this demonstration as Messrs Cobden and Bright.' (As pacifists, the Radical leaders regarded all such military parades as unnecessarily provocative.)

In mid September, Albert was laid low with recurrent stomach cramps, chills and aches. His physician diagnosed exhaustion and recommended rest. But Albert was determined not to delay his

★ The queen hit the bull's-eye, firing from a fixed rest at 400 yards, and the rifle won the competition. But the Whitworth, whose design Albert had encouraged, was never adopted by the British Army, because the War Office considered its bore too small for military effectiveness. (Subsequent rifles would have even smaller bores.)

visit to Coburg, and he and Victoria left as scheduled on
22 September. It was an inauspicious trip: en route they received
news of the death of Albert's stepmother, Duchess Marie; in
Coburg itself, Albert was almost killed when the carriage he was
driving crashed into a goods wagon. He leapt to safety at the last
moment, sustaining nothing more serious than cuts and bruises.
But the queen knew how close to death he had come and thanked
God for his 'wonderful' escape.

Albert was more concerned with his nagging illness. He seemed
to sense it might be terminal, and this made his visit to Coburg all
the more nostalgic. At one of his favourite beauty spots he began
to cry, telling his brother Duke Ernest that 'he was well aware that
he had been here for the last time in his life.' His condition
worsened on the journey home, with a persistent migraine and the
now familiar cramps and chills.

The prince's ailments continued on into 1861, though the queen
was distracted for a time by the death of her mother on 15 March.
Assailed by feelings of guilt and remorse, Victoria took her grieving
to excessive proportions, eating alone and ignoring official papers
for almost a month. 'I hope this state of things won't last,' Clarendon told the duchess of Manchester, 'or she may fall into the
morbid melancholy to wh[ich] her mind has always tended.'

By early summer the queen was over the worst of her torpor,
though her husband's chronic ill health had not been helped by
the extra burden her temporary withdrawal from public life had
placed on him. There was also the worry of Britain being dragged
into the American Civil War, which had erupted in April when
eleven Southern states seceded from the Union and formed the
Confederacy. The South was determined to preserve its distinctive
way of life, particularly the right to own slaves. But as three
states that had remained in the Union – Maryland, Kentucky and
Missouri – were also pro-slavery, President Abraham Lincoln was
loath to trumpet abolition. Instead he insisted that the Union's
chief war aim was to reverse secession. Palmerston and many
Britons saw this as hypocrisy. After all, the United States had been
created by secession from Great Britain. Support for the South,

therefore, could be justified as support for a people's right to self-determination (not that the British Empire encouraged such choice). There were also powerful commercial reasons for siding with the Confederacy, which supplied the cotton industry in Lancashire with most of its raw material, a trade that was threatened by the Union blockade of southern ports. For both these reasons, Palmerston's government was quick to recognize the Confederacy as a 'belligerent', meaning it was not obliged by law to regard the South's soldiers and sailors as rebels. But it held back from conferring nation status on the Confederacy, and Britain itself remained neutral.

Victoria and Albert's sympathies also lay with the South, and both feared that the North might attempt to recoup its territorial losses by invading Canada. In a letter to Palmerston of 30 May,[*] the queen urged sending artillery to Canada, as 'the Colony' had no arms industry. The navy also needed to be strengthened, she wrote, because 'it is less likely that the remnant of the United States could send expeditions by land to the North while quarrelling with the South, than that they should commit acts of violence at sea.'

The royal family's fears were realized on 8 November when the British mail steamer *Trent* was intercepted by a Union warship and forced to hand over two of its passengers, both Confederate diplomats on their way to urge the governments of Britain and France to accord their country nation status. Palmerston condemned the piracy as a 'gross outrage and violation of international law' – though his legal officers had assured him it was anything but – and instructed Russell,[†] the foreign secretary, to draft an ultimatum that demanded an apology and the immediate release of the diplomats. When Victoria and Albert saw the draft, on 30 November, they were far from satisfied. It was, the queen informed Russell, 'somewhat meagre' and would have benefited from 'the expression of a hope that the American captain did not

[*] Drafted by Albert and amended by his wife.
[†] Lord John Russell had been raised to the peerage as the first Earl Russell of Kingston earlier that year.

act under instructions, or, if he did, that he misapprehended them'. This get-out clause for the Union government was actually suggested by Albert, who drafted the queen's reply, and it was included by Palmerston in the final version of the dispatch that was sent in early December. A relieved Lincoln duly released the diplomats and declared that the Union warship's captain had been acting without authority.

Albert's diplomacy has been credited with averting a war between Britain and the United States. Feelings were certainly running high on both sides of the Atlantic, with *Punch*'s John Bull warning his American counterpart: 'You do what's right, my son, or I'll blow you out of the water.' But Union public opinion, already inflamed by war with the South, would never have allowed its government to submit to naked threats. Lincoln needed a way to back down with honour, and Albert's suggestion provided it. The prince's instinctive understanding of politics was never put to better use. The question is: would Palmerston, for all his belligerence in public, have authorized the sending of a dispatch that gave Lincoln no room for manoeuvre? The answer is probably no. Either way, the prince's timely intervention in the Trent Affair was to be his last political act.

So sick had he become by early December that as he drafted the queen's reply to Russell's ultimatum he could barely hold his pen. Two recent excursions were partly to blame for his sudden deterioration: the first on 22 November, when it had rained incessantly during his inspection of new premises for the Staff College at Sandhurst; and the second, four days later, when he had travelled to Cambridge to speak to his wayward eldest son. Now twenty, the fun-loving but feckless Bertie had done little to alter his parents' poor opinion of him. A case in point was his recent spell of military service in Ireland. The plan had been for him to learn the basic requirements of each officer grade – one rank a fortnight – until he was competent enough to command a regiment on parade. But he preferred carousing to square-bashing, and by the time his parents arrived in Ireland in late August he was still serving as a captain. His mother hardly noticed. 'Bertie marched past with his company,' she wrote to her uncle Leopold, 'and did not seem at all so very small.'

Back from Ireland, Bertie returned to Cambridge University, where he had been studying, on and off, since January. Reports had long since reached his parents that he was mixing with the wrong people, drinking, gambling and smoking cigars. Albert regarded an early marriage as essential and had selected as a potential bride the beautiful Princess Alexandra of Denmark, ignoring the fact that her country's standoff with Prussia over the disputed provinces of Schleswig-Holstein meant that a dynastic alliance would put Britain in a ticklish diplomatic position, not least because the queen's eldest daughter was married to the heir to the Prussian throne.* Bertie was less enthusiastic, and the reason became clear in mid November when a rumour reached Windsor that he had been having an affair since the summer with an Irish actress called Nellie Clifden. His upright father was appalled, telling Bertie that the scandal had caused him the 'greatest pain' he had felt in his life. Bertie admitted the affair but insisted it was over. This failed to mollify his outraged mother, who felt that she could never look upon her son again 'without a shudder'.

Albert was determined to have it out with his fornicating son and, though seriously ill and in no condition to travel, took a special train to Cambridge on 26 November. Ignoring a persistent drizzle, he and Bertie went for a long walk, during which the heir to the throne promised to mend his ways. Albert, in turn, forgave his son and assured him there would be no witchhunt of his brother officers who had led him astray. But the emotional and physical effort of the trip left Albert more exhausted than ever.

In early December, having penned the Trent memorandum, Albert took to his bed in Windsor Castle. He found it hard to sleep, and even soup and brown bread caused vomiting. On

---

* Nevertheless the marriage eventually took place at Windsor on 10 May 1863. A year later Denmark and Prussia went to war over Schleswig-Holstein, with the pro-German queen urging her foreign minister, Russell, not to favour her daughter-in-law's country over her son-in-law's. With Britain remaining neutral, Denmark was quickly overrun and the provinces annexed by Prussia.

7 December his illness was diagnosed by Sir William Jenner, the queen's physician extraordinary, as 'gastric & bowel' (or typhoid) fever. Yet Jenner insisted he knew how to treat the illness and that it would take at least a month to run its course. A day later the royal physicians detected slight signs of improvement, prompting a relieved Victoria to inform her uncle Leopold that 'our beloved invalid goes on well'. He was even better on the 9th. 'He seemed much more himself,' recorded the queen. 'When he took his broth, he quite sat up, as usual, & shows great strength, but is now entirely in bed.'

The next two days saw further grounds for optimism. Albert's pulse was 'good', noted the queen on the 10th, '& everything so far, satisfactory'. Victoria clung to Jenner's assurance that the fever would run its course if there were no '*unfavourable*' symptoms. 'I cannot sufficiently praise', she wrote on 12 December, 'the skill, attention, and devotion of Dr Jenner, who is the *first fever* doctor in Europe.'

Yet Albert's symptoms did worsen: his breathing quickened, his temperature rose and he lapsed into bouts of delirium. (He imagined he could hear the birds singing at his family home in Coburg.) On the 13th – a Friday – the queen was told that Albert was sinking fast, and their children were summoned accordingly. Hope flared briefly on the 14th, when yet another doctor thought 'there was ground to hope the crisis was over.'★ But it was a false dawn, and at 4.30 p.m. a medical bulletin declared the prince to be in a 'most critical state'. By now Princess Alice, who had kept a constant bedside vigil for days, had been joined by her siblings Bertie, Helena, Louise and Arthur. Of the remaining four children, Victoria was in Berlin with her husband,† Alfred at sea, the haemophiliac Leopold in France for his health and Beatrice, at four, too

---

★ If Prince Albert really had been suffering from typhoid fever, such an outcome would not have been out of the question. But Albert's most recent biographer is convinced that that was not the case, and that a long, slow disease like stomach cancer is much more likely. If so, there was nothing the doctors could have done (see Weintraub, *Albert*, 430).

† Now Crown Prince Frederick of Prussia.

young for such a heart-rending scene. For some time the queen held Albert's thin, motionless hand. But eventually she could take no more and fled the room in tears.

The end came at 10.45 p.m. Identifying Albert's change of breathing as the death rattle, Princess Alice sent for her mother. The queen rushed back in and cried: 'Oh, yes, this is death! I know it. I have seen it before.' She then collapsed on his lifeless body, muttering endearments, before her children gently led her away.

The shock of being widowed at the relatively young age of forty-two caused Victoria to suffer an almost total emotional collapse. 'My *life* as a *happy* one is *ended*!' she wrote to her uncle Leopold six days later. 'The world is gone for *me*! If I *must live* on (and I will do nothing to make me worse than I am), it is henceforth for our poor fatherless children – for my unhappy country, which has lost *all* in losing him – and in *only* doing what I know and *feel* he would wish, for he *is* near me – his spirit will guide and inspire me. But oh! To be cut off in his prime of life – to see our pure, happy, quiet, domestic life, which *alone* enabled me to bear my *much* disliked position, CUT OFF at forty-two – when I *had* hoped we would grow old together (though *he* always talked of the shortness of life) – is *too awful*, too cruel!'

This depth of anguish was not just because the queen loved Albert dearly, and knew too well the pain of losing a father in childhood, but also because she leant so heavily upon him in every aspect of her private and public life. Virtually all her official correspondence, for example, was either drafted or approved by Albert. Without him to guide her, how would she cope? Not well, according to Disraeli. 'Nothing great or small was done but by [Albert's] advice,' he noted in his diary on 16 December. 'I have myself . . . heard him at dinner, suggest to her in German to enquire about this, that, and the other; and the questions never failed to follow . . . The worst consequence possible is one, unluckily, not unlikely: that without being absolutely incapacitated for affairs, she may fall into a state of mind in which it will be difficult to do business with her, and impossible to anticipate what she will approve or disapprove.'

Disraeli's fears were soon realized. For five weeks the queen saw nobody but the members of her own household, not even the prime minister. Her withdrawal from public life would last much longer: until February 1866, to be exact, when she reluctantly agreed to reopen parliament. During that time she wore nothing but black, though the members of her household were allowed to revert to the semi-mourning colours of white, mauve and grey after a year. Even royal servants were expected to wear a black crêpe armband until 1869.

In a desperate, and some would say macabre, attempt to preserve Albert's memory, the queen insisted that in each of their homes her husband's dressing room and study were to be kept as if their former occupant were still alive. Towels and linen were changed daily, his nightclothes laid out and hot water brought in the morning for shaving. Each night the queen would kneel on Albert's side of the bed before walking round to her own. As for her future conduct, Victoria was determined to act as Albert would have done. '[It] is *my firm* resolve', she assured her uncle Leopold, 'that *his* wishes – *his* plans – about every thing, *his* views about *every* thing are to be *my law*! And *no human power* will make me swerve from *what he* decided and wished . . . I am *also determined* that *no one* person, may *he* be ever so good, ever so devoted among my servants – is to lead or guide or dictate *to me*. I know *how he* would disapprove of it.' Palmerston was only too well aware of the problems that such a course of action would produce for the government of the day. 'Her determination', he wrote to Russell in late December 1861, 'to conform to what she from time to time may persuade herself would have been at the moment the opinion of the late Prince promises no end of difficulties for those who will have to advise her. We must deal with her with the most gentle hand.'

The measure of the queen's, not to mention Britain's, loss was summed up by Disraeli. 'With Prince Albert,' he wrote, 'we have buried our Sovereign. This German Prince has governed England for twenty-one years with a wisdom and energy such as none of our Kings have ever shown.' Even the British press, initially so hostile, had come to appreciate Albert's qualities. 'He was a man of elegant mind,' commented the *Observer*, 'of cultivated tastes, of a clear understanding, and of high and lofty aspirations for the public good . . . Peace to his ashes! A good husband, a good father, a wise prince, and a safe counsellor, England will not soon "look upon his like again".'

Perhaps Albert's greatest achievement was that he helped to rescue the institution of monarchy from the depths to which it had sunk by the 1830s and reinvented it as a pillar of the emerging constitutional state. The queen's habit of holding each minister 'to the discharge of his duty' by constantly desiring to be 'furnished with accurate and detailed information about all important matters' was in fact, wrote Charles Greville in 1857, 'the act of Prince Albert, who is to all intents and purposes King, only acting entirely in her name'. Greville added: 'All his views and notions are those of a Constitutional Sovereign, and he fulfils the duties of one, and at the same time makes the Crown an entity, and discharges the functions which properly belong to the Sovereign.'

Albert's vision of a modern monarchy, with executive duties shared between Windsor Castle and Downing Street, was probably never achievable for long. But it is tempting to speculate on the role the monarchy might have played in British politics had he not died when he did, and had Victoria not withdrawn for so long into mourning and seclusion. That he would have 'deplored', in the words of one biographer, 'the glamorous, ornamental, impotent Crown that emerged in the next century' is not in doubt. Whether he could have prevented it is another matter.

The echoes of history are uncanny. In 1861, almost twenty years after the disasters of the First Afghan War, a Scottish MP moved a vote of censure on the government of the day for misleading the House of Commons about its Afghan policy. His charge was that Lord Melbourne's Whig government had deliberately edited an envoy's report on the situation in Afghanistan to make it appear that he preferred an alliance with the former ruler Shah Shuja than with the incumbent Dost Mohamed, when in fact the reverse was true. As one of only two members of Melbourne's government still in office (the other was Russell), Palmerston vigorously defended the policy in a speech that lasted an hour and a half. He did not deny that the envoy's full report had been withheld, arguing instead that the government had a right to present only the parts of a report on which its decisions had been based. Even some Opposition MPs agreed, with Disraeli insisting that the government had a discretionary right to suppress sensitive information. The motion was subsequently defeated by 168 votes to sixty-one, and Palmerston remained in office. A century and a half later, another British prime minister would face similar charges of doctoring intelligence reports to justify a pre-emptive war, this time in Iraq. He too would survive. The real reason for both wars, of course, was regime change.

For those born during the twentieth century, the idea that an earlier Britain routinely fought wars of aggression might come as something of a surprise. Both World Wars, Korea, the Falklands and even the First Gulf War were all, in the most basic sense, 'just' wars provoked by a third party's aggression. Part of the reason for the furore over the Iraq (or Second Gulf) War is that pre-emptive conflicts have become, for the British at least, extremely rare. The last genuine example (if you discount Younghusband's armed incursion into Tibet in 1903) was the Zulu War in 1879. But during the early years of Victoria's rule, with the empire steadily expanding, wars of aggression (if not always strictly pre-emptive) were far more commonplace than we might like to admit. You can dress the Opium, Sind, Second Sikh, Burma and Persian Wars in whichever clothes you choose – autocratic rulers refusing the march of progress, extending British trade, strategic security, prestige – but in the end it all comes down to power. We had it and were prepared to use it if we did not get our own way.

Not that all of Victoria's early wars were either aggressive or acquisitive. The First Sikh War, at least, was essentially defensive, though a reckoning with the Punjab was bound to have taken place sooner or later. The Indian Mutiny was a rebellion that needed to be put down. And the Crimean War was fought by

Britain and France, at least at the outset, to curb Russian aggression. But when, in June 1854, the Russians withdrew from the principalities of Moldavia and Wallachia, the allies' original strategic war aim, the fighting could and probably should have ended. That it did not was because the allies wanted to capture Sevastopol and strike a blow that would cripple Russian naval power in the region for a generation. The invasion of the Crimea, therefore, was the point at which the allies' war became one of aggression.

Of course not all aspects of 'imperialism' – whether practised by Britain in the nineteenth century or the United States today – are necessarily pernicious. The imposition of law and order, improved communications and more stable trading conditions will always be welcomed by certain sections of a conquered people. Others marginalized by the previous regime might even encourage foreign intervention. Yet it is hard to get away from the immutable fact that few indigenous peoples like to have their rulers forced upon them by foreigners. Nor do they appreciate the benefits of 'civilization' when they include – as they did during Victoria's early reign – the bombardment of ancient cities like Canton, the looting of national treasures like the Koh-i-Nor diamond and the wanton destruction of fabulous edifices like the Great Bazaar in Kabul and the Summer Palace at Peking.

The irony of Britain's rapid imperial expansion during the early years of Victoria's reign is that little of it was directly sanctioned by the home government. None of her early prime ministers, even 'gunboat' Palmerston, was pro-imperialist per se. Most tended to regard territorial empire as an expensive luxury, believing instead in the power of trade and moral prestige. 'At no time in the first half of Victoria's reign', writes James Morris in his brilliant imperial trilogy,

was Empire a central preoccupation of British statesmanship. Imperial episodes sometimes captured the centre of the stage . . . but no politician had tried to give the Empire an ideological meaning, or to convince the small and privileged electorate that theirs must be an imperial future. On the whole the Tory Party was the party of Empire, as the trustees of tradition and pride, while the Liberals were the champions of free trade and liberty: but neither could be described as a party of imperialism – a word which indeed carried for the English distasteful undertones of foreignness.

With little political capital to be made from imperial ventures, and mindful of the expense, home governments tended to discourage territorial expansion. That it took place at all, therefore, was chiefly the responsibility of individuals on the ground: diplomats like Auckland, soldiers like Napier, trading houses like Jardine Matheson & Co. and, occasionally, mavericks like 'Rajah' Brooke.* To those at home it seemed as if the empire was growing without thought or design, or, as the Victorian historian J. R. Seeley put it, 'in a fit of absence of mind'.

Writing in 1883, Seeley was referring specifically to the expansion of empire in the eighteenth century, though his comment was just as relevant to the Victorian period. Seeley himself thought that it was time to move beyond the haphazard, improvised empire of the past. Only by knitting together the mainly white dominions into a 'Greater Britain', he argued, could the empire hope to compete with the superpowers of the future. But the government was no more minded to listen to such talk in 1883 than it would have been in 1843.

When Albert died in December 1861, leaving Victoria to rule alone, the British Empire was about to enter its final period of huge expansion: chiefly in Africa. By Victoria's own death, on 22 January 1901, the empire was at its zenith, covering a quarter

---

* The son of a wealthy judge, James Brooke joined the Bengal Army in 1819 but was badly wounded in the First Burma War and forced into early retirement. He returned to South Asia in a private schooner and landed at piracy-plagued Sarawak in northern Borneo, the nominal possession of the sultan of Brunei, in 1839. Over the next decade, with the unofficial support of the Royal Navy, he largely eliminated piracy, head-hunting and slavery. Rewarded with a knighthood and the title of 'White Rajah', he and his descendants ruled Sarawak until it was belatedly declared a British protectorate in 1888.

38. The remains of one of the barracks in Wheeler's entrenchment, by Felice Beato.

39. The storming of the Kashmir Gate at Delhi, 14 September 1857.

40. The ruins of the Lucknow residency, by Felice Beato.

41. Sir Colin Campbell leading the Punjab Rifles and his beloved 93rd
Highlanders in the attack on the Sikandarbagh, 17 November 1857, by Major
Henry Hope Crealock.

42. The meeting of Sir Colin Campbell and the besieged general Sir James Outram at Lucknow on 17 November 1857. Campbell shook Outram's hand with the words: 'How do you do, Sir James?' Lithograph by Harry Payne.

(*Top left*) 43. Major-General Sir Hope Grant, the commander of the British expedition to China in 1860, by Felice Beato. A talented musician, Grant never went anywhere without his cello and would practise assiduously, even on campaign.

(*Top right*) 44. Lieutenant-Colonel Garnet Wolseley of Grant's staff, by Felice Beato. He regarded Grant as 'the best of men and the bravest of soldiers'.

(*Left*) 45. A Pathan officer of the Punjab Irregular Cavalry, by Felice Beato.

46. The fort at Pehtang that the British occupied without a fight on 1 August 1860, by Felice Beato. They found mocked-up wooden guns and 'no trace of recent occupation', though the entrance was mined with enormous shells 'fitted with percussion locks'.

47. The front of the northern Taku fort, showing the embrasure through which the British entered during the allied assault of 21 August 1860, by Felice Beato.

48. The interior of the northern Taku fort, strewn with dead Chinese defenders, by Felice Beato.

49. The rear of the northern Taku fort and its cavalier, showing the Chinese line of retreat, by Felice Beato.

50. The top of the walls of Peking from the Antung Gate, by Felice Beato. The gate was opened by its Chinese defenders on 13 October 1860, just minutes before the allied bombardment was due to begin.

51. The Imperial Summer Palace at Peking after it was burnt by British troops on 18/19 October 1860 as retribution for the murder of allied prisoners. By Felice Beato.

52. Lord Elgin's procession to the Forbidden City in Peking to sign the peace treaty, 24 October 1860, by Major Henry Hope Crealock. To emphasize his status as the representative of a sovereign, Elgin insisted on his sedan chair being carried by eight porters, a privilege jealously guarded by the Chinese emperor.

53. Prince Kung, the brother of the Chinese emperor Hsien Feng, who signed the peace treaties with the allies. Wolseley thought him 'a nice-looking, yellow-faced Tartar, of middle height and good features' who appeared a 'gentleman amidst the crowd of bilious, bloated, small-pox-marked faces of the mandarins around him'.

of the earth's land mass and a quarter of its population.* It was the greatest imperial experiment the world had ever seen.

Yet Albert's death was very much the end of an era – not only because the queen withdrew from public life for many years after his death, but also because, even when she did return in 1866, she was never as effective or influential a monarch as she had been with him at her side. Albert's demise coincided, moreover, with a change in the fundamental character of empire. Before the Indian Mutiny of 1857–9 most Britons saw the empire as a means of spreading civilization through trade and the imposition of superior codes of behaviour. So bloody were the events of the mutiny, however, that when it was over many Britons concluded that the subject peoples of the empire were not capable of being civilized. Imperial rule became, therefore, not a mission but a duty: or, as Rudyard Kipling so eloquently put it, 'the White Man's burden'.† It also became, with the demise of the HEIC, more formal. Influence gave way to ability as the colonial service and officers corps became more meritocratic and professional. New public schools like Cheltenham, Wellington and Marlborough began to churn out idealistic, dutiful young men who were keen to do their bit.

There was also a shift in the axis of imperial expansion from Asia to Africa that reflected the changing commercial and strategic concerns of the British government. During Albert's marriage to Victoria only a couple of minor wars were fought in Africa (on the Cape frontier), whereas ten were fought in Asia. Yet, of the fifteen significant wars fought by Victoria's troops after his death, eleven took place on the 'dark continent'.

And the empire itself became more popular as the century wore on. Recent research has shown that few Britons knew much about the empire during the early years of Victoria's reign. Even the

---

* Encompassing an area of 12.7 million square miles and a population of 444 million.

† Kipling's famous 1899 poem of the same name was actually an appeal to the United States to shoulder its imperial responsibilities. It begins: 'Take up the White Man's burden – /Send forth the best ye breed – /Go bind your sons to exile/To serve your captives' need.'

ruling classes had little interest in imperial issues, with parliamentary debates on the colonies rare and poorly attended. This all changed in the last third of the century, thanks to Disraeli's attempt to popularize the empire (by making Queen Victoria, for example, empress of India), competition with other imperial powers (hence the infamous 'Scramble for Africa') and the expansion of the franchise – in 1867 and again in 1884 – which put the future of the empire into the hands of millions of ordinary voters. From the 1880s onwards, an active minority of 'imperialists' did much to raise the profile of the empire in the public consciousness, forming movements such as the 'British Empire League', campaigning for the adoption of 'Empire Day' as a national holiday, and organizing lectures, exhibitions and publications. But if the middle classes did eventually become more enthusiastic about empire, this was not because they had been turned into chest-beating jingoists, but because they had come to think of it as a philanthropic exercise, in which the British were preparing colonial nations for eventual self-rule.

At their simplest level, Victoria's Wars can be seen as little more than the flexing of Britain's imperial muscle. 'What does Imperialism mean?' asked the nineteenth-century Liberal philosopher Robert Lowe, with more than a hint of sarcasm. 'It means the assertion of absolute force over others . . . if by the menace of overbearing force we can coerce a weaker state to bow before our will, or if, better still, we can by a demonstration of actual force attain the same object, or, best of all, if we can conquer our adversary in open fight, and impose our own conditions at the bayonet's point, then, as Dryden sings, "these are imperial arts and worthy of thee".'

Yet the climate in which Britain exercised her power changed considerably during Victoria's reign. Broadly speaking, for most of the first thirty years, certainly until Albert's death, she operated as the world's sole superpower, much as the United States does today. The French, beaten at Waterloo, were still dogged by internal political ructions, including revolutions in 1830 and 1848, though the latter ushered in the rule of Napoleon III, who promised, albeit fleetingly, a return to the days of *La Gloire*; the German and Italian nations were yet to be unified; the glories of the Spanish, Portuguese and Dutch Empires had long faded; the industrial and naval power of the United States was growing but still a long way from challenging Britain's maritime supremacy; even the Russians were a threat only in certain well-identified regions – the Near East and Afghanistan – and did not pose any significant danger to Britain's ocean-going might. Pax Britannica was the order of the day, and Britain's wars were mostly ones of consolidation and coercion against 'inferior' indigenous peoples, rather than wars seeking to expand the empire or maintain the traditional European balance of power. The Crimean War is the exception, though part of the reason the British became involved was because they wanted to safeguard the Suez route to India and the Far East.

By contrast, most of Victoria's later wars were fought by Britain with half an eye on her European rivals. The rise of a Prussian-dominated Germany, the resurgence of France after her disastrous defeat by Prussia in 1871, the ambitions of a nascent Italy and the relentless Asian expansion of imperial Russia – all posed serious threats to Britain's position as the pre-eminent world power. The imperial pretensions of France and Germany, in particular, but also of Italy, Portugal and Belgium resulted in the unedifying 'Scramble for Africa' that, in half a generation, 'gave Europe virtually the whole continent: including thirty new colonies and protectorates, 10 million square miles of new territory and 110 million dazed subjects, acquired by one method or another'. All of Britain's many African wars during this period, from the Zulu War of 1879 to the Boer War of 1899–1902, have to be seen in the context of this vicious European rivalry. They were no longer fought chiefly to extend British trade and influence, but rather to prevent other European powers from muscling into territories that Britain regarded as strategically vital for the safety of her steamer routes to the East, via Suez and the Cape. It is no coincidence, therefore, that the vast majority of these African wars took place on the continent's southern and north-eastern tips. Late-Victorian Britain was no longer the world's only superpower, though she was still pre-eminent at sea, and her wars reflect the way an increasingly tense Europe altered the priorities of empire. It was a rivalry that required two world wars to resolve.

# Author's Note

My fascination with Victoria's wars began as a boy reading the Flashman novels. The roll-call of famous (not to say infamous) British actions during the first quarter century of the Victorian era is nothing short of extraordinary: the retreat from Kabul, the charge of the 3rd Light Dragoons at Mudki (earning them the nickname the 'Mudki-wallahs'), the 'Thin Red Line', the charges of the Light and Heavy Brigades at Balaklava, the Cawnpore massacres, the storming of Delhi, the two reliefs of Lucknow, the capture of the Taku forts and the burning of the emperor's summer palace at Peking. Incredibly Flashman was (unwillingly) present on all these occasions – or so George Macdonald Fraser would have us believe.

In reality, no soldier could have participated in all. The vagaries of a military career prevented even the most gung-ho from serving in every war. Hence my decision to frame the story with the perspectives of two civilians who were constantly involved: Queen Victoria and her husband Prince Albert. The more I dug, the more I discovered that the royal couple played a far more central role in foreign affairs and the conduct of war than is generally believed. Where Albert led, the queen tended to follow. The obvious cut-off point for the book, therefore, was Albert's untimely death in 1861.

I have been writing about the wars of the Victorian period for almost a decade, and this book benefits from much of that earlier research. I would like to thank, in particular, Edmund and the Honourable Mrs Brudenell, William Dalrymple, Major-General P. B. Foster, Hugh Hinde, Dr Alastair Massie, Lord Raglan, Dr Kaushik Roy and Professor Hew Strachan.

I was given invaluable help by the staffs of the following institutions: British Library, Gwent Record Office, London Library, National Archives, National Archives of Scotland, National Army

Museum, National Archives of India, National Library of Scotland, Royal Archives. I am extremely grateful to Her Majesty Queen Elizabeth II for permission to quote from the Royal Archives.

The production of the book has been superb. Particular thanks to Eleo Gordon, Stephanie Collie, Colin Brush, Elisabeth Merriman, Douglas Matthews, Andrew Farmer and Donna Poppy. But my greatest debt of gratitude is, as ever, to my wife, Louise, and three daughters. It can't be much fun having a husband and father constantly preoccupied by war. So thank you.

# Timeline

**24 May 1819**   Princess Victoria, daughter of the duke and duchess of Kent (née Princess Victoire of Saxe-Coburg-Saalfeld), is born in Kensington Palace.

**20 June 1837**   King William IV dies and his niece, Princess Victoria, succeeds to the British throne at the age of eighteen.

**28 June 1838**   Queen Victoria is crowned in Westminster Abbey.

**March 1839**   Chinese commissioner confiscates 20,000 chests of British-owned opium in the southern port of Canton. Start of the First Opium War (1839–42).

**10 March 1839**   Invasion of Afghanistan by Lieutenant-General Sir John Keane's Army of the Indus. Start of the First Afghan War (1839–42).

**22 July 1839**   Keane's troops successfully storm the Afghan fortress of Ghazni.

**6 August 1839**   Keane's troops enter Kabul and install Shah Shuja as the new amir. The deposed amir, Dost Mohamed, flees north to the Hindu Kush.

**10 February 1840**   Queen Victoria marries her first cousin Prince Albert of Saxe-Coburg-Gotha in the Chapel Royal at St James's Palace.

**July 1840**   British expeditionary force reaches China and occupies Ting-hai on the island of Chusan.

**21 November 1840**   Queen Victoria gives birth to her first child, Princess Victoria. A further eight children would follow over the next seventeen years.

**December 1840**   Dost Mohamed surrenders to Sir William Macnaghten, British envoy in Afghanistan, and is exiled to Ludhiana in northern India.

**27 May 1841**   Major-General Sir Hugh Gough captures Canton.

**August 1841**   Lord Melbourne's Whig administration is defeated in a general election and replaced by Sir Robert Peel's Tories.

**2 November 1841**   Start of the anti-Shuja revolt in Kabul. The insurgents murder Sir Alexander Burnes, British resident, with his brother, staff and sepoy guard.

**22 November 1841**   Akbar Khan, Dost's eldest son, arrives in Kabul to take control of the insurrection.

**23 November 1841**   Brigadier-General John Shelton is badly defeated by Afghan rebels in the Behmaru Hills.

**23 December 1841**   Macnaghten and one of his assistants are murdered by Akbar Khan as they try to negotiate the safe withdrawal of the Kabul garrison.

**1 January 1842**   Major-General William Elphinstone, the British commander in Afghanistan, signs an agreement with Akbar Khan for the safe conduct of all British troops to Peshawar.

**6 January 1842**   The British garrison – 4,500 troops and 12,000 civilians – begins its ill-fated retreat from Kabul.

**12 January 1842**   Dr William Brydon reaches the safety of Jelalabad Fort, the only European to do so.

**April 1842**   Shah Shuja is murdered in Kabul.

**16 April 1842**   Major-General George Pollock relieves the Jelalabad garrison.

**23 April 1842**   General Elphinstone dies in captivity at Tezeen.

**19 June 1842**   General Gough captures Shanghai.

**29 August 1842**   Chinese envoys sign the Treaty of Nanking, ceding Hong Kong to Britain and opening four new treaty ports to foreign trade.

**15 September 1842**   General Pollock recaptures Kabul.

**Mid October 1842**   British troops begin their withdrawal from Afghanistan. Dost Mohamed is later released from British custody and reinstalled as amir. In retribution for the murder of Macnaghten, General Pollock destroys the magnificent Great Bazaar in Kabul.

**17 February 1843**   Major-General Sir Charles Napier defeats the amirs of Sind at Miani.

**20 February 1843**   Napier announces the deposition of the amirs and the annexation of Sind.

**24 March 1843**   Napier defeats the remnants of the amirs' forces at Hyderabad.

**12 December 1845**   Sikh Army crosses the Sutlej and invades British territory. Start of the First Sikh War (1845–6).

**18 December 1845**   General Sir Hugh Gough defeats the Sikh vanguard in a hard-fought battle at Mudki.

**21/22 December 1845**   Gough narrowly defeats the Sikhs at Ferozeshah.

**28 January 1846**   Major-General Sir Harry Smith routs the Sikhs at Aliwal.

**10 February 1846**   Gough destroys the main Sikh Army at Sobraon, effectively ending the war.

**9 March 1846**   Sikh sirdars sign the Treaty of Lahore, ceding the Jullundur Doab to the British and agreeing to a British resident.

**16 March 1846**   Kashmir is sold to Gulab Singh, ruler of Jammu, creating the new state of Jammu and Kashmir.

**25 June 1846**   Corn Laws are repealed, but Peel's Tory administration is defeated over the Irish Coercion Bill and replaced by Lord John Russell's Whig–Radical coalition.

**20 April 1848**   Lieutenants Patrick vans Agnew and William Anderson are murdered by mutinous troops in the southern Punjab city of Multan. Start of the Second Sikh War (1848–9).

**22 November 1848**   Gough's vanguard repulsed by Sikh troops at Ramnagar. Sikhs withdraw across the Chenab River.

**13 January 1849**   Gough narrowly defeats the Sikhs at Chilianwalla.

**21 February 1849**   Gough routs the Sikhs at Gujerat, effectively ending the war.

**29 March 1849**   Ten-year-old Maharaja Dalip Singh, nominal ruler of the Punjab, is forced to abdicate and his state is annexed.

**February 1852**   Lord John Russell resigns and Lord Derby forms a minority Conservative government.

**15 March 1852**   Lord Dalhousie, governor-general of India, issues the Burma government with an ultimatum to cease interfering with

British shipping and trade. When no reply is received, he dispatches an expeditionary force under Major-General Henry Godwin. Start of the Second Burma War (1852–3).

**12–14 April 1852**   Godwin captures Rangoon.

**9 October 1852**   Godwin captures Prome.

**17 December 1852**   The Conservative budget is defeated and Lord Derby resigns the next day. He is replaced by Lord Aberdeen's coalition of Peelites, Whigs and Radicals.

**20 December 1852**   Lord Dalhousie announces the annexation of Pegu Province by the HEIC.

**19 March 1853**   Ensign Garnet Wolseley is badly wounded during the capture of Myat-Toon's jungle stronghold near Donabyu.

**22 June 1853**   Russian troops invade the Danubian principalities.

**30 June 1853**   King Mindon of Ava (Burma) agrees to the cession of Pegu and hostilities cease.

**4 October 1853**   Turkey (Ottoman Empire) delivers Russia an ultimatum to evacuate the Danubian principalities within fourteen days. When Russia refuses, the two countries are at war.

**30 November 1853**   Russian Black Sea fleet destroys a Turkish squadron at Sinope.

**22 December 1853**   British and French ships enter the Black Sea to protect Turkish shipping.

**28 March 1854**   British and French governments declare war on Russia. Start of the Crimean War (1854–6).

**May 1854**   Anglo-French expeditionary force lands at Varna in modern Bulgaria to protect the Turkish capital of Constantinople.

**19 June 1854**   Russia, under pressure from Austria, raises the siege of Silistria and begins the evacuation of the Danubian principalities.

**14 September 1854**   Anglo-French-Turkish expeditionary force invades the Crimea.

**20 September 1854**   British and French troops defeat the Russians at the Battle of the Alma River.

**17 October 1854**   Siege of Sevastopol begins with a huge allied bombardment.

**25 October 1854**   Russians get the better of the Battle of Balaklava, but fail to capture the British supply base. Heroic but costly charge of the Light Brigade.

**5 November 1854**   British and (some) French troops repulse a huge Russian attack at the Battle of Inkerman.

**29 January 1855**   Aberdeen's government resigns after losing a vote of no confidence and is replaced by Lord Palmerston's Whig–Radical coalition.

**2 March 1855**   Tsar Nicholas I of Russia dies of pleurisy and is succeeded by his son, Alexander II.

**24 May 1855**   Allied amphibious operation captures the port of Kertch.

**6 June 1855**   Successful allied assault on the Russian outer works at Sevastopol. The British capture the Quarries and the French the Mamelon-Vert.

**18 June 1855**   Separate British and French attacks on, respectively, the Grand Redan and the Malakhov Tower are both beaten off with heavy casualties. Fortieth anniversary of the Battle of Waterloo.

**28 June 1855**   Lord Raglan, British commander, dies 'of a broken Heart'. He is replaced first by Major-General Sir James Simpson and later by Major-General Sir William Codrington.

**8 September 1855**   British troops again fail to capture the Grand Redan, but the French assault on the Malakhov succeeds, and the Russians are forced to evacuate the main part of Sevastopol.

**16 November 1855**   Turkish city of Kars, in Asia Minor, falls to the Russians after an epic siege.

**30 March 1856**   Russia signs the Treaty of Paris, agreeing to the demilitarization of the Black Sea, the return of Kars, the cession of part of Bessarabia and the relinquishment of her right to protect Turkey's Christians.

**8 October 1856**   Chinese coastguards impound the Chinese-owned but British-registered vessel *Arrow* at the mouth of the Canton River.

**23 October 1856**   Royal Navy bombards Canton and razes the viceroy's palace. Start of the Second Opium War (1856–8).

**1 November 1856**   The Indian government declares war on

Persia after the shah refuses to withdraw his troops from Herat in western Afghanistan.

**29 November 1856**   British expeditionary force captures the Persian port of Bushire.

**8 February 1857**   Major-General Sir James Outram routs a Persian force at Kush-ab.

**4 March 1857**   Persia signs a peace treaty in Paris, promising to withdraw from Herat and renouncing all claims over Afghanistan.

**Late March 1857**   Unaware of the peace deal, Outram captures Mohumra on the Euphrates.

**10 May 1857**   Indian troops rise at Meerut and head for Delhi. Start of the Indian Mutiny (1857–9).

**27 May 1857**   General the Honourable George Anson, commander-in-chief of India, dies of cholera at Karnal. Lieutenant-General Sir Patrick Grant is his temporary successor.

**3 June 1857**   Lord Elgin diverts troops from the China expedition to India.

**8 June 1857**   Major-General Sir Henry Barnard, commanding the Delhi Field Force, defeats the rebels at Badli-ki-Serai and establishes a camp on the ridge north of Delhi.

**26 June 1857**   Queen Victoria decorates sixty-two veterans of the Crimean War with the Victoria Cross, the first recipients of the new all-ranks gallantry award.

**27 June 1857**   Massacre of Europeans at Satichaura Ghat in Cawnpore after Major-General Sir Hugh Wheeler had agreed terms with Nana Sahib to evacuate the entrenchment.

**15 July 1857**   Nana Sahib orders the massacre of 200 British women and children in the Bibighar at Cawnpore.

**17 July 1857**   Havelock retakes Cawnpore.

**31 July 1857**   Lord Canning, governor-general of India, issues his famous 'Clemency Resolution', provoking a storm of protest in the British press.

**13 August 1857**   General Sir Colin Campbell, Anson's permanent successor as commander-in-chief, arrives at Calcutta.

**20 September 1857**   Delhi is recaptured by Major-General Archdale Wilson after a fierce six-day assault.

**25 September 1857**   First Relief of the Lucknow Residency by Brigadier-General Henry Havelock and Major-General Outram.

**16/17 November 1857**   Second Relief of the Lucknow Residency by Campbell.

**24 November 1857**   Havelock dies of dysentery during the evacuation of the residency.

**29 December 1857**   Anglo-French force captures Canton.

**20 February 1858**   Palmerston's Whig–Radical coalition is defeated over a new terrorism bill and is replaced by Lord Derby's Conservatives.

**21 March 1858**   Campbell captures Lucknow.

**3 April 1858**   Major-General Sir Hugh Rose captures Jhansi.

**20 May 1858**   Allied gunboats capture the five Taku mud forts at the mouth of the Peiho River in China.

**17 June 1858**   The rani of Jhansi is killed during a skirmish with British cavalry near Gwalior city.

**19 June 1858**   Rose captures Gwalior.

**3 July 1858**   China signs the Treaty of Tientsin, opening up the hinterland to Christian missionaries and eleven more ports to foreign trade. End of the Second Opium War.

**2 August 1858**   The India Bill – transferring the administration of the subcontinent from the HEIC to the crown – receives the Royal Assent.

**1 November 1858**   Queen Victoria's 'Proclamation' – the formal announcement of the transfer of authority from the company to the crown – is read out across India.

**10 June 1859**   Derby's Conservative government loses a vote of no confidence and is replaced by Palmerston's Liberals.

**25 June 1859**   Rear-Admiral James Hope tries and fails to recapture the Taku forts. Start of the Third Opium War (1859–60).

**8 July 1859**   Canning declares a 'State of Peace' throughout India.

**1 August 1860**   Anglo-French force lands at the mouth of the Pehtang River in north China.

**21 August 1860**   Allied troops capture the Taku forts.

**18 September 1860**   Allies rout the Chinese Army at Chang-kia-wan after British envoys and their escort are taken hostage.

**21 September 1860** Allies defeat the Chinese at the Yang-Liang Canal near Peking. Emperor Hsien Feng flees north to Jehol.

**6 October 1860** The allies begin their advance on Peking; the next day French and (some) British troops loot the emperor's fabled Summer Palace (the Yuen-ming-Yuen).

**8 October 1860** Three British hostages are released. More are handed over during the next four days, but twenty do not survive their barbaric torture.

**13 October 1860** Chinese surrender Peking just minutes before the allies are due to open their bombardment.

**18/19 October 1860** British troops burn the Summer Palace in retribution for the murder of their countrymen.

**24 October 1860** Prince Kung, the emperor's brother, ratifies the Treaty of Tientsin and signs a separate convention declaring Tientsin a free port and ceding the territory of Kowloon (opposite Hong Kong). End of the Third Opium War.

**14 December 1861** Prince Albert dies at Windsor Castle after a long illness, most likely stomach cancer.

# Bibliography

All sources published in London unless otherwise indicated.

## Primary Sources, Unpublished

### Official Documents

#### ORIENTAL AND INDIA OFFICE COLLECTION (OIOC), BRITISH LIBRARY, LONDON

Bengal Military Consultations
India Military Consultations

#### THE NATIONAL ARCHIVES (TNA), KEW

War Office (WO)

### Private Papers

#### BRITISH LIBRARY (BL), LONDON

Gordon Letters: letters of General Sir Charles Gordon
Maxse Papers: papers of Lieutenant Frederick Maxse, RN, and Lieutenant 'Fitz' Maxse
Peel Papers: papers of Sir Robert Peel

#### FAMILY PAPERS (FP)

Swinley Letters: letters from Captain G. H. Swinley, Bengal Horse Artillery, to sister, 30 Apr. 1846 (courtesy of Major-General Peter Foster, Royal Artillery)

#### GWENT RECORD OFFICE (GRO), CWMBRAN

Raglan Papers: papers of the first Baron Raglan

NATIONAL ARCHIVES OF SCOTLAND (NAS), EDINBURGH

Dalhousie Papers: papers of the tenth earl and first marquess of Dalhousie

NATIONAL ARMY MUSEUM (NAM), LONDON

Biddulph Letters: letters of Captain George Biddulph, 3rd Bengal Irregular Cavalry

Bingham Diary: diary of General G. W. P. Bingham

Blunt Papers: papers of James Blunt (Lucan's interpreter)

Brydon Diary: diary of Dr William Brydon, 5th Bengal Native Infantry

Dawes Journal: journal of Lieutenant Michael Dawes, Bengal Artillery

Greathed Papers: papers of William W. H. Greathed, Bengal Engineers

Hall Papers: Colonel Montagu Hall, 'Reminiscences of the Indian Mutiny'

Hargood Letters: 'Extract from the Letters Received from my son, Lieutenant William Hargood, First Madras Fusiliers'

Noel Letters: copies of letters written by Captain E. A. Noel, 31st Foot

Pennycuick Papers: papers of Lieutenant-Colonel John Pennycuick, 24th Foot

Plumb Letter: letter from Private Henry Plumb, 24th Foot, to his brother and sister

Raglan Papers: papers of the first Baron Raglan

Rowley Diary: diary of Captain R. H. R. Rowley, Royal Artillery

Souter Letter: typescript of a letter from Lieutenant Thomas A. Souter, 44th Foot, to his wife, describing the retreat from Kabul

Wilson Correspondence: correspondence of Sir Archdale Wilson

Wilson Letters: letters of Sir Archdale Wilson to his wife

NATIONAL LIBRARY OF SCOTLAND (NLS), EDINBURGH

Grey Diaries: diaries of Veterinary Surgeon Edward Simpson Grey, 8th Hussars

ORIENTAL AND INDIA OFFICE COLLECTION (OIOC), BRITISH LIBRARY, LONDON

Anderson Diary: diary of Captain William Anderson, Shah Shuja's Force

Birrell Diary: typescript copy of the diary of Lieutenant-Colonel (later General) David Birrell, Bengal Army

Canning Letters: letters of Viscountess Canning

Carter Journal: journal and scrapbook, dated 1839–61, of Sergeant-Major George Carter, Bengal Army

Colvin Diary: diary of John Russell Colvin (1807–57), Bengal Civil Service

Dalhousie Letters: letters of the tenth earl and first marquess of Dalhousie

De Norman Diary: diary of William de Norman, June 1859–Sept. 1860

Douglas Letters: letters of Captain James Douglas written during the First Afghan War

Elphinstone Papers: papers of Major-General William Elphinstone and John, thirteenth Baron Elphinstone

Napier Dispatches: 'Dispatches of Major-General Sir R. Napier'

Nicolls Letters: letters received by General Sir Jasper Nicolls, 1839–42

Lawrence Papers: papers of Sir John (Lord) Lawrence

Lyveden Papers: papers of Robert Vernon Smith, the first Baron Lyveden

Pester Letter: extract from a letter, dated 5 March 1846, by Lieutenant Hugh Pester, 63rd NI, describing the Battles of Mudki, Ferozeshah and Sobraon

ROYAL ARCHIVES (RA), WINDSOR CASTLE

Victorian Archive: RA VIC

Queen Victoria's Journal: VIC/QVJ

## Primary Sources, Published

### Parliamentary Papers

PP, House of Commons, 1852–3, XXVII: First Report from the Select Committee on Indian Territories (2 May 1853)

PP, House of Commons, 1854–5, IX: Report of the Select Committee on the Army before Sebastopol

PP, House of Commons, 1857, XXX: Papers Relative to the Mutinies in the East Indies

PP, House of Commons, 1859, V: Report of the Commissioners Appointed to Inquire into the Organization of the Indian Army

PP, House of Commons, 1859, XVIII: A Copy of the Evidence Taken before the Court Appointed for the Trial of the King of Delhi

## Published Documents, Diaries, Letters and Memoirs

Anglesey, marquess of (ed.), *Sergeant Pearman's Memoirs* (1968)

Appleyard, Major-General F. E., *A Résumé of Thirty-four Years' Army Service* (privately printed, 1904)

Bancroft, N. W., *From Recruit to Staff Sergeant* (1979; first pub. 1885)

*Bentinck Correspondence*: C. H. Philips (ed.), *The Correspondence of Lord William Cavendish Bentinck: Governor-General of India 1828–1835*, 2 vols. (Oxford, 1977)

Broughton, Lord, *Recollections of a Long Life*, 6 vols. (1909–11)

Calthorpe, The Honourable S. J. G., *Letters from Head-Quarters; or, The Realities of the War in the Crimea*, 2 vols. (1856–7)

*Creevey Papers*: Sir Herbert Maxwell (ed.), *The Creevey Papers* (1903)

*Dalhousie Letters*: J. G. A. Baird (ed.), *Private Letters of the Marquess of Dalhousie* (1910)

Duberly, Mrs Henry, *Journal Kept during the Russian War* (1855)

Fitzherbert, Clifford (ed.), *Henry Clifford, VC: His Letters and Sketches from the Crimea* (1956)

Forbes-Mitchell, William, *The Relief of Lucknow* (1962; first pub. 1893)

*Freedom Struggle*: S. A. A. Rizvi and M. L. Bhargava (eds.), *Freedom Struggle in Uttar Pradesh: Source Material*, 6 vols. (Lucknow, 1957)

*Gardner Memoirs*: Hugh Pearse (ed.), *Memoirs of Alexander Gardner* (1890)

Godwin, Major-General Henry, *Burmah: Letters and Papers Written in 1852–1853* (Uckfield, 2004)

Gough, General Sir Hugh, *Old Memories* (1897)

Gowing, Timothy, *A Soldier's Story; or, A Voice from the Ranks* (Nottingham, 1883)

*Greville Diary*: Philip Whitwell Wilson (ed.), *The Greville Diary*, 2 vols. (1927)

*Greville Memoirs*: Roger Fulford (ed.), *The Greville Memoirs* (1963)

*Hansard's Parliamentary Debates*, third series

*Hardinge Letters*: Bawa Satingder Singh (ed.), *The Letters of the First Viscount Hardinge of Lahore to Lady Hardinge and Sir Walter and Lady James 1844–1847*, Royal Historical Society, fourth series, vol. 32 (1986)

Harris, Mrs G., *A Lady's Diary of the Siege of Lucknow* (1858)

Hawley, Captain Robert Beaufoy, *The Hawley Letters*, Society for Army Historical Research, special publication no. 10 (1970)

Hewitt, James (ed.), *Eyewitnesses to the Indian Mutiny* (Reading, 1972)

Hibbert, Christopher (ed.), *Queen Victoria in Her Letters and Journals* (1985)

Humbley, W. W. W., *Journal of a Cavalry Officer: Including the Memorable Sikh Campaign of 1845–1846* (1854)

Jones-Parry, S. H., *An Old Soldier's Memories* (1897)

Kavanagh, T. Henry, *How I Won the Victoria Cross* (1860)

Knollys, Henry (ed.), *Life of General Sir Hope Grant*, 2 vols. (Edinburgh, 1894)

*Lang Journal*: David Blomfield (ed.), *Lahore to Lucknow: The Indian Mutiny Journal of Arthur Moffatt Lang* (1992)

Lawrence, Lieutenant-General Sir George, *Reminiscences of Forty-three Years in India* (1874)

Lawrence, Sir Henry, *Essays, Military and Political* (1859)

Lowe, Thomas, *Central India: During the Rebellion of 1857 and 1858* (1860)

Loy Smith, George, *A Victorian RSM* (1997)

Lunt, James (ed.), *From Sepoy to Subedar: Being the Life and Adventures of Subedar Sita Ram, a Native Officer of the Bengal Army* (1970; first trans. and pub. by Lieutenant-Colonel J. T. Norgate in 1873)

Mitchell, Albert, *Recollections of One of the Light Brigade* (Tunbridge Wells, 1884)

Napier, Sir Charles, *Defects, Civil and Military* (1853)

Napier, Captain Robert, *Personal Narrative* (1846)

Paget, General Lord George, *The Light Cavalry Brigade in the Crimea* (1881)

Roberts, Field Marshal Lord, *Forty-one Years in India: From Subaltern to Commander-in-Chief* (1898)

Russell, William H., *The Great War with Russia* (1895)

*Russell's Dispatches from the Crimea*, ed. by Nicolas Bentley (1970)

Sale, Lady, *A Journal of the Disasters in Afghanistan, 1841–1842*, ed. by Patrick Macrory (1969)

Sattin, Anthony (ed.), *An Englishwoman in India: The Memoirs of Harriet Tytler 1828–1858* (Oxford, 1986)

Sleeman, Major-General Sir William, *Rambles and Recollections of an Indian Official* (1843)

*Speech of Major-General the Earl of Lucan in the House of Lords, Monday, March 19, 1855* (1855)

*State Papers*: G. W. Forrest (ed.), *Selections from the Letters, Dispatches and Other State Papers 1857–1858*, 4 vols. (Calcutta, 1893–1912)

Steevens, Lieutenant-Colonel Nathaniel, *The Crimean Campaign with the Connaught Rangers* (1878)

*Stockmar Memoirs*: E. von Stockmar (ed.), *Memoirs of Baron Stockmar*, 2 vols. (1873)

Swinson, Arthur, and Scott, Donald (eds.), *The Memoirs of Private Waterfield: Soldier in Her Majesty's 32nd Regiment of Foot 1842–1857* (1968)

Temple Godman, Richard, *Letters Home from the Crimea*, ed. by Philip Warner (1999)

Thackwell, E. J., *Narrative of the Second Sikh War in 1848–1849* (1851)

Thomson, Captain Mowbray, *The Story of Cawnpore* (1859)

Tuker, Lieutenant-General Sir Francis (ed.), *The Chronicle of Private Henry Metcalfe* (1953)

*Two Native Narratives of the Mutiny in Delhi* (1898)

Vibart, Edward, *The Sepoy Mutiny* (1898)

*Victoria Girlhood*: Viscount Esher (ed.), *The Girlhood of Queen Victoria: A Selection from Her Majesty's Diaries between the Years 1832 and 1840*, 2 vols. (1912)

*Victoria Journal*: Queen Victoria, *Leaves from the Journal of Our Life in the Highlands from 1848 to 1861* (1868)

*Victoria Letters 1*: A. C. Benson and Viscount Esher (eds.), *The Letters of Queen Victoria: A Selection of Her Majesty's Correspondence between the Years 1837 and 1861*, 3 vols. (1908)

Wightman, J. W., 'One of the "Six Hundred" on the Balaklava Charge', *Nineteenth Century*, vol. 31, 1892

Wolseley, Field Marshal Viscount, *The Story of a Soldier's Life*, 2 vols. (1903)

Wood, Sir Evelyn, *From Midshipman to Field Marshal*, 2 vols. (1906)

## Newspapers and Journals

*Bengal Hurkaru*
*Hindoo Patriot*
*Morning Chronicle*
*The Times*
*United Service Magazine*

## Secondary Sources

### Books and Articles

Allen, Charles, *Soldier Sahibs: The Men Who Made the North-West Frontier* (2000)

*The Army Purchase Question* (1958)

Barat, Amiya, *The Bengal Native Infantry: Its Organization and Discipline 1796–1852* (Calcutta, 1962)

Barley, Nigel, *White Rajah: A Biography of Sir James Brooke* (2002)

Beckett, Ian, *The Victorians at War* (2003)

Blake, Robert, *Disraeli* (1969; first pub. 1966)

Bond, Brian (ed.), *Victorian Military Campaigns* (1967)

Brighton, Terry, *Hell Riders: The Truth about the Charge of the Light Brigade* (2004)

Cadell, Sir Patrick, 'The Outbreak of the Indian Mutiny', *Journal of the Society for Army Historical Research*, vol. 33, 1955

Campbell, Christy, *The Maharajah's Box* (2001; first pub. 2000)

Chambers, James, *Palmerston: 'The People's Darling'* (2004)

Collett, Nigel, *The Butcher of Amritsar* (2005)

Cook, Hugh, *The Sikh Wars* (1967)

David, Saul, *The Homicidal Earl: The Life of Lord Cardigan* (1997)

— *The Indian Mutiny: 1857* (2002)

De la Billière, General Sir Peter, *Supreme Courage: Heroic Stories from 150 Years of the Victoria Cross* (2004)

Dempsey, John, 'Storming the Taku Forts', *Royal Magazine*, vol. 34

Featherstone, Donald, *Weapons and Equipment of the Victorian Soldier* (Poole, 1978)

Ferguson, Niall, *Empire: How Britain Made the Modern World* (2004; first pub. 2002)

Fortescue, The Honourable J. W., *A History of the British Army*, 13 vols. (1927)

Hanes III, W. Travis, and Sanello, Frank, *The Opium Wars: The Addiction of One Empire and the Corruption of Another* (2003)

Harding, D. F., *Smallarms of the East India Company 1660–1856*, 4 vols. (1997–9)

Haythornthwaite, Philip J., *The Colonial Wars Source Book* (1995)

Herman, Arthur, *To Rule the Waves: How the British Navy Shaped the Modern World* (2005)

Hernon, Ian, *The Savage Empire: Forgotten Wars of the Nineteenth Century* (Stroud, 2000)

Hibbert, Christopher, *The Destruction of Lord Raglan* (1961)

— *The Great Mutiny: India 1857* (1980)

Holmes, Richard, *Redcoat: The British Soldier in the Age of Horse and Musket* (2001)

— *Sahib: The British Soldier in India* (2005)

Hopkirk, Peter, *The Great Game: On Secret Service in High Asia* (Oxford, 1991; first pub. 1990)

Hurd, Douglas, *The Arrow War* (1967)

James, Lawrence, *The Rise and Fall of the British Empire* (1994)

— *Raj: The Making and Unmaking of British India* (1997)

Jenkins, Roy, *Gladstone* (1995)

Judd, Denis, *The Lion and the Tiger* (2004)

Kaye, J. W., *History of the War in Afghanistan*, 2 vols. (1851)

Kinglake, Alexander, *The Invasion of the Crimea*, 8 vols. (1863–87)

Knollys, J. (ed.), *Life of General Sir Hope Grant*, 2 vols. (Edinburgh, 1894)

Longford, Elizabeth, *Victoria R.I.* (1964)

— *Wellington*, 2 vols. (1969–72)

Maclagan, Michael, *'Clemency' Canning* (1962)

Macrory, Patrick, *Signal Catastrophe: The Retreat from Kabul 1842* (1966)

Malleson, Colonel G. B. (ed.), *Kaye and Malleson's History of the Indian Mutiny of 1857–1858*, 6 vols. (1888)

Massie, Alistair, *The National Army Museum Book of the Crimean War* (2004)

Metcalf, Thomas, *The Aftermath of Revolt: India 1857–1870* (Princeton, 1965)

Morris, James, *Heaven's Command: An Imperial Progress* (1981; first pub. 1973)

Mukherjee, Rudrangshu, *Awadh in Revolt 1857–1858* (Delhi, 1984)

Napier, Lieutenant-Colonel The Honourable H. D., *Field Marshal Lord Napier of Magdala* (1927)

Packenham, Thomas, *The Scramble for Africa: 1876–1912* (2003; first pub. 1991)

Palmer, Alan, *The Banner of Battle: The Story of the Crimean War* (1987)

Palmer, J. A. B., *The Mutiny Outbreak at Meerut in 1857* (Cambridge, 1966)

Panmure, Lord, *The Panmure Papers* (1908)

Ponting, Clive, *The Crimean War* (2004)

Porch, Douglas, *Wars of Empire* (2000)

*The Register of the Victoria Cross* (Cheltenham, 1997)

Rhodes James, Robert, *Albert, Prince Consort* (1983)

Royle, Trevor, *Crimea: The Great Crimean War 1854–1856* (1999)

Seeley, J. R., *The Expansion of England: Two Courses of Lectures* (1886)

Sen, S. N., *1857* (Delhi, 1957)

Small, E. Milton, *Told from the Ranks: Recollections of Service* (1898)

Stokes, Eric, *The English Utilitarians and India* (1959)

— *The Peasant Armed: The Indian Revolt of 1857* (Oxford, 1986)

Strachan, H. F. A., 'The Origins of the 1855 Uniform Changes: An Example of Pre-Crimean Reform', *Journal of the Society for Army Historical Research*, vol. 55, 1977

— *Wellington's Legacy: The Reform of the British Army, 1830–1854* (Manchester, 1984)

— *From Waterloo to Balaklava: Tactics, Technology and the British Army 1815–1854* (Cambridge, 1985)

Sweetman, John, *Raglan: From the Peninsula to the Crimea* (1993)

Taylor, P. J. O., *What Really Happened During the Mutiny* (New Delhi, 1997)

Thomas, Donald, *Charge! Hurrah! Hurrah!* (1976)

Trotter, L. J., *The Earl of Auckland* (1893)

Wake, Joan, *The Brudenells of Deene* (1959)

Ward, Andrew, *Our Bones are Scattered: The Cawnpore Massacres and the Indian Mutiny of 1857* (1996)

Weintraub, Stanley, *Victoria: Biography of a Queen* (1987)

— *Albert: Uncrowned King* (1997)

Woodham Smith, Cecil, *Florence Nightingale: 1820–1910* (1950)

— *The Reason Why* (1958)

— *Queen Victoria: Her Life and Times 1819–1861* (1972)

Woodward, Llewellyn, *The Age of Reform: England 1815–1870* (Oxford, 1992; first pub. 1962)

Ziegler, Philip, *Melbourne* (1976)

## Unpublished Theses

David, Saul, 'The Bengal Army and the Outbreak of the Indian Mutiny', Ph.D. thesis, University of Glasgow, 2001

Shibly, A. H., 'The Reorganization of the Indian Armies 1858–1879', Ph.D. thesis, SOAS, University of London, 1969

# Source Notes

## Abbreviations

Fortescue | The Honourable J. W. Fortescue, *A History of the British Army*, 13 vols. (1927)
VC Register | *The Register of the Victoria Cross* (Cheltenham, 1997)
Victoria Letters 1 | A. C. Benson and Viscount Esher (eds.), *The Letters of Queen Victoria: A Selection of Her Majesty's Correspondence between the Years 1837 and 1861*, 3 vols. (1908)
Victorian Campaigns | Brian Bond (ed.), *Victorian Military Campaigns* (1967)
Weintraub | Stanley Weintraub, *Victoria: Biography of a Queen* (1987)
Wolseley | Field Marshal Viscount Wolseley, *The Story of a Soldier's Life*, 2 vols. (1903)
Wood | Sir Evelyn Wood, *From Midshipman to Field Marshal*, 2 vols. (1906)

## Prologue

1 'alone' . . . '*I am* Queen': RA VIC/QVJ/1837: 20 June (E).

2 'quite alone' . . . *in gratitude*: ibid.

2 '*very fine*' . . . '*good man*': ibid.

2 '*Everyone appeared touched*': Broughton, *Recollections*, V, 51.

2 '*not at all nervous*': RA VIC/QVJ/1837: 20 June (E).

2 '*very important*': ibid.

3 '*It was an unsystematic affair*': Morris, *Heaven's Command*, 26.

# 1. The Young Queen

**8** '*damnedest millstone*' . . . '*House of Commons*': Creevey Papers, 277.

**9** '*a pretty little Princess*': Stockmar Memoirs, I, 78.

**10** '*How old!*': *Victoria Girlhood*, I, 190.

**11** '*I have no doubt*': 12 Sept. 1838, *Greville Diary*, II, 37.

**12** '*Oh, you must*': Ziegler, *Melbourne*, 261.

**12** '*Talked with him*': *Victoria Girlhood*, I, 207.

**12** '*are* sexual *though*': *Greville Memoirs*, 156.

**12–13** '*much pleased*' . . . '*poor old Palace*': *Victoria Girlhood*, I, 210–11.

**13** '*There was never anything*': 27 June 1837, *Greville Diary*, II, 28.

**13–14** *On the day itself* . . . '*on the other side*': Victoria's journal, 28 June 1838, *Victoria Letters 1*, I, 121–2.

**14** '*the undoubted Queen*' . . . '*God Save the Queen*': Weintraub, 114.

# 2. Afghanistan

**15** '*great pomp and splendour*': Macrory, *Signal Catastrophe*, 51.

**15** '*very interesting*': Victoria's journal, 26 Dec. 1833, *Victoria Girlhood*, I, 89.

**16** '*I came*': Macrory, *Signal Catastrophe*, 50.

**16** '*quiet and unobtrusive*': ibid., 44.

**16** '*extending the blessings*': Trotter, *Auckland*, 15.

**17** '*judge as to what steps*' . . . '*commercial character*': Macrory, *Signal Catastrophe*, 46.

**18** '*We are in a mess here*': ibid., 56.

**19** '*Russian and Persian intrigue*' . . . '*against the Persians*': ibid., 67.

**20** '*decided remonstrance*' . . . '*directly concerned*': Colvin Diary, 15 June 1838, OIOC, MSS Eur/E539.

**20** '*He is a man of undoubted ability*': Trotter, *Auckland*, 53.

**20** '*wild and unmeasured*' . . . '*scanty population*': Lieutenant-Colonel H. Fane to the *Morning Herald* [n.d.], OIOC, MSS Eur/F89/50.

**20** *was originally comprised of*: The British Contingent of the Army of the Indus included two cavalry (the 4th Dragoons and the 16th Lancers) and four infantry regiments (the 2nd, 3rd, 13th and 17th Regiments of Foot). Also involved was one of the Company's European infantry regiments. The remaining troops were all Indian.

**21** '*I used to dispute*': Macrory, *Signal Catastrophe*, 82.

**22** '*aggrandizement and ambition*' . . . '*Afghanistan established*': Trotter, *Auckland*, 66–7.

**22** '*principal and real reason*': Lieutenant-Colonel H. Fane to the *Morning Herald*, op. cit.

**23** '*most efficient*' . . . '*the Bayonet*': Wellington to F. Somerset, 9 Nov. 1835, in Strachan, *From Waterloo to Balaklava*, 31.

**24** '*merely a useful standby*': ibid., 62.

**24** *Officers came . . . from the traditional ruling castes*: In 1830, for example, 21 per cent of British officers were aristocrats, 32 per cent landed gentry and 47 per cent middle class (Strachan, *Wellington's Legacy*, 110).

**24** '*It is the promotion by purchase*': *The Army Purchase Question*, 22.

**24** *cost a minimum of £450*: The fixed price for an ensign's commission in a regiment of foot; a cornetcy, the lowest cavalry rank, cost a minimum of £840.

**25** '*thoughtless youths*': Strachan, *Wellington's Legacy*, 54.

**25** *bounty money*: This was earmarked to cover the cost of 'necessaries' – equipment not provided by the colonel – and often fell short of the sum required.

**25** '*the scum of the earth*': Wellington to Earl Bathurst, 2 July 1813, quoted in Longford, *Wellington*, I, 321.

**25** *deterred 'young men'*: *Bentinck Correspondence*, II, 1,430.

**26** '*perhaps the best*': Vincent Eyre, quoted in Macrory, *Signal Catastrophe*, 174.

**26** '*a huge chasm*': ibid., 89.

**27** '*attended by great trouble*': Birrell Diary, OIOC, MSS Eur/D1026.

**29** '*a most miserable mud town*': Macrory, *Signal Catastrophe*, 91.

**29** '*a pack of dogs*' . . . '*his subjects*': ibid., 93.

**29** *Any delay*: Captain James Douglas to his brother, 15 May 1839, Douglas Letters, OIOC, MSS Eur/C181.

**29** '*Welcome to the son of Timur*': Macrory, *Signal Catastrophe*, 94.

**29** '*none of the Sirdars*' . . . '*British camp outside*': diary, 8 May 1839, Pennycuick Papers, NAM, 7604/9.

**29** '*Candahar is a square*': Captain James Douglas to his brother, 15 May 1839, op. cit.

**30** '*some no doubt*' . . . '*no resistance*': Keane to Sir Jasper Nicolls, Aug. 1839, Nicolls Letters, OIOC, MSS Eur/D1118.

**30** '*On the morning of the 21st*': ibid.

**31** '*The scene at this moment*': Captain James Douglas to his father [n.d. but *c.* July 1839], op. cit.

**32** '*the gateway being blocked up*': Birrell Diary, op. cit.

**32** '*The Afghans*' . . . '*he had met with*': Keane to Sir Jasper Nicolls, Aug. 1839, op. cit.

**32** '*The character of the scene*': Macrory, *Signal Catastrophe*, 101.

**33** '*managed to scale*': Captain James Douglas to his father [n.d. but *c.* July 1839], op. cit.

**33** '*Our success*': ibid.

**33** '*a cocked hat*': Macrory, *Signal Catastrophe*, 106.

**33** '*It was more like a funeral*': Kaye, *History of the War in Afghanistan*, I, 461.

**34** '*Shah Shuja*' . . . '*is King*': Captain James Douglas to his father [n.d. but *c.* Aug./Sept. 1839], op. cit.

**34** *Order of the Bath*: Respectively Knight Commander (KCB), Knight Grand Cross (GCB) and Companion (CB) of the Order of the Bath.

**35** '*I cannot but congratulate you*': Macroy, *Signal Catastrophe*, 14.

**35** 'no *expedition*': Victoria's journal, 7 Oct. 1838, *Victoria Girlhood*, II, 47.

**35** '*uneasy*' . . . '*right thing*': ibid., 63.

**35** '*You should see*' . . . '*possession in the East*': ibid., 146.

**36** 'All,' *she replied*: Victoria's journal, 9 May 1839, *Victoria Girlhood*, II, 171.

**37** '*It is a high trial*': 12 May 1839, *Greville Diary*, II, 73.

**37** '*Mrs Melbourne*' . . . '*done nothing*': Weintraub, 126.

**37** '*for such an event*' . . . '*but not more*': *Victoria Letters 1*, I, 177–8.

**38** '*grown and changed*' . . . '*struck me at once*': Victoria's journal, 10 Oct. 1839, *Victoria Girlhood*, II, 262–3.

**38** '*beautiful blue eyes*': ibid., 11 Oct. 1839.

**38** *make her decision* '*soon*': ibid., 13 Oct. 1839.

**38** '*I think it is a very good thing*': ibid., 14 Oct. 1839.

**38** '*He came to the closet*': ibid., 15 Oct. 1839.

**39** '*My future lot*': Weintraub, 135.

**39** '*For if once you get the English people*': ibid., 133.

**39** '*abominable infamous Tories*': ibid., 134.

**40** '*It is MY marriage*': ibid., 139.

**40** '*Nothing could have gone off better*': Victoria's journal, 10 Feb. 1839, *Victoria Girlhood*, II, 321.

**40** '*I do not think it is* possible': *Victoria Letters 1*, I, 217.

**40** '*unhappy condition*' . . . '*will be a Prince*': Weintraub, 144, 149.


# 3. The Retreat from Kabul

**41** *Brigadier-General Abraham Roberts*: The father of Frederick Roberts, then eight, who would become one of Victoria's most successful battlefield commanders, and the first man to command both the Indian and British Armies; he would retire as Field Marshal Earl Roberts, VC.

**42** *defeating a British force in Kohistan*: At the Battle of Purwandurrah, 2 Nov. 1840, when a portion of the 2nd Bengal Light Cavalry had disgraced itself by fleeing from a smaller body of Afghan horse, leaving its five European officers to charge on alone (four were killed). The 2nd was subsequently disbanded.

**42** '*all travellers and caravans*': Captain James Douglas to his father, 11 May 1840, Douglas Letters, OIOC, MSS Eur/C181.

**42** '*most certainly as great a scoundrel*': Macrory, *Signal Catastrophe*, 131.

**43** '*The climate there is good*': Elphinstone to his brother Lieutenant-Colonel James Elphinstone, 24 Dec. 1840, Elphinstone Papers, OIOC, MSS Eur/F89/54.

**43** '*in a shocking state of gout*': Macrory, *Signal Catastrophe*, 136.

**43** '*My command I do not think enviable*': Elphinstone to his brother James, 5 Apr. 1841, op. cit.

**43** '*The City is extensive*': ibid., 19 May 1841.

**44** '*At different periods*': First Elphinstone memorandum [n.d.], Elphinstone Papers, OIOC, MSS Eur/F89/54.

**44** '*violent fever*': ibid.

**44** *'My medical attendants'*: Elphinstone to Lord Elphinstone, 26 July 1841, Elphinstone Papers, OIOC, MSS EUR/F89/47.

**45** *'I am quiet and prepared'*: Victoria to King Leopold of the Belgians, 24 Aug. 1841, *Victoria Letters 1*, I, 299.

**45** *'kicking up a row'*: Macrory, *Signal Catastrophe*, 141–2.

**45** *'frequent conversations'* . . . *'did not extend to Cabool'*: First Elphinstone memorandum, op. cit.

**46–7** *'pure insanity'* . . . *'know what street fighting is'*: Lawrence, *Reminiscences*, 62.

**47** *'cut to pieces'*: Hopkirk, *The Great Game*, 241.

**47** *'How easily we could have quelled'*: Lawrence, *Reminiscences*, 69.

**48** *'did not think much'*: First Elphinstone memorandum, op. cit.

**48–9** *'unable to get about'* . . . *'carrying them into effect'*: Second Elphinstone memorandum (found in his effects) [n.d.], Elphinstone Papers, OIOC, MSS Eur/F89/47.

**49** *'not only disastrous but dishonourable'* . . . *'wisest course'*: Lawrence, *Reminiscences*, 90.

**50** *'to resist the distant fire'*: Lieutenant Vincent Eyre, quoted in Macrory, *Signal Catastrophe*, 174.

**51** *'Our squares broke'* . . . *'then in communication'*: Lawrence, *Reminiscences*, 93.

**51** *'For when our men'*: ibid., 94.

**51** *'impracticable'* . . . *'death to dishonour'*: ibid., 95–6.

**52** *'a want of carriage'* . . . *'increase of numbers'*: First Elphinstone memorandum, op. cit.

**52** *'no more military operations'* . . . *'within three days'*: Lawrence, *Reminiscences*, 100–108.

**52** *But little or no supplies . . . over to the British*: ibid., 109–15.

**53** *The following morning . . . moment's notice*: First Elphinstone memorandum, op. cit.

**53–4** *At noon . . . bruised Mackenzie*: Lawrence, *Reminiscences*, 116–20.

**54** *Determined not to be taken . . . twice in the chest*: Captain George Broadfoot to Lord Elphinstone, 26 Apr. 1842, Elphinstone Papers, OIOC, MSS Eur/F89/54; Macrory, *Signal Catastrophe*, 197.

**54** *'Your own will soon be'*: Lawrence, *Reminiscences*, 121.

**54** *When Elphinstone learnt . . . no effective resistance*: First Elphinstone memorandum, op. cit.

**54** *'would no doubt have stormed'*: Lawrence, *Reminiscences*, 138.

**54–5** *Akbar was not to be trusted . . . 'impracticable'*: First Elphinstone memorandum, op. cit.

**55** *Shah Shuja tried to persuade Elphinstone*: Lawrence, *Reminiscences*, 141.

**55** *'troops moved off'*: ibid., 143.

**57** *'There were no tents'*: Sale, *Journal*, 97.

**57** *'Already all discipline and order' . . . 'to defend them'*: Lawrence, *Reminiscences*, 146.

**58** *'extreme inclemency'*: First Elphinstone memorandum, op. cit.

**58** *'forced to lie down'*: Lawrence, *Reminiscences*, 149.

**58** *'supplies of every kind'*: First Elphinstone memorandum, op. cit.

**58** *'saying that I would much prefer remaining' . . . 'but go I must'*: Lawrence, *Reminiscences*, 151.

**59** *'The pressure of non-combatants*: First Elphinstone memorandum, op. cit.

**59** *Akbar . . . had tried to stop the slaughter*: Lawrence, *Reminiscences*, 153–4.

**59** *'Slay them!' . . . 'not the first'*: Sale, *Journal*, 104n.

**59** *'Sepoys and camp followers'*: Lawrence, *Reminiscences*, 154.

**59–60** *'The flesh from the men's feet'*: Anderson Diary, 9 Jan. 1842, OIOC, MSS Eur/C703.

**60** *Akbar further 'proposed'*: Lawrence, *Reminiscences*, 157.

**60** *'being desirous to remove' . . . 'food, covering or fire'*: First Elphinstone memorandum, op. cit.

**60** *'Little or no resistance was made'*: ibid.

**60** *'regretted his utter inability'*: ibid.

**61** *'great number'*: Brydon Diary, 10 Jan. 1842, NAM, 8301-60.

**61–2** *'strongly adverse' . . . 'unexpected detention'*: First Elphinstone memorandum, op. cit.

**62** *'telling us to push on'*: Brydon Diary, 12 Jan. 1842, NAM, 8301-60.

**62** *'We had not gone far'*: ibid.

**63** *'wounded and dying' . . . leading the rest into the valley*: ibid., 13 Jan. 1842.

**64** *Those on foot . . . to the left of the road*: Anderson Diary, 13 Jan. 1842, OIOC, MSS Eur/C704.

**64–5** '*Some Affghan horsemen*' . . . '*led me away to a village*': Lieutenant Thomas Souter to his wife [n.d.], Souter Letter, NAM, 6912-6.

**65–6** '*inquire into the state of the country*' . . . '*coming to my assistance*': Brydon Diary, 13 Jan. 1842, op. cit.

**66** '*As he got nearer*': quoted in Macrory, *Signal Catastrophe*, 236.

**67** '*scour the plains*': Brydon Diary, 13 Jan. 1842, op. cit.

**67** '*This day my ears were saluted*': Dawes Journal, 13 Jan. 1842, NAM, 6508-50.

**67** '*Many valuable officers*': *Victoria Letters 1*, I, 372.

**67** *The full scale*: Lord Fitzgerald to the queen, 10 Mar. 1842, ibid., 385.

**68** '*only twice or thrice*': Trotter, *Auckland*, 166.

**68** '*Oh, but ye've been*': Macrory, *Signal Catastrophe*, 251.

**69** '*He was wounded at Jugdulluk*' . . . '*cares of others*': Major Eldred Pottinger to Lieutenant-Colonel James Elphinstone, 26 Apr. 1842, Elphinstone Papers, OIOC, MSS Eur/F89/47.

**69** '*severe fall*' . . . '*Envoy & others for information*': Second Elphinstone memorandum, op. cit.

**69–70** '*opinions*' . . . '*unprejudiced in the Army*': Major Eldred Pottinger to Lieutenant-Colonel James Elphinstone, 26 Apr. 1842, op. cit.

**70** '*military leaders*' . . . '*want of skill*': Lawrence, *Reminiscences*, 167.

**70** '*It is extremely interesting*': Henry Loch to Elphinstone [n.d.], Elphinstone Papers, OIOC, MSS Eur/F89/54,

**70** '*some signal and decisive blow*': Trotter, *Auckland*, 181.

**70** '*at the earliest practicable moment*': ibid., 190.

**71** '*in heaps of fifties and hundreds*': Captain Julius Backhouse, quoted in Macrory, *Signal Catastrophe*, 258.

**71** *the remaining 105 hostages*: They included twenty officers (half of them wounded), ten ladies, two soldiers' wives, twenty-two children, thirty-eight men of the 44th Foot, seven of the 13th Light Infantry and six Bengal Horse Artillerymen.

**71** '*To my daughter and myself*': Sale, *Journal*, 157.

**71** '*some lasting mark*': Macrory, *Signal Catastrophe*, 265.

**72** '*be withdrawn to the Sutlej*' . . . '*British Government*': ibid., 266.

**72** '*There is not a Moslem heart*': quoted in James, *Raj*, 98.

**73** '*distributed in and about*' . . . '*feel daily more!*': queen to King Leopold of the Belgians, 31 May 1842, *Victoria Letters 1*, I, 398–9.

**73** '*signal victory*': Lord Fitzgerald to the queen, 7 June 1842, ibid., 401.

**73** *The outlook was a little brighter*: ibid., 4 July 1842, 407.

**73** '*brilliant exploits*' . . . '*all*': ibid., 23 Nov. 1842, 442.

**73** '*brilliant successes*': queen to Peel, 25 Nov. 1842, ibid., 443.

**74** *Yet the queen could not help feeling*: ibid.

## *4. Sindis and Sikhs*

**75** '*completely routed*': Lord Ripon to the queen, 5 June 1843, *Victoria Letters 1*, I, 602.

**76** '*the shape of a jockey's cap*' . . . '*being covered*': Carter Journal, 24 Jan. 1845, OIOC, MSS Eur/E262.

**76** '*His tent is but a small*': ibid., 5 Feb. 1845.

**78** '*Peccavi*': James, *Raj*, 105.

**78** '*foul stain*': ibid.

**78** '*very unwise*': queen to Peel, 23 Apr. 1844, *Victoria Letters 1*, II, 9.

**78–9** *He was still in the latter post* . . . *personal loyalty to Peel*: *Hardinge Letters*, Introduction, 3–4.

**82** '*a handsome debauched woman*': Hardinge to Sir Walter James, 8 Feb. 1845, ibid., 49.

**83** '*The Rani was dragged away*': *Gardner Memoirs*, 259.

**84** '*silently collected*': Hardinge to his wife, 8 Mar. 1845, *Hardinge Letters*, 58.

**84** '*not to recognize a successor*': Hardinge to Sir Walter James, 20 Feb. 1845, ibid., 52.

**85** *Lal Singh hinted*: E. R. Crawford, 'The Sikh Wars' in *Victorian Campaigns*, 39.

**88** *less than a third of whom were British*: Only four of the thirteen infantry regiments and one of the five cavalry regiments were British. They were: the 9th (East Norfolk), 31st (Huntingdonshire), 50th (Queen's Own) and 80th (South Staffordshire Volunteers) Regiments of Foot; and the 3rd Light Dragoons.

**88** '*besides numerous elephants*': Humbley, *Journal*, 47–9.

**90** '*Arrived at Moodkee*': Napier, *Personal Narrative*, 4.

**91** '*when leather breeches*': Bancroft, *From Recruit to Staff Sergeant*, 4.

**92** '*We sustained*' . . . '*disembowelled*': ibid., 42.

**93** '*Conceive a brigade*': Reynell Taylor to his father, 1 Jan. 1846, in Allen, *Soldier Sahibs*, 66.

**94** *872 casualties*: E. R. Crawford, 'The Sikh Wars', op. cit., 41.

**94** '*attached himself*': Cook, *The Sikh Wars*, 48.

**94** '*Most deeply do we lament*': queen to Hardinge, 6 Apr. 1846, *Victoria Letters 1*, II, 78.

**94** '*Underneath this stone*': Sale, *Journal*, 159.

**94** '*There were NO arrangements*': Captain G. H. Swinley, BHA, to his sister, 30 Apr. 1846, Swinley Letters, FP.

**95** '*no supplies*': Hardinge to Lord Ripon, 27 and 28 Dec. 1845, in *Hardinge Letters*, 134n.

**95** '*never again to witness*' . . . '*where they were*': Napier, *Personal Narrative*, 6.

**95** '*splendid dress*' . . . '*never forget*': Biddulph to his mother, 1 Jan. 1846, Biddulph Letters, NAM, 5910/115,

**97–9** '*It being found*' . . . '*on the other*': Bancroft, *From Recruit to Staff Sergeant*, 49–50.

**100** '*On passing our Artillery*': Birrell Diary, OIOC, MSS Eur/D1026.

**101** '*In the most dense dust*': Allen, *Soldier Sahibs*, 68.

**101** '*murderous, but glorious*' . . . '*this is only policy*': Noel Letters, NAM, 7910-64.

**101** '*rode forward*': Napier, *Personal Narrative*, 9.

**102** '*Had the enemy known*': ibid.

**102** '*After this*': Birrell Diary, op. cit.

**102** '*the fate of India trembled*': Cook, *The Sikh Wars*, 64.

**102–3** '*I consulted*' . . . '*political considerations*': Napier, *Personal Narrative*, 14.

**103** '*The C.C. came to me*' . . . '*fight it out*': Hardinge to Sir Walter James, 30 Dec. 1845, op. cit., 135.

**103** '*Seeing that we were losing*': Swinley to his sister, 30 Apr. 1846, op. cit.

**104** '*Can you imagine*': ibid.

**104** '*verdict*' . . . '*their leaders*': E. R. Crawford, 'The Sikh Wars', op. cit., 43.

**104** '*It is a perfect riddle*': Swinley to his sister, 30 Apr. 1846, op. cit.

**104** '*The sights were most harrowing*': Bancroft, *From Recruit to Staff Sergeant*, 56.

**105** '*We have been in the greatest peril*': Peel Papers, BL, Add. MSS 40475.

**106** *keen to negotiate a peace*: Hardinge to Sir Walter James, 3 Feb. 1846, op. cit., 143.

**106** '*at least*' *35,000 men*: *Hardinge Letters*, 145.

**108** '*Thank God*': quoted in Cook, *The Sikh Wars*, 89.

**108** '*Their guns*': Birrell Diary, op. cit.

**108** '*On we went*': Anglesey (ed.), *Sergeant Pearman's Memoirs*, 55.

**109** '*We drove the enemy*': Lieutenant Hugh Pester to unknown correspondent, 5 Mar. 1846, Pester Letter, OIOC, MSS Eur/F18/11.

**109** '*bloody foam*': Bancroft, *From Recruit to Staff Sergeant*, 82.

**109** '*clip the state*': Hardinge to Sir Walter James, 16 Feb. 1846, op. cit., 146.

**110** '*the ablest scoundrel in all Asia*': Hardinge to Lady James, 19 Feb. 1846, ibid., 151.

**110** '*Conceive a beautiful little boy*': ibid.

**110** '*dirtiest place*' . . . '*very offensive*': Pester Letter, op. cit.

**110** '*In the tent*': Anglesey (ed.), *Sergeant Pearman's Memoirs*, 59.

## 5. '*I know it to be just, politic, and necessary*'

**112** '*admiration*' . . . '*great anxiety*': queen to Sir Henry Hardinge, 4 Mar. 1846, *Victoria Letters 1*, II, 75–6.

**112** '*her extreme satisfaction*': ibid., 6 Apr. 1846, 77–8.

**113** '*slightly pompous*': Blake, *Disraeli*, 241.

**113** *gave '*the semblance*'*: quoted in Weintraub, *Albert*, 175.

**114** '*I had to part with Sir R. Peel*': queen to King Leopold of the Belgians, 7 July 1846, *Victoria Letters 1*, II, 87.

**114** *It was '*weak*'* . . . '*people together*': ibid., 14 July 1846, 89.

**114** '*One of the most brilliant*': queen to Lord Hardinge, 8 July 1846, ibid., 88.

**115** '*venal and selfish*': Allen, *Soldier Sahibs*, 80.

**115** '*I have seldom seen*': ibid., 81.

**115** '*We had not been many days*': ibid., 82.

**116** '*Half a dozen foreigners*': ibid.

117 ' '*Why do you take possession*': ibid., 144.

117 '*entirely free*': Dalhousie to Sir George Couper, 26 July 1847, *Dalhousie Letters*, 18.

117 '*assist men to avoid harmful acts*': Stokes, *The English Utilitarians*, 55.

119 '*the head of the youth*': Allen, *Soldier Sahibs*, 150.

119 '*Postpone a rebellion!*': Cook, *The Sikh Wars*, 141.

120 'Because *my predecessor*': Dalhousie to Sir George Couper, 14 Oct. 1848, *Dalhousie Letters*, 35.

120 '*restoring order*': E. R. Crawford, 'The Sikh Wars' in *Victorian Campaigns*, 56.

121 '*A party of the enemy horse*': Anglesey (ed.), *Sergeant Pearman's Memoirs*, 72–3.

122 '*astonishment*' . . . '*charging, charge*': ibid., 74.

123 '*The C.-in-C.'s movement was excellent*' . . . *Gough's supplies and supports*: Dalhousie to Sir George Couper, 22 Dec. 1848, op. cit., 38–9.

124 '*Every one was plundered*' . . . '*shot him dead*': Corporal John Ryder, quoted in Swinson and Scott (eds.), *The Memoirs of Private Waterfield*, Appendix C, 168-70.

126 '*formed in an extended line*' . . . '*in great force*': Dalhousie to the duke of Wellington, 22 Jan. 1849, Dalhousie Papers, NAS, GD46/6/323.

126 '*As [Gough] was making his arrangements*': Dalhousie to Sir George Couper, 20 Jan. 1849, op. cit., 44–5.

128 '*Well away we went*' . . . '*was a wonder*': Anglesey (ed.), *Sergeant Pearman's Memoirs*, 91–2.

129 '*Let it be said*': quoted in Cook, *The Sikh Wars*, 169.

129 '*When we first took up the charge*: Private Henry Plumb to his family, 21 Mar. 1849, Plumb Letter, NAM, 7104-23-2.

130 '*Our brigade retired in disorder*': ibid.

131 '*Poor Boy*': unidentified officer to his father, 15 Jan. 1849, Pennycuick Papers, NAM, 7604-9.

131 '*But for that manoeuvre*': Sir Charles Napier to Major Kennedy [n.d.], ibid.

132 '*These miserable creatures*': Dalhousie to Sir George Couper, 20 Jan. 1849, op. cit., 46.

**132** '*The Surgeon & myself*': unidentified officer to his father, 15 Jan. 1849, op. cit.

**133** '*make him a Brevet Bishop*': quoted in Cook, *The Sikh Wars*, 177.

**133** '*We couldn't see the enemy*' . . . '*poured in grape*': Carter Journal, 24 Jan. 1845, OIOC, MSS Eur/E262.

**134** '*We have gained a victory*': Dalhousie to Sir George Couper, 20 Jan. 1849, op. cit., 44, 47.

**135** '*Her Majesty's Government*': Dalhousie to the duke of Wellington, 22 Jan. 1849, op. cit.

**136** '*In and around the village*': Swinson and Scott (eds.), *The Memoirs of Private Waterfield*, 101–2.

**137** '*The battle was now at its highest*': Anglesey (ed.), *Sergeant Pearman's Memoirs*, 102.

**137** '*We overtook numbers*': Captain Delmar, quoted in ibid., 103.

**138** '*This day Ranjeet Singh has died*' . . . '*so powerful an enemy*': Dalhousie to the queen, 24 Mar. 1849, *Victoria Letters 1*, II, 217.

**139** '*for himself, his heirs*' . . . '*five lakhs of rupees*': quoted in Campbell, *The Maharajah's Box*, 39.

**139** '*the British colours were hoisted*': Dalhousie to Sir George Couper, 30 Mar. 1849, *Dalhousie Letters*, 62.

**139** '*I cannot*': quoted in Campbell, *The Maharajah's Box*, 39.

**139** '*His Lordship*': *The Times*, 31 Aug. 1882.

**140** '*home authorities*' . . . '*perfect tranquillity*': Dalhousie to Sir George Couper, 30 Mar. 1849, op. cit., 62.

**140** '*quite approves*' . . . '*reward for his services*': *Victoria Letters 1*, II, 220–21.

**140** '*so well versed*': queen to King Leopold of the Belgians, 6 Mar. 1849, ibid., 215.

**140** resigned on '*general grounds*': Dalhousie to Sir George Couper, 19 Mar. 1849, op. cit., 60.

**140** '*Government could hardly have done otherwise*': ibid., 20 Apr. 1849, 67–8.

**140** '*I wish you could see it*': Colonel Robert Adams to Mrs Lena Login [n.d.], quoted in Campbell, *The Maharajah's Box*, 40.

**141** '*If a strong man*' . . . '*conquered their enemies*': Dalhousie to the queen, 15 May 1850, *Dalhousie Letters*, 242.

**141** '*One, that means of mischief* ' . . . '*resting place*': Campbell, *The Maharajah's Box*, 41.

**142** '*My little friend*': *Dalhousie Letters*, 156–7.

**142** '*I am convinced*': 12 Mar. 1853, ibid., 249.

**143** '*and all its wonders*': Campbell, *The Maharajah's Box*, 45.

**143** '*He is 16 and extremely handsome*': RA VIC/QVJ/1854: 1 July.

**143** '*striking good looks*': Campbell, *The Maharajah's Box*, 61.

**143** '*small, lithe, and very handsome*': Weintraub, 238.

**144** '*which would enable them*' . . . '*under our rule*': queen to Dalhousie, Balmoral, 2 Oct. 1854, *Victoria Letters 1*, III, 59–61.

**144** '*I should like to have it in my power*': Campbell, *The Maharajah's Box*, 67.

**145** Did he think it '*improved*' . . . '*the Koh-i-Noor*': ibid., 68.

## 6. Burma

**146** '*Our beloved wedding day*' . . . '*full Highland dress*': RA VIC/QVJ/1850: 10 February.

**146** '*more backward*' . . . '*simplicity of character*': quoted in Longford, *Victoria R.I.*, 271.

**147** '*The Prince is indolent*': Weintraub, *Albert*, 101.

**147** '*any subject she pleased*': ibid., 104.

**147** '*extremely strait-laced*': 6 Sept. 1841, *Greville Diary*, II, 206.

**147** '*insisted on spotless character*': 7 Sept. 1841, ibid., 207.

**148** '*the obvious but up to that time*': quoted in *Encyclopaedia Britannica*, XXII, 1,030.

**149** a '*cross between a muff*': Weintraub, *Albert*, 153.

**149** with the South Eastern Railway calculating: Strachan, *Wellington's Legacy*, 201.

**150** '*tempting idea*': quoted in Weintraub, *Albert*, 231.

**150** '*His loss*': queen to King Leopold of the Belgians, 17 Sept. 1852, *Victoria Letters 1*, II, 394.

**151** '*tawdry, cumbrous and vulgar*': 16 Nov. 1852, *Greville Diary*, II, 346.

**151** '*The car!*': quoted in Longford, *Wellington*, II, 403.

**151** '*I can remember*': Wolseley, I, 23–4.

**153** '*This must not happen again*': queen to Lord Palmerston, 17 Feb. 1850, *Victoria Letters 1*, II, 234.

**153** '*most anxious*' . . . '*other hands*': memorandum by Prince Albert, 3 Mar. 1850, ibid., 235–6.

**154** '*domestic intrigue*' . . . '*injustice and wrong*': Chambers, *Palmerston*, 321–2.

**154** 'to prevent any mistake' . . . '*sent off* ': queen to Lord John Russell, 12 Aug. 1850, *Victoria Letters 1*, II, 264.

**155** '*attend to the directions*' . . . '*old system*': Palmerston to Russell, 13 Aug. 1850, ibid., 264–5.

**155** '*I have the greatest pleasure*': queen to King Leopold of the Belgians, 23 Dec. 1851, ibid., 344–5.

**157** '*mischievous aggression*': Hernon, *The Savage Empire*, 26.

**157** *costing the British £13m and . . . almost 15,000 men*: ibid., 43.

**158** '*We can't afford*': *Encyclopaedia Britannica* (1973), VII, 6.

**158** '*an old man in a wig*': Wolseley, I, 28.

**159** '*The gunboat*': Herman, *To Rule the Waves*, 461.

**160** *seventeen killed and 132 wounded*: Fortescue, XII, 479.

**160** '*Key of Burma*': ibid., 481.

**160** '*were not unwilling to go*': quoted in Barat, *The Bengal Native Infantry*, 285.

**160–61** '*assemble their men*' . . . '*practically it was*': Dalhousie to General Sir William Gomm, 10 Mar. 1852, Dalhousie Letters, OIOC, MSS Eur/Photo Eur. 309.

**161** '*Oh! So they are fond of walking*' . . . '*dying in hospital*': Sattin (ed.), *An Englishwoman in India*, 82.

**162** '*the very act*': Lunt (ed.), *From Sepoy to Subedar*, 85.

**162** '*whether within or beyond*': Bengal Army Regulations 1855, OIOC, L/MIL/17/2/442, 220.

**162** '*In Bengal*': evidence of Philip Melvill, 14 Dec. 1852, PP, HC, 1852–3, XXVII, 8.

**162** '*They have never objected*': evidence of Colonel Leslie, 26 Aug. 1858, PP, HC, 1859, V, 94.

**162** *After the Battle of Chilianwalla*: Thackwell, *Narrative of the Second Sikh War*, 190.

**162** *At the siege of Multan . . . rejected this charge*: evidence of Colonel Patrick Grant, PP, HC, 1852–3, XXVII, 127–8.

**162–3** '*march to the trenches*' . . . *performance of duty*: evidence of Colonel John Hill, 26 Aug. 1858, PP, HC, 1859, V, 95–6.

**163** *furnished the sepoy with a 'pretext'*: United Service Magazine, Aug. 1858 and July 1857, 604 and 318–19.

**165** '*looked forward*': Wolseley, I, 8–9.

**165–6** '*great bulk*' . . . '*kept them cool*': ibid., 10–11, 51–2.

**166** '*small pugree*' . . . '*upon their enemy*': ibid., 39.

**168–70** '*to move slowly*' . . . '*to be moved*': ibid., 63–71.

**170** '*gallantry in leading the storming party*': Major E. A. Holdich, quoted in ibid., 73.

## 7. The 'sick man' of Europe

**171** '*was to satisfy the "interests"*': Blake, *Disraeli*, 328.

**172** '*I could have said*': ibid., 338.

**172** '*Disraeli's enemies*': ibid., 340.

**172** '*Our Government*': Victoria Letters 1, II, 430.

**173–4** '*Turkey is a dying man*' . . . '*exists today*': Palmer, *Banner of Battle*, 6–7.

**175** '*close alliance*' . . . '*arrangements are made*': ibid., 14.

**177** '*looking the crisis*': Chambers, *Palmerston*, 361.

**177** '*waiting timidly*': ibid., 362.

**178** '*the only likelihood*': Royle, *Crimea*, 73.

**178** '*It is evident*' . . . '*in his place*': Victoria Letters 1, II, 452n.

**179** '*It was evident*' . . . '*morally and constitutionally*': ibid., 454–5.

**179** '*We have taken*': queen to Clarendon, 11 Oct. 1853, ibid., 455–6.

**180** '*disadvantage of the course*' . . . '*could be obtained*': Prince Albert's memorandum, 16 Oct. 1853, ibid., 456–7.

**180** '*Peace is an Excellent thing*': Chambers, *Palmerston*, 364.

**181** '*under the banner*': ibid.

**181** '*The English people*': The Times, 12 Dec. 1853.

**182** '*threatened steps*': queen to Clarendon [n.d.], Victoria Letters 1, II, 470.

**182** '*War with Russia*': Loy Smith, *A Victorian RSM*, 77.

**182** '*provided for by the Constitution*': Aberdeen to the queen, 6 Jan. 1854, Victoria Letters 1, III, 4.

**183** '*I still say*': Chambers, *Palmerston*, 369.

**183** '*The Regiment halted*': Lieutenant the Honourable Hugh Annesley, quoted in Massie, *The Crimean War*, 5.

**184** '*It was a* touching': queen to King Leopold of the Belgians, 28 Feb. 1854, *Victoria Letters 1*, III, 17.

**184** '*No nation*': Wolseley, I, 82.

**185** '*Almost all the Civil departments*': ibid., 82–3.

**185** '*Every ordnance storehouse*': ibid., 83.

**186** '*This Army is a shambles*': Hibbert, *The Destruction of Lord Raglan*, 8.

**186–7** *Criticism of the top-heavy shako . . . by a lower shako*: H. F. A. Strachan, 'The Origins of the 1855 Uniform Changes: An Example of Pre-Crimean Reform', *Journal of the Society for Army Historical Research*, vol. 55, 1977, 85–117.

**188** '*In the early spring*': Wolseley, I, 80.

**188** '*The army thought small*' . . . '*British civilization*': Strachan, *Wellington's Legacy*, 268.

**190** '*Hey, bring my arm back*': Hibbert, *The Destruction of Lord Raglan*, 3.

**190–91** '*He possesses great professional*' . . . '*personnel of the army*': Sweetman, *Raglan*, 170.

**193** '*protested strongly*': ibid., 172–3.

**193** '*Few of them*': Woodward, *The Age of Reform*, 268.

**194** '*the elementary principles*': Strachan, *Wellington's Legacy*, 128.

**194** '*thoroughly ignorant*': Wolseley, I, 80.

**194** '*want of scientific knowledge*' . . . '*how to retire*': quoted in Woodward, *The Age of Reform*, 268n.

**196** '*He is a regular charlatan*': Royle, *Crimea*, 114.

**196** '*[The] Eye tooth*': Palmer, *Banner of Battle*, 61.

**197** '*to check and repel*': Royle, *Crimea*, 184.

**197** '*to concert measures*' . . . '*poured into the Crimea*': Newcastle to Raglan, 29 June 1854, TNA, WO 6/74/5.

**198** '*of a most serious character*': Massie, *The Crimean War*, 21.

**198** '*My information is*': Raglan to Lady Westmorland, 4 Aug. 1854, GRO, Raglan Papers, letters from 1854 to June 1855, Box D.

**198** '*The cholera is amongst us!*': Duberly, *Journal*, 53.

## 8. Crimea

**200** '*Six hundred sail*': Mitchell, *Recollections*, 37.

**200** '*For nearly a mile*': Loy Smith, *A Victorian RSM*, 96.

**201** '*fifty rounds of ammunition*': Wood, I, 29.

**201** '*I never saw such a scene*': Paget, *The Light Cavalry Brigade in the Crimea*, 18.

**202** '*animated controversy*': Massie, *The Crimean War*, 31.

**203** '*one of the most magnificent*': Loy Smith, *A Victorian RSM*, 102.

**203** '*very strong by nature*' . . . '*key of the position*': Massie, *The Crimean War*, 32–3.

**205** '*As soon as the enemy's round shot*': Gowing, *A Soldier's Story*, 16.

**206** '*had to pass through a Vineyard*': Massie, *The Crimean War*, 39.

**206** '*The fire [was] heavy*': ibid., 41.

**207** '*We were busy*': Appleyard, *A Résumé of Thirty-four Years' Army Service*, 11.

**207** '*The mass of English troops*': Royle, *Crimea*, 226–7.

**208** '*The Duke at this time*': Massie, *The Crimean War*, 44.

**208** '*When formed in line*': ibid.

**208** '*To my dying day*': ibid., 45.

**209** '*I kept on shouting*': ibid., 45–6.

**209** '*Above 20 guns*': ibid., 46.

**210** '*We had merely to pour our fire*': ibid.

**210** '*On crowning the hill*': ibid.

**210–11** '*[The Russian] dead*' . . . '*nothing to shout for yet*': Mitchell, *Recollections*, 55.

**211** '*that there were one thousand*': Russell, *The Great War with Russia*, 116.

**212** '*Lord Raglan & his staff*': Massie, *The Crimean War*, 54.

**213** '*We were out for hours*': Russell, *The Great War with Russia*, 75.

**216** '*great intelligence*' . . . '*perfect security*': Aberdeen to the queen, 1 Oct. 1854, *Victoria Letters 1*, III, 55–6.

**216** '*strengthening the alliance*': queen to Clarendon, 10 Oct. 1854, ibid., 61–2.

**217** '*We have received*': queen to King Leopold of the Belgians, 13 Oct. 1854, ibid., 63–4.

**219** '*We have four miles of beds*': Royle, *Crimea*, 252.

**219** '*could not maintain*': Massie, *The Crimean War*, 64.

**221** '*preparatory to an early attack*' . . . '*reported to him*': NAM, Blunt Papers, 5610/47.

**221** '*I went into most of them*': ibid.

**221** '*As usual we thought*': Lieutenant Frederick Maxse, RN, to his mother, 28 Oct. 1854, Maxse Papers, BL, Add. MSS 73526.

**222** '*to the left of the second line*': NAM, Blunt Papers, 5610/47.

**222** '*cowardly curs*': Lieutenant Frederick Maxse to his mother, 28 Oct. 1854, op. cit.

**222** '*We were much annoyed*': Mitchell, *Recollections*, 80.

**222** '*We could hear the yells*': Russell, *The Great War with Russia*, 140–41.

**223** '*covered with running Turks*': Duberly, *Journal*, 117–18.

**223** '*towards Balaklava*': Sweetman, *Raglan*, 247.

**223** '*Remember, there is no retreat*': Kinglake, *The Invasion of the Crimea*, IV, 124–5.

**223** '*Gathering speed*': *Russell's Dispatches from the Crimea*, 122.

**224** '*trying to get round*' . . . '*with a flea in their ears*': Massie, *The Crimean War*, 80.

**224** '*condescending to form square*': Lieutenant Frederick Maxse to his mother, 28 Oct. 1854, op. cit.

**224** '*towards the ridge*': Kinglake, *The Invasion of the Crimea*, IV, 133.

**224–50** '*The enemy seemed quite astonished*': Temple Godman, *Letters Home from the Crimea*, 75.

**225** '*There they were*': ibid.

**225** '*In five minutes*': Russell, *The Great War with Russia*, 151.

**225** '*Well done the Heavy Brigade*': Temple Godman, *Letters Home from the Crimea*, 76.

**225** '*The ground was strewn*': ibid.

**226** '*We lost a corporal*': ibid., 78.

**226** '*The wounds*': ibid., 102.

**226** '*My lord*' . . . '*orders to remain here*': Hibbert, *The Destruction of Lord Raglan*, 141.

**226** '*within reach*': Kinglake, *The Invasion of the Crimea*, IV, 209–10n.

**227** '*Cavalry to advance*': *Speech of Major-General the Earl of Lucan in the House of Lords, Monday, March 19, 1855*, 8–9.

**227** '*we soon saw them*': Lieutenant Frederick Maxse to his mother, 28 Oct. 1854, op. cit.

**227** '*Lord Raglan wishes*': *Speech of Major-General the Earl of Lucan*, op. cit., 9.

**228** '*Tell Lord Lucan*': Hibbert, *The Destruction of Lord Raglan*, 142; Brighton, *Hell Riders*, 104.

**228** '*what any cavalry should do*': Lieutenant Frederick Maxse to his mother, 28 Oct. 1854, op. cit.

**228** '*instead of being formed*': *Speech of Major-General the Earl of Lucan*, op. cit., 9.

**228** '*uselessness*' and '*dangers*' . . . '*There are your guns!*': Lucan to Raglan, 30 Nov. 1854, quoted in ibid.

**229** '*neither enemy nor guns*' . . . '*end of the [north] valley*': ibid.

**229** '*appeared to be surprised*': NAM, Blunt Papers, 5610-47.

**229** '*momentary talk*': J. W. Wightman, 'One of the "Six Hundred" on the Balaklava Charge', *Nineteenth Century*, vol. 31, 1892, 852.

**229** *It has been suggested*: Thomas, *Charge!*, 242.

**230** '*say the spot*' . . . '*we must attack*': Lieutenant 'Fitz' Maxse to his mother, 28 Oct. 1854, Maxse Papers, BL, Add. MSS 73527.

**230** '*Lord Cardigan*' . . . '*attack the enemy*': Kinglake, *The Invasion of the Crimea*, IV, 401.

**230** '*its contents*' . . . '*read the order to him*': 'Exploratory Statements Laid before Mr Kinglake by Lord Lucan', ibid.

**230** '*no more reason*': *Speech of Major-General the Earl of Lucan*, op. cit., 20.

**231** '*Here goes the last of the Brudenells*' . . . '*Sound the advance!*': Russell, *The Great War with Russia*, 165.

**231** '*Hell had opened upon us*': Wightman, op. cit., 853-4.

**232** '*struck by a shot*': Mitchell, *Recollections*, 84.

**232** '*yet for about thirty yards further*' . . . '*Close in!*': Wightman, op. cit., 854.

**232** '*It was the maddest thing*': David, *The Homicidal Earl*, 409.

**233** '*We got by them*': Paget, *The Light Cavalry Brigade*, 188-92.

**233-4** '*My horse was shot dead*' . . . '*on his back*': Wightman, op. cit., 856-7.

**234** *107 killed* . . . *almost 400*: Official Return of the Adjutant-General, 26 Oct. 1854, quoted in Loy Smith, *A Victorian RSM*, 213-15.

**234** '*What do you mean, sir*': Cardigan's statement in Kinglake, *The Invasion of the Crimea*, IV, 402.

**234–5** *'You have lost the Light Brigade'* . . . *'Raglan's report'*: Speech of *Major-General the Earl of Lucan*, op. cit., 11–12.

**235** *'From some misconception'* . . . *'imperative' to obey*: ibid., 11–16.

**235** *'There was nothing in that'* . . . *'all other precautions'*: Sweetman, *Raglan*, 264, 271–2.

**235** *'[Lucan] ought to have had the moral courage'*: Wake, *The Brudenells of Deene*, 408.

**236** *'Went down on the plain'*: Lieutenant Frederick Maxse to his mother, 28 Oct. 1854, op. cit.

## 9. Stalemate

**238** *'We cut their Army'*: Loy Smith, *A Victorian RSM*, 148.

**241** *'We retired gradually'*: Lieutenant Frederick Elton, quoted in Massie, *The Crimean War*, 98.

**241** *'The Picquet of the 2nd Div.'*: Captain John Crosse, quoted in ibid., 102.

**243** *'We were I should think'*: Lieutenant George Carmichael, quoted in ibid., 106.

**243** *'They were armed'*: ibid., 108.

**244** *'He immediately ordered me'*: Colonel Charles Windham, quoted in ibid., 110.

**244** *'Poor Cathcart'*: Airey, quoted in ibid., 110.

**244** *'I had endeavoured'*: duke of Cambridge, quoted in ibid., 112.

**245** *'Not a muscle'*: Captain the Honourable Edward Gage, quoted in ibid., 115.

**245** *'An immense force'*: Lieutenant Mark Walker, quoted in ibid., 116.

**246** *'I advanced'*: Lieutenant George Carmichael, quoted in ibid., 120–21.

**247** *'very efficient'*: Lieutenant-Colonel Frederick Haines, quoted in ibid., 121.

**247** *10,729 killed*: Royle, *Crimea*, 290.

**247** *'What a fight on the 5th!!'*: Airey, quoted in Massie, *The Crimean War*, 122.

**248** *'We have not a single'*: *Victoria Letters 1*, III, 65n.

**248** *'will never be forgiven'*: Albert to Aberdeen, 11 Nov. 1854, quoted in Weintraub, *Albert*, 312.

**248** '*We now know*': *Victoria Letters 1*, III, 66.

**249** '*glorious, but alas!*' . . . '*excellent an officer*': ibid., 66–7.

**249** 'beyond praise': ibid., 66.

**249** '*The Queen desires*': Newcastle to Raglan, 27 Nov. 1854, quoted in Royle, *Crimea*, 292.

**249** '*I find that the men*': journal of Staff Surgeon C. Pine, quoted in Massie, *The Crimean War*, 126.

**250** '*I find myself*': Royle, *Crimea*, 128.

**250** '*The Clubs*': Weintraub, 241.

**250** '*The Duke's excitement*': ibid.

**250** '*The winter is setting in*': Temple Godman, *Letters Home from the Crimea*, 86–7.

**251** '*I don't think*': ibid., 100.

**251** '*The English*': Royle, *Crimea*, 300.

**252** '*I saw* nine *men*': Lieutenant-Colonel George Bell, quoted in Massie, *The Crimean War*, 136.

**252** '*I regret to say*': Nightingale to Raglan, 29 Dec. 1854, ibid., 155.

**252** '*Many were landed dead*': Henry Bellow's journal, 15 Jan. 1854, ibid., 157.

**254** '*The noblest Army*': *The Times*, 23 Dec. 1854.

**254** '*There are people*': ibid., 30 Dec. 1854.

**255** '*men in the trenches*': TNA, WO6/70/202.

**255** '*Did you ever see*': Kingscote to the Honourable Richard Somerset, 7 Feb. 1855, GRO, Raglan Papers, Box D.

**255** '*to be resisted*': *Victoria Letters 1*, III, 91.

**256** 'no *other alternative*': queen to King Leopold of the Belgians, 6 Feb. 1855, *Victoria Letters 1*, III, 128.

**256** '*Things are very much on the mend*': Kingscote to the Honourable Richard Somerset, 7 Feb. 1855, op. cit.

**257–8** '*It is no longer the camp of misery*': Fitzherbert (ed.), *Henry Clifford, VC*, 193.

**257** '*I have visited the camps*' . . . '*worthy of credit than I am*': Raglan to Panmure, 2 Mar. 1855, TNA, WO33/1.

**258** '*any details of your arrangements*' . . . '*in your own*': Panmure to Raglan, 19 Mar. 1855, ibid.

**259** '*perish rather than surrender*': Royle, *Crimea*, 337.

**260** '*great qualities*' . . . '*great secrecy*': memorandum of 2 May 1855 in Hibbert, *Queen Victoria in Her Letters and Journals*, 131.

**260** '*We should thank Austria*': Royle, *Crimea*, 349.

**261** '*The very earth*': Wolseley, I, 151.

**262** '*As the signal went up*': Wood, I, 79.

**263** '*ridiculously small*': Wolseley, I, 157.

**263** '*The loss I have experienced*': Massie, *The Crimean War*, 197.

**263** '*The deaths*': Kingscote to the Honourable Richard Somerset, 9 June 1855, op. cit.

**264** '*When I saw how stoutly*': Massie, *The Crimean War*, 198.

**264–6** '*formed of two faces*' . . . '*where I lay insensible*': Wood, I, 86–93.

**266** '*If the attack*' . . . '*expose itself to defeat*': Raglan to Panmure, 19 June 1855, quoted in Massie, *The Crimean War*, 207.

**267** '*An army encamped*' . . . '*gratefully acknowledged*': Report of the Select Committee on the Army before Sebastopol, PP, HC, 1854–5, IX, Part 3, 142–3.

**268** '*I have seen the Doctor*': Airey to Miss Charlotte Somerset, 26 June 1855, GRO, Raglan Papers, Box D.

**268** '*Even then*': Raglan's nephew to 'Min', 12 July 1855, ibid.

**268** '*for upwards of an hour*': Calthorpe, *Letters from Head-Quarters*, II, 363.

**268** '*His disease*': Dr Fowle Smith to A. Kinglake, 1877, quoted in Massie, *The Crimean War*, 208.

**268** '*He died of a broken Heart*': Airey to Major-General George Wetherall, 4 July 1855, ibid.

**268** '*The soldiers thought little of him*': Captain Robert Hawley to his father, 29 June 1855, *The Hawley Letters*, Society for Army Historical Research, special publication no. 10 (1970), 63.

**269** '*It is thought*': Joseph Leggatt to his father, 12 July 1855, GRO, Raglan Papers, Box D.

**270** '*deep and* heartfelt grief' . . . '*taken from them*': queen to Major-General James Simpson, 30 June 1855, *Victoria Letters 1*, III, 164.

**270** '*Words cannot convey*': queen to Lady Raglan, 30 June 1855, ibid.

**270** '*It is quite evident*' . . . '*self possession*': Panmure to the queen, July 1855, NAS, Dalhousie Papers, GD45/8/144.

**271** '*Under no circumstances*': Panmure to the queen, 31 July 1855, ibid.

**271** '*General Simpson writes*': ibid., 27 Aug. 1855.

**272** '*Men of other Regts.*': Captain Edmund Legh, quoted in Massie, *The Crimean War*, 225.

**273** '*The moment we were out*': Lieutenant-Colonel Daniel Lysons, ibid., 228–9.

**273** '*At last our ammunition*': Steevens, *The Crimean Campaign*, 278–9.

**274** 'Never *had to perform*': Captain Hopton Scott, 9th Foot, quoted in Massie, *The Crimean War*, 232.

**274** 'There was *a sad* deficiency': Brigadier-General Charles Ridley, quoted in ibid., 232.

**274** '*There he stood*': Lieutenant-Colonel Anthony Sterling, quoted in ibid., 233.

**275** '*Never saw I*': Arthur Taylor, quoted in Royle, *Crimea*, 414.

**275** '*I stood in the Redan*': Captain Henry Clifford, quoted in ibid.

**275** '*Albert said*': *Victoria Journal*, 98–100.

**276** '*Russia has not yet been beat enough*': Royle, *Crimea*, 435.

**277** '*The honour and glory*': queen to Clarendon, 15 Jan. 1856, *Victoria Letters 1*, III, 207.

**277** '*Much as the Queen*': ibid., 31 Mar. 1856, 235.

**278** '*That so* good *a Peace*': queen to King Leopold of the Belgians, 1 Apr. 1856, ibid.

**278** '*The treaty left England*': Weintraub, *Albert*, 333.

**278** '*revealed as a sham*' . . . '*at its outset*': Royle, *Crimea*, 501.

**279** '*enervating mental*': ibid., 503.

**280** '*I wish we had her*': Woodham Smith, *Florence Nightingale*, 264.

**280** '*Tell the others*': Weintraub, 256.

**281** '*There was really* no one': queen to King Leopold of the Belgians, 21 July 1856, *Victoria Letters 1*, III, 254.

**281** '*vulgar looking thing*': Paget, *The Light Cavalry Brigade*, 117.

**281** '*to those Officers*': De la Billière, *Supreme Courage*, 3.

**281** '*poor looking*' . . . '*once invented a hat*': *The Times*, 27 June 1857.

**282** But a recent book: De la Billière, *Supreme Courage*, 4.

**282** '*are deemed brave*': queen to Panmure, 5 Jan. 1856, *Victoria Letters 1*, III, 203.

**282** '*no one could be called*': ibid., June 1856, 298.

## 10. *The Devil's Wind*

**285** '*The only real benefit*': Ferguson, *Empire*, 166.

**286** '*carry the city*': Hanes and Sanello, *The Opium Wars*, 178.

**286** '*Hereafter Chinese officers*': ibid., 179.

**287** '*The gate of China*': ibid., 185.

**287** '*most despicable cause*': ibid., 186.

**288** '*a man of the people*' . . . '*a set of barbarians*': Chambers, *Palmerston*, 423–4.

**288** '*physically quite unable*': Prince Albert to Palmerston, 3 Mar. 1857, *Victoria Letters 1*, III, 290.

**289–90** '*full of agitation*' . . . '*gratifying day*': RA VIC/QVJ/1857: 26 June.

**291** '*Delhi is in the hands*': Canning to Robert Vernon Smith, 19 May 1857, Lyveden Papers, OIOC, MSS Eur/F231/5.

**291** '*no fear*' . . . '*foreign agency*': Palmerston to the queen, 26 June 1857, *Victoria Letters 1*, III, 298.

**292** not be '*of a nature to offend*': Malleson (ed.), *Kaye and Malleson's History of the Indian Mutiny*, I, 379–80.

**292** '*You will defile it*' . . . '*where will your caste be?*': Major-General J. B. Hearsey to Colonel R. J. H. Birch, 11 Feb. 1857, *State Papers*, I, 25.

**292–3** '*no extraordinary precaution*' . . . '*objectionable fat*': evidence of Colonel A. Abbott, 23 Mar. 1857, PP, HC, 1857, XXX, 261.

**293** '*turned out to be well founded*': Canning to Vernon Smith, 7 Feb. 1857, Lyveden Papers, OIOC, MSS Eur/F231/4.

**293** '*Come out, you* bhainchutes': testimony of Havildar Shaik Pultoo, 6 Apr. 1857, *State Papers*, I, 124.

**294** '*I know that at present*': Lieutenant Edward Martineau to Captain S. Becher, 5 May 1857, quoted in Palmer, *Meerut*, 32.

**295** '*traced to the preaching*': Anson to Lord Elphinstone, 10 May 1857, Elphinstone Papers, OIOC, MSS Eur/F87/Box 6A/No. 4.

**295** '*to win away the allegiance*': *Bengal Hurkaru*, 29 May 1857.

**296** '*the old race*': Malleson (ed.), *Kaye and Malleson's History of the Indian Mutiny*, I, 344.

**296** *as many as three quarters*: Sleeman, *Rambles and Recollections*, 624.

**296** *'seizing of Oudh'*: Lunt (ed.), *From Sepoy to Subedar*, 161.

**297** *'commanded by a fair-faced beardless Ensign'*: Napier, *Defects, Civil and Military*, 255–7.

**297** *'above all others'*: Lawrence, *Essays*, 27–8.

**298** *'dangerously discontented'*: ibid., 395.

**298** *'never, as a general rule'*: memo by Lieutenant-General Sir Patrick Grant to the governor-general, 29 June 1857, PP, HC, 1859, V, Appendix 66, 496.

**299** *'The principal cause'*: Lunt (ed.), *From Sepoy to Subedar*, 174.

**299** *'In all mutinies'*: Napier, *Defects, Civil and Military*, 61–2.

**299** *'The plot for revolt'*: Lieutenant-Colonel F. W. Burroughs to Captain I. H. Chamberlain, Jan. 1860, *Freedom Struggle*, I, 347.

**300** *'answers began to pour in'* . . . *'regular form of government'*: statement of Sitaram Bawa to H. B. Devereux, 28 Jan. 1858, ibid., 372–6.

**301** *'that they would get a bad name'*: evidence of Colonel G. M. Carmichael-Smyth, 25 Apr. 1857, *State Papers*, I, 230–32.

**301** *'The real case'*: Cornet John MacNabb to his mother, 10 May 1857, quoted in Cadell, *Journal of the Society for Army Historical Research*, vol. 33, 1955, 120–21.

**301–4** *'loudly calling'* . . . *'at their mercy'*: Lieutenant Alfred Mackenzie, quoted in Vibart, *The Sepoy Mutiny*, 219.

**304** *That evening* . . . *'idle words'*: Gough, *Old Memories*, 21–3.

**304–5** *The conclusion drawn* . . . *exactly what happened*: address by Major F. J. Harriott, 9 Mar. 1858, PP, HC, 1859, XVIII, 246.

**305** *'they had leagued'*: additional evidence of Ahsanullah Khan, PP, HC, 1959, XVIII, 268.

**305** *'Dohai Badshah!'*: examination of Ahsanullah Khan, 12 Feb. 1858, ibid., 198–9.

**305** *'The officers of the cavalry'*: examination of Ghulam Abbas, 29 Jan. 1858, ibid., 137.

**306** *'to march at once'*: *Two Native Narratives*, 85.

**306** *'promising monthly salaries'*: ibid., 60.

## *11. Retribution*

**309** '*Cawnpore is now the most anxious position*': *State Papers*, II, Introduction, 144n.

**310** '*Tattered in clothing*': Thomson, *The Story of Cawnpore*, 88.

**311** '*It is not easy to describe*': Mr Shepherd's narrative, *State Papers*, II, Introduction, 138.

**312** '*General Havelock is not in fashion*': *State Papers*, II, Introduction, 106–16.

**313** '*Their fire*': Havelock to the DAG, 12 July 1857, *State Papers*, II, Introduction, 87.

**313** '*In [the first] ten minutes*': quoted in Stokes, *The Peasant Armed*, 59.

**313** '*It was evident*': Havelock to the DAG, 20 July 1857, *State Papers*, II, Introduction, 99.

**314–15** '*who were lying down*' . . . '*heavy cannonade*': ibid., 100–101.

**315** '*The frightful massacre*': Lieutenant William Hargood to his parents, 18 July 1857, NAM, Hargood Letters, 5206-10.

**316** '*if they were left alive*': deposition of Futteh Sing, *State Papers*, III, Appendix, ccxxvi.

**316** '*The place was literally running*': Bingham Diary, NAM, 5903-105.

**317** '*ask the poor fellows*': Tuker (ed.), *The Chronicle of Private Henry Metcalfe*, 34.

**317** '*could not . . . move*': Havelock to Sir Patrick Grant, 31 July 1857, *State Papers*, II, Introduction, 199.

**317** '*Whenever a rebel is caught*': Hewitt (ed.), *Eyewitnesses*, 122.

**318** '*It is rumoured*': Vernon Smith to Canning, 9 Oct. 1857, OIOC, Lyveden Papers, MSS Eur/F231/5.

**318** '*Upon entering*': Wolseley, I, 273.

**319** '*Our Indian empire*': *Hansard's*, third series, CXLVI, June–July 1857, 537–44.

**319** '*The moment*': *Victoria Letters 1*, III, 299.

**319** '*I think it most advisable*': Vernon Smith to Canning, 27 July 1857, OIOC, Lyveden Papers, MSS Eur/F231/4.

**319** '*The last accounts*': queen to Palmerston, 2 Aug. 1857, *Victoria Letters 1*, III, 306.

**320** *'the neck of the insurrection'*: OIOC, Lyveden Papers, MSS Eur/F231/5.

**320** *'Nothing remains'*: Canning to the queen, 4 July 1857, *Victoria Letters 1*, III, 300.

**320** *'fearful responsibility'*: Wilson to his wife, 17 July 1857, NAM, Wilson Letters, 6807-483.

**320** *'He was utterly devoid'*: Captain Richard Barter, 75th Highlanders, quoted in Hibbert, *The Great Mutiny*, 334.

**321** *'I trust'*: Vernon Smith to Canning, 10 Aug. 1857, OIOC, Lyveden Papers, MSS Eur/F231/4.

**321** *'loyalty and patriotic readiness'*: queen to the duke of Cambridge, 12 July 1857, RA VIC N15/57.

**322** *'temper stern justice'*: Malleson (ed.), *Kaye and Malleson's History of the Indian Mutiny*, II, 367–8.

**323** *'It would be a fatal policy'*: Allen, *Soldier Sahibs*, 283.

**323** *'Hold on to Peshawar'*: Maclagan, *'Clemency' Canning*, 113.

**324** *'Nicholson impressed me'*: Roberts, *Forty-one Years in India*, 33.

**325** *'Fortunately for us'*: Wolseley, I, 268.

**326** *'The troops which have come in'*: Campbell to Lawrence, 12 Sept. 1857, OIOC, Lawrence Papers, MSS Eur/F90/19A.

**326** *'that the measures hitherto taken'*: queen to Palmerston, 22 Aug. 1857, *Victoria Letters 1*, III, 308.

**326** *'should be found insufficient'*: Palmerston to the queen, ibid., 309.

**326** *'The Queen'*: queen to Palmerston, ibid., 309–10.

**327** *'The Government incur'*: ibid., 25 Aug. 1857, 312.

**327** *'almost naked'* . . . *'every kindness'*: Lady Canning to the queen, 20 July 1857, OIOC, Canning Letters, MSS Eur/Photo Eur 321/2.

**327–8** *'Major Holmes'* . . . *'down a well'*: ibid., 10 Aug. 1857.

**328–9** *'That our thoughts'* . . . *'trying & difficult'*: queen to Lady Canning, 8 Sept. 1857, ibid., MSS Eur/Photo Eur/321/1.

**329** *'Hold your fire'*: Vibart, *The Sepoy Mutiny*, 138.

**329** *'Considering that the country'*: Wilson to his wife, 27 Aug. 1857, NAM, Wilson Letters, 6807-483.

**329** *'the power of knighting you'*: Malleson (ed.), *Kaye and Malleson's History of the Indian Mutiny*, II, 494.

**329** *'Every day disaffection'*: Roberts, *Forty-one Years in India*, 116–17.

**330** '*Everyone felt*' . . . '*quite broken down*': Field Marshal Earl Roberts to Sir William Lee Warner, 3 Dec. 1911, NAM, Wilson Correspondence, 5710-38.

**330** '*Delhi must be taken*': Roberts, *Forty-one Years in India*, 118.

**330** '*I have seen lots*': Allen, *Soldier Sahibs*, 314.

**331** '*I saw my captain*': Hewitt (ed.), *Eyewitnesses*, 60.

**331** '*As long as we rushed on*': *Lang Journal*, 92.

**331–2** '*All this greatly agitated*' . . . '*shoot him, if necessary*': Roberts, *Forty-one Years in India*, 129–32.

**332** '*We are now holding*': NAM, Wilson Letters, 6807-483.

**332** '*Our force is too weak*': ibid.

**333** '*have been most virulent*': ibid.

**333** '*If Havelock could only relieve Lucknow*': ibid.

**334** '*so long and gloriously fought*': Malleson (ed.), *Kaye and Malleson's History of the Indian Mutiny*, III, 352–3.

**334** '*though he had never resigned*': Hibbert, *The Great Mutiny*, 259.

**334** '*I hope to be able to hold on*': *State Papers*, II, Introduction, 100.

**334** '*no carriage*': Inglis to Havelock, 25 Aug. 1857, *State Papers*, II, 34–5.

**335** '*the dead and dying*': NAM, Hall Papers, '1857' (54), 11919/11.

**335** '*I esteemed it to be*': Havelock to Norman, 30 Sept. 1857, *State Papers*, II, 221–2.

**336** '*At dusk*': Harris, *A Lady's Diary*, 120.

**336** '*Everyone is depressed*': Hewitt (ed.), *Eyewitnesses*, 150–51.

## 12. The '*jewel of her Crown*'

**337** '*He went to see them*': Canning to the queen, 25 Sept. 1857, *Victoria Letters 1*, III, 317.

**338** '*As we neared the Alambagh*': Roberts, *Forty-one Years in India*, 166.

**338–9** '*a large three-storied*' . . . '*out of him*': Wolseley, I, 282–5.

**339–40** '*I am Sir Colin Campbell*' . . . *just in time*: Kavanagh, *How I Won the Victoria Cross*, 74–93.

**340** '*Outram showed his military acumen*': Roberts, *Forty-one Years in India*, 168.

**341** '*We circled*': Wolseley, I, 297–8.

**341–2** '*the iron tyre*' . . . '*would have done this*': ibid., 302–3.

**342** '*Inch by inch*': Roberts, *Forty-one Years in India*, 182.

**343** '*I steadied my men*': Wolseley, I, 310.

**343–4** '*To the astonishment*' . . . '*ill and worn*': ibid., 314–15.

**344** '*How do you do, Sir James?*': Hibbert, *The Great Mutiny*, 345.

**344** '*I advise you*' . . . '*93rd Highlanders*': Wolseley, I, 315.

**344** '*never been so enraged*': Hibbert, *The Great Mutiny*, 345.

**345** '*although hidden*' . . . '*everything and everybody*': Wolseley, I, 318.

**345** '*I die happy and contented*': Hibbert, *The Great Mutiny*, 350.

**345** '*a martyr to duty*': Roberts, *Forty-one Years in India*, 199.

**345** '*It was a strange procession*': ibid., 200.

**346** '*Our star was in the ascendant*': Forbes–Mitchell, *The Relief of Lucknow*, 93.

**346** '*Thank God!*': queen to Lady Canning, 26 Dec. 1857, OIOC, Canning Letters, MSS Eur/Photo Eur 321/2.

**346** '*They did not arrive*': Lady Canning to the queen, 11 Oct. 1857, ibid., MSS Eur/Photo Eur 321/1.

**346** '*just when they seemed*': queen to Lady Canning, 25 Nov. 1857, ibid., MSS Eur/Photo Eur 321/2.

**346–7** '*ascertain how far*' . . . '*I could not write*': queen to Lady Canning, 22 Oct. 1857, ibid.

**347** '*For the perpetrators*': Maclagan, '*Clemency*' *Canning*, 141.

**348** '*The chase continued*': Roberts, *Forty-one Years in India*, 214.

**351** '*rapid march*': Lowe, *Central India*, 300.

**351–2** '*boldly attacked*' . . . '*mainstays of the mutiny*': Grey Diaries, NLS, MS 15395, 31.

**353** '*My man stood 50 yards*': Wood, I, 141.

**354** '*We declare it our Royal will*' . . . '*instigators in revolt*': Taylor, *What Really Happened*, 213–14.

**354** '*It is a source of great satisfaction*': queen to Canning, 2 Dec. 1858, *Victoria Letters 1*, III, 389.

**355** '*Have arrested the Nana Sahib*' . . . '*Release at once*': Ward, *Our Bones are Scattered*, 530.

**355** '*War is at an end*': Maclagan, '*Clemency*' *Canning*, 232.

**357** '*We have not been elected*': Allen, *Soldier Sahibs*, 339.

**357** '*If I fired*': Collett, *The Butcher of Amritsar*, 328.
**357–8** '*massacre*' . . . '*British way of doing business*': ibid., 382.
**358** '*impossible for the British to leave*': ibid., 402.

## 13. China

**359** '*If you send me troops*': Hanes and Sanello, *The Opium Wars*, 196.
**360** '*My difficulty*': ibid., 206.
**361** '*giving me latitude*': ibid., 213.
**362** '*manly and consistent*': ibid., 224.
**363** '*sunk or stranded*': De Norman Diary, 27 June 1859, OIOC, MSS Eur/A216.
**365** '*We must in some way*': Hanes and Sanello, *The Opium Wars*, 234.
**366** '*If you humiliate*': ibid., 235.
**366** '*It is the opinion*': John Selby, 'The Third China War 1860' in *Victorian Campaigns*, 77–8.
**367** '*He was the best of men*': Wolseley, II, 87.
**367** '*dear old fellow*': Roberts, *Forty-one Years in India*, 165.
**367** '*If Roberts*' . . . '*help a woman again!*': ibid., 265.
**368** '*possessed keen, bright views*' . . . '*sophisms of theology*': Wolseley, II, 5–6.
**368** '*We came in sight*': De Norman Diary, 9–16 July 1860, OIOC, MSS Eur/A216.
**368** '*plucky, cheery and very strong*' . . . '*to keep in any order*': Wolseley, II, 9, 25.
**370** '*in excellent condition*': Napier, *Field Marshal Lord Napier of Magdala*, 128.
**371** '*The eastern coast*': Greathed Papers, NAM, 6711-1/8, 43–4.
**371** '*We suspicious Britishers*': Wolseley, II, 20.
**371** '*magnificent spectacle*' . . . '*hoped-for destination*': ibid., 20–21.
**372** '*On the 1st August*': Greathed Papers, NAM, 6711-1/8, 47–8.
**372** '*an old campaigner*': Wolseley, II, 23.
**372** '*Picture a somewhat fierce*': ibid., 23–4.
**374** '*no trace of recent occupation*': Greathed Papers, NAM, 6711-1/8, 50–51.

**374** *'suffered much'*: Wolseley, II, 24.

**374** *'The principal drill'*: Haythornthwaite, *The Colonial Wars Source Book*, 242.

**374–5** *'The beach was a busy scene'* . . . *'to walk or ride'*: Greathed Papers, NAM, 6711-1/8, 55–7.

**375** *'This valuable reconnaissance'*: ibid., 59–60.

**375** *'were slow in their disembarkation'*: Wolseley, II, 25.

**376** *'They act in every respect'*: Fortescue, XIII, 408.

**376** *'I advanced by brigades'*: Napier to Captain Robert Biddulph, 24 Aug. 1860, Napier Dispatches, OIOC, MSS Eur/B116, 4.

**376** *'the range and accuracy'*: ibid., 5.

**376** *'The first gun'*: Rowley Diary, NAM, 8108-33.

**377** *'streamed out in a long line'*: Napier to Captain Robert Biddulph, 24 Aug. 1860, op. cit., 5.

**377** *'As soon as the enemy's movements'*: ibid.

**377** *'apparently regardless'* . . . *'and they fled'*: ibid., 6.

**379** *'Let dusky Indians whine'* . . . *'type of all her race'*: Hurd, *The Arrow War*, 212–13.

**380** *'all military science'*: Fortescue, XIII, 412.

**380** *'tall black pillar'* . . . *'at an end'*: Wolseley, II, 32.

**381** *'edge of the outermost'*: Napier to Captain Robert Biddulph, 26 Aug. 1860, Napier Dispatches, OIOC, MSS Eur/B116, 12.

**382** *'covered with killed and wounded'*: Wolseley, II, 34.

**382** *'considerable number'* . . . *'before he fell'*: ibid., 35.

**382** *'which firing over the heads'*: Napier to Captain Robert Biddulph, 26 Aug. 1860, op. cit., 13.

**382** *'All the time'*: John Dempsey, 'Storming the Taku Forts', *Royal Magazine*, vol. 34, 307.

**383** *'But foot by foot'*: Napier to Captain Robert Biddulph, 26 Aug. 1860, op. cit., 13.

**384** *'dead and dying'* . . . *'might go free'*: Wolseley, II, 36.

**384** *'particularly with regard'*: De Norman Diary, OIOC, MSS Eur/A216, 78–9.

**384** *'demurred at the hardship'*: ibid.

**386** *'The blockheads'*: Hanes and Sanello, *The Opium Wars*, 257–8.

**386** *'everything'*: De Norman Diary, 11 Sept. 1860, op. cit.

**386** *'tall dignified man'* . . . *'also intelligent'*: Hanes and Sanello, *The Opium Wars*, 258.

**387** *the commissioners signed a letter*: 'The China War in Brief', Greathed Papers, NAM, 6711-1/8, 5.

**387** *'pending the return'* . . . *to await Parkes's return*: ibid., 6–7.

**388** *'I will send Wolseley'* . . . *never to return*: Wolseley, II, 64.

**388** *'Suddenly we heard'*: Knollys (ed.), *Life of General Sir Hope Grant*, II, 136–7.

**389** *'The French went off'*: Rowley Diary, 18 Sept. 1860, op. cit.

**390** *'We must have one more fight'*: Rowley Diary, 19 Sept. 1860, op. cit.

**390** *'They were mounted'*: Wolseley, II, 68–9.

**391** *'strewn with dead Tartars'*: Rowley Diary, 21 Sept. 1860, op. cit.

**391** *'helped at this work'*: Wolseley, II, 70.

**392** *'October 6 saw us'*: ibid., 76.

**393** *'General Montauban'* . . . *'Emperor of China'*: ibid., 77–8.

**393** *'It was pitiful'*: Hanes and Sanello, *The Opium Wars*, 273.

**393** *'For some days afterwards'*: Wolseley, II, 78.

**394** *'You would scarcely conceive'*: Gordon Letters, BL, Add. MSS 52389, no. 27, 9 Oct. 1860.

**395** *'take the broadest view'*: 'The China War in Brief', Greathed Papers, op. cit., 9.

**395** *'I had sentries posted'*: Hanes and Sanello, *The Opium Wars*, 273.

**395** *'the lives and property'* . . . *'respected'*: 'The China War in Brief', Greathed Papers, op. cit., 10.

**395–6** *'I found myself'* . . . *'elbows pinioned'*: Selby, 'The Third China War 1860', op. cit., 100–101.

**396** *'harsh and rude'*: 'The China War in Brief', Greathed Papers, op. cit., 8.

**396** *'hostilities to be temporarily suspended'*: Hanes and Sanello, *The Opium Wars*, 281.

**397** *'Their hands and feet'*: 'The China War in Brief', Greathed Papers, op. cit., 7.

**398** *'I took my place'*: Wolseley, II, 81–2.

**398** *'In a few minutes'*: Rowley Diary, 13 Oct. 1860, op. cit.

**398** *'None of this'*: Hanes and Sanello, *The Opium Wars*, 284.

**399** *'as a lasting mark'*: 'The China War in Brief', Greathed Papers, op. cit., 11.

**399** '*dense clouds of smoke*': Wolseley, II, 83.

**399** '*hastened the final settlement*': Selby, 'The Third China War 1860', op. cit., 103.

**399** '*could find nothing suspicious*': Wolseley, II, 85.

**399** '*surrounded by Imperial officers*': 'The China War in Brief', Greathed Papers, op. cit., 11.

**399** '*Prince Kung*': Wolseley, II, 86.

**400** '*he had been himself* ' . . . '*in his hands*': 'The China War in Brief', Greathed Papers, op. cit., 12.

**400** '*The public here*': Selby, 'The Third China War 1860', op. cit., 103.

**400** '*I most sincerely*': Napier to Colonel Baker, 26 Oct. 1860, in Napier, *Field Marshal Lord Napier of Magdala*, 157.

**401** '*It was necessary*': Elgin to Russell, 25 Oct. 1860, in Selby, 'The Third China War 1860', op. cit., 103.

**401** '*It was absolutely necessary*': Chambers, *Palmerston*, 471.

## Epilogue: 'Oh, yes, this is death!'

**403** '*excellent telegraphic news*': queen to Russell, 16 Dec. 1860, RA VIC/C12/83.

**403** '*The French*': Weintraub, *Albert*, 389.

**404** '*wonderful* escape*': ibid., 393.

**404** '*he was well aware*': ibid., 394.

**404** '*I hope this state of things*': ibid., 400.

**405** '*the Colony*' . . . '*violence at sea*': *Victoria Letters 1*, III, 562.

**405** '*gross outrage*': Palmerston to the queen, 29 Nov. 1861, ibid., 595.

**405–6** '*somewhat meagre*' . . . '*misapprehended them*': queen to Earl Russell, 1 Dec. 1861, ibid., 598.

**406** '*You do what's right*': Weintraub, *Albert*, 422.

**406** '*Bertie marched past*': queen to King Leopold of the Belgians, 26 Aug. 1861, ibid., 577.

**407** '*greatest pain*': Albert to the prince of Wales, 16 Nov. 1861, in Weintraub, *Albert*, 406.

**407** '*without a shudder*': Weintraub, 293.

**408** '*gastric & bowel* fever*': RA VIC/QVJ/1861: 7 December.

**408** '*our beloved invalid*': queen to King Leopold of the Belgians, 9 Dec. 1861, *Victoria Letters 1*, III, 599.

**408** '*He seemed much more himself*': RA VIC/QVJ/1861: 9 December.

**408** *pulse was 'good'*: ibid.: 10 December.

**408** 'unfavourable' *symptoms* . . . 'first fever *doctor in Europe*': queen to King Leopold of the Belgians, 12 Dec. 1861, *Victoria Letters 1*, III, 601.

**408** '*there was ground to hope*': Weintraub, *Albert*, 430.

**409** '*Oh, yes, this is death!*': ibid., 431.

**409** '*My* life': *Victoria Letters 1*, III, 602–3.

**409** '*Nothing great or small*': Weintraub, *Albert*, 436.

**410** '*[It] is* my firm *resolve*': ibid., 438.

**410** '*Her determination*': Chambers, *Palmerston*, 488.

**410** '*With Prince Albert*': Weintraub, 307.

**411** '*He was a man of elegant mind*': Weintraub, *Albert*, 433.

**411** '*to the discharge of his duty*' . . . '*to the Sovereign*': 19 Oct. 1857, *Greville Diary*, II, 362–3.

**411** '*deplored the glamorous, ornamental*': Weintraub, *Albert*, 443.

**413** '*At no time in the first half of Victoria's reign*': Morris, *Heaven's Command*, 380.

**414** '*in a fit of absence of mind*': J. R. Seeley, quoted in ibid., 381.

**416** '*What does Imperialism mean?*': Morris, *Heaven's Command*, 388.

**417** '*gave Europe virtually the whole continent*': Packenham, *The Scramble for Africa*, xxiii.

# Index

*Note*: Ranks and titles are generally the highest mentioned